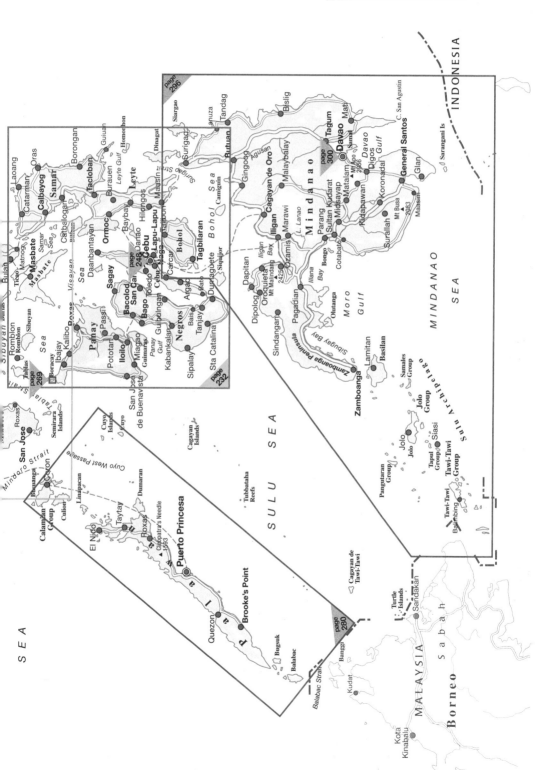

# INSIGHT GUIDES
# PHILIPPINES

## APA PUBLICATIONS  L
Part of the Langenscheidt Publishing Group

# INSIGHT GUIDE
# PHILIPPINES

## Editorial

*Project Editor*
**Tom Le Bas**
*Series Manager*
**Rachel Lawrence**
*Designer*
**Ian Spick, Lucy Johnston**
*Map Production*
**Original cartography Cosmographics, updated by Apa Cartography Department**
*Production*
**Tynan Dean, Linton Donaldson and Rebeka Ellam**

## Distribution

*UK*
**Dorling Kindersley Ltd**
A Penguin Group company
80 Strand, London, WC2R 0RL
sales@uk.dk.com

*United States*
**Ingram Publisher Services**
1 Ingram Boulevard, PO Box 3006,
La Vergne, TN 37086-1986
ips@ingramcontent.com

*Australia and New Zealand*
**Woodslane**
10 Apollo St, Warriewood, NSW 2102,
Australia
info@woodslane.com.au

*Worldwide*
**Apa Publications GmbH & Co.
Verlag KG (Singapore branch)**
7030 Ang Mo Kio Avenue 5
08-65 Northstar @ AMK
Singapore 569880
apasin@singnet.com.sg

## Printing

**CTPS-China**

© 2013 Apa Publications (UK) Ltd
*All Rights Reserved*

*First Edition 1980*
*Twelfth Edition 2013*
*Reprinted 2015*

## CONTACTING THE EDITORS

We would appreciate it if readers would alert us to errors or outdated information by writing to:
**Insight Guides, PO Box 7910, London SE1 1WE, England.
insight@apaguide.co.uk**

# ABOUT THIS BOOK

The first Insight Guide pioneered the use of creative full-color photography in travel guides in 1970. Since then, we have expanded our range to cater for our readers' need not only for reliable information about their chosen destination but also for a real understanding of that destination. Now, when the Internet can supply inexhaustible – but not always reliable – facts, our books marry text and pictures to provide those much more elusive qualities: knowledge and discernment. To achieve this, they rely heavily on the authority of locally based writers and photographers.

## How to use this book

This book is carefully structured to convey an understanding of the Philippines and its culture, and to guide readers through its myriad sights and attractions:

◆ The **Features** section, indicated by a pink bar at the top of each page, covers the natural geography and eventful history of the Philippines as well as key aspects of its culture: its people, religions, festivals, crafts, cuisine and architecture.

◆ The main **Places** section, indicated by a blue bar, is a complete guide to all the sights and areas worth visiting across the archipelago. Places of special interest are

# Contents

The entire book was updated by Taiwan-based journalist and travel writer **Ralph Jennings**. Stationed in Beijing before moving to Taipei in 2006, he has covered East Asia for a range of international media organizations, and spends a large amount of time in the Philippines.

The update builds on the work of numerous writers who have contributed to earlier editions, including **Alfred Yuson**, **Doreen Fernandez**, **Augusto Villalon**, **Gina T. Mission** and **Julie Gaw**.

New photography for this edition was provided by Insight regular **Chris Stowers**, who spent months travelling around the country to search out the best images to bring the pages to life.

This 12th edition of the guide was copy-edited by **Jane Hutchings**, proofread by **Jan McCann** and indexed by **Penny Phenix**.

## Map Legend

| | |
|---|---|
| — · — | International Boundary |
| — — — — | Regional Boundary |
| — — — — | Province Boundary |
| ● | National Park/Reserve |
| — — — — | Ferry Route |
| Ⓛ Ⓜ | LRT (Light Rail) or MRT (Metro Rail) |
| ✈ ✈ | Airport: International/Regional |
| 🚌 | Bus Station |
| ❶ | Tourist Information |
| ✉ | Post Office |
| ✝ ✝ ✝ | Church/Ruins |
| ✝ | Monastery |
| ✡ | Synagogue |
| ☾ | Mosque |
| 🏰 | Castle/Ruins |
| ∴ | Archaeological Site |
| ☊ | Cave |
| 𝟏 | Statue/Monument |
| ★ | Place of Interest |

The main places of interest in the Places section are coordinated by number with a full-colour map (eg ❶), and a symbol at the top of every right-hand page tells you where to find the map.

coordinated by number with the maps.

♦ The **Travel Tips** listings section, with a yellow bar, provides all the practical information you'll need, divided into six key sections: transportation, accommodations, eating out, activities, an A–Z section of essential practical tips, and a handy section on language.

## The contributors

The challenge of stringing the 7,107 islands that make up the Philippines into a coherent read was undertaken by **Tom Le Bas**, senior commissioning editor at Insight's London office. This 12th edition has been completely overhauled with new chapters and a new-style Travel Tips section, building on earlier editions put together by **Francis Dorai** and **Scott Rutherford**.

**Maps**

**Inside front cover:**
The Philippines.
**Inside back cover:** Manila.

# THE BEST OF PHILIPPINES: TOP ATTRACTIONS

The must-see sights of this far-flung archipelago range from awe-inspiring landscapes to some of Asia's finest beaches and Spanish colonial architecture.

△ **Boracay.** Leave the cares of the world behind on this idyllic island of perfect beaches, luxurious resorts, and water adventures. See page 269.

▽ **Corregidor Island, Cavite.** Get an on-site crash course on how the successive armies of Spain, Japan, and the US sought to defend the Philippine capital. See page 142.

△ **Ifugao rice terraces.** Perhaps the most spectacular sight in the Philippines, this amazing terraced landscape in the highlands of central Luzon was sculpted some 2,000 years ago. See page 202.

▽ **Ati-Atihan festival.** The frenetic, colorful and noisy festivities on the island of Panay each January commemorate the sale of land to 13th-century refugees from Borneo. See page 268.

△ **Intramuros, Manila.** For a sense of Manila's rich history, wander through this district of handsome Spanish colonial architecture. See page 122.

▷ **Vigan, Ilocos Sur.** Stroll or take a horse-drawn carriage down some of the country's best-preserved streets from the Spanish era, stopping at cafés inside historic mansions to sip San Miguel Pilsen. See page 175.

◁ **Fort San Pedro, Cebu.** Step inside the massive stone walls to an era when the "Pearl of the South" was under siege as the Spanish struggled for a toehold in the Philippines. See page 249.

△ **Palawan.** This barely developed island in the far west of the Philippines is endowed with beautiful white-sand beaches, prime dive sites and extensive tracts of jungle. See page 277.

▽ **Volcanoes.** In a country littered with volcanic peaks such as Apo, Mayon, Pinatubo, and Taal, enlist the help of a trained guide for a rewarding trek up one of the great cones. See page 104.

▽ **Jeepneys.** A hop onto one of these brazenly embellished and garishly painted vehicles – the local answer to urban mass transit – is an essential experience for any visitor to the Philippines. See page 139.

# THE BEST OF PHILIPPINES: EDITOR'S CHOICE

Breathtaking landscapes, exciting adventure activities, absorbing museums, and a dynamic culture are among the attractions of the Philippines. Here, at a glance, are our recommendations, plus some tips that even Filipinos won't always know.

## BEST BEACHES

**Baler, Aurora**. A string of accessible surfing beaches halfway up Luzon's east coast. See page 189.

**Boracay**. The Philippines' world-famous resort has fabulous beaches, luxurious resorts, and offshore adventures. See page 269.

**Dauin, Negros Oriental**. Snorkelers can wade into a marine sanctuary covered with coral gardens and their colorful underwater life. See page 259.

**Puerto Galera, Mindoro**. A complex of beaches relatively close to Manila appeals to divers, swimmers, and seaside party-goers. See page 221.

**Samal Island, Davao**. This island features sleepy palm-lined, white-sand beaches just a quick hop from urban Davao. See page 304.

## BEST DIVE SITES

**Alona Beach, Bohol**. This coastal trading post of dive shops, guides, and boat rentals acts as a hub for the offshore reefs and seawalls. See page 245.

**Apo Island, Negros Oriental**. This islet draws scuba divers to follow schools of colorful fish swimming past the coral just offshore. See page 259.

**Apo Reef National Park, Mindoro Occidental**. The coral ecosystem in a 34 sq km (13 sq mile) reef, home to some 400–500 coral species, has rebounded from years of damage by dynamite fishing. See page 220.

**Batangas**. This well-developed resort area, two to three hours' drive from Manila, stands out for its convenience and class A beaches. See page 147.

**Busuanga Island, Palawan**. Dive to see dugongs and other marine life, or search for World War II shipwrecks. See page 284.

**Moalboal, Cebu**. A 35-meter (115ft) wall drops right off from Panagsama Beach. See page 255.

**TOP:** Beach resort, Palawan. **LEFT:** a typical beach near Puerto Galera. **ABOVE:** diving off Bohol Island.

## BEST WILDERNESS AREAS

This almost perfectly conical, and still active, volcano invites intrepid trekkers. See page 210. **Sierra Madre National Park, eastern Luzon**. The country's largest national park covers grand mountain landscapes while sheltering endangered species such as the Philippine eagle. See page 189.

**Chocolate Hills, Bohol**. The sunrise over these hills, named for their confectionery-like appearance in summer, leaves a lasting impression. See page 247.

**Mt Banahaw, Laguna**. A mountain that has been held sacred for thousands of years. See page 148.

**Mayon volcano, Albay**.

**Sohoton National Park, Western Samar**. Tour gigantic caves, underground rivers, and see natural arches. See page 239.

**St Paul Underground River, Palawan**. Vertical cave walls form caverns and narrow passageways along an aquamarine river deep in the jungle. See page 286.

**ABOVE:** kayaking in Coron Bay, Calamian Islands.

## BEST ENTERTAINMENT DISTRICTS

**Balibago, Angeles, Pampanga**. An entertainment-intensive boomtown near Clark Airbase. See page 164.

**P. Burgos Street, Makati**. Manila's upmarket financial district doesn't close at 5pm but rages on with a strip of lively bars. See page 134.

**Ermita and Malate, Manila**. This district inland from Roxas Boulevard stitches together Latin bars, gay bars, and everyday clubs with hotels and a bookstore. See pages 127, 128.

**White Beach, Boracay**. The hundreds of resorts, bars, and restaurants throw what amounts to a party along the palm-studded beach at night. See page 269.

## BEST HISTORIC SITES

**Butuan, Agusan del Norte**. Some consider the area the cradle of Philippine civilization, and three museums showcase the local archeology. See page 318.

**Kadaugan sa Mactan, Cebu**. Spanish explorer Ferdinand Magellan's fatal encounter with the local hero Lapu-Lapu is dramatized on the waters off Mactan Island. See page 252.

**Lights and Sounds of Rizal, Manila**. National hero Jose Rizal's final hours before his execution are re-enacted in this open-air audio-visual presentation. See page 125.

**Museo Dabawenyo, Davao**. Free guides explain the city's history, Mindanao's indigenous groups, and local forays into modern art. See page 300.

**Vigan, Ilocos Sur**. Stroll among some of the country's best-preserved streets and houses from the Spanish era. See page 175.

**TOP:** Chocolate Hills, Bohol. **RIGHT:** White Beach, Boracay.

**ABOVE:** bottlenose dolphin at Ocean Adventure.
**RIGHT:** Ati-Atihan Festival.
**BELOW:** decoration on a Manila jeepney.

## BEST FAMILY HANGOUTS

**Davao Crocodile Park**. Get up close to these fearsome beasts, plus pythons and other creatures. See page 302.
**Museo Pambata (Children's Museum), Manila**. Explores themes ranging from the environment and science to the human body. See page 127.

**Ocean Adventure, Subic Bay**. Marine theme park with dolphins, whales, sea lions, and plenty of interaction. See page 167.
**Manila Ocean Park**. A visit starts with the indoor aquarium, showcasing marine life from around the world, and ends with a seal show outside. See page 126.

## BEST CULTURAL ICONS

**Ati-Atihan Festival, Kalibo**. At the most famous and raucous of Philippine festivals, the line between spectators and participants gets increasingly blurred as the day progresses. See page 268.
**Batanes**. Spend a night in one of the far-flung villages in the islands off Luzon's north coast to experience one of the country's most isolated cultures. See page 181.
**Jeepneys**. A ride on this often brazenly embellished and garishly painted mode of transportation is an essential Philippines experience. See page 139.
**Moriones Festival, Marinduque**. A spectacular festival featuring men wearing masks (moriones) and colorfully dressed as Roman soldiers. See page 223.
**Metropolitan Museum of Manila, Metro Manila**. The works of local artists are on display along with gold artifacts and pottery dating to the 8th century. See page 129.

**ABOVE:** durian fruit seller, Magsaysay Park, Davao.
**BELOW:** Divisoria Market, Manila.

## BEST SHOPPING

**City Market, Baguio.** Look for unusual weavings, carvings, and other crafts at this crossroads of the Cordilleran mountain tribes. See page 194.

**Batak Village, Puerto Princesa.** This indigenous Batak community along the highway sells basketry, kitchenware, and musical instruments. See page 283.

**Divisoria, Manila.** An intense shopping experience awaits at this bargain-basement flea market with thousands of stalls. See page 136.

**Greenhills Shopping Center, Manila.** Look for freshwater and South China Sea pearls as well as cheap electronic goods. See page 134.

**Mall of Asia, Manila.** Asia's largest commercial complex testifies to the favored Filipino leisure pursuit of shopping. Outdoor eateries serve local cuisine. See page 132.

## TRAVELERS' TIPS

**Book ahead whenever possible.** Online hotel bookings can lower room rates and guarantee a spot during holidays. Advanced purchases of ferry tickets save time standing in long sweaty lines, followed by disappointment that the boat is full.

**Be assertive with taxi drivers.** By law, taxi drivers should use their meters, but many give excuses for why they won't do this. A quoted set price to a destination *(contrata)* is usually around three times the normal fare.

**Be firm with touts.** Don't be pressured by touts at airports, bus and boat terminals. Be firm, agree on the price before you begin a journey, and keep in mind that any tout's first stated price is way over the going rate. Bargaining on the price is expected on almost everything for sale in the Philippines.

**Carry exact change and count what comes back.** Someone who is out to cheat may just try to pocket the small difference between a price and the amount tendered.

Merchants may not carry change for P1,000 bills, causing delays as they search for a third party who does. When change comes back, count it. Errors are common.

**Prepare for outages.** The internet is often down in the Philippines. Consider prepaid mobile phone cards instead of email. Power goes off regularly in some outlying regions, such as Palawan.

**Be flexible.** Restaurants may stock only two-thirds of their menu offerings. Be open to second choices.

# ASIA'S MAVERICK

**Geographically within Southeast Asia, yet far removed culturally, the Philippines has a marked Latin temperament which sets it apart from its neighbors.**

Three centuries of Spanish rule and 48 years of United States government have left their mark on this Southeast Asian archipelago of 103 million people. The indigenous population, some of whom look more African than Asian, have further influenced the dominant Filipino culture that traces its roots to the Malays. Add the widespread use of English as a second official language, and a preference for detached houses over high-rise apartments, and it's sometimes possible to think you could be in the United States. Spanish place names and devotion to Catholicism also give visitors a sense of being in Latin America. The Philippines has an extraordinary legacy. It is the maverick of Asia.

Today on almost every island, white-sand beaches open into clear, coral-studded waters. Popular resorts such as Alona Beach, Boracay, and Puerto Galera attract scuba divers, who can get trained for a deep-sea adventure within days after arrival. The mountains that dominate the interior of every large Philippine island appeal to travelers wishing to embark on rigorous treks. Between the coasts and the cones, tourists trust in the local barbecued chicken, songs, smiles, and eagerly imparted travel advice.

The Philippines is part of a giant mountain backbone from Japan to Indonesia. It stretches 1,840km (1,140 miles) north to south and up to 1,000km (690 miles) wide. Its land area is slightly bigger than that of New Zealand. A total of 111 cultural, linguistic, and racial groups live in the country. Some 70 languages are spoken, with Tagalog far the most dominant one.

Capitalism and democracy both run deep in the country, but due to government inefficiency, people remain poor, with 26.5 percent below the national poverty line. Some 10 percent of the US$261 billion economy comes from money sent home by Filipinos, who form a huge diaspora working abroad. The country's reputation improved in the mid-1990s under the economic strategies of President Fidel Ramos, but has stumbled again under successive leaders, bringing back corruption and inefficiency.

**PRECEDING PAGES:** Taal volcano crater lake, Cavite Province; Durian stall, Magsaysay Park, Davao; Inabuyutan Island in the Bacuit Archipelago, Palawan.
**LEFT:** jeepney in front of the Philippines Stock Exchange. **ABOVE, FROM LEFT:** house in Leyte Province; traditional dancer.

# ISLAND NATION

The Philippine archipelago stretches from its largest, most populated island of Luzon in the north to uninhabited southern atolls small enough for just a thatched hut and a few coconut trees.

I f one number sticks in your mind after a visit to the Philippines, it's probably 7,100. This estimate of the total number of islands in the archipelago regularly appears in tourism literature because it's so large yet also so singularly descriptive of the country's geography. The actual total is 7,107, and about 1,000 of those are inhabited.

For purposes of easy analysis, the archipelago divides into northern, central, and southern island groups. In the north is the large island of Luzon and the nearby, smaller islands of Mindoro, Romblon, and Marinduque. Most of the population, wealth, and dominant Tagalog-speaking Filipino ethnic groups are clustered on Luzon, which is anchored by the 12 million-population capital Manila. The country's most prominent industrial belt sits south of Manila on the Batangas peninsula, and one of its most fertile farming areas bounds the capital to the north. Luzon as home to Mt Mayon and Mt Pinatubo is largely volcanic, but some of its mightiest mountains form solid, barely penetrable ranges, such as the Sierra Madre, in the far north. It's also known for the flat Central Plains farming area and the drier wind-battered Batanes islets off the north coast.

The central group of islands is known as the Visayas. Poorer and culturally distinct from Luzon, they range from Samar and Leyte in the east through Cebu to Negros and Panay in the west. Fisheries dominate the economy, with tourism an increasingly vital source of income because of the region's

endless coastline. Divers work the waters of Bohol, Boracay, Cebu, and tiny Apo Island off the coast of Negros in search of underwater life. Some of the country's most fabled beaches occur in the Visayas. Mountainous patchworks of farms and jungles make up the island interiors.

The southernmost part of the country consists of Mindanao plus its attendant Sulu Sea islands. Poorer and known for its range of indigenous peoples – including Muslim groups still at war with the government – Mindanao is a large and relatively undeveloped island, home to the country's highest peak (Mt Apo: 2,956 meters/9,698ft) and some of its most extensive tracts of rainforest. Muslim towns

---

**LEFT:** rice paddies, Bicol Peninsula.
**RIGHT:** Coron Island, Palawan.

*The Asian bearcat, or binturong, lives in Palawan. The nocturnal creature resembles a cross between a raccoon and a bear, with a long tail and retractable, hooked claws for climbing trees. Asian bearcats eat mainly fruits and leaves.*

eruption, such as that of Mt Pinatubo in 1991, wreaks further deadly havoc. Much of the country is located on the Pacific rim of fire and is prone to earthquakes. On the plus side, fertile soil and abundant rainfall make the Philippines a productive place for rice, coconuts, and a range of fruits.

## Island communications

also populate the islets of the Sulu Sea, southwest of Mindanao, up to the strait dividing the Philippines from Malaysia.

To Mindanao's northwest lies Palawan, a long north-south island known for remote

Filipinos once lived largely in tribal villages in the mountains. Then, more than 800 years ago, ethnic Malays came from other parts of Southeast Asia to set up coastal communities. Beasts and boats provided transportation in those days.

jungles, quiet beaches, and offshore reefs, as well as a fabled lack of infrastructure. Throughout the archipelago one will find countless barely visited islets of coral reef-rimmed white-sand beaches. Some have nothing but the beach and a few trees. The visitor can ask pumpboat operators on larger islands about getting out to one.

Located between the Pacific Ocean and South China Sea, the archipelago is surrounded by a rich marine life, from tiny squid to massive marlins, on which it is both economically and nutritionally dependent. Late-year weather brings regular typhoons from the Pacific, flooding villages and setting off deadly landslides after sustained rainfall. The odd volcanic

While some parts of the country still work that way, people in most of the Philippines get around on a network of two-lane roads and a range of public transportation, from jerrybuilt tricycle taxis to air-conditioned buses. That has facilitated widespread domestic migration, intermarriages and new urban jobs for people from poor parts of the countryside. Some of today's highways, such as the one running north of Manila through the plains of Pampanga, are as modern as anything anywhere in the world. A long list of airports, including some on faraway islands – served by Cebu Pacific, Philippine Airways, and others – further aids business and migration.

That said, some Filipino farmers barely make

it to market once a week because they must walk down muddy dirt roads from their mountain fields to the nearest town. For them, the market is a major social event as well as a place to sell pigs or produce.

Television and widespread early education have functioned in different ways since the early 1900s to homogenize the country's ethnic and linguistic groups, giving everyone a bite of English – plus a lot more Tagalog. Filipinos are fond of the cheap mobile phone text message to communicate extensively with friends or family in other cities, easing the pains of internal migration for jobs. Transportation and commu-

## FLORA AND FAUNA

The so-called Wallace Line that defines the geographical habitat of most Philippine plants and animals is named after English naturalist, explorer, and writer Alfred Russel Wallace (1823–1913), who first noted the zoological differences between the Asian and Australian continents. This zoological division runs up the Lombok Strait between Indonesian islands Bali and Lombok. It continues north through the Makassar Strait that separates Borneo and Sulawesi, turns east into the Pacific and then north again to encompass the Philippines. All animals to the east

nications had effectively connected most of the country by 1990.

Some members of minority ethnic groups in the highlands of Luzon and in the harder-to-reach parts of Mindanao and Palawan islands stayed out of the 20th-century shifts in transit and communications, keeping them semi-autonomous yet poorer and far less plugged in to national affairs than their fellow country people in the cities and lowlands. Some of those groups have a legacy of resisting colonists, while others simply lack the money or skills to move into the mainstream.

**ABOVE, FROM LEFT:** Zamboanguita Beach, Negros Island; Mt Isarog, Bicol Peninsula.

### RICE FARMING

Rice, the staple food of the Philippines, is the most common crop cultivated in upland volcanic areas. Yet despite the abundance of rice fields, what is planted locally is often insufficient to sustain an ever-growing population. The International Rice Research Institute in Los Baños, near Manila, works to develop new varieties of faster-yielding rice and improvements in cultivation methods to increase output.

Rich volcanic soil remains the farmer's chief ally. Coupled with abundant rainfall throughout the year, the most productive farms are clustered beneath the archipelago's numerous volcanoes.

of the line, including those of the Philippines, owe their biological heritage to species originating in Asia.

When sea levels fell during the last Ice Age, a series of land bridges cut through the shallow waters between Philippines' Palawan and Mindanao and Indonesia's Sulawesi and Borneo. Like the tentacles of an octopus, these land bridges made possible a temporary alliance of flora and fauna, which led to adaptations and mutations in isolation when the land links sank again.

Sixty species of Bornean plants are found in the southern islands of Mindoro, Palawan, and Mindanao. Flora identified with Sulawesi and Moluccas of Indonesia are widespread in the Philippines, mainly ferns, orchids, and the dipterocarp, a tree that makes up the country's primary tracts of forests, as it does in Thailand and Indonesia.

In Palawan and nearby Calamian islands, the same species of mousedeer, weasel, mongoose, porcupine, skunk, anteater, and otter are found in Borneo's interior. Species of Palawan shrews, as well as a rare bat found in Mindanao, have kin in Sulawesi.

Fish in the waters of eastern Sumatra and western Borneo are like those in southwestern

### DYNAMITE AND DEFORESTATION

The Philippines, like many resource-rich but impoverished countries, suffers from its share of environmental degradation. Despite efforts by the government and NGOs since the 1970s, illegal logging persists in Aurora, Ilocos Sur, and Quezon provinces, according to news reports, as well as parts of Mindanao. Illegal logging has been blamed for soil erosion that has set off countless mudslides.

A second environmental threat to the Philippines is dynamite fishing. Some 12 percent of commercial operators fished this way in 1999, according to reports. The practice kills all marine life in a blast area, either sinking the fish or making them rise to the surface. Blast fishing is lucrative and hard to patrol. Some tourist areas charge visitors a fee to help restore the local seas.

Much of the country's wildlife remains hidden from general view. At least 130 species of Philippine fauna now stand on the United Nation's list of endangered and threatened species. In an encouraging move, the government has set up 60 national parks, four marine parks, and 10 wilderness areas.

To see some of the country's signature wildlife up close, visit the Palawan Wildlife Rescue and Conservation Center (formerly known as the Crocodile Farming Institute) in Puerto Princesa. Visitors can see the endangered Philippine crocodile and Asian bearcats.

Philippines, as are the fish between Mindanao and Papua New Guinea. Many Malaysian and Bornean birds make their home in Palawan.

There is evidence of an even older land bridge that connected northern Philippines with Taiwan at a time when that island was itself connected to the Asian mainland. The

> Research on the evolution of anteaters, orchids, and other species proves links between the Philippines and neighboring islands to the southwest, now part of Indonesia.

have helped to form a distinctly Filipino architectural style. The 1,000 orchid species found in the Philippines include the *waling-waling* of western Mindanao. The pinkish endemic flower is one of the largest orchid species in the world but hard to find in the wild due to habitat encroachment.

The Philippines would be a mostly forested country, but more than 70 percent of its original forests have fallen to loggers. Vast tracts of hardwood stands still survive in the protected areas of Palawan and Mindanao.

Back from the beaches, dry forests of heavy, highly prized woods grow slowly, rarely exceeding

remains of the stegodon, a pygmy elephant, have been dug up here as well as in Taiwan.

## Plant life

Botanists have discovered more than 12,000 different species of plants in the Philippines, namely types of ferns, orchids, and vines in the jungles. Tourists will see mangroves growing in the sea and palms along the coast. Bamboo and rattan, both sought after by crafts people, rise from the inland soil. Locals in Mindoro, Panay, and the Cagayan Valley use the rough cogon grass to thatch the roofs of houses that

**ABOVE, FROM LEFT:** farmer, Northern Mindanao; orchids, Luzon's Islands.

### THE PHILIPPINE EAGLE

The endangered *haribon*, or Philippine eagle, is the national bird of the Philippines and the second-largest bird in the world, after the Californian condor. The eagles once soared freely over much of Luzon, Samar, and Leyte. They would eat small animals, including bats, snakes, and flying lemurs. The Philippine eagle is thought to be monogamous, challenging its long-term survival in the wild. Today fewer than 100 *haribon* remain.

The Philippine Eagle Center (see page 303) near Davao may be the eagle's last hope. The center has successfully bred eagles in captivity, with an aim of reintroducing the young back to the wild.

30 meters (100ft) in height. Characteristic species include the molave (of the teak family), kamagong, ebony, and narra.

## Birds

One-third of nearly 560 recognized bird species are endemic, an unusually large number for any country. Of these, 66 are "island-endemic," occurring on only one island.

Common birds include the white-collared kingfisher, with its iridescent coat of turquoise blue, which makes itself at home near water. One of the most peculiar bird species is the Luzon bleeding heart dove, endemic to south-central Luzon and outlying Polillo Island. Grayish green on the back and upper mantle, the bird's white chest feathers are interrupted by a splotch of red. Among the country's newest recognized bird species are Lina's sunbird and the Panay striped babbler. Ornithologist

> Scientists exploring the Sierra Madre range in Luzon said in 2010 they had discovered a new species of monitor lizard. The biologists called the yellow and black, 2-meter (6.6ft) -long reptile the Northern Sierra Madre Forest Monitor.

### MINDORO'S DWARF BUFFALO

Few visitors will spot the endangered native *tamaraw*, or dwarf buffalo, of Mindoro Island – the country's largest indigenous land mammal. Hunting, shifting agriculture, deforestation, and cattle ranching have reduced the herds from 10,000 a century ago to only 260–300 *tamaraw* today, mostly in the grasslands of Mt Iglit in Baco National Park.

The government holds a few animals in captivity in Mindoro, with the hope of breeding more for eventual release into the wild. Local charities have also done their bit. The city tourism in San José, Mindoro, arranges day trips by van from the town to a *tamaraw* viewing area in the mountains.

Robert Kennedy of the Cincinnati Museum Center in the US discovered and named the babbler in 1989.

Palawan's endemic *Papilio trojano*, with bold black and green markings, has a wingspan of 18cm (7ins), but it's a butterfly, not a bird.

## Mammals

Among the country's 180 mammal species are leopard cats, oriental small-clawed otters, civets, and wild boar – a staple food for the local inhabitants. Native primates include flying lemurs and lorises of the tropical forests. The nocturnal tarsier is the world's smallest primate. It lives in Bohol, Samar, Mindanao, and elsewhere in Southeast Asia. Visitors can see these tiny monkey-like creatures in their native habitat at the Philippine Tarsier Sanctuary in Corella, Bohol.

Thousands of fruit bats with wingspans of 1.8 meters (6ft) roost in the lauan trees of Cubi Point at Subic Bay. They head out every night around 8pm to feed and return to roost by 5am. Most visitors to Subic will also see long-tailed macaques walking fences along the roadside, looking for a hand-out from visiting tourists – though feeding them is not recommended. Visitors to Honda Bay on Palawan will see giant fruit-eating bats flock over from an offshore island around sunset after a day's rest.

Philippines gives home to 488 species of coral and 1,000 different fish species. Among the more visible creatures are octopus, cuttlefish, and squid. Sea turtles can also be found on much of the coastline. The snorkeler out for a casual dip will easily turn up schools of tiny fish bearing a rainbow's worth of colors. On Apo or Tubbataha reef, look for manta rays and (harmless) sharks of the white-tipped and black-tipped types. Any of 20 dolphin species may pop up behind your boat in the waters off Dumaguete or Puerto Galera, for example.

Pearls are harvested in Philippine waters, from the natural South Sea pearls to the fresh-

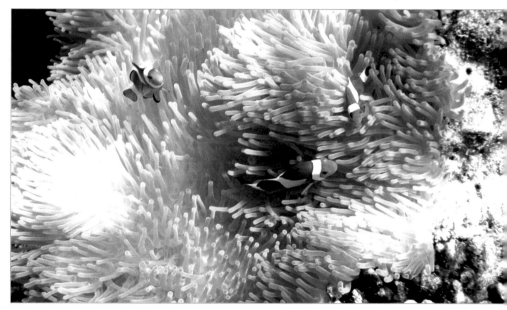

New species are always turning up in the Philippines. The Panay cloudrunner, for example, is one of 15 new mammals found and classified in the past 25 years and documented only in 1996. The 1kg (2lbs) gray, nocturnal rodent resembles a fox squirrel in appearance. Still, little is known of its native existence in the mountains of Panay in the Visayas.

## Marine life

With almost 36,300km (22,500 miles) of coastline (nearly twice that of the US), the

water, cultivated pearls of Mindanao province. Marlins and tuna are among the more prized commercial fish.

Perhaps the most unique underwater species is the massive whale shark or *butanding*, discovered in the Philippines in numbers larger than anywhere else on the planet. They congregate off the coast of Donsol, on the Bicol peninsula, from February to May every year (see page 214). Despite its protected status, unscrupulous villagers have slaughtered several of the 20-meter (66ft) -long giants, selling the meat to traders en route to the lucrative Taiwan market.

For more details on Philippine marine life, see Living Seas on page 272.

**ABOVE, FROM LEFT:** resident of the Philippine Tarsier Sanctuary in Corella, Bohol; coral and clownfish.

# DECISIVE DATES

## Early days

### Prehistory

Migrants cross land bridge from Asian mainland and settle in an archipelago that would become the Philippines.

### AD 900

Chinese establish coastal trading posts over the next 300 years.

### 1400

Muslim clergy start to bring Islam to the Philippines from Malaya.

## Colonial intrusions

### 1521

Explorer Ferdinand Magellan lands on Cebu and claims the region for Spain. Lapu Lapu (Rajah Cilapulapu), in defending his island of Mactan, slays Magellan.

### 1543

Next Spanish expedition led by Ruy de Villalobos lands in Mindanao. He names the archipelago "Filipinas," after Crown Prince Felipe II.

### 1565

Miguel Lopez de Legazpi sails from Mexico and gains a foothold in Cebu.

## Rise of Nationalism

### 1872

Uprising in Cavite, south of Manila. Spain executes Filipino priests Jose Burgos, Mariano Gomez, and Jacinto Zamora, martyrs to the cause of nationalism.

### 1892

Thinker Jose Rizal founds La Liga Filipina, is arrested and exiled to Dapitan, Mindanao. Andres Bonifacio founds the Katipunan with aim to revolt.

### 1896

Spanish colonists imprison and kill hundreds of Filipinos in Manila. Bonifacio and the Katipunan launch the Philippine revolution. Rizal is executed.

### 1898

The United States defeats Spain in a war. Treaty between the United States and Spain grants the US authority over the Philippines.

### 1899

War breaks out between the United States and the Philippines.

### 1935

Manuel Quezon elected president. The Philippines is made an American common-wealth with the promise of independence in 1945, but World War II intervenes.

## World War II

### 1941

On December 22, Japanese land on Luzon.

### 1942

Japanese overrun Manila. Quezon proposes and Roose-velt rejects Philippine neutrality.

### 1943

Japanese install puppet republic, under brutal rule, with Jose Laurel as president.

### 1944

MacArthur and Osmeña land in Leyte and begin the Allied effort to retake the archipelago.

### 1945

Allies recapture Manila, which is subject to intense bombardment. Much of the city is destroyed.

## Problems and opportunities

### 1946

On July 4, the Philippines is granted independence.

### 1965

Ferdinand Marcos defeats Diosdado Macapagal in his bid for re-election to the presidency.

### 1970

Peso devaluation fuels price increases, food shortages, unemployment, and unrest.

Students stage a series of anti-Marcos, anti-US demonstrations.

**1972–81**
Martial law imposed. Marcos accumulates a vast fortune. His wife, Imelda, dominates Manila government.

**1981**
Martial law lifted but Marcos keeps power to rule by decree. Marcos re-elected in contest boycotted by opposition.

**1983**
Leading opposition leader Benigno Aquino returns to Manila from US exile and is assassinated on arrival at Manila airport.

**1984**
"Parliament of the street" holds frequent anti-Marcos demonstrations. Spiraling economic crises.

**1985**
General Fabian C. Ver and 25 others are charged with slaying Aquino, but are acquitted. Marcos announces a snap election.

**1986**
Violence escalates before elections, at least 30 are killed on election day. Election rigging enrages Filipinos and millions join in uprising against Marcos regime. On February 26, Marcoses flee. Corazon Aquino elected to presidency.

**PRECEDING PAGE:** Vigan Heritage Village, Ilocos Region. **ABOVE, FROM LEFT:** Lapu Lapu Monument, Mactan Island; the assassination of Jose Rizal, as depicted by Lights and Sounds of Rizal, Manila; President Benigno Aquino III.

New constitution drafted.

**1987**
Ceasefire breaks down, and the military kills 13 peasant demonstrators near the presidential palace. Public ratifies constitution after third military mutiny put down. Concern about renewed human rights abuses. Pro-Aquino forces win majorities in House and Senate elections.

**1988**
Marcoses indicted by a US grand jury for fraud and embezzlement.

**1989**
Ferdinand Marcos dies in Hawaii. Amid coup threats, government calls on the US for air support to help Aquino government.

**1991**
Dramatic eruption of Mt Pinatubo. Americans pack up and leave the Philippines.

## Pragmatic revival

**1992**
Fidel Ramos, Aquino's defense secretary and a strong ally who backed her during coup attempts, wins presidential election. His pragmatic leadership defies traditional perceptions of inept Filipino government. Foreign investors return.

**1998**
Former action-movie star Joseph Estrada is elected president.

**2000**
Impeachment proceedings begin against Estrada on charges of corruption.

**2001**
Estrada's impeachment fails, and triggers massive street protests. After the military withdraws its support, Estrada is removed from office. His vice-president, Gloria Macapagal-Arroyo, takes over.

**2002**
US military joins the Philippines in large-scale exercises in the southern Philippines to rescue kidnapped American tourists.

**2009**
Fifty-seven journalists are massacred in a rebel-controlled province, an act linked to the 2010 election campaign.

**2010**
Benigno Aquino III, son of former president Corazon Aquino, wins the presidential race; a year later his government holds landmark talks with Muslim rebels.

**2011**
Gloria Macapagal-Arroyo prepares to stand trial on charges of graft and election fraud stemming from her presidential term.

**2012**
China and the Philippines clash over Scarborough Shoal in the contested South China Sea, seeding a high-level diplomatic dispute.

# BORN OF FIRE AND WATER

**When furious underwater action between vast tectonic plates blew lava up through the earth, the Philippine archipelago took form. Archeological sites reveal evidence of human occupation dating back 40,000 years.**

Some 43 million years ago the bottom of an ancient ocean opened to spew up bits of earth. Islands rose precariously, threatened on every side by huge waves. They needed to be anchored, if people were to live on them.

Echoes of this motif of unstable land can still be heard in the creation myths told by the indigenous tribes of the Philippines. A number of the archipelago's more than 7,100 islands continue to grow, while almost every year, typhoons threaten low shorelines and monsoon rains tear at mountain ranges as if in memory of when land first emerged.

The area is prone to earthquakes because the Philippine tectonic plate is squeezed between the vast Pacific and Asiatic plates. In the distant past, the Pacific Plate – the world's largest – slid along its northwest track, and the smaller Philippine Plate buckled and was ground into the adjacent Asiatic Plate. In a process called subduction, the much heavier Pacific Plate slipped under the Philippine Plate and threw up vast amounts of molten material deep in the earth. When the Philippine Plate buckled, fissures formed and the trapped molten mass poured forth in colossal volcanic eruptions in over 200 known volcanoes in the archipelago.

Northern Luzon sits on the western edge of the Philippine Plate, while the remaining islands rest on the eastern edge of the Asiatic Plate. A narrow belt running southeast from Zambales Province to Legaspi in Albay Province roughly follows the boundary

**LEFT:** Filipino tribesman. **RIGHT:** seventeenth-century map of Asia.

## BATTLE OF SEA AND SKY

All Filipinos have their own favorite creation myths which have nothing to do with geological theory.

One such story has it that several million years ago, there was a violent battle between the sea and sky. Their quarrel was started by a cunning bird that sowed discord in the hope of opening up dry land.

The sea vented its might at the sky, hurling huge walls of water at it, and the sky spat down islands and rocks to quell its crashing waves. Bombarded by the sheer number and weight of the islands and rocks, the sea was forced to admit defeat and retreat. The bird achieved its purpose and the Philippine archipelago was born.

between the two plates. This belt contains the most vigorous of the Philippine's two dozen active volcanoes, including Pinatubo, Taal, Banahaw, Iriga, and Mayon.

Around 2 million years ago, at the beginning of the Pleistocene epoch, the archipelago was already formed. But events were taking shape in the earth's polar regions, causing three successive ice ages that lowered sea levels by 100 meters (330ft). One large land area reached out into the Pacific Ocean from the Asian continent. Only the South China, Sulu, and Celebes basins remained as seas.

## Early inhabitants

Early humans soon followed grazing herds onto the newly exposed grassy plains. Over thousands of years, bands of early hunters pushed farther out into the continental bulge. At times, the rising waters isolated them on islands for scores of generations. Some took to the sea while others took to the mountains, developing unique patterns of life as varied as the plants and animals they followed.

Much of early human history remains rooted in speculation, but in the Philippine archipelago it is remarkably well documented. Archeologists have dated human occupation

### EARLY MILESTONES

Archeological digs show that the Negritos, a broad term for indigenous people of dark complexions, reached the Philippines around 25,000 years ago by a land bridge from the Asian mainland. Waves of Indonesians followed by sea from 3000 BC, while Malays got a firm foothold around 200 BC. Most of today's Filipinos have grown out of intermarriages between indigenous and Malay people. Modern Filipino language and cuisine, was heavily influenced by the Malays, who also introduced arts, literature, and a system of government.

A few centuries before the Spanish arrived in the 16th century, Filipinos involved in trade had also met Arabs and Hindus from India.

During the 14th century, the increasingly powerful Muslim trading communities on nearby Java began to exert their influence and in 1380 Islam entered the Philippines via Borneo. Muslim and Chinese traders in the Philippines fostered a new social order that included slaves and bonded servants.

In 1450, the Muslim sultanate of Jolo was established on the islands between Borneo and Mindanao, which today is the country's most dangerous area for travel because of the violent anti-government Muslim presence. Also in the 15th century, a Muslim sultanate called Maguindanao was founded on Mindanao as Islam continued to spread.

of the Cagayan Valley, on northern Luzon, to more than 40,000 years ago. No human skeleton has yet to be found, but scientists agree that the flake and cobble tools unearthed in beds of stegodon, rhinoceros, and other fossils are proof of Paleolithic human life. On Palawan, human skeletal remains have been dated to more than 20,000 years ago.

A Neolithic site in Dimolit, Cagayan, has yielded the earliest pottery in the Philippines, dating to 5,000 years ago. Another Neolithic site is at Callao, in the Cagayan Valley, where stone tools and pottery were excavated and dated to 4,000 years ago. The fabled rice ter-

links with China as early as that period. In addition, historians have uncovered accounts of trade missions to China. Chinese records show that several tributary missions were made to China between the 10th and 15th centuries.

Among the most spectacular archeological finds is a 14cm (16ins), 21-carat, solid gold figure discovered in Agusan del Norte in 1917. Looking similar to an Indo-Javanese queen or a deity in the Mahayana Buddhist or Hindu pantheon, it suggests a link between the Philippines and Asian tradition as early as AD 1000. It is now kept in the Field Museum of Natural History in Chicago.

races of the Ifugao people have been identified as being 2,000 to 3,000 years old.

Finds at the Butuan site in Agusan del Norte, Mindanao, and in caves on Palawan show that the early inhabitants were engaged in far-reaching trade. Ancient boats, gold ornaments, pottery, and evidence of metalworking unearthed at Butuan point to long-distance maritime commerce as early as the 10th century. Excavations on Palawan yielded burial jars, porcelain, and stoneware from China's Sung dynasty (960–1279), indicating strong trade

**ABOVE, FROM LEFT:** rice cultivation dates back to 2,000–3,000 years ago; Iron-Age pottery at the Cagayan Museum and Historical Research Center.

### GOLDEN VOLCANOES

A "seamount" was detected in 1998 off the coastal town of Tabango on Leyte island. Oceanographers have confirmed that this possibly volcanic "Tabango Underwater Mountain," with a nearly perfect cone, rises from depths of 300 meters (1,000ft) and broke free of the sea's surface to grow 10 meters (33ft) from 1992 to 1997.

Other Philippine islands rest on underwater mountains formed by the outpourings of molten rocks from the earth's interior. The activity has allowed a mineral deposition and is believed to have left some deposits of gold, formed over 1.5 million years. People still seach for gold in parts of Luzon.

# Le Petit Journal

Le Petit Journal
CHAQUE JOUR 5 CENTIMES

Le Supplément illustré
CHAQUE SEMAINE 5 CENTIMES

## SUPPLÉMENT ILLUSTRÉ

Huit pages : CINQ centimes

ABONNEMENTS

|  | SIX MOIS | UN AN |
|---|---|---|
| SEINE ET SEINE-ET-OISE | 2 fr. | 3 fr. 50 |
| DÉPARTEMENTS | 2 fr. | 4 fr. |
| ÉTRANGER | 2 50 | 5 fr. |

Douzième année

DIMANCHE 14 AVRIL 1901

Numéro 5

# LA GUERRE AUX PHILIPPINES
## Capture d'Aguinaldo

# FOREIGN DOMINATION

After centuries of intrusion by Spanish, British, American, and Japanese forces, nationalist uprisings and violent reprisals, the Philippine call for freedom and independence was finally answered.

Since prehistoric times, the Philippine islands have been populated by peoples of Malay origin. Most of them lived simply in scattered villages at river mouths. Their houses were made of bamboo and palm-thatch. They grew rice and fished for a living. Until 3,000 years ago, contact with the outside world was minimal. The following centuries saw arrivals by Chinese, Indian, Arab, and Indonesian traders. They brought pottery, textiles, iron weapons, tools, and jewelry to barter for pearls, coral, and gold. They also made commercial and political imprints that endure to this day.

Unlike the Chinese settlers who exercised substantial commercial power but little political influence, the traders that came from the south in 1400 introduced Islam, an influence that swept through the Sulu Archipelago. The new faith consolidated groups that later vigorously resisted foreign rulers and, more recently, Philippine national rule.

## The Spanish arrive

The archipelago's recorded history began half a world away in a small, dusty town in southwestern Spain. The Treaty of Tordesillas was inked in 1494, dividing between Spain and Portugal the yet-unexplored world. Everything to the east of a line 370 leagues west of the Cape Verde Islands in the Atlantic belonged to Portugal and everything west was Spain's.

The Portuguese set off to navigate Africa's Cape of Good Hope in search of the riches of the Spice Islands, while the Spanish headed across the vast Pacific. The captain of Spain's

**LEFT:** rebel leader Emilio Aguinaldo is captured.
**RIGHT:** Lapu-Lapu monument, Mactan Island.

search was a Portuguese who had taken up the flag of Castile and the Spanish name Hernando de Magallanes; to the English-speaking world, he is Ferdinand Magellan.

Magellan took 109 days to cross the Pacific Ocean but missed every island in the vast body of water, save the tiny atoll of Poka Puka and Guam. In 1521, he made landfall on the island of Homonhon, off the southern tip of Samar in the Philippines. Calling the new lands Lazarus, after the saint's day on which he first sighted them, Magellan sailed on through the Gulf of Leyte to Limasawa island. There he celebrated the first Mass in the Philippines' history.

Six weeks later, Magellan was dead. He had sailed to the island of Cebu, where he Christianized the local *rajah* (king) and his followers. However, a chieftain of Mactan – the island where Cebu's international airport now sits – rebelled against the Rajah of Cebu and his foreign guests. Chieftain Lapu Lapu and his 2,000 men defended their island against 48 armor-clad Spaniards in April 1521. A white obelisk today marks the spot where Magellan was slain.

It was not until 1565 that Spain, under Miguel Lopez de Legazpi, gained a foothold in Cebu. Over the next few years, the Spanish pushed northward, defeating Muslim chieftain Sulayman and taking over his fortress of Maynilad, facing what is now Manila Bay. Here,

> Chinese junks converged in Manila yearly from 1572 to 1815, carrying silk and other luxuries from Persia and India. The Spanish eagerly bought the goods for re-export to Mexico on the Manila Galleon, for payment in Mexican silver.

for sparing the city from being razed. But his troops looted the city anyway, and civil governor Dawson Drake stripped the governor's palace of its lavish fittings and shipped them home in cases marked "Rice for Drake."

The Spanish retreated north of Manila to

in 1571, Legazpi built the Spanish walled city of Intramuros.

Bands of conquistadors, newly arrived from Mexico, fanned out from Intramuros to conquer Luzon and the Visayas. They met ineffectual opposition, and soon entrenched themselves as lords of great estates worked by the natives, called *indios*, in the manner as applied to Mexican "Indians." The friars who accompanied them rapidly converted the population, building churches, schools, roads, and bridges, while accumulating vast land holdings for the Catholic Church.

Late in 1762, as a minor episode in the Seven Years' War with Spain, Intramuros was seized by England's General William Draper, who collected almost 4 million pesos in exchange

the province of Pampanga, where they set up a new seat of government. Due to a lack of reinforcements, the British could not hold on to Intramuros, and were dislodged in early 1764.

## Rise of the nationalists

In the late 18th and early 19th centuries, the Spanish introduced important political, economic, and social reforms, allowing limited Filipino participation in government. They also introduced cash crops such as sugar, tobacco, indigo, and hemp; at the same time, they put an end to the galleon monopoly on foreign commerce.

But by that time, the nationalist movement had taken root, led by the liberal clergy, professionals, and a clique of Filipino students studying in Spain. A minor uprising sprang up in Cavite, near Manila, in 1872, causing the Spanish authorities to panic. Three well-known Filipino priests – Jose Burgos, Mariano Gomez, and Jacinto Zamora – were garrotted after being convicted of inspiring subversion.

Their deaths fanned the fire of nationalism during the last two decades of the 19th century. Three leaders emerged: Jose Rizal, Andres Bonifacio, and Emilio Aguinaldo. Rizal led the Propaganda Movement to promote equality for the Filipinos. Bonifacio headed a secret society named Katipunan, which advocated armed insurrection, while Aguinaldo led the Philippines' first declaration of independence in 1898.

The Katipunan organized a major revolt in 1896. Many revolutionaries were captured and executed, including peace advocate Rizal.

## Revolutionary rivalry

With Rizal's death, the remaining revolutionaries were divided into two rival camps led by Bonifacio and General Aguinaldo, who was more skilled in battle. The latter had Bonifacio arrested, and under controversial circumstances, the Katipunan founder was executed.

This would have meant the end of the revolution, had not the crafty Aguinaldo offered the Spanish a truce in return for his voluntary deportation to Hong Kong with some payment as well. Once in exile, the revolutionary leader formed a junta and purchased more arms, while seizing the opportunity to seek support from Asian neighbors such as Japan. In 1898, he returned to Manila and had himself inaugurated as president of the first Philippine republic. Independence was won – for a day – as the Filipino intelligensia gathered in Malolos, a town north of Manila, and wrote the charter for the first constitutional republic in Asia.

In the meantime, Spain and the United States had gone to war over Cuba. Admiral George Dewey sailed into Manila Bay and engaged the aging Spanish fleet in what historians describe as a mock confrontation. Filipino revolutionary troops had already surrounded Manila and were preparing to march in and cap the victory when Aguinaldo hesitated, believing that their alliance with the Americans would seal the fate of Spain. Unknown to him, Dewey had allowed the Spanish admiral a face-saving gesture. In return, the old colonists made way for the new. So the Americans took over.

Distrust of the Americans developed and grew, until the first exchange of fire between Filipino and American troops on the San Juan bridge on the outskirts of Manila on February 4, 1899. Hostilities erupted and ushered in guerrilla warfare that lasted until 1902, taking at least 300,000 civilian and military lives from both sides.

With the end of the Spanish-American War, Spain had ceded the Philippines, Puerto Rico,

### A TOAST TO INDEPENDENCE

General Emilio Aguinaldo and his revolutionaries celebrated the ratification of the Declaration of Philippine Independence with an elaborate French banquet at the Barasoain Church in Malolos on September 29, 1898. Even the menu was in French. Two prominent chefs from Sulipan, a town celebrated for its French culinary excellence, served a feast that included crab, oysters, buttered prawns, salami *de Lyon*, and salmon Hollandaise. These were washed down with wines and champagne, not to mention Chartreuse and Cognac. The revolutionaries may not have spoken French, but that day they manifested great ability at eating French.

**ABOVE, FROM LEFT:** nineteenth-century depiction of the death of Ferdinand Magellan; American troops torturing a Filipino native.

and Guam to the United States, and paid an indemnity of US$20 million. Filipinos now realized the Americans offered not independence but just another style of colonialism.

Aguinaldo's luck had run out, too. He found himself pursued by American troops

*American rule proved benign for the most part, bringing lessons in English and in self-government. It's no accident that today most Filipinos speak a measure of English, and government institutions are based on those in the US.*

to the wilderness of northern Luzon, and was finally captured in Palanan, Isabela, on March 23, 1901. Aguinaldo ordered all revolutionaries to accept American rule, but the other generals refused and many were captured and executed.

## Liberation at last

The Americans, defining their role as one of trusteeship and tutelage, promoted rapid political, economic, and social development. Then World War II intervened.

On December 22, 1941, Japanese forces landed in the Philippines and fought their way

### THE MACARTHUR SUITE

The MacArthur Suite is one of the Manila Hotel's special attractions. The three-room complex in a newer wing of the historic downtown hotel memorializes rooms actually occupied by the general upon his triumphant retaking of Manila. It was there he was known to have had a tryst with Filipina actress Elizabeth "Dimples" Cooper. Some Catholics were scandalized over that episode, but by and large Manileños turned a blind eye to the affair.

Today the suite goes for US$650 per night. It includes a study, a powder room, and views of Manila Bay.

down the Bataan Peninsula of Luzon. Despite the heroic resistance of General Douglas MacArthur's American and Filipino troops, the Japanese stormed the fortress island of Corregidor, occupied Manila, and eventually overran the whole archipelago.

On leaving Corregidor, MacArthur had pledged, "I shall return." He kept his word. In 1945, the American-Filipino troops fought their way back into Manila. The liberation of the Philippines may have cost enormous losses in lives and property, but Filipinos greeted the moment with jubilation.

**ABOVE:** Leyte Landing Memorial at Red Beach where General MacArthur landed in 1944.

# A Hero for All Seasons

**Physician Jose Rizal wrote novels that planted seeds of revolution in the Philippines, though he declined to help overthrow the Spanish. But it was too late.**

No self-respecting town in the country is without a statue of the man, or does not have a major street named after him. Reverence for thinker Dr Jose Rizal, who died a martyr at age 35 in the last years of Spanish rule, has spanned a century and spread to foreign lands.

Born on June 19, 1861, in the town of Calamba in Laguna Province, Rizal was to live a short but eventful life. He had initially studied ophthalmology to cure his mother's eye condition; he was also a physician, naturalist, botanist, engineer, linguist, sculptor, musician, composer, poet, dramatist, novelist, reformist, thinker, and writer.

Rizal's two novels – *Noli Me Tangere (Touch Me Not)* and *El Filibusterismo (The Filibusterer)* – were written and published in Europe at the time he led a movement for political reforms. The novels were deemed incendiary by powerful friars.

He was exiled to Dapitan, Mindanao, for four years after returning from Europe. There he set up a school, fixed up the waterworks, and wrote music. He also won the heart of Josephine Bracken, an Irish woman who had accompanied her foster father to his eye operation. Their brief seaside romance was marred only by a stillborn son.

## Exile and imprisonment

Emissaries from Andres Bonifacio's Katipunan, which favored armed struggle, offered to help Rizal escape so he could return to Manila to lead the revolution. Instead, the writer who advocated non-violence volunteered to serve as a doctor for the war in Cuba. But when his ship docked at the first port on the way to the Americas, a telegram came, ordering his return to Manila.

He was placed under arrest on the grounds of complicity in the revolution, and a quick trial sentenced him to death by musketry. In his cell in Fort Santiago, Rizal composed a long poem in Spanish, *Mi Ultimo Adios (My Last Farewell)*. He concealed it inside an oil lamp, which he handed to his sisters on the eve of his execution.

He walked calmly to his death at dawn on December 30, 1896, to a field by Manila Bay called Bagumbayan, later renamed Luneta for its crescent shape. Rizal protested against having to be shot in the back, for he was no traitor. As the shots rang out, he attempted to twist his body to face the rising sun at the moment of death. His last words were *"Consummatum est"* ("It is finished").

His martyrdom set the country aflame. A revolution broke out, and soon Asia had its first independent republic, cut short by the Americans' entry into the Pacific. The new colonial power recognized Rizal as a national hero.

## Tributes worldwide

On the centennial of his death, a monument to Rizal was unveiled in Madrid, the capital of the colonial government that had executed him by firing squad. Rizal busts or markers can be found on a plaza in Heidelberg, Germany, at a residential building in London, in cities across the United States where Filipino American communities have strong representation, and in Latin America.

An international conference on Rizal in 1997 took place in Jakarta to give tribute to a man described by Malaysian Deputy Prime Minister Anwar Ibrahim as "the pride of the Malay race," a reference to the historical ethnic origins of many Filipinos.

**RIGHT:** national hero Jose Rizal.

# THE DEMOCRATIC ERA

Freed at last from colonialism, Filipinos lived through the excesses of the Marcos years before Fidel Ramos began turning the country around, setting an example which more recent presidents have found hard to follow.

After World War II, the American authorities devoted themselves first to desperately needed emergency relief, then to the Philippines' long-delayed independence – proclaimed on July 4, 1946 – and finally to the colossal task of post-war rebuilding and development.

The country's democratic era through to the present day has been dominated by a few political dynasties known for their charm and tenacity. Voters are resigned to dynastic entitlement to power as a fact of life, while upstart rivals face physical harm, including assassination, if they make a credible bid for office.

## Marcos moves center stage

Manuel Roxas served as the first president of post-war, independent Philippines, but died before finishing his term and was succeeded by Elpidio Quirino, his vice-president. Quirino won the election in 1949 and served a full term. Despite advances in foreign relations, domestic issues cost him his re-election bid. Voters instead picked Ramon Magsaysay. But Magsaysay died in a plane crash, leaving the top job to his vice-president, Carlos Garcia, who was credited with stimulating business. Garcia also came up short and lost in 1961 to his own vice-president, Diosdado Macapagal.

Macapagal's victory ushered in serious efforts at instituting some measure of land reform. He led the way for the formation of Maphilindo, an alliance with Malaysia and Indonesia, which led to the creation of ASEAN, the Association of Southeast Asian Nations.

### HELL OF A DEAL

Manuel Quezon, Sergio Osmeña, and Manuel Roxas had all distinguished themselves by leading missions to the United States to seek early sovereignty for their country. It was the fiery, eloquent (particularly in Spanish and most notably for expletives) Quezon who is credited with uttering the immortal line: "Better a government run like hell by Filipinos than one run like heaven by Americans."

To which, of course, generations of Filipinos, especially the many who lobbied for and who may still entertain notions of American statehood, have caustically replied: "Well, thanks to our Filipino leaders, we're still in hell."

**LEFT:** President Benigno Aquino III. **RIGHT:** Ex-president Ferdinand Marcos and his wife Imelda.

Ferdinand Marcos defeated Macapagal in 1965 to win the presidency. Once again, the rule of rotation prevailed and, in 1969, Marcos became the only Philippine president to gain re-election. He was the seventh president, and seven years after he took office, Marcos imposed martial law in 1972. The official line given out was that the republic was in peril. Confronted with student unrest, Muslim revolts in Mindanao, and a rural communist insurgency, Marcos faced little resistance from either the opposition or the military, which he mollycoddled.

On September 23, 1972, the country awoke to an absence of media; no newspapers, radio, or

*President Macapagal decreed an end to the commemoration of Independence Day on July 4, the day Americans celebrate their own. June 12, the day Aguinaldo proclaimed independence in 1898, is now Philippines National Day.*

tv broadcasts. Soon the word was out. Raids and arrests were made left and right by the military. Hours later, a television station was allowed to transmit news from Malacañang Palace: Martial law was in effect and the executive order had been signed two days earlier. A curfew was in

### THE GUY

Former Secretary of National Defense Ramon Magsaysay had succeeded in turning back rebellious peasants. Then in 1953, Magsaysay ran against Elpidio Quirino, who was seeking re-election, and won. (His election campaign slogan: "Magsaysay is my guy.")

The Guy, as he was called, was well loved for his simple ways. Nationalists, however, were sure he was no more than a stooge of the CIA.

Magsaysay failed to finish his term. He died in a plane crash on Mt Manunggal, off Cebu City, on March 17, 1957, and Filipinos grieved at the loss of this down-to-earth leader with an easy charm.

place. Citizens were told that discipline would save the nation. Marcos started erecting monuments to himself and accumulating a vast fortune for himself as well as his "cronies."

Marcos and his wife Imelda – called the Conjugal Dictatorship by disenchanted Filipinos – prospered until the 1983 assassination of the popular opposition leader, Benigno "Ninoy" Aquino, Jr. On his return to the Philippines after self-imposed exile in America, Aquino was shot dead under highly suspicious circumstances just after stepping off the plane at Manila airport. The assassination fanned discontent. Faced with a restless populace, Marcos called a snap election in February 1986 to renew his mandate. Amid unsubtle election fraud, he was proclaimed the winner over Aquino's widow Corazon (Cory). But Marcos was losing ground; his political cronies began to jump ship and, in that same month, a four-day bloodless revolution climaxed with a standoff between Marcos's tanks and citizens at a busy highway that ran between two military camps in Manila.

Marcos and his wife were bundled off in an American plane to Hawaii. Marcos died there in 1989. Imelda was later to return to the Philippines. The specter of the Marcos regime lingered long after his departure as he left behind a depressed economy and an exhausted treasury.

## Aquino's daunting task

The overthrow of Marcos was made complete by the inauguration of Corazon Aquino as president. She had her work cut out: overhaul the government and military, revive the economy, weed out corrupt bureaucratic practices, and restore public trust – in essence, rebuild the nation.

It was a massive task, made worse by continuing communist insurgency, political infighting, persistent undermining of her mandate by Marcos supporters, and deeply embedded bureaucratic corruption. In the process, Aquino survived seven coup attempts – and for one of which she was forced to ask for American military assistance.

The woes of economic stagnation eventually dampened the initial exhilaration that accompanied Aquino's victory. Symbolic of the times were the daily electrical outages called brownouts in Manila. Brownouts remain common in rural areas.

The most important signal of the end of the post-Marcos era was the withdrawal of the American military. The US presence at that time centered around Subic Bay Naval Base and Clark Air Force Base, both north of Manila. The bases were a significant factor in the economy and the Americans claimed that the area's security depended on them, but as they also served US interests, the Filipinos felt the US should pay substantially more for the leases.

The bilateral posturing ended abruptly in 1991 with the eruption of Mt Pinatubo. Clark was covered in volcanic ash, so the Americans packed

up and left. A year later, after the Senate decided against a new lease on Subic, the Americans hauled up anchor and sailed away. Clark is now an industrial zone with the Clark International Airport (also known as Diosdado Macapagal airport), while Subic is a duty-free freeport zone with dozens of companies using its facilities.

## Pragmatic revival

In the 1992 presidential election, Fidel Ramos, Aquino's defense secretary and a strong ally during the coup attempts, won a seven-way presidential election with just 24 percent of the vote. Ramos too faced numerous problems.

### THE LEGEND OF FERDINAND MARCOS

Ferdinand Marcos was a dynamic orator and a brilliant politician, possessed of a brutal determination to get his way. He was also unusually talented in his ability to manipulate the patronage system to secure excessive material gain. He billed himself a war hero, but his medals for valor were later proven to be fake. The son of an Ilocos congressman, Marcos took up law studies and became a champion debater. After his father had been defeated in a local election by Julio Nalundasan, the victor was brushing his teeth one night by a window when he was shot dead. Marcos was indicted for the crime. He defended his own case and won acquittal.

**ABOVE, FROM LEFT:** the funeral procession of the opposition leader Benigno Aquino Jr, who was assassinated in 1983; former president Corazon Aquino.

*With hindsight, Corazon Aquino's transitional administration accomplished little, but at that time, it was an important symbol, which helped boost the esteem of the country.*

The Philippines had been sparring with China over groups of small islands – including the Spratlys – in the South China Sea. Since the late 1990s, military units have periodically been sent to the area to signal Manila's claim. Chinese construction of semi-permanent mini-barracks on one islet in 1999 did nothing to soothe nerves.

Besides a population that is increasing at a higher rate than even Thailand and Indonesia, the most immediate domestic problem has been the Muslim secessionist movement in Mindanao, which has claimed over 60,000 lives since the 1970s. Ramos successfully engineered peace and autonomy for the region with the return to the political system of the majority of the Muslim rebels, including their primary leader. Many former guerrillas have become regulars in the national army, but radical splinter groups are still a threat. Violence erupted again in 2009 when armed men linked to a Mindanao provincial governor killed 12 journalists and 30 others.

## THE PHILIPPINE ECONOMY

Much business activity in the Philippines remains outside the scope of government monitoring. Estimates on the size of that sector, which covers informal trade and direct sales, range from 25 percent to 40 percent of the gross national product. As an estimated 14 million Filipinos live or work abroad in places such as Dubai, Hong Kong, and the United States, dollar remittances have been a significant boost to the economy. From just a little over US$1 billion in 1990, those remittances total around US$20 billion annually.

The economy grew under President Ramos, but suffered in late 1997 from the Asian economic downturn. Joseph Estrada, elected as president in 1998, hurt the economy further as his presidency was plagued by corruption scandals.

Corruption still holds back new infrastructure and other programs. Transparency International gave the Philippines a perceived corruption score of 2.6 out of 10 for 2011 and ranked it 129th cleanest in the world, toward the bottom of its scale.

Despite problems in government, private industries such as mining, offshore natural gas, automotive manufacturing, and microchip production have given the Philippine economy a foundation. The country's 2011 GDP expanded 3.72 percent to the 46th economy in the world.

During Ramos' single six-year term, the future started looking better – and more certain – for Filipinos. Ramos promised to strengthen the economy and enable the Philippines to share in the prosperity enjoyed by Asian rivals such as Malaysia, Korea, and Taiwan. He also promised improvements in electrical power supplies and in other areas of infrastructure, not to mention a general housecleaning of the corrupt political system. Such promises had often been heard but seldom kept. But Ramos kept his.

After years of instability and natural disasters, the Philippines finally began to show signs of solid improvement. One of Ramos's first tasks was to put Manila's lights back on – reliably – by having private industry build oil-burning power plants, eliminating the dreaded brownouts.

The new political stability and major economic reforms allowed for economic turnaround. Decades-old protectionism and state intervention gave way to economic liberalization and industry deregulation. The telephone industry, which used to be a private monopoly, was opened to new players. Full deregulation of the petroleum industry was accomplished and the privatization drive included the public utilities.

## Economic hotspots

The Philippines' strengths are its strategic location in the heart of the world's fastest-growing region, abundant natural resources, a Westernized business environment, and a high level of English proficiency. In recent years the language factor has made the Philippines one of the top bases for call centers outsourced from North America and Europe.

Although much of the economic activity is in Metro Manila, the recovery spawned dynamic growth centers elsewhere in the archipelago. North of the capital, the Subic Bay Freeport Zone has gone from a military base to an economic zone that offers generous investment incentives.

Modern industrial estates have sprouted south of Metro Manila, an agro-industrial corridor that takes up the excess from factories in the overcrowded capital. A law allowing foreigners to lease land for up to 75 years has encouraged investors from Japan and North America.

Much of the growth has focused on industrial

estates and financial centers, including central business districts adjacent to the financial district of Makati, in the Ortigas area, and in south Metro Manila. Agriculture has continued to be the economy's weak spot. Most farmers work as landless tenants, and two-thirds of all poor families live in rural areas.

The high level of poverty has led a number of investors to underestimate the potential of the domestic market. But many urban Filipino consumers are young, highly literate, and ambitious consumers. The success of newer shopping malls, a growth in retail chains and the proliferation of fast-food outlets testify to urban spending power.

Visitors who have been to overcrowded shopping malls in Metro Manila and Cebu may wonder where the people's purchasing power comes from, given official statistics on poverty and unemployment. But such numbers miss the strength of the informal, undocumented economy and money coming back from Filipinos working overseas.

## New starts

The presidency of Joseph Estrada, a former actor who was elected in 1998, was plagued by corruption scandals. In January 2001 he was forced out of office by massive street protests. He went on trial through 2007 on charges of plunder and perjury involving hundreds of millions of pesos.

**ABOVE, FROM LEFT:** demonstrations in the US against Fidel Ramos; Metro Manila, the nerve center of the Philippine economy.

*A tribute website, www.noynoy-aquino.com, calls President Benigno "Noynoy" Aquino III an "enthusiast" of shooting and billiards, who enjoys music, particularly "jazz, bossa nova and OPM (Original Pilipino Music)."*

A legal body equivalent to a court of appeals found him guilty of plunder, though innocent of perjury, and sentenced him to life imprisonment.

His vice-president Gloria Macapagal-Arroyo, appointed as successor, served the remaining four years of his term and went on to win the next election in 2004. She pardoned Estrada in October 2007. While initial hopes of a quick fix after the Asian economic crisis proved optimistic for the Philippines, Macapagal-Arroyo targeted problematic areas such as corruption in government and inefficiencies in the infrastructure. But her momentum would eventually be reversed. In late 2011, out of office for more than a year, she was arrested and charged with electoral fraud. She denied the charges as her case unfolded in court.

In June 2010 Benigno Aquino III took office as president. The son of former president Corazon Aquino and the assassinated Senator Benigno Aquino Jr is credited with reacting

## SOUTH CHINA SEA DISPUTE

President Benigno Aquino III has amplified his country's voice as part of a long-standing effort to stick up for a claim over hundreds of uninhabited but fishery-rich South China Sea islets. The Philippines faced off against China in 2012 over the Scarborough Shoal near Zambales Province.

China, Taiwan, Vietnam, and the Philippines compete for claims to the islets, with occasional naval clashes since the 1970s west of Palawan and north of Borneo. China and Vietnam, both seeking oil or natural gas deposits, have become particularly aggressive. The US military has effectively backed smaller claimants such as the Philippines.

quickly to damage from typhoons and agreeing to negotiate with state's chief domestic enemy: restive Muslim rebel groups from Mindanao. He came under fire briefly in 2010 for the country's handling of a hostage incident that left eight Hong Kong tourists slain on a bus in Manila.

Aquino started 2012 with a push to assert Philippine claims to the South China Sea, which is rich in fisheries and possibly undersea oil or natural gas reserves. His government has cozied up to the country's arch-ally the United States for protection.

**ABOVE:** President Benigno Aquino III (fourth from right) leads events to mark the 25th anniversary of the fall of the Marcos dictatorship.

# "Imeldific" Imelda

**Long after returning from exile, the extravagant wife of former Philippine strongman Ferdinand Marcos grabs headlines in the Philippines and still stands by her man**

Imelda Marcos threw two parties when she turned 70 on June 2, 1999. The first was in Rizal Park, attended by the usual motley gathering of so-called Marcos loyalists. The second celebration involved 1,000 bejeweled guests at a sit-down dinner at Manila Hotel. Madame Meldy showed up with a ruby-and-diamond tiara, necklace and bracelets. Together, the parties show a continuing loyalty to her embattled late husband and a focus on personal wealth that still wows the world.

The woman born in 1929 and dubbed one half of a "Conjugal Dictatorship" fled with the ex-president to Hawaii in 1986 amid popular discontent over his iron grip, but returned after Ferdinand Marcos died in 1989.

A continuing saga of the recovery of the fabled Marcos billions unfolds sporadically, destroying the reputation of government lawyers. Ten thousand Filipino human rights victims who filed a class action suit in a Honolulu court were awarded a legal victory, but must contend with the Philippine government over the division of the token amounts recovered. Compromise solutions are ever in the works.

## An enigma

Imelda confuses all, both enemies and protectors. One day, she laments her family's reliance on the kindness of strangers; the next, she boasts that they practically own the entire country. All are public statements, as she thrives in the media limelight.

Her only consistency is that she stands by her man. Imelda regularly pulls out a handkerchief and wipes a corner of her eye, while insisting that Ferdinand Marcos was not just a brilliant hero, but a practical man who built his wealth before he turned dictator.

Born to poor relations of the landed Romualdez

**RIGHT:** the inimitable Imelda Marcos.

clan of Leyte Province in the Visayas, she never forgot or forgave her early station in life. She won a beauty contest and, as Miss Manila, was swept off her feet by the dashing Marcos in a whirlwind seven-day courtship. As a partner, she enhanced Marcos's political campaigns, singing onstage and providing glamor, or as how she describes herself, "the heart that gave the poor a glimpse of beauty."

As Ferdinand Marcos consolidated power, Imelda became Metro Manila Governor and Minister of Human Settlements. Her love of the grand gesture prompted the building of cultural and film centers to showcase "the good, the true and the beautiful." In 2004, the documentary film *Imelda* swept inter-

national film festivals. Imelda, despite having participated in its making, attempted to have its screening blocked in Philippine cinemas. The documentary was shown anyway.

## Congresswoman at 81

In 2010 the 81-year-old former first lady won a congressional seat representing a part of her late husband's native Ilocos Norte Province.

In another comeback sign, ex-president Macapagal-Arroyo stopped the auction of jewelry collections confiscated from Imelda as she protested the sale of treasures worth an estimated P15 million. But Imelda Marcos is still known the world over for having owned 3,000 pairs of shoes, a testament to her glamorous tastes.

# FILIPINOS

**Naturally hospitable and welcoming to outsiders, the Filipino also retains a strong sense of kinship within the wider family, which influences many areas of daily life.**

*Spanish mestizo are largely of Catalan, Andalusian, or Basque descent, and some are from Italian territories ruled by Spain at the time of colonization.*

As of early 2012, about 103 million people live in the Philippines, a rapid rise from 27 million in 1960. It is one of the most densely populated countries in the world. Although Filipinos pack the often jerrybuilt cities for jobs, many stick to the rural areas where they plant fields or fish the seas.

Filipinos are generally descended from a proto-Malay stock, preceded only by nomadic aborigines who crossed land bridges from mainland Asia before these were submerged to isolate the archipelago. Those early Philippine inhabitants intermarried into Chinese settlements and later with the Spanish during their 333-year period of colonization. Many present-day Filipinos, or *Pinoys* as they call themselves, are of mixed heritage, known as Spanish *mestizo*. It's unclear how many live in the Philippines today, but estimates range from 3.5 million to 36 million.

Descendants of the Spaniards live largely in cities, but even in the countryside it is not uncommon to come upon fair-skinned residents with obvious *mestizo* features.

## Family support

An extended support system remains both the main strength of Filipino society and the customary source of corruption. Kinship ties of both blood and marriage, often up to three generations removed, are kept well defined and operative on all levels and facets of life. Clans operate as custodians of common experiences, and in memory of geographical and racial origins. They act as disciplinary mechanisms, placement agencies, and informal social security systems. When there is a marriage between two clans, it is as much an alliance as a binding of two individuals.

Within the sometimes tyrannical embrace of the clan, members of all ages find their place in an orderly self-policed world. Children are cared for by an array of helpful aunts, uncles, cousins, and grandparents, and the elderly are given care and reverence through to their last days.

Asians outside the Philippines, such as in China and South Korea, follow similar traditions of intense family unity. But as those

*The naturally easy-going, good-humored Filipinos are more open to outsiders than peers elsewhere in East Asia. Doors open quickly to new house guests, and Filipino-foreign marriages are anything but rare.*

countries have modernized past the level of the Philippines, advances in their legal systems, banking, and commerce have increased faith in doing transactions with people outside the family.

### Yes SIR

Sociologists have coined the phrase "smooth interpersonal relationships", or SIR for short, to indicate the key premise of human contact among Filipinos: face-to-face communication must be kept smooth at all times by gentle speech, no matter how unpleasant the message. Direct confrontation is generally avoided. When forced to deliver a negative message, Filipinos are fond of emissaries and subtle indirection, out of respect for the sensitivity of the other party. (Filipino hospitality workers are so keen on calling male guests "sir" that multiple uses of the honorific can slow conversation.)

Part of the SIR ritual is to use polite forms of address when conversing with strangers, especially older people and those of high social rank. Tagalog is packed with such terminology. Words include *po* and *ho* to end sentences, *opo* and *oho* to say yes, and *hindi po* and *hindi ho* to say no. Even in face-to-face conversation, one refers to a new acquaintance, an older person, or a dignitary in the third person-plural *sila*. The intention is to maintain a respectful distance, beginning on the verbal level, from which to slowly establish a pleasant relationship.

*The concept of hiya,* literally translated as shame, but also defined as a delicacy of sensitivity to the feelings of others, prevents individuals from taking each other for granted. Related to *hiya* is *pakiramdaman*, or feeling each other out. Beyond words, Filipinos often intuit or divine what the other means to communicate.

A second, essential strand in the fabric of social relationships is *utang na loob*, or debt

of gratitude. As elsewhere in Asia, favors long bestowed are never forgotten and always returned in an invisible bond of reciprocity. Of course, *utang na loob* (both individual and collective) has also been responsible for sluggish bureaucracies resistant to impersonal but rational management procedures.

A third Filipino concept is *pakikisama*, which can be defined as "getting along" or submitting to group will. Although this tradition may suppress individual expression or trying out new ideas, when positively applied *pakikisama* has tremendous power to mobilize individual energies for collective goals.

Perhaps the crowning glory of local sociology is the Filipino expression traced to a linguistic root of *Bahala na,* or "leave it to God." This is a typical Filipino reaction to crises and insoluble problems. Development experts have often decried *Bahala na as* passive and fatalist, holding back further development in the country.

### Ethnic and minority groups

Ethnic minorities continue to play a major role in the Philippines. Over 80 ethnic groups are scattered in relative isolation about the islands, usually in the mountains far from even second-tier cities. Some inhabit accessible villages, where visitors can catch glimpses of native customs and lifestyles.

**PRECEDING PAGES:** Valentine's Day Parade, Ilocos region. **ABOVE, FROM LEFT:** workers in Metropolitan Manila; mother and child in Bukidnon Province, Northern Mindanao.

Of the total Philippine population, some 10–25 percent are classified as cultural or ethnic minorities. Most of these people live separately from mainstream Filipinos who are of Malay heritage and city or coastal-dwellers. Some 60 percent of the country's ethnic minorities are made up of Muslim groups living in Mindanao and the Sulu Archipelago. The remaining peoples – comprising mostly animists – inhabit the mountain provinces of northern and central Luzon, and the big island's highland plains. Some populate the rainforests and isolated seashores of Mindanao and Palawan islands. Major ethnic groups include the following:

**Mangyan:** The dark-skinned highland tribes of Mindoro island – Iraya, Tagaydan, Tatagnon, Buid, Alangan, and Hanunoo – are collectively known as Mangyan. These reclusive farmers have been largely displaced by newer arrivals.

**Tagbanua:** The Tagbanua tribe of Palawan island has retained a unique animist culture despite intrusions. They wear scanty dress, maintain a religion intimately joined with nature, and carve bamboo tubes with an old alphabet of Hindu origin.

**Negrito:** The Aeta, Ati, Dumagat, and Ita are collectively known as Negrito, or the

## FINE-TUNED HOSPITALITY

Meeting people makes traveling as fun as any beach or cathedral. A foreign visitor with the name of a local resident is usually fed and shown around town. Others can make equally hospitable friends on the street, in bars, and lounging at the seaside.

Conversation often starts with questions about family, a topic that allows both sides to go into detail about parents, siblings, children, and their global whereabouts. Filipinos generally know a bit about world geography as a family member has probably worked abroad. Since there are no major ongoing feuds with foreign governments (China is on the watch list from 2012, however), Filipinos harbor little suspicion toward foreign

visitors, though cannot hide their pride in having thrown off colonial rule.

**Body language:** Strong and fixed eye contact between males is considered aggressive. Eyebrows raised with a smile are a silent "hello" or "yes" to a question. One might be pointed toward a direction with pursed lips. Politeness is important, even during inevitable disputes between travelers and local merchants.

If foreign guests are invited to a Filipino home, they should give special acknowledgment to elders. Use the honorifics *lolo* and *lola* for grandparents and other elders. Greet them by putting their right hand to your forehead in a time-honored gesture of respect.

Philippines' Aborigines. Numbering some 40,000, these short, dark-skinned, and curly-haired people are facing cultural extinction. The Aeta live in the mountain jungles of Negros, Samar, and Leyte; in the rolling hills of Zambales, and Nueva Ecija on Luzon; and along the shores of northern Luzon.

**Mountain people:** There are five major ethnic groups spread across the Cordillera highlands of northern Luzon: Ibaloi, Kankanaey, Ifugao, Kalinga, and Apayao. These proud, uncon-quered tribes have evolved robust indigenous cultures and traditions due to their relative seclusion. They live in one place all year and

> The Tausug were the first tribe in the Philippines to follow Islam. The "people of the current," as they are known, lead a combative life, with violence a form of expression.

have a highly developed agricultural economy. They worship tribal ancestors or spirits of nature and may be suspicious of "intruders" from the lowlands.

**Ibaloi and Kankanaey:** The Ibaloi tribes of the western and southern Cordillera grow rice, cof-fee, and vegetables, and raise livestock on their terraced hillsides. They also mine precious metals such as gold and copper in the upland region of Lepanto.

**Ifugao:** The Ifugao of the eastern and central Cordillera are the architects of the most famous rice terraces in the world; the Banaue rice ter-races were first constructed 2,000 to 3,000 years ago and cover at least 260 sq km (100 sq miles) of steep mountainside in Ifugao Province. The Cordillera minorities proudly trace their ancestry to Taiwan and mainland Asia and have hosted conferences that bring people in from abroad to explore or just celebrate those cross-national ties.

**Muslims:** Considered as a whole, the Muslims of the south – also called Moros – constitute the largest cultural minority. Some claim Mindanao and the Sulu Archipelago far-ther to the south as their own holy land. The Muslims, fiercely independent and combative,

are classified into five major groups: Tausug, Maranao, Maguindanao, Samal, and Badjao.

In contrast to the more bellicose Tausug, the Maranao are the graceful "people of the lake" who live by Mindanao's Lake Lanao at 700 meters (2,300ft) above sea level. In cool and aloof isolation, they continue to uphold their complex but vigorous sultanates.

The Maguindanao are the "people of the flood plain," inhabiting a less hospitable area in Cotabato Province, where land is periodi-cally flooded by overflowing rivers. The largest group of Muslims, the Maguindanao live on agriculture and fishing.

The Samal are the poorest and least inde-pendent of the major Muslim groups. Many of them live in villages perched on stilts above coastal waters.

The Badjao, a nominally Muslim group, are the country's fabled "sea-gypsies," true wander-ers of the Sulu seas. They are born on the water and live upon their tiny craft for a lifetime – turning tawny in the sun and salt.

A unique cultural group living on Basilan Island off Mindanao are the Yakan. A gentle people of partial Polynesian origin, with mixed Muslim and animist beliefs, they are known for their skill in textile weaving. On backstrap looms, they turn cottons and silks into geomet-ric works of art.

**ABOVE, FROM LEFT:** the extended family often plays a big role in bringing up children; Mindanao tribesman.

More than 10 non-Muslim tribes also inhabit the Mindanao interior. Of those, the T'boli tribe of Lake Sebu in Cotabato make crafts and elaborate costumes. They are also admired for brasswork, which finds its way into statues, belts, chains, and tinkling anklets worn by heavily ornamented tribal women.

## The modern Filipino

The present-day Filipino covers the spectrum of cappuccino-sipping yuppie at a trendy café near frenetic Manila Bay to the coconut-sap gatherer shimmying up a tree somewhere in the distant outlying islands. City folk have the money,

through gainful employment or social class, to afford designer coffee as well as hot rods and name brands of whatever.

In the cities, namely Manila and Cebu, visitors will see many pockets where poverty rules and the shanty dweller has degenerated into levels below country folk, since they are unable to find honorable work. Urban shanty denizens often start in the countryside, where they are unable to find work, and then show up in cities where it's also tough to get a toehold in the job market. Some of the more desperately poor people in Manila live in squalid, jerry-built shacks along rivers. Others live outdoors and

> To combat the fashionable Filipino habit of late arrivals, which was said to be hurting productivity, the education secretary launched the We Are Time Conscious and Honest (WATCH) campaign in all schools to instill a sense of time in students.

panhandle or pickpocket for a living, a caution to tourists carrying valuables. In extreme cases, money seekers in upscale parts of Manila resort to scams that start with claims to know the traveler or invitations to get into a car.

Manila is not the Philippines, a visitor is often told. Out in the boondocks (a Tagalog word drawn into the American lexicon in the colonial years), daily existence is a far cry from the sophisticated, if often anarchic, features of big city life. People living in jungles just a few paces behind the luxury beach resorts are earning only a few dozen pesos a day from farming

## CHINESE ASSIMILATION

Long before the Spanish conquest, the Chinese had settled in the Philippines as independent traders, itinerants, or pillaging corsairs. The legendary pirate Limahong attacked Pangasinan in northern Luzon in the 16th century and, when cornered by a Spanish expeditionary force, dug an extensive channel to escape to the gulf. Many of Limahong's men stayed to intermarry with the natives, thus producing the first Chinese *mestizo* in the Philippines.

Although occasionally the butt of jokes, well-assimilated Chinese descendants never suffer from strong prejudice. Kidnap bands targeted wealthy Chinese in the mid-1990s, but this was more an indication of

ineffective policing than anything else. During that time, many well-to-do Chinese kept their heads down, for fear of attracting unnecessary envy or attention.

Former President Corazon Aquino and Cardinal Sin, the prime movers behind the People Power reaction against the Marcos dictatorship, are both descended from Chinese migrants from Fujian. Second- and third-generation "Chinoys" (a combination of Chinese and "Pinoy") are very much a part of the managerial pool of Filipinos; in fact, many Chinese business leaders have become strong pillars of the economy. Among them are the country's richest man, the developer SM Group's founder Henry Sy, and billionaire Andrew Tan.

or net fishing in the oceans. They may rely on remittance income from relatives in Hong Kong or Dubai, for example, or hope to sell a piece of land to the next guy who comes along with designs to build a beach resort.

People in the lowlands of the rural Philippines often live in spacious, ornate, one-story or two-story family houses. Up higher, where roads are rutted, sometimes flooded or even nonexistent, families occupy single-room huts, growing whatever they can on land that may be as unforgiving as the roads.

Filipinos tend to turn first to family when fighting threats of poverty. The government also runs a social security system, offers food subsidies, and parcels out child allowances. For longer-term relief, people may apply for public employment or space in the country's credit-based livelihood programs.

In cities, middle-class families (often extended ones) live in small, solid houses of one to two stories. Wealthier urbanites, often from the educated professional ranks or the managerial class, live in bigger houses or high-rise condominiums. Those homes may be in gated, guarded subdivisions. Billboards in Manila indicate that a spacious flat in a new, serviced high-rise in the Makati financial center is the country's ultimate

> One of the country's most pressing social issues is drug abuse, especially to get people off the powerful and addictive methamphetamine-like drug called shabu. Some 7 percent of youth are thought to be using the drug.

housing dream. Middle-class Filipinos earn on average P10,000 to P30,000 (US$230–700) per month, too little for the glitz of Makati, but enough to take care of family, get a car, and pursue an after-work passion such as art or music.

Regardless of economic status, early education is taken seriously. Most children put in 12 years at school, bringing adult literacy to around 93 percent.

## The diaspora

Propping up the national economy is the ever-growing number of Filipinos working overseas, whose common denominator is that they all send foreign currency home. There is the OCW (Overseas Contract Worker), since euphemized further into OFW for (Overseas Filipino Worker). Legions leave their families for extended terms in the oilfields of the Middle East and factories in Taiwan and South Korea.

There are also Filipino seamen and domestic helpers. Some have left teaching positions in the Philippines to earn a steady income in Hong Kong, Singapore, Australia, North America, and Europe. English skills may open doors in markets where the language is prized but spoken with little fluency. Roving bands of musicians dominate the bars in Asia. In Tokyo and Osaka, Filipino workers sing and dance at local nightspots, and their bands bring covers

of Western tunes to the massive tourist-business hotels of Beijing. Professionals, such as doctors, nurses, engineers, and computer experts, have found career jobs in Europe and the US.

The extent of the Filipino diaspora nearly rivals that of the numerically superior Chinese and buoys an otherwise tough local economy. Most of them return within a few years, having saved enough to start small businesses, only to be replaced by the next generation of OFWs and adventurers who are convinced they can profit similarly from a spell abroad.

**ABOVE, FROM LEFT:** around 20 percent of the population of Mindanao are Muslim; boats are the main form of transport for many people in coastal areas.

*It's not unusual to run into locals with proud stories about a son in Dubai or unrequited dreams of working for two or three years in the US simply for the financial security it would bring.*

As Filipino workers spread across the world, using their English skills and flexible attitudes toward work to find jobs, some invariably stay outside the country for good. Fil-Ams, or Filipino Americans, make up a sizeable minority in the US. The official count stands

at 3.4 million. They tend to cluster in bigger cities and may be concentrated around particular employers.

There is now strong interaction between Filipino Americans and Filipinos, with the younger generation of Filipinos raised in the States passionately retracing their roots. Nearly every family in the Philippines has relations or friends who have relocated to the Americas, although differences in culture and economic status have tested ties to the homeland. Fil-Am athletes and entertainers also have started coming home to roost, bolstering professional basketball and the domestic movie industry.

Other overseas work destinations are less accommodating. In Hong Kong, a popular Asian destination for the OFW, Filipinos – almost all women – usually work as domestic helpers despite sometimes having higher degrees from home. They earn an average of US$490 per month. Although many of the 100,000 workers in Hong Kong appear happy on the outside as they hold mirthful mass picnics in a central business district on Sundays, advocacy groups complain of racial slurs, such as "cockroach," posted online, plus routine discrimination in social settings. They are also pushing to be included under Hong Kong's laws against removal or deportation.

In Taiwan, about 90,000 men and women from the Philippines work in factories on restrictive contracts signed in advance by labor brokers. Conditions are rough, pay around just US$700 per month, and legal disputes, common when contracts cannot be renewed, suddenly landing workers back in Philippine villages where their foreign income had been helping impoverished family members. A few are allowed to live in Taiwan long-term to work in bars or as domestic helpers, though the Filipino social scene is nothing like that of Hong Kong. Not far from Taiwan, a group of Filipinos has also surfaced in Palau, a well-off South Pacific island where hotels and dive shops hire them as service workers.

Another group of Filipinos has found work in the United Arab Emirates, mainly in Dubai. In that Middle Eastern country, some 280,000 Filipinos do jobs in construction, design engineering, real estate, marketing, and medical services. Some also work as domestic helpers. Their minimum salaries are about US$400.

## Women's status

Today's Filipina emerged from a checkered history. She is still emerging, playing dual or even multiple roles: at home a teacher, abroad a "Japayuki" dancing scantily in a Tokyo bar, or a domestic helper in Hong Kong. Add to that nurse and beauty queen, scholar and chambermaid, torch singer, and ambassador. Regardless of today's occupation, women in the Philippines largely trace their origins to a long line of priestesses.

Early tribes relied on women to perform sacred rites. Known as *catalonan* to the Tagalog, or *babaylan* to the Bisaya – the priestess healed with herbs and received the spirits in trance. When the Spanish missionaries came, she sought to poison those strangers and burn their altars. But she later became Christian, and proved to be the colonist's delight. She wound up helping him pacify warlike tribes and became an adopted waif to be melted in the Castilian mold.

The friar, who was father figure to whole villages, fancied her a naive child, tender-heartedly teaching her his alphabet. She once worshipped nature and ancestral spirits, but her sudden embrace of Christianity found her praying endlessly and placing flowers on the altar. In her innocence, she proved too tempting a morsel for the friar fathers, and time and again was seduced.

Ilocos, took to the battlefield in place of slain husbands.

Later, with the same earnestness she had reserved for catechism, the Filipina worshipped at the American altar of formal education. Americans also prodded her into giddy new experiences – voting for the first time, shedding the *saya* (long skirt), bobbing long tresses, speaking her mind. Her ambitions were awakened. Today, one encounters the Filipina in a great variety of professions, jockeying for public office, running modern corporations, sitting in international commissions, and governing the country.

Friar children, though illegitimate, enjoyed a slightly higher status as Castilian progeny. For mothers who adored fair-haired saints with blue eyes, they aroused special devotion. To be white was the subject of many silent prayers.

The revolution against Spanish rule was a chance to gamble for freedom. Men plodded and fought; women hid his arms, carried his secret documents, nursed his wounds, and aided his escape. Brave widows, foremost among them Gabriela Silang of the

**ABOVE, FROM LEFT:** many Filipinos have Chinese heritage; the elderly are revered in Philippine society; guests at a wedding in Manila.

### MALL MANIA

It's no accident that Manila is home to the largest mall in this part of the world, the SM Mall of Asia. In smaller cities, from Davao to Tagbilaran, multi-story shopping arcades dominate central business districts. Most are atrium-style mixes of clothiers, electronics, and fast-food outlets. Bigger ones include an anchor supermarket or department store.

Malls are a core part of Filipino leisure culture. Some say it's the free air-con. Others say malls offer an easy way to relax with family or a platform to show off new clothes – to gawk and be gawked at. People more often than not walk out with bags in their hands.

# RELIGION IN THE PHILIPPINES

Unusually for an Asian country, the Philippines is a largely Catholic nation. The population worships in highly ritualistic displays and in forms that show a strong attachment to folk tradition, underpinned by ancient animist beliefs.

The story is told that when the explorer Ferdinand Magellan landed in the thriving coastal kingdom of Cebu, it was not his sonorous promise of friendship with a white king, nor the gleam of Spanish cannons, nor the symbol of the cross that won the day. Rather, it was a local queen's first beguiled look at a statue of the Christ child, the Santo Niño. The idol was alien as could be, but presented along with the magnanimity of the crown, scepter, and tenacity of the newly arrived Europeans, the queen of a children-loving kingdom could hardly resist conversion to the new faith. That was in 1521.

At the mass baptism that ensued, the queen received the icon as a gift from the chronicler of the expedition and promised that it would replace the *anito* (idols) of her people. The

*Filipinos follow the Catholic faith as closely as their peers in Latin America or at the religion's source in Europe. Churches dominate city centers and weekend social activities.*

promise was not kept for very long; the records show a rapid return to animism after the first round of conquistadors left. But after Miguel Lopez de Legazpi got a foothold in Manila in the late 1500s and established firm Spanish rule, Christianity dug in alongside, as it did throughout Latin America in the 1700s when colonists from Spain or Portugal used their religion to edge out local indigenous beliefs.

**LEFT:** statue of Jesus, Naga City. **RIGHT:** Magellan's Cross commemorates the conversion of the Cebu islanders to Christianity.

## ANIMISM

Before the arrival of the Spanish, Filipinos believed that spirits dwelled within inanimate objects such as lakes, mountains, and wind. People would make offerings to particular trees that were thought to house benevolent gods and would avoid sleeping under other trees considered to be hideouts for malevolent spirits. Some Filipinos also believed in totemism, meaning essentially that humans had kindred animal spirits such as crocodiles or snakes.

Although animists today make up only 1 percent of the population, the personification or deification of nature still influences folk belief and permeates mainstream religious activities.

In that process, the souls of departed ancestors, the spirits of nature, and mythical monsters were replaced by (and in many cases, incorporated with) an extended Christian family consisting of both the human and divine. God, of course, played the stern father, various saints were kindly aunts and uncles, the Virgin Mary was the merciful mother, and her child, the darling of the family. After generations of inculcation, women were convinced that true femininity lay in devotion, chastity, and obedience, while children were to perfect their trust in the Father. In lieu of visible manifestations of God, the local friars and governors took their

place. The focus of Christian teachings varied from region to region between the Virgin Mary and the Child Jesus.

In the shrines and churches of Luzon, where women's equality with men had long ago extended into roles of power as priestesses, Mary became the standard-bearer of Catholicism. In the Visayas of Queen Juana, where children to this day are indulged in extended childhood, the Santo Niño was king.

Unlike almost every other part of Asia, because of three centuries of Spanish rule, the Philippines is a staunchly Christian nation, with about 80 percent embracing the faith through traditional baptism as infants. The rest of the population may be divided among Islam (7

percent), practiced for centuries in Mindanao, the Aglipayan church (about 1 percent), and the Iglesia ni Cristo (Church of Christ), or INC (3 percent). Small numbers are Buddhist, Taoist, and animist.

## Miracles and the Virgin Mary cult

Propaganda was part and parcel of the missionary kit. Friars made sure that every important event was attributed to divine intervention. Thus Mary and her son, along with the various patron saints of particular places, became agents for fire prevention, earthquake-proofing (especially of churches), and fending off marauders' attacks. They became deities of rain, fertility, and the entire range of human needs.

It would seem that many of the wishes, pleas, and heart-cries were indeed granted. Tradition continues to claim that in such a place and at such a time, crops were saved from destruction by locust and drought, floods were diverted, and brigands turned away by heavenly protectors. At least 50 major icons of Mary and the Holy Child in the Philippines are associated with stories of miracles. Several of them have been recognized by the Vatican as authentic miracle workers.

Practically all large Christian towns and cities have their own special image of the Virgin and Child: polished ivory by the classic skills of medieval European carvers; stained ebony fashioned by Mexican artisans; intricately carved in soft wood by Chinese sculptors (many displaying the almond eyes of their own immortals); or hewn from hardwoods by the persevering hands of local Filipino craftsmen. There is hardly a Catholic home without its own Virgin and Child enshrined, usually near the master bedroom.

Just a generation ago, it was standard practice to affix a Maria or a Jesus Maria to a Filipino child's given name, and wealthy Filipinos often embark on extended pilgrimage tours to Lourdes, Jerusalem, or any new foreign site where a miraculous apparition has been reported, such as Medjugorje in the former Yugoslavia, or Naju in South Korea. Closer to home, any news of a sighting or simulacrum (sometimes the shape of Our Lady is perceived to have appeared in a tree trunk or on an otherwise greasy kitchen wall) instantly draws hordes of devotees, together with an equal legion of candle-sellers and soft-drink vendors.

Older people still recall how rose petals bearing the image of Our Lady's face rained on the town of Lipa in Batangas in the 1950s, or how a decade later the Blessed Mother reportedly appeared to some children in the tiny island of Cabra north of Mindoro.

On December 8, the Feast of the Immaculate Conception, Catholic schoolchildren enjoy a holiday, and their parents might attend a lengthy procession of motor-driven and illuminated floats with rococo carvings. The processions inch forward past an adulatory throng in a slow-moving display of richly dressed statues of the Virgin Mary.

## Shows of devotion

The Philippines is aflame with festivals, but for sheer religious drama, none rivals the Peñafrancia Festival held in September in Naga City. The 15-day celebration that draws thousands of devotees and tourists centers on the image of Our Lady of Peñafrancia, the patroness of Bicolandia where Naga is located. Barefoot male devotees called *voyadores*, numbering in the hundreds, take turns carrying the 284-year-old image on their shoulders. Eventually, the image is set on an elaborately adorned pagoda atop a large boat. Cheering throngs gathered

*The Virgin is ever present in garden shrines – grottoes simulating her recorded apparitions in Fatima, Lourdes, and Carmel. The usual spot is on a mound, hillock, or mountainside that is carved out with tortuous steps to the shrine.*

by the river banks witness its passage up the Naga River. A similarly grandiose fluvial procession called Pagoda sa Wawa is staged yearly in Hagonoy, Bulacan.

One of the most enduring images of the People Power revolution was the sight of a blue-robed icon that never left the side of the principal military rebel, General Fidel Ramos, who would become president after Corazon Aquino. A modern shrine to that icon, now named Our Lady of Edsa, has since been erected by the historic highway with a towering bronze statue

of an Asian-looking Virgin Mary rising as religious counterpoint to a busy mall and soaring highway infrastructure in Manila.

## Offshoots

Aside from the mainstream Catholicism, there is the Aglipayan religion. Officially called the Philippine Independent Church, it was started by Gregorio Aglipay in the early 1900s as a breakaway, nationalistic faction of Catholicism. More clearly visible from the wealth of solemn-looking roadside churches with clean white or pastel facades and soaring Gothic spires, the Iglesia ni Cristo (Church of Christ), or INC,

claims additional non-Catholic followers. INC, with 5 million members worldwide, has made strong inroads with its strict tithing practices.

The INC is noted for hewing to a collective decision during elections, so that it has emerged as a powerful political bloc often courted by aspirants to national office.

The late 1980s saw the proliferation of various charismatic movements, preaching the importance of leading a spirit-led and spirit-filled life. It started with a return to fundamentalism practiced by so-called born-again Christians. Soon every radio and television station had its own evangelist preaching versions of revivalism mixed with theatrical come-ons such as singing and dancing.

**ABOVE, FROM LEFT:** San Agustin Church in the Intramuros district of Manila; Catholic devotees at the annual Peñafrancia Festival in Naga City.

The most successful televangelist to date is "Brother Mike" Velarde, a former radio broadcaster who found his true (and lucrative) calling by establishing the El Shaddai group, which counts millions among its followers. His extravaganzas, held every Saturday at various open-air fields in Metro Manila, can attract as many as a million people. Always smartly attired, Velarde holds his crowd in thrall, sometimes for over 24 hours, with a curious mix of Bible sayings, rhetorical speeches, songs, and prayers. When Velarde asks his faithful to wave their handkerchiefs in the air, they need no second cue. The Catholic Church usually tolerates El Shaddai's activities as

*As many as 1 million Filipinos are attracted to the weekly extravaganzas of "Brother Mike" Velarde of El Shaddai. The nattily attired leader holds his Manila crowds in thrall.*

an extension of charismatic faith, but once sanctioned Velarde over allegations that he had been amassing personal wealth through tithing.

Jesus might not be who most of us imagine, claims a group called *Watawat ng Lahi* (Flag of the Race). It believes that Philippine national hero Jose Rizal was a reincarnation of Christ and, as such, will come again. Its headquarters is perched on top of a hill near the town of Calamba, Rizal's birthplace in Laguna Province. Through a trance medium, some in the group speak in the *Banal na Tinig*, the holy voice of prophecy. At that time, everyone in the hall falls silent while resonant tones echo around it. The day, says the Voice, is not long in coming when the new age shall be known in the Philippines by the building of a golden church and a golden palace, and the waving of a golden flag.

## Islam

Islam touched the shores of the Philippine Islands in the 13th century, before the Spanish arrived, when it was spreading through other parts of Southeast Asia. The religion came via Malaysia, where several Islamic governments had been established, with Muslim traders who had originated in the Persian Gulf or the coastline of southern India.

With Islam came a specialized system of government and new dimensions of culture. One dimension was a political structure known as the sultanate, where a sultan in charge would assume both religious and secular authority.

When Spanish colonizers put pressure on the rule of sultans, Muslims in the southern Philippines, where they were most concentrated, resisted as the dominant non-Muslims from the north took resources. The Spanish reign created a divide between Christians and Muslims, who became holdouts lasting to the present, as manifested in the bloodshed on the southern island of Mindanao.

### VOLUNTARY CRUCIFIXION

On Good Friday, a spectacle showing the extent of devotion to Catholicism in the Philippines is played out in various barrios in Pampanga and Tarlac on the plains north of Manila. People seen as sinners – mostly men – sacrifice themselves for the community by being nailed to wooden crosses in a grisly re-enactment of Christ's suffering. Medics are on hand to treat injuries. This display of Christ's Passion may also include a last supper, a carrying of the cross, and the seven last words.

The Catholic Church occasionally frowns on such practices, but for the most part it remains content to let this folksy if gory devotion continue.

**LEFT:** devotees light candles at the Lady of Del Pilar shrine, Zamboanga. **RIGHT:** Muslim girls at the Taluksangay mosque, Zamboanga.

# Superstitions and Taboos

**Modern education aside, Filipinos may still attend grueling rituals or hire people with magic powers as guides to cure a range of ills.**

Philippine folk superstitions reveal a sense of fatalism and fear of the unknown. Although the combined influence of Western cultural hegemony and the Catholic Church has challenged

these age-old beliefs, many have survived – albeit in somewhat diluted form – into the modern age.

## Childbirth

Some believe that a pregnant woman should shun soft drinks as they might overly increase the size of the fetus and that she should not stand by doors, which could cause a difficult labor. When the baby is due, a spiritual doctor may recite prayers to keep spirits away during labor and ensure the child's obedience. After birth, the expelled placenta may be buried along with pen and paper to make the baby smart. And the baby's first feces should be massaged onto its infant gums like toothpaste to ensure strong teeth. The litany of Filipino childbirth superstitions goes on and on.

While modern Filipinos may not admit belief in them, most are inclined to follow some as a safety measure.

## The subok

It could be any Good Friday in the lush hills of lakeside Tanay town in Rizal Province. A gathering of men, hollow-eyed from fasting and overnight meditation, shuffle their feet around the courtyard of an old church. Creaking and groaning, a flower-decked *carroza* float emerges from the dim interiors, carrying the Santo Sepulcro, a wooden statue of the dead Christ. There is a rush toward it, then a scramble to insert objects in the folds of the robes, under the feet, in the hands.

The image – now loaded with handkerchiefs, bronze medals, pieces of paper inscribed with Latin phrases, and images of Christ and the Virgin Mary, pebbles, tektites, bones, prayer books, crucifixes, catfish eyes – is encircled by a chain of linked hands.

A man, in his forties, walks forward. He sharpens a long *bolo* knife in deliberate motions. Then he suddenly starts hacking away at his stretched left arm. Neither cuts nor blood appear. Then weapons are passed around – horse-hair whips, revolvers, more *bolo*. Throughout the rest of Good Friday afternoon and Holy Saturday, each person will test the efficacy of his own talisman – asking to be shot at, whipped or stabbed. Some get hurt. Others leave the *subok* unscathed, exuding a profound solemnity.

## The magbabarang

On the island of Siquijor the *magbabarang* or sorcerer collects special bees, beetles, and centipedes (collectively called *barang*), chosen because they all have an extra leg. They're moved into a bamboo tube for Fridays, when the *magbabarang*

**LEFT:** a flagellant at the Good Friday procession in Pampanga. **ABOVE:** potion making.

performs a ritual from which his name derives. He takes a list of names and addresses of supposed wrongdoers, writes them on separate pieces of paper, and puts them in the bamboo tube. If the papers have been torn to shreds when he opens the tube, it means the insects are willing to attack the owners of the names.

The *magbabarang* proceeds to tie a white string on the extra legs of his assistants. He then lets them loose, with instructions to lodge themselves inside the victim's body, bite his internal organs and wreak havoc in his system until he dies. Then they go back to their master. If the strings are red with blood, the hex was successful. If clean, the victim was innocent after all and thus was able to resist the magic.

## The bolo-bolo

B*olo-bolo* magic healers in Siquijor swallow water, gargle, and spit it out a window. Then they open their mouths wide to show that they're empty. After praying in a low mumble, they dip one end of a bamboo tube into the glass, stick a reed into their mouths and blow. Soon the water darkens and worms wriggle in the glass. The three-minute ritual is claimed to cure illnesses, and bolo-bolos believe it's sacrilegious to accept pay for service.

## Psychic surgery

Most of what is known in the West today, both good and bad, about the gray areas of the occult in the Philippines stems from the discovery of Pangasinan psychic surgery in the late 1940s by a few Americans. The first major healer encountered by the Americans was Eleuterio Terte. His method was a simple laying on of hands, similar to the practice of any number of spiritual healers in Brazil, Hawaii, England, and the southern United States.

Shortly after World War II, Terte is said to have noticed bodies opening spontaneously under his hands. By the mid-1960s, when Harold Sherman, an American researcher, came to document psychic surgery, Terte had already trained 14 of the 30 surgeons now known the world over as Filipino faith healers.

Diagnosis follows meditation and before an operation. During surgery, with short, cavalier slashes of the finger 50cm (18ins) away from the diseased part, bodies appear to open up without a single knife stroke. Then after a few gropes, turns, pulls, and twists, the healer pulls out a supposed

organ, or an eyeball, quickly dabs alcohol-soaked cotton on blood-drenched areas and finally closes the cut.

The body parts may be deposited in bottles of alcohol, which then become the much-prized booty of visiting scientists and the scientific minded. Laboratory examinations show the contents either to be genuine, diseased human tissue, or to be animal parts. Some may have vanished through evaporation, theft, or chemical breakdown.

A recent theory purports that Filipino faith healers are descendants of the kahuna, the ancient healers of old Tahiti and Hawaii. The kahuna disappeared with the coming of Christianity to Polynesia.

Psychic healers have fallen out of favor in the past couple of decades as Western education, including textbook science and religion, cast glaring doubt on their practices. Desperately afflicted Filipinos less and less often travel to Pangasinan, once well noted for its concentration of celebrated faith healers. The phenomenon that peaked in the 1970s also fails to draw the large number of foreigners as it once did.

For a casual tourist, finding a psychic or sorcerer could be a problem, as these healers live in low-key, out-of-the-way places. But around Easter every year, the magically inclined on Siquijor island hold their Witches Festival. During the open event, potions are brewed and spells are cast under the watch of shamans.

**RIGHT:** a black magic practitioner, Siquijor Island.

# FIESTA FANTASTICA

The Philippines is known for its passionate, dramatic festivals. Most are rooted in the country's mixture of religions, from animism to Christianity. Diversions include fanciful giants and fully clothed roast pigs.

**F**estivals take place all year round in the Philippines. Most run for a few days to a week in specific communities, diverting traffic and sparking de facto holidays for local businesses. A festival tourist must plan carefully to see each event before it ends, yet not get stuck in traffic trying to reach a venue or land somewhere without a hotel booking. There are hundreds (if not more) festivals in the Philippines. Those described in this chapter, listed month by month, are just the highlights of the party; for a comprehensive list, see Travel Tips, page 360. For background on the Catholic origins of festivals described below, refer to the chapter Religion in the Philippines, page 62.

## January

Kalibo's Ati-Atihan festival, held in the third week of January, is the Philippines' most famous fiesta. *Ati-Atihan* refers to the dark-skinned Negrito aborigines, the original inhabitants of Panay Island where Kalibo is situated. In 1212, as legend has it, 10 Bornean lords escaping religious tyranny in the south fled northwards with their followers. Upon their arrival in Panay, they struck a deal with the local chieftain. The peace pact was later reinforced by a harvest feast prepared by the new arrivals for their Ati neighbors. Ever eager to please, the Bornean hosts welcomed the Negritos with gongs and cymbals, smeared soot on their faces and started dancing in the streets in merry imitation of their Ati guests. The Christ-child

LEFT: dancers at the colorful Lanzones festival, Camiguin Province. RIGHT: young girl at the Sinulog festival in Cebu.

figure of Santo Niño, a highlight of today's festivities, was introduced only in later years.

As column upon column of sooted locals dressed as Ati people beat on drums and cymbals, and march in syncopated rhythm, wild dancing breaks out everywhere. The unceasing and deafening Ati-Atihan beat magnetizes everyone to join in the madcap fun. The Ati-Atihan is so popular that it has been replicated in other parts of the Visayan islands, albeit with localized twists. A visitor to Kalibo couldn't miss this festival even in a backwater hotel room with earplugs.

Also in January, the Sinulog festival takes place in Cebu to honor the Santo Niño (child Jesus), once the patron saint of the whole province of

Cebu. Dance contests and music parties follow religious rites during the festive period.

## February

The giant ring road encircling Manila, Epifanio de los Santos Avenue (better known as EDSA), was the focus for the bloodless February 1986 revolution that toppled former dictator Ferdinand Marcos. There was tension, of course, when the banners of revolt were first unfurled over Camp Crame in Quezon City. Despite their fears, hundreds of thousands of Filipinos converged on this road to form a protective human wall. Confronted with tanks and

*The crispy roast pig is so prized among the Balayan and Batangas that during a local fiesta, the pigs go on parade surrounded by barbed wire to deter greedy hands.*

troops, they brought their personal weapons of prayers, smiles, rosary beads, and flowers to bear on the forces of discredited authority. Marcos eventually fled the country.

Since then, Filipinos have celebrated the **anniversary of the EDSA People Power revolution** with Masses, stage shows, dancing,

### COMMERCIAL SPIRIT

Although spiritual in origin, many Philippine festivals are heavily commercialized. Some organizers allow sponsors to display their company names at venues for a fee, while others have retooled the mechanics of the events themselves to reel in tourists. Events may be held at malls or hotels, which use the chance to gain publicity.

Festivals also give civic groups and aspiring politicians a chance for some self-promotion. They may give speeches or employ other means of advertising. At a city fiesta in Vigan in early 2012, for example, local hog-feed producer Pigrolac mounted a multistory-high inflated pig in a central park.

displays, singing, and fireworks. The portion of EDSA between Aguinaldo and the EDSA Shrine on Ortigas Avenue takes center stage for the anniversary events. About 20,000 people gathered for the 2012 memorial.

## March and April

Holy Week turns into a colorful frenzy of celebration throughout the Philippines. Most notably, the heart-shaped island of Marinduque south of Luzon becomes the stage for an epic spectacle: the **Moriones** festival that re-enacts the biblical story of Longinus and his miracle.

The drama unfolds as the villages of Boac, Gasan, and Mogpog are converted into an immense stage. The all-male participants don masks carved from coral wood to resemble Roman soldiers wearing perpetual scowls. On Ash Wednesday they roam the streets to terrorize – not for real, naturally – the locals. On Good Friday, a stand-in for Jesus is crucified with help from the one-eyed Longinus. When he thrusts a spear into Jesus' side, the blood spurts into his blind eye and restores his full sight. By Easter Sunday, the Moriones (masked participants) and thousands of spectators crowd into an open-air arena alongside the Boac River. Christ's resurrection is then dramatically re-enacted. Longinus reappears, now a convert.

These tributes to the Virgin Mary climax in a glittering parade of crowns and costumes on the last Sunday of May.

The Santacruzan is a Spanish legacy that commemorates the search for the True Cross of Christ. According to legend, Constantine the Great was converted to the Christian faith through the vision of a flaming cross in heaven, which is said to have led him to victory in battle. Queen Helena, the first Christian empress and who was canonized after her death, led a pilgrimage in search of the Cross, and claimed to have found it in Jerusalem in AD 324.

Throughout the archipelago, every town and

Soldiers suddenly pursue Longinus and bring him to trial. He is thrown before Pontius Pilate, judged, and then ceremoniously beheaded. With his mask held high by a Roman soldier, the body is carried on a bamboo stretcher to the church, bringing an end to the Moriones Festival.

## May

The first of May heralds a month of fiestas, flowers, and maidens parading in pretty gowns. This month also brings the twin processions of the **Flores de Mayo** and the **Santacruzan**.

community stages its own Santacruzan. The fiesta is managed by a *hermana* or *hermano mayor* (big sister or brother) or a *capitana* (lady-in-charge), who recruits girls to be the *sagalas* (maidens) of the night. The procession that closes the Santacruzan is heady with romance, pronouncing these girls adults for the first time. In this spirit, the Santacruzan has become a puberty rite sublimated into a religious ceremony.

Santacruzan festivals occur throughout the Philippines and are particularly accessible in mid-sized cities such as Iloilo and Dumaguete.

Separately, the popular **Pahiyas** feast honors San Isidro de Labrador, the patron saint of farmers from the town of Lucban in Quezon Province. The town's houses are decorated for

**ABOVE, FROM LEFT:** masked Roman soldiers at the Moriones festival, Marinduque Island; *lechon* (roasted pig) parade in Quezon City.

the mid-May event with colorful *kiping* (leaf-shaped rice wafers) and other farm produce. Go to Lucban in the morning to catch the Pahiyas procession.

## June

Lechon, or whole roast pig, presides over any Filipino fiesta table. So revered is this succulent dish that the people of Balayan in Batangas have highlighted the feast of their patron saint, St John, with a tribute to golden red-colored *lechon*. On the eve of the fiesta, an anniversary ball is held at the town plaza, where a *lechon* queen is crowned. Next morning, after Mass at

After the parade, most of the *lechon* are taken to their respective homes or club headquarters, where the feasting and drinking begins in earnest. Some groups may surrender their prized roast to the crowds of merrymakers who in turn stuff themselves.

## July

The festival of **Santa Ana Kahimonan Abayan**, held in late July in the northern Mindanao city of Butuan, grew out of an era when human-eating crocodiles infested the Agusan River. Faced with this common enemy, the townspeople implored their patron saint to give them boun-

the Immaculate Conception Church, participants bring together at least 50 *lechon* skewered on long bamboo poles.

Skewered as they may be, these pigs still wear clothes. The attire of each roasted animal reflects the theme of the participating civic and social organizations. Medical associations, for instance, present their pig wearing a doctor's uniform, complete with stethoscope and mask.

As the *lechon* go on parade, pranksters hurl water or beer over the pigs, drenching their bearers and onlookers. A wet free-for-all ensues and the only objects left unscathed are the few *lechon* clad in raincoats. The **Parada ng Lechon** remains one of the most riotous fiestas held in the Philippines.

> Whenever calamity threatened Christian settlements in the early days of Spanish rule, friars led everyone to church in quest of a "miracle." In time, the pre-Catholic guardian spirits of harvest feasts were replaced by Christian saints.

tiful harvests and safe passage across the river. Santa Ana heard their prayers and destroyed the creatures.

Today, the river-people honor their patron saint by staging a waterborne Mass celebrated by a line-up of priests. The statue of Santa Ana is borne high on the shoulders of devotees and positioned on the middle of a riverboat. Several priests, sacristans, and a choir lead an ensuing Mass. After the Mass, the choir's chants and the beating of drums fire the celebration into a frenzy. The Santa Ana Kahimonan Abayan festival also gives various local tribes a chance to sell their wares and perform dances.

## August

Lucban, site of the Pahiyas (see May), goes back into party mode again with a festival for **gigantes**, or giants. Four-meter-high (14ft) papier-mâché *gigantes* strut through the Quezon town to represent Juan Cruz, a farmer, his wife, and their two children.

parade, the bull scampers around the town plaza, scattering spectators as fireworks shoot off from inside.

Also in August, the city of Davao in Mindanao celebrates **Kadayawan**, which is a non-religious, week-long festival giving thanks for the city's bounties. The parades, dances, and costume competitions particularly celebrate the city's flowers, fruits, and multiethnic legacy, a tribute to tribes based in the mountains outside Davao.

## September

The tiny statue of **Our Lady of Peñafrancia**, patroness of the Bicol region in southern

Manning the **gigantes** on bamboo frames over the shoulders, especially while balancing on stilts, requires great discipline and tolerance of bodily discomfort. But the men inside the figures have vowed to perform the service in thanksgiving for an answered prayer. With much skill, after months of practice, they can march, dance, curtsy, and bow before the spectators, and even peer through the second-floor windows of houses they pass along the way. Heightening the fun is the *toro*, an enormous papier-mâché bull painted bright red and rigged with firecrackers. Throughout the

**ABOVE:** smiling masks at the Masskara festival in Bacolod.

Luzon, is one of the most revered Christian images in the Philippines. Come September, thousands of devotees travel by any means to catch a glimpse of her at the festival in the city of Naga.

The religious observance begins on the second Friday of September, nine days before the actual feast day. From her shrine, male devotees carry the statue on their shoulders to the Metropolitan Cathedral. Thousands of eager arms stretch up from a sea of bodies desperate to touch the image, while shouts of *Viva la Virgen* fill the air. Nine days later, the statue goes back to her shrine by way of the Naga River, escorted by a flotilla of outrigger canoes, bamboo rafts, and brightly decorated motorboats. As dusk approaches, candles light the way, giving the river procession the semblance of jewels against a backdrop of darkness.

## October

Bacolod, the capital city of the sugar-producing province of Negros Occidental, hosts laughter-filled homecoming Negrenses – natives of the island of Negros – and a horde of visitors for the big annual party called **Masskara**.

Masskara is coined from two words: *mass*, meaning crowd, and the Spanish word *cara*, or face; thus the double meaning for "mask" and

"many faces." The Masskara festival was first conceived in 1980 to add color and gaiety to the city's celebration of its Charter Day anniversary, on October 19. The symbol of the festival – a smiling mask – depicts the Negrenses' happy spirit, despite periodic economic downturns in the sugar industry. So masked faces grin or laugh through molded clay or papier-mâché worn by costumed men and women who dance in the streets.

People from all over the Visayas islands flock to the town plaza for a week of raging fun. They join Bacolodnons in trying their luck in mask-making contests, greased-pig catching

### LONG CHRISTMAS

Filipinos pride themselves on celebrating the longest **Christmas** in the world. Officially, the religious observance starts on December 16, when almost everyone rises early for the first of the nine-day series of pre-dawn Masses. It is in part a social event, with the focus as much on meeting friends, neighbors, and relations, as on savoring the delicacies offered at church side stalls. The climax is Midnight Mass on Christmas Eve. After this, families go home for the Media Noche, the post-midnight feasting, and only after this may presents be unwrapped. On Christmas Day children are brought round to their godparents' for more gifts.

December 28 is **Holy Innocents' Day**, commemorating the martyrdom of Christian infants mentioned vaguely in the Bible. This is the Yuletide version of April Fool's Day, when pranks abound. December 30 marks Dr Jose Rizal's martyrdom, followed by **New Year's Eve** and **New Year's Day** merrymaking, including 24 hours of loud fireworks. On the first Sunday of January, the **Feast of the Three Kings**, children awake to discover the shoes they have lined up the day before overflowing with goodies. These are mixed in with some dirt, which serves as evidence that during the night a camel, or three, had entered the house like Santa. And with this, the official Christmas season ends.

games, pole climbing, and sack races. Hot dancers participate in disco king and queen contests; hungry people take up coconut-milk drinking, and banana- and bread-eating competitions. The more energetic and athletic sports aficionados compete in basketball or motocross races. The festival culminates with a Masskara parade on Sunday.

## November

The walled city of Intramuros in midtown Manila relives its colonial golden age with exhibitions of historical artifacts, cultural presentations at Fort Santiago, and parades of women

Conception. This is a parade of some 75 statues of the Blessed Virgin Mary brought from all over the country, many of which are believed to be miraculous. Glittering with gold and festooned with flowers, the image-bearing floats are paraded at sunset from the old San Agustin Church to the Quirino Grandstand beside the bay in Rizal Park.

Separately, people throughout the Philippines celebrate **All Saints' Day** on November 1. It's a time to visit the gravesites of deceased family members, offer prayers, and decorate tombs. Among the adornments are candles, flowers, and toys.

clad in the traditional Maria Clara costume of the Spanish era.

The related Casa Manila choral competition, called *Centar Villancios*, is held for visitors to enjoy the Spanish and Tagalog Christmas carols popular during the 18th century. It is a trip back into colonial times and a re-enactment of that elegant age. Manileños love it.

This **Intramuros Festival** goes on until December, when it culminates in the procession of the Feast of Our Lady of the Immaculate

## December

One evening in the week before Christmas, at sunset, lanterns as big as 13 meters (40ft) in diameter go on parade in the town plaza of San Fernando in Pampanga. The finest lanterns vie for the coveted Star of Bethlehem title. Cash prizes awarded are also nothing to sneer at.

The air is meanwhile cool and filled with the sound of Christmas carols. Townspeople dance to the beat of a lively brass band, and children scramble up a trellis to grab at candies as part of a traditional game.

Life for the housewives of San Fernando is turned upside down as visitors flock by to sample traditional Noche Buena (Christmas Eve) specialties of chicken *relleno*, roast pig, and *bibingka*.

**ABOVE, FROM LEFT:** the annual lantern parade at the University of the Philippines; the Pahiyas harvest festival is held in honor of San Isidro Labrador, the patron saint of the farmer and worker.

# A THRIVING ARTS SCENE

The Filipinos are the minstrels of Asia, making a name on stages from Beijing to Dubai. Dance, painting, and pop music have meanwhile matured at home.

D espite the wide reach of Filipino artists, it's hard to pinpoint a particular filming style, musical beat, or English-language writing technique that clearly says "this is Filipino," as so much of it has been influenced by Spaniards, Americans, and Muslims. Filipino stars often train overseas or became famous because of exposure outside the Philippines. But home-grown film, music, and writing have been used to spread anti-government sentiments since the days of nationalist hero Jose Rizal.

## Rural roots

Going back to the countryside, traditional Filipino arts have included pottery, weaving, woodcarving, indigenous music, and poetry inscribed on bamboo tubes. Those art forms still exist, as collectors or souvenir shoppers will find throughout the country. Performing arts also trace some of their roots back to indigenous people in pre-colonial times.

Colonization introduced newer arts, unleashing a creative energy seldom matched in the rest of Southeast Asia.

## Dance

The history of dance shows how native art forms merged with trends from Europe and, more recently, the United States.

On the more traditional side, performers of the Muslim dance called singkil carry two large gilded fans and dress to exude wealth

and privilege. The female performers approach attendants carrying bamboo poles and dance between the moving staffs. The poles, crossed together on the floor, beat faster and louder, clacking furiously. This showpiece number is often performed by professional folk dancers, and one such group, called the Bayanihan (literally, working together), has become an internationally known troupe that aims to preserve and popularize traditional Filipino dance forms outside the country.

Traditional dance written and choreographed by Filipinos can also be seen in Manila. Popular companies are Ballet Philippines, Philippine Dance Company, Filipinescas, and the Ramon Obusan Dance Company.

**LEFT:** Pangalay dancers perform at the Cultural Center of the Philippines, Manila.
**RIGHT:** Traditional dance merges native art forms with European traditions.

The country's best-known classical ballerina is Lisa Macuja, who made her name with the Kirov Ballet in Russia in 1984. Before her, the diminutive but masterful Maniya Barredo had performed outstandingly as a prima ballerina with the Atlanta City Ballet in the United States. Barredo has retired, while Macuja resumed her career and now works as artistic director of Ballet Manila. The best-known young choreographer today is Agnes Locsin, who fuses modernism with ethnic myths and legends. Dubbed a "neo-ethnic" choreographer in local media, Locsin's performances include Moriones, and La Revolucion Filipino.

and from rock music to show band repertoires, Filipino singers and musicians are noted for their self-styled covers of Western music.

Overseas Filipino musicians first emerged in Japan in the early 20th century, but American influence lurked in the background. Filipinos took with them music, jazz for example, that they had picked up during American colonial days, and relied on American recruiters to find jobs in Asian establishments that wanted to create a Western or international ambiance. So old is the musical legacy overseas that countless ordinary workers now seek to become the next superstar.

Ballroom dancing has become such a phenomenon that open-air areas, like a concrete section of Rizal Park in Manila, are regular venues for this activity. More recently, the country has pushed onto the world hip-hop stage with a band called The Philippine All-Stars. The group formed in 2005 and won World Hip-Hop Dance Championships in 2006 and 2008. The band aims to raise the profile of Philippine dancing and, in 2010, it opened a dance school in San Juan city, Ilocos.

## Music

Wherever one travels in Southeast Asia, there are sure to be Filipino bands performing in top hotels and nightclubs. From jazz to pop

*Whatever is on the Top 40 charts abroad quickly gathers steam in the Philippines. In 2012 one of the most popular songs was "Teach Me How to Dougie" by US hip-hop artists Cali Swag District.*

American influence clearly shows in the overseas Filipino musical hall of fame: Lea Salonga was key to making the musical *Miss Saigon* a resounding success, and Paolo Montalban made a name for himself on American stage, film, and television. Until his death a few years ago, Bobby Enriquez, known as "the Wildman" from Montreaux to Chicago, was toasted in the international jazz circuit for his inimitably energetic assault on the piano. Another cult figure, Sugar Pie de Santos, has cut jazz albums in the US.

At home, European and American pop tunes have been translated into Tagalog or sung in *Taglish* (a mixture of Tagalog and English). But more significantly, OPM, or Original Pilipino Music, has made such great strides that bestselling albums are now mostly original collections of Pilipino pop, rock, and folk music.

Some Filipinos follow Ryan Cayabyab, composer of musicals and ballets. He sings and plays the piano, as well, and led a band

Sandwich, and Sugarfree. Another popular OPM band, Bamboo, sent out shockwaves when it broke up in 2011. The band Eraserheads, which does jams and a range of rock music, remains an enduring favorite at home.

## Theater

Another Western tradition, the stage play, was eagerly assimilated by Filipinos, especially the Spanish-influenced passion plays. These plays developed into street theater under the broader term of fiesta. The fiesta is the ultimate street theater, complete with drama, religious passion, and enthusiastic audience participation.

in the 1990s called Smokey Mountain. In the 1980s, prolific actress Sharon Cuneta branched out into popular music, pushing her fame to new heights. Religious music composer Gary Grenada and folk singer-composer Joey Ayala have earned fans for what amounts to Philippine soul music. Grenada helped headline an anti-government "Protest Broadcast" that followed the killing of 57 people, including 38 journalists, on the embattled island of Mindanao in 2009.

Inside the iPods of Filipino youth post-2000 can be found hundreds of laid-back rock 'n' roll tunes of local bands such as Rivermaya,

**ABOVE, FROM LEFT:** *burnay* pots; budding guitarists.

### TRADITIONAL MUSIC TODAY

Traditional music lives on in the Philippines despite the pervasive influences of the outside world. Indigenous music is still being composed, for example, for brass or bamboo percussion instruments. In Mindanao and the Sulu islands *kulintang* ensembles create melodies using rows of gongs.

Folk music is best sampled at Malate's Hobbit House (www.hobbithousemanila.com) in central Manila. There the legendary Freddie Aguilar, who is known all over Asia for his monster hit ballad *Anak* (Child), has performed regularly over the years. His *Bayan Ko* (My Country) became the anthem of the anti-Marcos movement in the 1980s.

Filipino theater is generally coupled with dance and music. Comedy is wrapped into the traditional fiesta, as actors say something about the historical conflict between Christians and non-believers through their music and dance. In cosmopolitan Manila, the *zarzuela*, a musical comedy form seemingly adapted from the Italian opera, enjoys an occasional revival.

Younger Filipinos hold the theater sacred. Every college or university has its own stage, and Western drama flourishes on campus. Contemporary playwrights also write in local languages to produce fiery comedies and dramas.

Undoubtedly, the biggest Filipino name to date in theater is Lea Salonga, who became an international star after her performance as Kim in the musical *Miss Saigon*. The best-known full-length play written by a Filipino in English is *Portrait of the Artist as Filipino* by the late Nick Joaquin. The drama about high society in Manila during World War II is often re-staged and has been made into a movie.

## Literature

Before the arrival of the Spanish, the indigenous people had a distinct oral tradition that included creation myths, native legends, and folk tales. Proto-historic peoples even used a syllabic writing system called alibata. The country's first printed book, *Doctrina Christiana*, written in Spanish, appeared in the 16th century. For almost 300 years in the archipelago, the printed word was mostly Spanish, and typically related to religious themes.

National hero Jose Rizal set the standard for prose and poetry with his pre-revolutionary *Noli Me Tangere* and *El Filibusterismo*, which he wrote in Spanish. After 1930, English and the increasing use of Tagalog replaced Spanish as media for literary expression. During American rule, the short story was a popular form among writers and continues to this day, with competing story volumes outnumbering novels on some modern bookshelves. A book of stories by T.P. Bocquiren, for example, looks at sad stories from poor neighborhoods, while Vic H. Groyon's The Names and Faces of People relates struggles of the country's middle class.

### SCREEN PLAUDITS

The Philippines' movie industry has a long history but remains one of the world's lesser known entities. Revered director Lino Brocka generated rave reviews with his first non-commercial movie, *Tinimbang Ka Ngunit Kulang* (You Were Weighed But Found Wanting), in the 1970s, which tells of a small town's outcasts seen through a young man's eyes. Brocka made several political films, including *Bayan Ko* (My Country), an anti-Marcos film. He was posthumously declared a National Artist for Film. Fellow Filipino director Ishmael Bernal made movies about gritty social realism, winning applause from circles abroad. One of his most acclaimed works was *Himala* (Miracle).

Independent movies thrive in Manila, with directors such as Kidlat Tahimik, Briccio Santos, Nick Deocampo, and Raymond Red making inroads into the cultist European market. Internationally acclaimed Brillante Mendoza won Best Director for his movie Kinatay (Butchered) at the Cannes Film Festival in 2009.

Many films are shot in just seven days to save money. Film piracy has been another tearjerker for the industry. A bigger threat comes from Hollywood. Already steeped in American culture, movie-goers in the Philippines eagerly embrace imports from the US. As a result, Filipino film-makers are producing only 40 movies per year compared to an annual 200 to 300 in the 1990s.

*Private funding helps keep the Philippine arts scene alive. Since 1951, the Carlos Palanca Memorial Awards for Literature have sponsored the annual literary competition. Cash prizes are awarded by sponsors in annual painting contests.*

One of the best-known Filipino novelists abroad, F. Sionil Jose, owns the Solidaridad Bookshop in Manila and continues to publish the regional journal *Solidarity*. The owner's short stories and an epic series of novels on people and land have been translated short but popular books sold in mainstream bookstores.

## Painting and sculpture

Throughout the 19th century, painting in the Philippines was heavily influenced by Spanish trends. Both Juan Luna and Felix Resureccion Hidalgo achieved international fame when they won prizes at the Madrid Exposition of 1884. Luna painted epics and scenes of social significance, while Hidalgo was best known for his neo-Impressionist scenes.

Contemporary Filipino artists are among the most productive in Asia, with their sculptural

into many languages and were published by Random House.

English-language writing continues to thrive, its dynamism recently enhanced by the success of Filipino American writers such as Eugene Gloria, who won the much-coveted US National Poetry Award in 1999.

Humor has also made its way onto the literary scene. Comedian-authors such as Gary Lising and Luis Joaquin Katigbak (author of The King of Nothing to Do) are making modern Filipinos laugh about themselves through

**ABOVE, FROM LEFT:** Lea Salonga and co-star in the Broadway musical *Miss Saigon*; contemporary artists produce an effigy for an anti-government protest.

*The first Filipino artist to achieve international recognition was Juan Luna. He won a gold medal at the Exposicion Nacional de Bellas Artes in Madrid in 1884.*

works adorning lobbies of hotels and corporate buildings. An oil painting by Anita Magsaysay Ho was purchased for a record US$400,000 at a recent auction in Singapore. Modern Filipina sculptress Alma Quinto, born in 1961, produced a multi-media animal titled Lolita's Pet that is worth hundreds of US dollars. Filipino contemporary Duddley Diaz made a mark in 1997 with a multimedia figurine titled Preacher No. 3.

# INDIGENOUS ARTS AND HANDICRAFTS

**Traditional village-based arts and crafts have found a new lease of life as esoteric art forms and decor accessories in modern Manila homes.**

Art spans the Philippines from Manila's museums to exterior decor of the most humble rural homes. Even the simple tools and weapons used by the early nomadic people were artistically designed. Effigies of the early people of the Philippines' 110 indigenous tribes have men and women donning a variety of headdresses, earrings, anklets, belly rings, bracelets, and necklaces. Such artistic expressions, influenced by religious beliefs and cultural practices, reached an apogee in the early Iron Age when people of Malay descent migrated in droves to the country.

Soon, visual art forms expanded to include woodcarvings, weaving, and pottery. Creative artisans, seeing the wealth of natural materials available – bamboo, rattan, nipa palm, *pina* and *abaca* (pineapple and hemp fibres), seashells, and marble – have used them to fashion a range of handicrafts, from tiny baskets to massive pieces of furniture. Today, travelers will find brilliant weaves, intricate beadwork, silver tribal jewelry, rustic wood figurines and dishes, ceramic pots, jewel-colored capiz-shell chandeliers, earthy *pandan* leaf mats and coasters, rattan basketry, and shiny brassware. Among the going favorites are change pouches shaped from leather into fish. Slit the fish's throat with a zipper to deposit coins.

The best range of crafts is found in Manila – in Ermita, Makati, and the Quiapo area – and also in specialty shops or malls, including those inside tribal theme villages open to the public. Airport gift shops in Cebu, Davao, and other cities sell samples of the handicrafts from their regions.

**ABOVE:** The Philippines' guitar-making industry is centered on Mactan Island just off the coast at Cebu City. Visitors can watch the local craftsmen at work or be entertained by a quality-control expert trying out a newly-made guitar.

**BELOW LEFT:** Ceramic *burnay* pots from the Ilocos region, Luzon.

**ABOVE:** Attractive ceramic jars known as *burnay* are made in and around Vigan in the Ilocos region of northern Luzon. They are designed for storing vinegar, fermented fish paste and the local wine.

## THE ART OF T'BOLI WEAVING

In the southermost part of Mindanao lies Lake Sebu, surrounded by rolling highlands and mountains. This is where the T'boli people live and produce the much sought-after *t'nalak* cloth. Made from pounded bark, the weave is a striking blend of primary colors. When sewn into traditional attire, the cloth is a perfect foil for the beautiful ethnic accessories worn by T'boli women.

For modern Manileños, however, the cloth is prized as tablecloths, bed covers and scarves. In the old days, T'boli women could weave *t'nalak* even with their eyes closed. But as the big cities beckon, young tribal people, including T'boli women, are lured by urban jobs and lifestyles. As a result, *t'nalak* weaving is in danger of vanishing.

**RIGHT:** Weaving cloth at Yakan weaving village, Zamboanga.

**ABOVE:** Religious keepsakes.

**LEFT:** Filipino crafts are often on display at the numerous festivals, such as the colorful masks at the Masskara festival that takes place in Bacolod every October.

# CROSS-CULTURAL CUISINE

Filipino food is a marinade of the country's multiethnic past, exotically flavored by the cuisines of Chinese, Spanish, and American settlers and featuring locally produced ingredients.

L ittle-known outside the country, cuisine in the Philippines offers an often delicious combination of Asian, American, and European inspired dishes with a local twist, drawing on the archipelago's rainy, warm climate, verdant farms, and abundant supplies of seafood.

Delicate broths overflow with prawns and vegetables. Chicken and pork are combined with ginger, garlic, or tamarind, and served fried, barbecued, wrapped in crêpes, or crisply roasted. Chinese noodle dishes, Spanish paella, and American steaks can be found alongside indigenous dishes cooked with coconut, and the pick of

> Filipino food was prepared by Malay settlers, spiced by Chinese traders, stewed in 300 years of Spanish rule, and hamburgered by American influence in the Philippine way of life. Food historian Monina A. Mercado.

the day's fish catch. Filipinos seldom serve things spicy. Desserts are a specialty, often infused with the juices of sweetly scented tropical fruits.

## Soups

Anchoring many a meal is *sinigang*. These soups blend meat, fish or prawns, and vegetables (such as green beans) stewed with tamarind, green mangoes, and acidic fruits or leaves. As in the soups of Thailand and Indonesia, the sourness is considered cooling, and to have a healing effect on the body.

**LEFT:** a vendor at the Zamboanga fruit market displays a ripe marang fruit, a cross between a jackfruit and a durian. **RIGHT:** grilled corn is sold at street stalls.

## Main dishes

Chicken forms a staple part of many dishes. There's chicken *tinola* made with ginger, papaya, and pepper leaves. Chicken *relleno* is stuffed with Spanish olives and sausages. Fried chicken dominates the fast-food scene. Chicken *adobo*, a foreigner favorite, is cooked with vinegar, bay leaf, peppercorns, and garlic. The name derives from the Spanish dish *adobado*. Filipinos have re-mastered the recipe with shellfish, vegetables, and a variety of sauces, including soy and liver.

Pork *adobo* is just as common, likewise *lechon* – slices of roasted suckling pig stuffed with tamarind leaves and cooked till crispy. Pork-filled spring roll, *lumpia*, includes heart-of-palm and shrimp. It's wrapped in a tissue-paper-thin crêpe and served with garlic and soy sauce.

One of the oldest dishes is *kinilaw*, made of raw fish or shrimp flavored with ginger, onions, and chilli. Vinegar or lime juice is added to a point when it reaches a still-fresh translucence. An archeological site in Mindanao had some *kinilaw* remnants that carbon-dated back at least 1,000 years. The name *kinilaw* also applies to sour salads. For fish eaters, the dish *sinanglay* mixes fish or crab with hot pepper wrapped in Chinese cabbage and cooked in coconut milk.

## Indigenous food

Native Filipino food belongs mainly to an Austronesian matrix, with resonances of the food of its Southeast Asian neighbors. People from the Bicol peninsula east of Manila make *laing*: fish, taro leaves, chilli, and coconut milk; the Ilonggo people make *binakol*, which is chicken with young coconut (traditionally, cooked in a coconut shell); the Ilocanos in the north all but invented *pinakbet* and make it with bitter melon, okra, tomatoes, and eggplant, steamed with anchovy sauce. Elsewhere, it may contain green beans and a sprinkling of pork to give it a salty kick. The native Tagalog are known for *sinampalu-*

On the wilder side, diners may run across *kare-kare*, a blend of oxtail, knuckles, and tripe, stewed with vegetables in peanut sauce. It's served with fish-based *bagoong* sauce.

## Rice and noodles

Rice is the Philippine staple, as in Vietnam and Malaysia – neighboring countries that have made a major impact on local cuisine. The variety of rice ranges from the prized tiny-grained *milagrosa* to the *malagkit*, or glutinous rice that features in leaf-wrapped, sweetened cakes known as *bibingka*, *puto*, *suman*, and *kutsinta*.

A series of noodle dishes known as *pancit* also puts the Philippines squarely on the pan-Asian culinary map.

*kang manok*, which is chicken flavored with green tamarind pods and tendrils. (The word *manok* is good to remember as it runs rampant on restaurant signboards. It simply means "chicken.")

## Chinese influences

From the Chinese merchants, who since the 11th century had been trading silk and pottery for sea and forest products, comes a list of entrées that have been a part of local cuisine for so long that most Filipinos do not even realize they are foreign. The early Chinese traders lived among the ordinary people, so their food was introduced to Filipino society at that level. Eateries offering Chinese dishes were the first to operate in the Philippines and they served dishes bearing

Spanish names for the sake of the clientele. *Pancit* is one such example. It comprises rice, mung bean, egg, and any type of noodle cooked with meat, seafood, and vegetables. Every region, town, and home has its own version of *pancit*, with different ingredients added. Chinese rice porridge has been re-adapted as *arroz caldo*, which is soft rice with chicken or tripe, flavored with *kasubha*, a spice less potent than saffron, and sprinkled with lime juice and roasted garlic. Also sourced to China, dumplings (*siomai*), stuffed buns (*siopao*), and noodle soups (*mami*, *lomi*) are sold at street stalls and restaurants.

## Spanish paella

Three hundred years of Spanish colonization have been imprinted, not just on everyday menus, but more especially on feasts and celebrations. Since Spanish cuisine called for ingredients not available in the tropics, the dishes took on an exclusive value and were found mainly on tables of the elite class. Those hard-to-get ingredients were olive oil, saffron, and pork sausages,

Paella, for example, which in Spain is a common dish cooked in the field, with meat such as rabbit or seafood, is in the Philippines a fiesta dish. The Philippine rendition pulls together a full-blown grocery list: sausages, ham, clams, crabs, chicken, pork, pimientos, saffron, olive oil, and wine.

With the introduction of Christianity came dishes associated with the celebration of Christmas: sugared brioches (*ensaymada*) dipped in thick hot chocolate, sliced Edam cheese, apples and oranges, chestnuts and walnuts, beef rolls, stuffed turkey, and ox tongue with mushrooms.

## American steaks

Thanks in part to recent American influence, younger people carry sandwiches rather than rice cakes in their backpacks. Steaks, chops, salads, and pies occur in restaurants. Filipinos prize American food's pre-packaging for easy consumption in fast-food restaurants, on the road, or at home.

Baked goods of American or Spanish descent are reflected in today's numerous bakeries, where pocket change buys bags full of churros, empanadas, banana bread, and round cakes with a dollop of sweetened fruit in the middle.

**ABOVE, FROM LEFT:** roasted chickens for sale; *pancit* noodles.

Some cakes are Chinese-inspired. Breakfasts of salty chopped beef, garlic rice, and eggs sunnyside up also mix Spain, the United States, and the Philippines.

## Sauces and condiments

The input of Filipino culture really comes in the sauces and dips. A cook may make *sinigang* broth with a particular, personalized degree of sourness. The diner, however, is free to fine-tune this to taste with different relishes or dipping sauces. There is *patis* (fish sauce) or *bagoong* (shrimp paste) with chopped onions, tomatoes, and cilantro. Each individual in a group of

diners may come away with a different experience, depending on the dips chosen.

The most popular condiments are hot chilli sauce, and soy sauce mixed with *calamansi* (small limes). Grilled items labelled *ihaw-ihaw* are taken with crushed garlic, vinegar, and chilli.

> *Despite flies, floor filth, and coughing customers, restaurant food is usually cooked well enough and served fast enough to keep out the bugs that might cause digestive problems for the novice diner.*

## Eating out in the Philippines

At regional specialty restaurants in the Philippines one faces an array of fresh fish, crustaceans, and rarities such as the coconut crab whose coconut diet accounts for the taste of its flesh. There are grill outlets that specialize in *pulutan*, which is food for drinking sessions. Some specialty restaurants serve cuisine that would have been found on the tables of the 19th-century elite.

Filipinos generally prefer to eat with forks and spoons rather than chopsticks. The fork should be held in the left hand during buffet-style meals to put food onto a spoon in the right hand.

## MANGO, MANGOSTEEN AND MORE

The Philippine mango, heart-shaped and golden, is hard to miss. Its sweet and firm flesh – celebrated in verse and song – is eaten fresh, juiced, dried, diced into a salad, cooked in syrup, made into jam, or added to crêpes and desserts. Lesser-known fruits are the brown-skinned lanzones that are pinched open to reveal white sweet-sour sections within. Filipinos say the locally grown durian, particularly abundant in Mindanao, "tastes like heaven" but "smells like hell." Meanwhile, the russet, husk-encased mangosteen is sweet throughout.

Other common fruits are bananas, custard apples, guavas, papayas, pineapples, soursop, star fruit, and easy-to-peel tangerines. Jackfruit, the largest tree-borne fruit in the world, exudes a pineapple or banana odor when opened and contains bulbs of banana-flavored flesh. Children go for the small, red tambis, known as a water apple because of its watery consistency. Filipinos are fond of using the sour calamansi, basically a kumquat, to make juice, with sugar added to suit individual taste. The tiny lemonsito is also pressed to make a refreshing lemon juice drink with added water.

Roadside stands sell fruits throughout the country, charging a modest price for a variety pack hand-selected by customers. Most fruits sold in the Philippines are grown in-country, but imported Fuji apples from Japan can be found at local supermarkets.

Chinese eateries range from bicycle carts offering salty, sweet or sour nuts, and fruits, and street corner shops that serve *lumpia* (spring rolls) and noodles, to luxurious restaurants serving 12-course meals. Spanish restaurants offer Asia's best Iberian cuisine. Leave room for *gambas al ajillo* (shrimps in olive oil and garlic), *almejas o mejillones al horno* (baked clams or mussels), and *champinones adobados* (marinated mushrooms).

Italian diners proliferate because pasta is akin to *pancit*, and the pizza that American chains have taught the young Filipino to love has acquired local toppings such as regional sausages, farmer's cheese, and salted egg. Thai, Vietnamese, and Korean restaurants are popular because the foods taste familiarly Asian.

(See also Travel Tips, page 348).

## Desserts

The coconut in the Philippines, as in any other Pacific Rim country, controls much of the dessert menu. Its mature flesh can be grated or squeezed out as coconut cream or milk. The water and flesh of the green nut can be drunk or made into sweets. The sap is fermented or distilled into the potent *lambanog*.

Coconut milk puddings make up a common dessert, along with *bibingka*, which is made from ground rice and sugar as well as coconut milk, then baked in a clay oven and topped with salted duck egg. *Leche* flan is a crème caramel made with coconut milk and flavored with the rind of local limes.

Tired of coconut? Get ice cream. It comes in flavors such as jackfruit, mango, and, well, coconut. If stumped by the dessert decision, try *halo-halo*: a colorful bowl of shaved ice and evaporated milk mixed with any number of fruits and sweetened beans.

## Drinks

Almost every drinks list in the Philippines, from roadside dining stalls to formal restaurants, covers canned fruit juices, soft drinks, locally brewed San Miguel beers, and instant coffee.

Most places will have mango, orange, and pineapple juice, probably sweetened artificially. Some restaurants serve sweetened Four Seasons brand drinks that merge the flavors of multiple fruits. Soft drinks include the usual cola

choices, and Royal Tru Orange soda. Bottled water is also available.

As for beer, it takes an unusual restaurateur to expand beyond the cheap, locally brewed San Miguel Pilsen and Light beers, but some proprietors will sell a darker variety too. Red Horse, a stronger, locally brewed beer akin to malt liquor, is also available in most stores and a few restaurants. Internationally known lager brands occasionally make a restaurant drinks list, and red wine – always imported – pops up with the same irregularity. Quality South American and Australian wines can be had for around P100–200 a glass. Another option is the

local brew, San Miguel, which can cost as little as P21 in the street, and usually no more than P100 at the finest establishments.

All coffee in the Philippines should be presumed instant except in dedicated coffeehouses and restaurants that advertise freshly ground beans. Coffee fanatics may ask around about where to get whole bean varieties in regions, such as Davao, that grow it. Tea, if offered at all, will be the common black type brewed from bags made by international mass-market labels.

It is best not to take any chances with tap water. Stick to bottled water, even for brushing your teeth and especially outside Manila. In larger cities, major hotels and restaurants serve filtered water.

**ABOVE, FROM LEFT:** tasty street food; glutinous rice dessert.

# THE SPORTING LIFE

**Filipinos are enthusiastic about many sports, notably basketball and boxing, but since most of the country is coastal or mountainous, travelers tend to choose diving, caving, hiking, and trekking.**

Participant sports popular with Filipinos often originated from periods of Spanish or American rule. *Arnis de mano*, which morphed into something akin to fencing, traces back to conflict between natives and Spanish colonizers. Boxing sustains its hit status in part because Filipino legislator Manny Pacquiao earned fame in 2012 as the world welterweight champion. Televised sports and American cultural influence give basketball a high score among younger men in the country.

Travelers may watch these local sports but, for their own exercise, tend to pursue a list of others in the outdoors. Some visit the Philippines only for diving, as witnessed by the fast growth in gear sales, permit courses, boat rentals, and underwater guides. Other fit, foreign aficionados of the local outdoors ply their way through caves with underground rivers or scale the steep sides of volcanoes that could blow anytime. Almost anywhere in the country, Filipinos can point the tourist toward local hiking trails.

## Basketball

Perhaps unexpectedly for an outsider imagining something more "indigenous", basketball is the national passion. Indeed, inch for inch, Filipinos are among the best players in the world, and the sport is marked by year-round amateur and professional tournaments.

Manila was the first Asian city to establish a professional league in 1976 with the birth of the Philippine Basketball Association (PBA). Star players become much-loved celebrities, and often double as movie or television icons.

### STICK FIGHTING

Few visitors to the Philippines have heard of *arnis de mano*, Filipino stick fighting. The ancient sport originated as a defense of the traveler against robbers, and is played with a 1-meter (3ft) -long hardwood stick, or *tungkod*. Opponents swing and parry at each other. Out of the movements of *arnis* evolved *eskrima*, a martial art that substituted the wooden sticks of *arnis* for bladed weapons.

The decline of these practices came as a result of their ineffectiveness against Spanish guns. Movements characteristic of *arnis* were later added in an approximation of dance and spectacle. *Arnis* is played regularly by aficionados in Manila.

**LEFT:** basketball is hugely popular in the Philippines.
**RIGHT:** jet-skiing at Puerto Galera.

*Filipino Rafael "Paeng" Nepomuceno has won the world bowling championships a record six times since the late 1980s. His female counterpart is Bong Coo.*

Two such individuals have even managed to have themselves elected to the Senate. Imports (American pros, mostly black) reinforce PBA teams in two of the three conferences held every year, with the last reserved as the All-Filipino Conference. Teams are owned by companies, which profit from the media exposure

Travelers to the Philippines may glimpse a roadside basketball game anywhere from Metro Manila to the outskirts of Puerto Princesa.

For more on basketball see page 363.

## Billiards

Billiards is the one sport where the Filipino has proven himself a global champion. The 2010 nine-ball world champion was Francisco Bustamante, of the Philippines. Ex-champion Efren "Bata" Reyes, also a Philippine national, whose exploits in the professional pool rooms in the United States and Europe were glorified through global sports television, became an

the whole year round from live television coverage of doubleheaders thrice a week.

Simplicity of equipment lies at the root of the appeal, and every town plaza sports a basketball court across from the church and town hall. Young boys go through their paces using a makeshift basket. Courts can be seen on roadsides in even remote rural areas, and the topic of basketball makes it easy to strike up conversation with local men.

At one time or another, nearly every Filipino male tries his hand at the game. Like his professional counterpart, the backstreet jock revels in showy creativity. He does not just pass the ball, but indulges in hangtime before executing a behind-the-back feed with a torrid scramble.

endearing hero. He started playing as a nine-year-old working as a "spotter" in his uncle's parlor in Manila, where he slept nightly on a pool table. Filipino players are known to rule the game with such superiority that at one time, the top three finishers in the annual US pro circuit were all Filipino campaigners. Other feared billiards masters have been "Amang" Parica, whom Reyes beat in the 1990s.

Such is Reyes' mastery of the game that when he was fielded into the national team for the Southeast Asian Games, he took only a few hours to familiarize himself with the larger balls and table used in snooker, and still came away with the gold medal. Filipinos are hoping billiards becomes an official Olympic event, confident it is where they stand the best chance of bagging that elusive and first Olympic gold.

## Boxing

Next only to basketball in popularity is boxing. Not only does it open doors for destitutes from distant provinces to rise in economic stature, but it is also one sport where Filipinos have proven themselves to be world-class.

Legendary boxers include Pancho Villa who dominated in the flyweight division in the 1930s. He boxed successfully in the United States, as well, and lived it up by posing with such Hollywood personalities as Mae West. Filipino

Flash Elorde was the world's junior lightweight champion for seven years in the 1960s.

More modern champions and top-class contenders include Luisito Espinosa, Gerry Peñalosa, and Manny Pacquiao. The latter was the World Boxing Organization's welterweight champion as of 2012 and considered the best pound-for-pound boxer anywhere in the world – in addition to other bests and awards. The boxer is also an actor and musician. Wildly popular at home for his sporting achievements, Pacquiao was elected in 2010 as a member of the House of Representatives.

---

**ABOVE:** group practicing *arnis de mano* (Filipino stick fighting).

---

> *Florencio Campomanes, who was a renowned national master in his younger days, headed FIDE, the world's top chess body, for well over a decade. He retired in 1997.*

## Chess

Since the post-war period, Filipino chess players have been some of Asia's best representatives. But only when Eugenio Torre (whose name appropriately means "rook") became the first Asian grandmaster in 1973 did thousands of chess aficionados battle it out in clubs, at corner stores, in barber shops, and under mango trees.

Torre inserted serious book study and single-mindedness to emerge national champion at age 18. He then represented Asia in high-rating tournaments, in the process winning over some of the world's chess superstars. For the legion of chess fanatics in the country, Torre's ascendancy only confirmed the remarkable national affinity for the game. The Philippine national team, led by Torre, placed a record-high seventh in the Chess Olympics held in Greece in the late 1970s.

Torre is now semi-retired, occasionally serving as a coach for national teams, which are sure to find talent as Filipino children still dedicate themselves to the game. Taking over as the country's top player is Joey Antonio, who finished third in the 2009 Asia Continental Chess Championship. He made it into the World Cup the same year.

## Cockfighting

Banned in most countries, cockfighting has had a long tradition in the Philippines. No self-respecting town will do without a cockpit (*sabungan*) and, every Sunday or public holiday, raucous crowds in tiers reaching the roof pack galleries around the central pits.

The pre-fight shouting is directed at the bookmakers (*kristo*), their arms stretched out like Christ as they acknowledge bets. The *kristo* are minor attractions in themselves for their uncanny ability to absorb all the bets and odds without writing anything down. Thousands of pesos change hands at each bloody duel; even houses, land titles, and car registrations have been placed as bets ahead of the contests that may last all night along with the flow of alcohol.

Combat proper begins after the arbiter has unsheathed the razor-sharp spur attached to

*A common joke is that a Filipino would sooner save his favorite gamecock, in the event of a fire, than his spouse. The sight of men lovingly fondling their potential champions adds credence to this claim.*

the right legs of both roosters and allowed each combatant a sharp peck at the other's neck. Thus teased and aroused into a fighting mood, the duelists fix upon each other with a chilly stare and in the next instance lunge at each other, their talons taut with intent to

Today, jockeys in colorful silks mount horses bred from imported stock. There are electronic totalizers, computers and photo-finish cameras, and air-conditioned booths with push-buttons that summon club personnel to place bets on the horses, plus cocktail lounges and bars. Racing in Manila is big business.

At the start of the day's races, fans gather in the compound fronting the grandstand beside the paddock, such as at the San Lazaro track in Manila. The Philippine horses make their entry, breathing gently, some skittish, kicking and throwing their heads in the air, ears laid back, eyes rolling, and tugging at the reins held by

destroy. The loser of the mid-air pecking and clawing battle scurries to one end of the arena, where it crumples into an ungainly, usually dead, heap.

For more on cockfighting, see page 363.

## Horse racing

Horse racing in the Philippines has come a long way from the 1860s, when fashionable races organized by the Manila Jockey Club were held twice a year at the Hippodrome. At that time, fans arrived in flamboyant carriages, the women in flowing skirts with parasols and the men with buttoned coats and Ascot ties. After the races, the gentlemen and their ladies would repair to a ball held at the same site.

trainers who talk soothingly, to calm the animals.

A Philippine racetrack is different from anything that horse-racing enthusiasts will have seen in Europe or America. There is no green turf (the track is of sand), there are no specialized hats, elaborate dresses, checkered suits, or other paraphernalia that have grown alongside the sport elsewhere. Enjoyment is derived purely from seeing the animals in motion.

The San Lazaro track complex on Felix Huertas Street is a near-perfect oval – its immensity telescoped by the tricky light of the early morning. It measures 1,300 meters (6 furlongs) around the track, which is made of sea sand over a soft rock and charcoal base. Encircling the outer track are dozens of stables, on top of which perch a number of stable lads, all eagerly monitoring the progress of their charges.

There is some fine, honest racing around San Lazaro, the horses running smoothly and with a dull thunder on the packed sand track. Cheers become roars at the end of each race as bettors see what they might have won.

While the Gran Copa Cup is the main event of the racing year, other highlights at San Lazaro are the Founders Cup, the Presidential Cup and the National Grand Derby. The National Grand Derby has also become one of the most colorful spectacles of local racing.

For more on horse racing, see page 363.

## Jai alai

Brought to the Philippines decades ago from the Basque area of Spain, *jai alai* presents an exciting spectacle because of the shattering speed at which the ball is thrown and returned. Players leap around the court with agility, clambering up the side wall or the wire netting separating the *fronton* (court) from the spectators to return a difficult ball.

The inauguration of a court in Manila in 1940 by President Manuel Quezon was billed at the time as the most elaborate sporting and social event in the capital's history. Cebu set up its own court in the 1970s.

But with the downfall of Marcos, *jai alai* was mothballed due to its reputed links with "crony" operators. It took over a decade before the Philippine Amusement and Gaming Corporation (Pagcor), a government agency, managed to reopen the franchise in Manila against objections from religious leaders.

Armed with renewed vigor, games were played every afternoon in Manila. These events with noisy spectators would run wild as betting was both legal and frantic.

*Jai alai* was once again closed down – this time by the Arroyo-Macapagal administration in August 2001. Prior to its ban, it was estimated that more than half a million bets were placed daily, involving 20 percent of the capital's population. It has since re-emerged in parts of the country, only to face a new legal challenge in 2011. That year the sport's legal status resurfaced once more after an appeals court barred the activities of *jai alai*

**ABOVE, FROM LEFT:** a fight at the Pasay City Cockpit, Manila; hiking among the black cliffs of El Nido, North Palawan.

operator Meridien Vista Gaming Corporation unless it could prove that it had the rights to do business in Cagayan Province.

## Hiking

As mountains dominate the interiors of most Philippine islands, national parks with networks of trails may perch somewhere in the peaks. Anyone with solid legs and lungs can find hikes on the country's larger islands. Combinations of bus, jeepney, and private van, tricycle-taxi, or motorcycle rides, costing a few hundred pesos per person, are not always comfortable but often required to reach prime

### HIKING PRECAUTIONS

Hiking is generally safe in the Philippines, although trails are not always well marked so it is best to hire a guide. As most hikes involve mountains, travelers should also monitor fast-changing weather for signs of heavy rain. Ask around about provisions sold along the trail before setting out. Blood-slurping insects thrive in the Philippines, so carry repellent.

Entry permits are unnecessary in most places, but are required for Mt Apo, Mt Banahaw, and Mt Kanlaon (available on site or through your guide service). The Pinoy Mountaineer website (http://www.pinoymountaineer.com) is a useful resource.

hiking spots. To avoid getting stranded, ask transport operators if they will be around after a hike, or book a return trip ahead of time.

Here are five of the country's best hikes:

**Mt Asog**, Camarines Sur. Start from Barangay Cabatuan in Iriga city for a four-hour hike around 1,140 meters (3,740ft) above sea level to a volcanic crater rim.

**Taal volcano**, south of Manila. Start from Talisay in Batangas for a 45-minute hike at just 300 meters (984ft) above sea level around the tiny but potentially explosive volcano.

**Mt Ampacao**, Sagada. Start from Ambasing Elementary School, for a climb of 386 meters

(1,266ft) above sea level. The hike of less than half a day dips into pine forests.

**Mt Talinis**, Dauin (Negros Oriental). Start from Barangay Bediao for a two- to three-day hike around 1,900 meters (6,230ft) above sea level past lakes, waterfalls, and forests.

**Mt Kalatungan** on Mindanao. Start from Barangay Mendis in Pangantucan city for up to 15 hours' worth of hikes through thick forests and tribal areas.

## Trekking

Hiking segues naturally into trekking, with the difference in many cases just a matter of time spent, technical difficulty of trails, and equipment needed. But that difference can mean

reaching a peak via the steep moon-like upper regions of a mountain rather than just plumbing the jungles at lower elevations.

Volcanoes such as Apo, Mayon, Isarog, and Pinatubo have earned a particularly strong following among trekkers. Lesser-known routes are also open on Mindanao and the island of Cebu. Guides cover the territory, while amenities such as equipment rentals anchor the staging areas. Among the guides are Philippine Adventures (tel: 02-887-0047) and Bagwis Outdoor (tel: 02-671-0010).

## Caving

Those unafraid of the dark, but excited by rivers, stalactites, galleries, and mountains of marble will enjoy a different sport in the Philippines.

Many caves in the archipelago act as tunnels for underground rivers, top among them St Paul on Palawan. On the island of Negros, look for the unusually long Odloman cave. It's 8.8km (5.5 miles) in length and up to 82 meters (269ft) high. And on Mindanao, the Banbow and Tatol caves have attracted attention for their rock formations.

Construction worker-style helmets and multiple sources of light are highly advised. Cavers should be at moderate fitness level, as rope climbing may be required. And always go into the dark with someone else. Ask around at hotels and tourist hubs such as airports about guide services. For more information, visit the Philippine Caving Society's website at www.philippinecavingsociety.com.ph.

## Snorkeling and swimming

It is possible buy or rent snorkels for sorties over coral gardens near the shorelines. Ask where to find the best coral just meters from the beach. Fair-skinned snorkelers should dab sunblock on their backs.

The country's calm seas also provide a natural swimming pool for beachgoers with no special equipment. Coastal resorts often skip building pools as guests can just jump into the waves. Swimming is safe, as rip currents are not a problem, though drop-offs can be steep and pumpboats may cruise annoyingly close to people in the water.

For more sports information see Travel Tips, page 363.

**LEFT:** exploring the Callao Caves in Cagayan Province.

# A Diver's Haven

**Most of the 7,107 Philippine islands drop off quickly into the ocean. The best way to explore this extraordinary underwater world is with scuba gear**

**D**ivers in the Philippines will swim in near perfect visibility with groupers and snappers. Some will photograph multicolored feather stars. They may float over coral gardens, past sharks (gentle ones), and around massive World War II wrecks.

Many of the islets mentioned in this guidebook beckon intrepid divers to plunge into waters that are seldom explored only for lack of amenities on land. More popular coastal magnets, such as Alona Beach, Puerto Galera, and Boracay, have grown a reputation among travelers largely, if not only, because of diving.

## Clownfish and coral

Would-be divers can usually choose an instructor on arrival in a beach town and get internationally recognized certification within days. Equipment is rented on the spot. Europeans, Japanese, and Korean expat diving guides cater to fellow nationals in bigger towns. Prices of instruction can be steep, however, with some rates quoted in the hundreds of euros.

Luzon's most accessible dive area is Anilao in Batangas, a few hours' drive south of Manila. Facing severe environmental degradation 30 years ago, the locals banded together to protect their coral reefs. Healthy again, coral, clownfish, and anemones now thrive in these waters.

Across the strait from Anilao, in Puerto Galera, swifter currents encourage tremendous coral growth and ample numbers of big fish. Another hour by pumpboat leads from Puerto Galera to Verde Island, where strong ocean currents attract plenty of marine life to an undersea wall.

---

**ABOVE:** snorkeling off Mactan Island.
**RIGHT:** scuba diving in the Sulu Sea.

One of the best Philippine dive sites, Apo Reef, a 34 sq km (13 sq mile) atoll-like reef in the Mindoro Strait, has suffered from dynamite fishing. But boats allow divers access to the reef's sheer walls and drop-offs, which are breeding grounds of tuna, barracuda, manta rays, and marine turtles.

## Underwater wrecks

Divers can visit several World War II wrecks in Subic Bay, though visibility tends to be hazy. The famed 19th-century battleship USS New York lies in 27 meters (90ft) of water, with El Capitan, a 130-meter (430ft) -long freighter, submerged just 12 meters (40ft) below. Coron Bay, off northern Palawan's

Calamian Island, also covers some of the Philippines' best wrecks accessible to divers.

Balicasag Island is Bohol's best-known dive site. One of the archipelago's finest walls is illuminated by shafts of sunlight. On Cebu Island, divers prefer Moalboal, where a 35-meter (115ft) wall drops right off the shores of Panagsama Beach and a variety of dives await in Pescador Island Marine Park.

The Sulu Sea's Tubbataha Reefs, off south Palawan, has surged in fame in recent years due to numerous glowing write-ups and a quest to stop illegal fishing. White-tip and hammerhead sharks, marine turtles, manta rays, and eagle rays are common in the open-sea area open to divers from February to June. For information on diving agencies see Travel Tips, page 363.

# AN ARCHITECTURAL PASTICHE

**Filipino architecture ranges from thatched bamboo huts to modern high-rises. Between those extremes, classic Spanish architecture still reigns in the historical towns of Vigan and Taal.**

Philippine architecture reflects the country's historical blend of influences from Borneo to Spain and the United States. A casual observer can see three main stages: the early native huts, the massive Spanish Baroque churches, and lately, the modern concrete-and-glass structures of the cities.

Native huts still dominate much of the countryside, especially on farms and right over the perimeter wall from the country's swankiest beach resorts. Baroque architecture turns up at the cores of cities, large or small. Though it usually defines just a church or

*Elevated on stilts, the nipa hut is protected from seasonal monsoon floods and the space beneath the house is used as a shelter for animals, a granary, a workbench, or an additional room for the family.*

two, the same style may apply to a few other nearby buildings. Concrete-and-glass structures loom around the Baroque holdouts in Manila, Davao, Cebu, and many provincial capitals. That style describes office complexes, high-end condominium towers, and the odd restaurant.

## Nipa huts

Before the arrival of the Spanish, people lived in small villages along coastlines or rivers. In its pre-Intramuros days, for example, Manila was a riverside fort safeguarded by wooden

palisades that protected settlements loosely strung along the Pasig River and the shores of Manila Bay. The bamboo and wood huts in the settlements were usually covered by *nipa* palm.

Travelers almost anywhere outside the cities, from just over the wall of a Palawan resort, or on a bus ride on Cebu Island, will see nipa huts in full form. One who gets close enough may on occasion be invited inside.

Construction of the squarish traditional huts has changed little over time. Designs vary by region, but common features include a steep roof over a one- or two-room living area raised on stilts. Floors may be of split bamboo to allow dirt and food scraps to fall through to

**LEFT:** Manila Cathedral. **RIGHT:** rural dwelling in Bukidnon province.

*Towns in the Spanish empire were built in a cuadricula, a chessboard of streets. At the center was a Plaza Mayor in which the cathedral stood opposite the government office.*

pigs and poultry. The stilts also serve to ward off wild animals.

The houses, usually called *bahay na nipa*, have just one major room, ventilated by windows with legs that hold the swinging shades open during the day. Houses may also have ladders

that can be taken away when the occupants are gone. Quite often, the lightweight structures collapse with earthquakes, burn quickly, or get blown away easily by typhoon winds. However, this type of house can be swiftly rebuilt with the abundant local materials such as bamboo, grass, and slats of wood.

## Urban developments

When the early settlements became towns during the colonial era, houses became sturdier as residents grew more affluent. These urban dwellings are modified variations of the simple hut, typically two-story structures

### A SMATTERING OF YOU NAME IT

Passengers can unwind on the often frustrating taxi ride from Manila airport toward Roxas Boulevard by staring out at the wide range of architectural styles along the roadsides. Most obvious are the grayish low-rise offices and budget hotels reminiscent of Americana in the 1970s. Packed in among those are dilapidated post-World War II houses or shops of two to three stories. Some of those sport peaked roofs, not nipa or tile but tin painted in just about any color, carried over in spirit from colonialism-influenced rural houses. This picture lacks overall scenic value, however, as the architectural styles clash along dirty streets that lack setbacks or landscaping. No shortage of smaller struc-

tures cry out for basic maintenance or a paint job.

Fancier modern edifices begin to sprout on the inland side of Roxas, with Manila Bay on the other. Along the boulevard's Ermita segment looms the US Embassy, a 1940s bayside compound that describes its own architecture as "simple yet elegant," consistent with "public buildings that were built during the American occupation of the islands." One may also glimpse Hotel H2O, luxury lodging built to resemble a pier over Manila Bay and with in-room aquariums. Skyscrapers in the same part of Manila like those in any multi-million-person downtown also darken horizons along the same stretch of Roxas.

reinforced with concrete and an iron roof. During the 19th century, wealthy Filipinos built houses with solid stone or brick lower walls, an overhanging wooden upper story with balustrades and *capiz*-shell sliding windows, and a tiled roof. Family quarters remained on the second story and were constructed completely out of wood; they were expanded to include a living room, at least two bedrooms, and an open porch behind the cooking area. The open area under the house was enclosed with stone or brick walls. Evolving into the Spanish colonial townhouse, a steep roof of terracotta tiles would cap each

change into American hands in 1898 introduced new nuances. In a matter of decades, modern yet mundane international-style buildings made of concrete and glass began to appear in Manila.

In the high-rise canyons of Makati, a once quiet suburb that has grown since the 1960s into a center of business and finance, swanky shopping malls and glass-clad skyscrapers dominate the skyline. One could be in the downtown area of any modern city in the world. Even individually designed single-family residences clustered around the business center are international in character.

dwelling. Rows of individual houses stood at the edge of narrow streets that were laid out in a *cuadricula*, a grid arrangement.

Tourists today can see these quiet neighborhoods, in striking contrast to the buzzing high-rise blocks of most Asian metropolises, on walks near the urban hearts of most cities.

## Foreign influences

The Spanish spent three-and-a-half centuries establishing cities and firmly entrenching Christianity by stringing the coastline with massive fortress-churches and convents. A

On Manila's more historic Roxas Boulevard, a palm-fringed parkway along the shores of Manila Bay, rows of new high-rises stand next to uneventful concrete medium-rises of 1970s vintage that overpower the few surviving international-style structures and Art Deco examples from the 1930s. Roxas Boulevard, nearby Rizal Park, and Intramuros became key elements in the 1904 Master Plan for Manila by Daniel Burnham, the American urban planner, who after a short stay in Manila established himself as one of the founders of modern American architecture in Chicago.

Burnham designed a Parisian system of parks, avenues, and waterways radiating from

**ABOVE, FROM LEFT:** Vigan Heritage Village, Illocos Sur; the ornate home of a former sugar plantation owner.

Intramuros. This district has been retained as a monument, although the moat has been filled in and it is now a golf course in the heart of the city.

At the bayfront section of Rizal Park are two neoclassical examples built a few years after the completion of the Burnham Plan, the Army and Navy Club (now the Metropolitan Museum of Manila) and the Elks Club (now the Museo Pambata).

Rizal Park, conceptualized as a tropical version of the expansive Mall in Washington DC, sweeps inland from Manila Bay to Taft Avenue. Taft Avenue was once a grand tree-lined way where the most imposing neoclassical government buildings were erected 80 years ago. These include a complex of three government buildings, two of which have become the National Museum. Taft Avenue effectively shifted the focus away from Spanish architecture and established the American footprint in Manila.

The Philippine Normal School and Philippine General Hospital, both built by American architects in the early 20th century, retain the tiled roofs, wide windows, and arcades of traditional Philippine architecture.

### PHILIPPINE BAROQUE CHURCHES

Spanish friars thought local structures of bamboo and thatch were improper for worship, so they directed Filipino and Chinese artisans to build large stone churches, vaguely following the Baroque style of Spain. Facades rising to a tip fronted rectangular churches and buttresses reinforced thick stone walls against earthquakes. Bell towers stood separately. Many of these churches survive, though some are in a poor state. The best examples are San Agustín (Intramuros, Manila), Santa Maria and Paoay churches (both in Ilocos) and Miagao Fortress Church (Panay), each of which is on the prestigious Unesco World Heritage List.

### Preserving the old

In pockets of the Philippines, local officials have pushed to conserve old architecture and city planning traditions. In Manila, a program to hold up the historic Intramuros district requires new structures to follow the traditional architecture of the late 19th century. The best example is Plaza San Luís, a series of new structures built in the old style, interconnected by courtyards that open into a museum, shops, restaurants, and a small hotel.

Among the examples of preserving old appearances, Casa Manila in Plaza San Luís re-creates the 19th-century home of an affluent Manileño. Its collection of art, period furniture, and decorative details is a mix of

Philippine, Chinese, and Spanish traits, and is the best example of the eclectic taste and the east–west fusion style of the era. Plaza San Luís stands next to the country's oldest stone church, San Agustin, and near the Ayuntamiento, the seat of the Spanish government and the customs house that was the eastern terminus of the Manila–Acapulco galleon route.

In the Ilocos Sur town of Vigan, the country's best surviving example of a 19th-century Spanish colonial town, a grid of streets pierces the entire historical district, framing broad views towards the plaza with rows of well-

Manila, once a Spanish center, is today considered one of the finest examples of this style. Built in 1615 by Chinese craftsmen, the building is noted for its exquisitely carved three-story facade and four-story octagonal bell tower.

The latter two features were redesigned by a wealthy citizen of the woodcarving town of Paete two centuries after construction. At that time, the Baroque movement had swept Europe, throwing echoes to the colonies, where the clergy was motivated to refurbish older structures.

Taal, two hours' drive south of Manila,

preserved houses built in the 18th and 19th centuries. This town is also protected by law from incursions by the gray dilapidated architecture that defines other urban areas. Vigan Cathedral and the Archbishop's Palace at Plaza Salcedo, the main plaza of the town, are magnificent examples of architecture from the Spanish colonial era.

Spanish architects also re-jigged European architecture to fit the Philippine climate, developing a style known as Tropical Baroque and found on a few remaining structures. A church in the town of Morong, southeast of

is another town with well-preserved 19th-century houses. Two typical *bahay na bato* houses are open to the public: the Agoncillo Museum and the Apacible residence. The Basilica of St Martin crowns the hill on which the town is built.

## Ingenious rice terraces

The most outstanding architectural monument in the Philippines may be a landscape: the rice terraces (see page 202) that lay out paddy fields in giant steps up the steep slopes of the Philippine Cordilleras. Traditions are kept alive from the maintenance of the terrace walls to the skillful engineering that allows constant irrigation.

**ABOVE, FROM LEFT:** colonial elegance in Vigan; rice terraces in Ifugao province.

# FORCES OF NATURE: VOLATILE VOLCANOES

**Volcanoes lying dormant for centuries have been known suddenly to turn active, spewing red-hot lava and causing widespread destruction. Thousands have died as a result of eruptions.**

From the archipelago's 7,107 islands soar more than 200 volcanic peaks, 18 of which are active. Nestled among these volcanoes are marshlands, rolling highlands, tropical woodlands, rainforests, both cold and hot, as well as mud springs, waterfalls, and extensive networks of caves and even subterranean rivers.

Postcards of Mayon Volcano, the most perfectly shaped volcano in the world alongside Mount Fuji in Japan and the most active in the country, continue to tickle the traveler's imagination. The rugged jungles that hug Mt Apo, the Philippines' highest peak and a dormant volcano, remain to this day the greatest challenge for local climbers. Taal Volcano, the world's smallest at 400 meters (1,312ft), awes the most jaded of tourists.

But volcanoes have a violent side: Mt Pinatubo's eruption in June 1991 left 847 people dead and more than 1 million displaced. Many of the victims died from diseases in evacuation centers. Devastation to land and property amounted to millions of dollars. The ash and sand, called *lahar*, created a new and surreal landscape that is now a tourist destination. Entrepreneurs have also cashed in by creating tourist souvenirs made of *lahar*.

**ABOVE:** The perfect conical form of Mt Mayon, one of the most destructive volcanoes in the Philippines.

**BELOW:** Some of the islands' most fertile farmland is situated precariously close to active volcanoes.

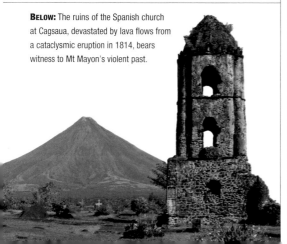

**BELOW:** The ruins of the Spanish church at Cagsaua, devastated by lava flows from a cataclysmic eruption in 1814, bears witness to Mt Mayon's violent past.

**ABOVE:** Volcanic eruptions are accompanied by huge ash clouds, as here at Mt Pinatubo in the deadly 1991 eruption.

## TIMELINE

**1814:** Mudflows from Mayon Volcano (2,462 meters/8,077ft) kill about 1,200 people.
**1911:** Ash flows from Taal Volcano (400 meters/1,312ft) kill 1,335 people.
**1951:** Hibok-Hibok Volcano (1,330 meters/4,370ft) in Mindanao belches ash flows that kill 500 people.
**1991:** An eruption of Mt Pinatubo (1,485 meters/4,871ft) leads to the death of 847 people and displaces 1 million.
**1993:** Mayon Volcano kills 78 people in an eruption.
**2007:** Mt Bulusan (1,565 meters/5,130ft) covers fields and villages as it spews ash 5km (3 miles) away.
**2008:** Mayon throws ash 200 meters (656ft) above the summit, and over the following two years authorities recorded a chain of volcanic movements that sparked evacuations.
**2011:** Bulusan sends ash and steam as high as 2km (1.2 miles) above the summit, forcing hundreds to evacuate.

**ABOVE:** Volcanic mudflows create fertile soils.

**BELOW:** Children playing in a lake created by mudflows from Mt Pinatubo, north of Manila.

**RIGHT:** The Philippine eagle is just one species that thrives in the wilderness areas on volcanic mountain slopes.

# INTRODUCTION

**A detailed guide to the entire country, with principal sites clearly cross-referenced by number to the maps.**

**M**anila, the capital and by far the largest city, is the usual starting point for most journeys in the Philippines. Increasingly, however, new international airline routes mean that visitors may also enter the country through Cebu City or Davao.

The first-time traveler from Europe or North America may find Manila intimidating in its chaos and frenetic energy.

But aside from the predictable scam artists, the city is safe on the whole and full of interest. It is an old city, with history that lingers in the architecture of Malacañang Palace, the thick stone walls of Intramuros, and the bustle of Chinatown. Day trips beyond Manila lead the curious to active volcanoes Taal and Pinatubo, to beach resorts or diving-friendly waters in Batangas.

Manila is on the southern part of Luzon, the largest island, located at the northern end of the archipelago. To the north are the lofty highlands of Baguio and Banaue, where cascading rice terraces spill over as far as the eye can see. On the northwest coast is the refined Ilocos region, home to jewels such as the well-preserved Spanish city of Vigan.

South of Luzon are the Visayas, a cluster of islands in the centre of the archipelago. The island, and city, of Cebu, anchor this region not only as a gateway to resorts and coral reefs, but also as a growing entrepreneurial city. Boracay, off the northern tip of Panay island, is famous throughout Asia for its long white-sand beach and endless parties. Increasingly, adventure tours are moving into such untouched locations as Samar and Leyte in the eastern Visayas.

The long, thin island of Palawan, west of the Visayas, is best known for its remote beach locations, difficulties of road travel, and pristine waters. Mindanao is the deepest south. On its sunny shores and cool mountains exist indigenous cultures not found in the northern islands. Mindanao has seen the kidnapping of tourists and fierce fighting between rebel groups and the government. Its southwestern areas are still not recommended for travelers. But cities such as Davao and Cagayan De Oro, as well as the country's highest peak Mt Apo, are safe for foreign travelers.

---

**PRECEDING PAGES:** a remote beach on Coron Island, Palawan; Manila Bay; the Chocolate Hills of Bohol Island. **LEFT:** Alona Beach, Panglao Island.
**ABOVE, FROM LEFT:** hiking on Mount Isarog; Manila Bay.

# Philippines

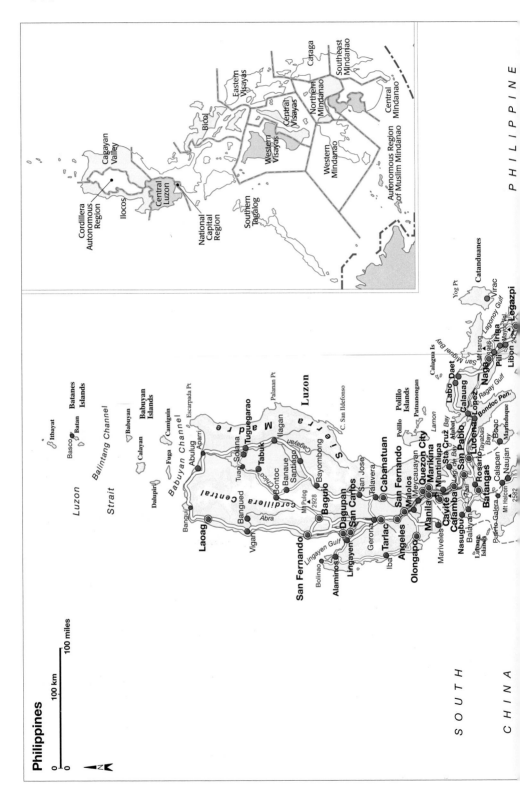

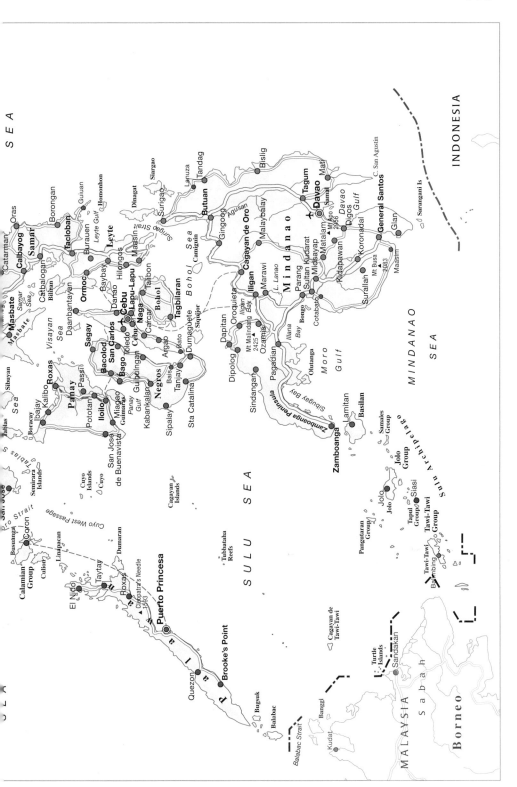

# LUZON

The country's main island features Spanish heritage, vast tracts of farmland, moody volcanoes, and the vibrant capital city Manila.

L uzon is the largest island in the archipelago, occupying over a third of the nation's total land area. That landmass extends from the rice basket of the broad, flat Central Plains, where sugar cane, coconuts, and tobacco grow, to mighty mountain ranges capped by Mt Pulog at 2,928m (9,606ft).

Key to its local pre-eminence over the centuries has been the national capital Manila's strategic bayshore location at the mouth of the Pasig river. The river opens into the 900 sq km (350 sq mile) Laguna de Bay, the Philippines' largest lake, in the city's eastern suburbs. Manileños like to escape the frenetic, polluted metropolis on the weekend for the provinces south of the lake, where beach resorts and upland trekking routes await.

Luzon has two of the first three cities founded by Spanish invaders in the late 1500s. After gaining a foothold in Cebu in 1565, Miguel Lopez de Legazpi seized Manila in 1571 and built thick stone walls near its shores. By 1572, the Spanish conquistadors had founded their third city on the northwest Ilocos coast at Vigan. Today a small town, Vigan remains one of the country's best-preserved Spanish-style cities.

Manila serves as a gateway to the mountainous rice terraces in Ifugao Province and to fishing-reliant beach communities where coral illuminates the underwater world. Further south, Quezon Province hosts indigenous wildlife in forests that had been denuded by loggers before parliament passed a bill in 2006 to reseed them with native fruit trees.

The island fortress of Corregidor and the once war-torn peninsula of Bataan are also found in this northern part of the archipelago. Among the island's hotbed of volcanoes are Taal and Mt Pinatubo, which angrily awoke from a 450-year slumber in 1991. The windswept Batanes Islands off the northern coast of Luzon offer hiking experiences, while the islands off the southern coast are speckled with scarcely developed white-sand beaches and coral-studded waters. Northeastern Luzon is known for a wealth of caves for exploring, plus the Cagayan River, the longest in the Philippines.

**LEFT:** the town of Banaue, Central Cordillera. **ABOVE, FROM LEFT:** Puerto Galera; Cagayan River.

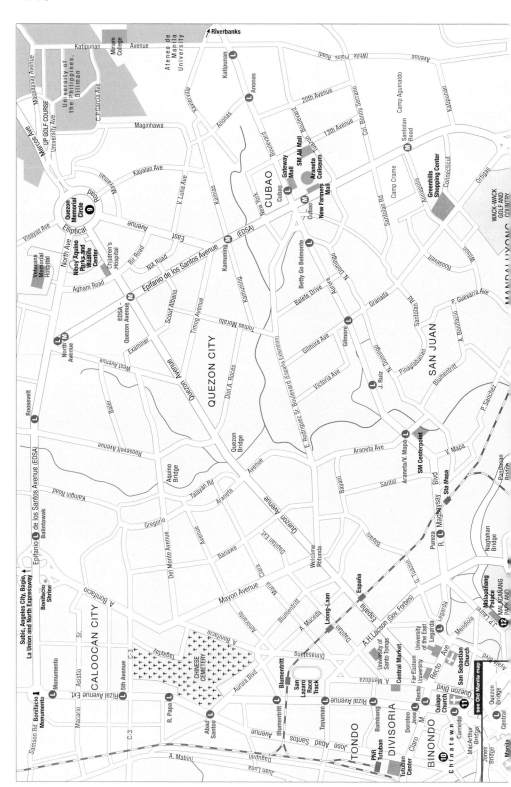

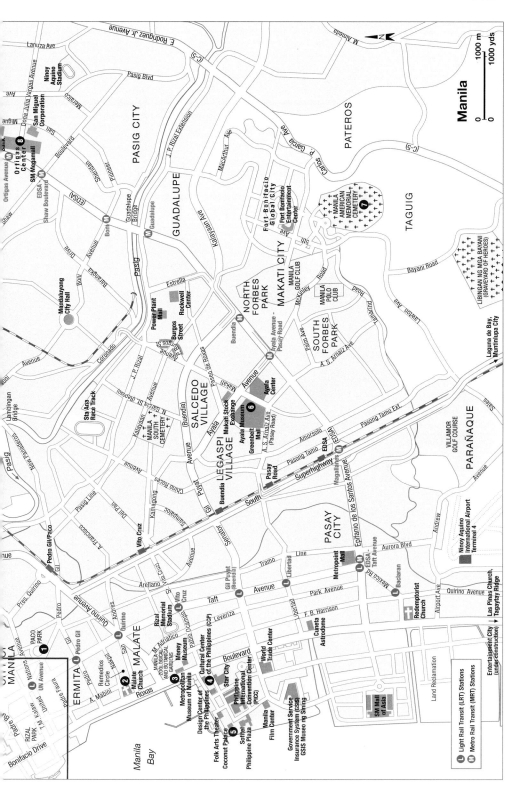

Manila

0   1000 m
0   1000 yds

Light Rail Transit (LRT) Stations
Metro Rail Transit (MRT) Stations

# MANILA

**Amid the hurly-burly of modern Manila, with its parks, museums, sky-high business districts, and vibrant nightlife, are reminders of the Philippine past in its Spanish architecture and Chinese enclaves.**

Manila

The Philippine capital, named after the white flowering *nilad* plant that once grew along the Pasig River where the city of 11.6 million people was founded, has the feel of an international metropolis: leafy landscaped parks, museums, five-star hotels, glitzy shopping malls, an endless choice of places to eat, sprawling suburbs. But in Manila the picture can change in a blink of the eye; just around the corner from a gleaming international hotel in one of the city's business districts you can witness the nation's rampant poverty: beggars, naked children living on curbs, and crumbling cement walls that shade groups of drug-crazed young men staring at passers-by under the watch of heavily armed guards in the doorways of common businesses.

As travelers are usually left alone by all but beggars and hawkers, they can freely use taxis and jeepneys to ply the main drags from history-rich Rizal Park south to the walled city Intramuros, a bayside aquarium, Malate's erotic nightlife district, and Asia's largest shopping mall. Most museums and monuments are found in the safe zone. Hardcore bargain shoppers will find whatever they ask for at the Divisoria bargain basement shopping area north of the Pasig River.

**LEFT:** view from Intramuros.
**RIGHT:** Divisoria flea market.

## Foreign influences

Manila has always been action-packed, if not always so peaceful. In 1571, Spanish conquistador Miguel Lopez de Legazpi reached the city founded 1,000 years earlier as a trading post. When increased maritime trade saw an influx of people and ideas from around the globe, the liberal attitudes of English and American traders, among others, helped raise the city onto a cosmopolitan plane.

Revolutionary rumblings came to a head in Manila in the 19th century,

**Main attractions**

INTRAMUROS WALLED CITY
LIGHTS & SOUNDS OF RIZAL SHOW
MUSEUM DISTRICT
MALATE NIGHTLIFE AREA
MALL OF ASIA
MAKATI
DIVISORIA MARKET

**TIP**

Manila taxi drivers usually speak English well enough to give passengers tips on where to go around town. If they're not angry about traffic, many are happy to chit-chat.

when Jose Rizal defined Filipino-Spanish relations in an 1886 novel. Taking Rizal's cue in 1892, Andres Bonifacio founded the Katipunan, a secret society promoting complete independence from Spain. Four years later, he led the first armed insurrection. After two years of guerrilla war against the Spanish, the revolutionaries found themselves beaten with the capture of their capital by the United States, which was at war with Spain. From 1898 to 1946, the people of the islands lived under another period of colonial, albeit benevolent, rule under the victorious US government. The Americans left an education system, democratic institutions, infrastructure technology, and Western mores.

Except for a few monuments and buildings, Manila was practically levelled during World War II as the Japanese sought a foothold. Young Filipino men allied themselves with the Americans against the Japanese, and Washington repaid the gesture by granting the Philippines independence in 1946.

## Intramuros

Though **Intramuros** is a far cry from the bustling Spanish city it once was, it has come a long way from the ravages of wartime. Formerly a jumble of broken buildings, portions of the old city have been renovated, including the *Ayuntamiento* (Municipal Hall), once the grandest structure here.

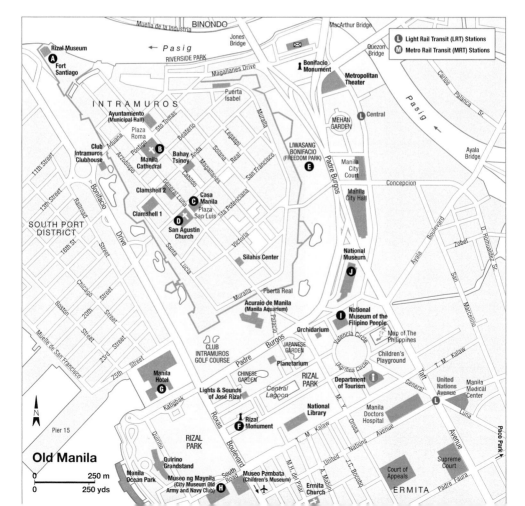

Old Manila

0    250 m
0    250 yds

Today travelers will find fully restored Spanish buildings hopping with cafés, bars, handicraft stores, and at least one boutique hotel. Walls aside, traffic of all types buzzes in and out of Intramuros, and there is no centralized admission.

Although Intramuros was laid out as a pentagon, its uneven sides more approximate a triangle. The old western wall fronted the sea before reclamation began a century ago, but is now flanked by Bonifacio Drive, which runs south to Roxas Boulevard. The perimeter of Intramuros measures nearly 4.5km (3 miles). Inside, following Legazpi's blueprint for the capital, succeeding Spanish governors built 18 churches, chapels, convents, schools, a hospital, printing press, university (in as early as 1611), palaces for the governor-general and the archbishop, soldiers' barracks, and houses for the assorted elite.

**Fort Santiago** Ⓐ (daily, 8am–6pm; charge) anchors this old walled city in the core of Manila, drawing visitors throughout the day for the wellspring of history lessons running from Spanish colonization through World War II. A stroll around the lavishly landscaped fort permits climbs onto the old wall, leads to a view of the grayish Pasig River, and allows a glimpse into a stone chamber where the Japanese jailed hundreds of Allied soldiers until they starved to death.

Within Fort Santiago is the **Rizal Museum** (Tue–Sat 8am–noon, 1–5pm; free with fort entrance), housing memorabilia of Philippine national hero Dr Jose Rizal, credited with fomenting the overthrow of Spanish rule. Nearby is Rizal's cell, where he wrote his last lines of poetry to the Filipino people.

Outside the fort area but still in the walled city, cross over to **Manila Cathedral** Ⓑ, an imposing Romanesque structure constructed of adobe. Like most Catholic churches, it's open to all, for free. A plaque on its facade reveals a relentless history, beginning in 1571, of reconstruction after the repeated ravages of fire, typhoon, earthquake, and war. Statues by Italian artists grace the facade. Fronting the cathedral is Plaza Roma, so-called since 1961

*Wealthy Spanish merchants who lived in houses like Casa Manila had all the modern conveniences of 100 years ago, including grand bathtubs. A small Spanish enclave still lives in Manila.*

**BELOW:** cannons on the Intramuros city walls.

*The Rizal Monument at Manila's Rizal Park is a tribute to national hero Jose Rizal.*

**BELOW:** San Agustin Church, Intramuros.

when Rome renamed one of its squares Piazza Manila, to commemorate the elevation of the first Filipino cardinal, Rufino J. Santos.

Part of a restoration plan for Intramuros is to replicate eight houses to illustrate different styles and periods through which local architecture has evolved. Some are already open to the public, including **Casa Manila** ⊙ (www.intramuros.ph; Tue–Sun 9am–6pm; charge) in the extensive Plaza San Luis. This restored Spanish merchant's house from the late 1800s features beautiful hardwoods throughout, plus *capiz* shell sliding windows. A hotel, restaurant, two cafés, and several gift shops operate in Plaza San Luis, which has space to expand on that repertoire. On General Luna Street is the three-story El Amanecer Complex, a reproduction of a 19th-century town home that now houses **Silahis Center** (tel: 02-527-3841; www.silahis.com; daily

10am–7pm), a destination for handicrafts shopping.

At the intersection of General Luna and Calle Real, Chinese *fu* dogs carved of granite guard the entrance to the courtyard of **San Agustin Church** ⊙ (daily 8am–noon, 1–6pm; charge), the only structure in Intramuros not bombed in World War II. The church facade is notable for its combination of styles, such as Doric lower and Corinthian upper columns, and the absence of one of its original twin towers, a victim of earthquakes in 1863 and 1889. The main door is carved *molave*, a Philippine hardwood, its panels depicting St Augustine and his mother, St Monica. Adjoining the church is a monastery-museum containing a trove of Philippine artifacts, religious art and Chinese, Spanish, and Mexican pottery. The cloister gallery exhibits paintings of the life of St Augustine.

Also visit the **Bahay Tsinoy** (tel: 02-526-6083; www.bahaytsinoy.org; Tue–Sun 1–5pm; charge) on Cabildo Street, a museum on Chinese people in the Philippines. Around the stone walls of the old walled city is **Club Intramuros** (02-846-6667; www. golfph.com/golf-courses/club-intramuros; office 9am–5pm), with an 18-hole golf course.

## Pasig River

From San Agustin Church, turn right at Calle Real to prowl the remains of Intramuros to Muralla Street on the east. Follow the walls or pass through one of the restored gates leading back to the Pasig River, or into a plaza, **Liwasang Bonifacio** ⊕ (Freedom Park). On this busy square is a statue of revolutionary leader Andres Bonifacio, with the Central Post Office just to the north. To the east stands the Art Deco Metropolitan Theater and Mehan Garden. Intersecting these landmarks is a complex sprawl of highway taking much of Manila's traffic north across the Pasig River. The

Pasig may not be the cleanest river to relax next to, but projects under former Manila Mayor Lito Atienza cleaned up some patches, opening several pocket parks and restaurant rows along its banks.

## Rizal Park

Formerly known as Luneta, **Rizal Park** is a large field with an elevated strolling ground, bounded by Roxas Boulevard and ending at the sea wall facing Manila Bay. On this section is Quirino Grandstand, from where officials preside over Independence Day parades and where religious congregations converge. In 1995, Pope John Paul II held Mass for an estimated 4.5 million admiring worshippers here, earning a spot in the Guinness World Records as the "largest Papal gathering."

In the central portion of Rizal Park stands **Rizal Monument 🅕**, a guarded memorial to the national hero. This spot also has the distinction of being Kilometer Zero, the point of reference for all road distances throughout the largest Philippine island, Luzon. Behind the monument is a series of plaques inscribed with Rizal's poem *Mi Ultimo Adios (My Last Farewell)*. A marble slab highlights the spot where Rizal met his martyr's death by firing squad, and an obelisk marks the site of the earlier executions of Filipino priests Gomez, Burgos, and Zamora. To the north side, along Burgos Street, are the Chinese Garden, Planetarium, Japanese Garden, and Orchidarium (small charge for each). Within the Orchidarium is Barbara's Restaurant, part of a small Manila chain. There is also an open area, used for wedding receptions and other intimate gatherings.

On the northern side of the park, at the exact spot where Rizal was executed for treason by the Spaniards, is the **Lights and Sounds of Rizal** (Wed–Sun, Tagalog 7–7.30pm, English 8–8.30pm; charge), a 30-minute audio-visual presentation in an open-air theater setting, dramatizing the most poignant moments of Rizal's final hours before his execution for treason.

**BELOW:** a scene from the Light and Sounds of Rizal presentation.

Northwest of the park is **Manila Hotel** . Although its charm and glamor have faded somewhat since 1912, the site of General Douglas MacArthur's former headquarters still has its allure. The National Library is along the Kalaw Street side of Rizal Park. To the west, on the bay at **Manila Ocean Park** (tel: 02-526-7777; www.manilaoceanpark.com; Mon–Fri 10am–7pm, Sat–Sun 9am–8pm; charge), marine life displays and sea-lion shows delight families with children. An underwater viewing tunnel allows close-up encounters with reef fish and other creatures.

Near the park's Central Lagoon, a group of speaking- and hearing-impaired people run a food kiosk, offering a cool spot from which to people-watch. Alternatively, head to the tried-and-true Harbor View Restaurant (tel: 02-524-1532) or the Seafood Wharf Restaurant (tel: 02-400-5066), in the old Army and Navy Club compound at the southwestern corner of the park, for a beer and *pulutan* (cocktail snacks Filipino-style) while watching the sunset over Manila Bay.

## Museum District

For a look at the city's historic development, visit the **Museo ng Maynila** (City Museum; tel: 02-524-5491; Tue–Sat 9am–6pm; free), housed in the century-old Army and Navy Club building bordering Rizal Park. Guided tours usually leave on the hour.

Two Greek-style buildings at Rizal Park's eastern edge house the **Department of Tourism** (DOT; tel: 02-524-2345) and the Department of Finance, home to the **National Museum of the Filipino People** (tel: 02-527-0278; Tue–Sun 9am–5pm; charge). Visit the DOT for travel information, or view one of the ethnographic displays in the front lobby. The Museum of the Filipino People, an anthropology and archeology adjunct to the National Museum, shows ethnographic displays and prehistoric burial jars.

Between the DOT area and Taft Avenue, which runs along the eastern side of the park, sprawls a topographic map of the Philippines (try viewing it from the light rail system) and a children's playground, featuring gigantic

**BELOW:** The National Museum.

prehistoric beasts cast in cement. Burgos Street, on the park's northern side, leads past the Old Congress Building, which once hosted the Philippine Senate and now houses the **National Museum** ❶ (tel: 02-522-5846; Wed–Sun 10am–4pm; charge), known for paintings by Philippine artist Juan Luna,

Northward is Manila City Hall, and beyond, Liwasang Bonifacio, from where three bridges head over the Pasig. From this point, a number of jeepneys and buses, starting from across the river, follow Taft Avenue to all points south.

This south-of-the-river section of the city is quite easy to get around in. On the westernmost side is Roxas Boulevard, running from Rizal Park to Parañaque, near the airport complex. Just south of the park, abutting the Roxas Boulevard seawall, are the sprawling grounds of the US Embassy. Next door is the impressive **Museo Pambata** (tel: 02-523-1797; www.museopambata.org; Children's Museum; Tue–Sat 8am–5pm, Sun 1–5pm; charge), which offers superb entertainment to children of all ages. Themed rooms and hands-on displays include a tunnel maze through the body.

## Ermita

From Taft, turn right at any of the streets beginning with United Nations Avenue, where the Manila Pavilion stands; this will lead to Ermita. The other side of Taft offers little except **Paco Park** ❶ (Mon–Thur 8am–5pm, Fri–Sun 8am–7pm; charge), a peaceful, circular promenade, originally a Spanish cemetery in the 1820s. Ermita has built its tourist reputation on its proximity to Rizal Park, the seawall along Manila Bay, and a wide assortment of hotels and restaurants in the backstreets. Ermita also offers nightspots, boutiques, antique shops, handicraft and curio stalls, and travel agency offices.

When the Spanish arrived, Ermita was a seaside village called Laygo, whose residents venerated a small female icon carved out of dark wood. Although stupefied at the statue's pre-Christian look, Legazpi's men turned the image to their advantage, telling

**BELOW:** Paco Park.

*Ermita was a hot spot for foreign men, second in Asia only to Bangkok, until Mayor Alfred Lim closed the bars and strip joints in the early 1990s. Ermita and Malate have since reinvented themselves, offering some of Manila's best nightlife. But a careful look will still turn up some of the pre-1990s glory.*

**BELOW:** the Blue Room jazz bar in Malate.

the villagers that the image's name was *Nuestra Señora de Guia* (Our Lady of Guidance), and that it had been brought by angels. They installed it in a wooden chapel not far from the spot where it was found: Ermita Church – reconstructed eight times – still stands at the original site on M.H. del Pilar Street. By the 19th century, the district had become an aristocratic suburb.

In line with the bohemian lifestyle of its younger residents and visitors, Ermita has given birth to a group called the Mabini painters, named after the street where their tiny galleries compete with stalls hawking cheap cultural souvenirs. Artists, writers, musicians and dancers here add to the city's eclectic mix. Near these galleries is Cortada Street, a tiny quarter for crafts and brassware from Muslim Mindanao in the south.

During daylight hours, browse the antique shops where pottery, religious icons, ethnic ware, old bottles, and assorted junk command varying prices on Mabini and del Pilar. By night, the area buzzes as locals make their way to Remedios Circle and Julio Nakpil

Street for dining, ranging from beer halls to top-end Chinese seafood restaurants. The selection on Nakpil covers Spanish cuisine at Casa Armas and modern European food at Sala. Look also for Pinoy-style pork and chicken favorites, including some served from a chain of stalls that surround massive common eating areas. For a calmer evening, check out the Solidaridad bookstore on Padre Faura Street with its broad selection of English-language literature titles.

## Malate

South of Remedios Circle, Malate's bars range from British-style pubs to those where Filipina hostesses accompany men as they drink. There is at least one beer hall. Nakpil and Orosa streets are home to drag shows, plus dance clubs for all persuasions. If still thirsty, swing past the Latin scene at Café Havana in Remedios Circle. Many spots are open 24 hours, though they look a bit hollowed out by late morning. Boutique hotels are scattered among the eats and drinks venues, likewise beggars and homeless

people. On the Roxas Boulevard edge of Malate, swankier nightclubs, with names such as Club Enigma and Studio 69, pull in those seeking some evening entertainment.

West of Remedios Circle stands **Malate Church ②** dedicated to Nuestra Señora de los Remedios (Our Lady of Remedies), patron saint of women in childbirth. Her image, brought from Spain in 1624, is still venerated on the main altar. In front of the church, bronze statues of Our Lady, and Rajah Sulayman – ruler of Manila until ousted by Legazpi in 1571 – make an odd couple as they face the sunset.

Further south, along Roxas Boulevard at Quirino Avenue, is a government complex that includes the Manila Hospital and the **Metropolitan Museum of Manila ③** (tel: 02-521-1517; www.metmuseum.ph; Mon–Sat 9am–6pm; charge). Gold and pottery showpieces go back to the 8th century, while paintings by the country's best-known artist Juan Luna await in another gallery. The museum offers regular talks on photography,

cartography, and the secrets of artists themselves.

The nearby Central Bank of the Philippines houses the **Money Museum** (tel: 02-524-7011; www.bsp.gov.ph/about/facilities_money.asp; Mon–Fri 9am–noon and 1–4pm; free), a comprehensive collection of Philippine money and other currencies from around the world. Behind the hospital on Adriatico Street are **Manila Zoological and Botanical Gardens** (tel: 02-525-8157; www.manila-zoo.org; daily 7am–6pm; charge).

A relaxing way to see Manila Bay is to stroll along the wide walkway between Roxas Boulevard and the water. "Baywalk" is most spectacular when the setting sun frames row after row of palms, but it becomes livelier as the evening progresses. Food kiosks and open-air restaurants bring refreshments and live entertainment after

*The Metropolitan Museum of Manila has a large collection of both contemporary and traditional art.*

**BELOW:** Malate Church.

dark. As of early 2012, a swathe of this promenade was lined by metal construction barriers, blocking bay views.

## Roxas

Past the Navy Headquarters, on the seaward side of Roxas Boulevard, is the immense **Cultural Center of the Philippines** ❹ (tel: 02-551-0323; www.culturalcenter.gov.ph), the centerpiece of reclaimed land called the CCP Complex.

The main building houses three theaters, two art galleries, a library, and a museum. The surrounding complex includes the Folk Arts Theater, the Design Center of the Philippines, Philippine Center for Industrial and Trade Exhibits (Philcite), and Philippine International Convention Center (PICC). Past the CCP is **Star City**, an amusement park with rides and theme areas that change seasonally. Roxas Boulevard then approaches Senator Gil Puyat Avenue, still called by its old name, Buendia. On the bayside is the **World Trade Center**, used as a trade and exhibit hall, convention center, and concert venue.

Architecturally, the Government Services Insurance System (GSIS) building to the southwest is the most interesting. It houses the Philippine Senate, a theater, and the **GSIS Museo ng Sining** (tel: 02-551-1301; Tue–Sat 8.45–11am, 1–4pm; free), featuring contemporary Filipino art by painters such as Fernando Amorsolo and Hernando Ocampo.

In the northwest corner is a former Marcos guesthouse, the **Coconut Palace** ❺ (tel: 02-832-0223; Tue–Sun 9–11.30am, 1–4.30pm; charge). Built entirely from indigenous materials such as coconut wood, the palace was intended to host Pope John Paul II during his 1981 visit, although he didn't stay here. Today's visitors can ogle at guest rooms such as the Visayas Room, showcasing thousands of shells; the Mountain Province Room, executed in the bold red and black colors of the highland people; and the Ilocos Room, with its priceless mother-of-pearl furniture. The Coconut Palace is available for private rentals, often hosting lavish parties for Manila's rich and famous. Call in

**BELOW:** Manila Bay.

advance to make sure there is space for the purpose of your visit.

Palm-fringed Roxas Boulevard continues to dominate the crescent of the bay, leading from the airport, just beyond its southern end, into the heart of the city. Hotels, restaurants, and nightclubs fill the area. Steel and cement are rising from Manila Bay as new commercial projects take shape on reclaimed land.

## Entertainment City

Filipinos have gambled legally for nearly 30 years. A nationwide chain of government-run PAGCOR-brand casinos brings them out for baccarat, poker, and slot machines, despite the ruinous addictions formed by some repeat gamblers. Add to that US$1 billion industry a legal online gaming network, plus simpler forms of betting such as lotteries and all-night cockfights.

The Philippines is now turning up the neon to bring foreign tourists to its casinos. PAGCOR, also a regulator, has given out four casino licenses for a midtown Manila megaproject due to rake in US$10 billion per year when it starts to open from 2013. PAGCOR Chairman Cristino Naguiat Jr told Insight Guides the project called Entertainment City will be particularly popular among Asians who travel to gamble. Foreign revenue already makes up 30 percent of the country's total gaming revenue, with Koreans and Chinese gamers contributing the most. After Entertainment City opens, Philippine gaming revenue will beat Las Vegas and reach up to a 10th of the worldwide total of an estimated US$100–150 billion, the chairman says.

The biggest of the four casinos at the square-kilometer Entertainment City complex – located on reclaimed land south of the Mall of Asia to the west of Roxas Boulevard – will have 5,400 machines and about 800 game tables. Hong Kong-invested Resorts World Bayshore will operate it. Resorts World

*The Cultural Center of the Philippines is a vast complex housing three theaters, two art galleries, and a library.*

**BELOW:** Resorts World casino, near Manila airport.

already operates a casino just outside Manila airport's Terminal 3 and aims to open a new one in Boracay.

Existing casinos usually adjoin large hotels in cities such as Cebu, Davao, and Manila. After checking any bags and standing for a security check, customers will find the same tables and rows of slots common to casinos anywhere. But Philippine casinos are known for laxer rules compared to peers elsewhere in Asia. Gamblers note lower minimum bets, more F&B freebies and chances to touch their own cards on the table instead of having the house do it.

## Pasay and Parañaque

One of the most popular places in all of Manila for its inhabitants is the **SM Mall of Asia** (www.smmallofasia.com), which was built in Pasay at the end of the Epifanio de los Santos Avenue (EDSA). Opened in mid-2006, this is the largest shopping mall in the Philippines and the sixth largest in the world, occupying 20 hectares (50 acres) and 1.9 million floor tiles on reclaimed land along Manila

**BELOW:** Makati financial district.

Bay. Mall management also claims it's the largest mall in Asia, replete with two outdoor food courts so long it's hard to see from end to end. Music, clothes, and books, as well as everyday sundries that a traveler might have been denied at a rural convenience store, are easy to find among the throngs of local shoppers out to spend time with family, enjoy free air conditioning, or flash new clothes. The mall is refreshingly child friendly, with ample places to rest, slurp ice cream, or make crafts with adult guidance.

A left turn under the Buendia flyover leads to Manila's business center, Makati. Down from the flyover is the Cuneta Astrodome, an inappropriately named box structure where professional basketball is played. Close to the end of Roxas Boulevard is Redemptorist Road, forking left to Baclaran, an area on the Pasay-Parañaque boundary famous for its *lechon* (roast suckling pig) stalls which fringe the **Redemptorist Church**.

NAIA Avenue, at the boulevard's end, turns left to **Ninoy Aquino International Airport**, as well as **Philippine Airlines' Centennial Terminal** and Terminal 3, anchored by Cebu Pacific with a network of domestic flights plus cheap routes around Asia. From NAIA Avenue, turn right at narrow Quirino Avenue and go past Parañaque to Las Piñas Church, which has a historic bamboo organ. Where Roxas Boulevard ends, a coastal road curves around the bay toward Cavite. An hour south is **Tagaytay Ridge**, the view point overlooking Taal Lake and its Volcano Island.

## Makati

From NAIA Avenue, take a short bus or taxi ride to Makati, the swank financial district of greater Manila, via **Epifanio de los Santos Avenue** (EDSA). Another **Makati** main street, **Ayala Avenue**, has been dubbed Philippine Wall Street.

Much of what Makati is today – skyscrapers, walled-in, residential "villages" for the well-to-do, modern shopping centers, first-class restaurants, and international hotels – can be traced to the Zobel de Ayalas, an old family of Spanish descent. Owners of a vast tract of swamps, the family initially sold off the land haphazardly. Then in the 1950s, the Ayalas hit on the idea of developing the area called Makati as the new residential and business capital of the Philippines, first building Forbes Park as the premier enclave for themselves and other exclusive residents. Businesses followed, gradually relocating from Escolta district north of the Pasig River. The first planned residential community in Makati, the gated, lushly landscaped Forbes Park on McKinley Road (at the end of Ayala Avenue), remains a premier housing area for business tycoons and expats.

The Ayala family continues to lead urban development, building even more world-class hotels, international restaurants, and modern shopping complexes in the business district, such as **Ayala Center**'s Glorietta and Greenbelt shopping malls. Rows of glittering boutiques have sprung up in this area in recent years, tempting shoppers with fashion's best-known names. Restaurants have begun to infiltrate residential areas, such as Legaspi and Salcedo Village, making Makati more of a walking-friendly neighborhood. Greenbelt also describes a nightlife district with bars, cinemas, coffeehouses, and restaurants.

Near Greenbelt, on Makati Avenue, the **Ayala Museum** ❻ (tel: 02-757-7117; www.ayalamuseum.com; Tue–Fri 9am–6pm, Sat–Sun 10am–7pm; charge) offers a collection of Philippine art from various historical periods, as well as the Fernando Amorsolo Gallery named after a noted Filipino painter.

Beyond McKinley Road and Forbes Park is the **Fort Bonifacio Global City** development, where the **Fort Bonifacio Entertainment Center** – nicknamed The Fort – stands. Many good restaurants and

**TIP**

The IRT (Light Rail Transit) and MRT (Metropolitan Rail Transit) are fast ways to move around the city, particularly during the rain, when flooded roads can cause traffic jams.

**BELOW:** SM Mall of Asia.

fun nightclubs can be found here. Nearby **Serendra** has fashionable bars, restaurants, and shopping.

Makati by night brings out crowds on **P. Burgos Street**. There a string of clubs, with names such as Rogues and the Ivory Jungle Bar, reels in mostly male customers for alcohol – and more.

Nearby is the peaceful, park-like **Manila American Memorial Cemetery** ❼ (daily 6.30am–5pm), where the remains of 17,200 Allied dead rest below rows of white crosses and stars of David. The **Libingan ng Mga Bayani** (Graveyard of Heroes) is close by, its eternal flame burning by the Tomb of the Unknown Soldier.

From Fort Bonifacio, it is easy to access the new C-5 Expressway, planned years ago to ease a little of Manila's rush-hour and weekend congestion. C-5 connects to the South Superhighway, running to the lakeshore towns of Laguna de Bay.

### Pateros

**BELOW:** young
Filipinas in Makati.

Makati abuts the riverside town of **Pateros**, center of the *balut* duck-egg

industry. The sandy soil of the area provides the local Pateros duck with an abundance of snails. A unique Filipino delicacy, *balut* is an embryonic duck boiled in its shell. *Balut* vendors sell their wares at night, their raucous cries of "bah-LOOOOT" carrying through to anyone hungry enough to feast on them. Filipinos often wager on the number of *balut* that can be eaten at one sitting, but a *balut*-eating mêlée frequently turns into a beer-drinking contest, and no one remembers to count. Balut are also hawked at cockfights elsewhere in the Philippines. Just don't try to eat *balut* on an empty stomach, warn the experienced ones.

## Ortigas Center and Greenhills

Beyond the Pasig River, northeast of Makati, spread Pasig City and Mandaluyong City. Straddling them is **Ortigas Center** ❽, a rival to Makati as the country's premier business district. The **San Miguel Corporation** and **Asian Development Bank (ADB)** are based in Ortigas, as is **SM Megamall**, a rival to the SM Mall of Asia. Plenty of malls, eateries, and upscale hotels dot the area. Northwest of the Ortigas Center sprawls the park-like landscape of the exclusive Wack-Wack Golf and Country Club. Further northwest along Ortigas Avenue you come to **Greenhills Shopping Center**, a haunt for those seeking to buy freshwater and South China Sea pearls, as well as good-quality knock-offs of designer labels and popular brand names. There are 2,000 stores, nearly 100 restaurants, and a cinema.

## Quezon City

North of Manila lies **Cubao**, Quezon City's commercial center. Cubao has been written off by some as a crude, traffic-infested jungle of shops and supermarkets that don't quite make the grade. This image is being revamped with the **Gateway Mall**. Its 200 stores are considered high-end, making Gateway a different kind of shopping magnet in mall-mad Manila. Another landmark is the **Araneta Coliseum**, billed as the world's largest domed coliseum in the 1960s, and used mainly for basketball and concerts today.

**Quezon City** was the country's official capital before its integration into Metro Manila. Though a few non-governmental organizations and several universities are based here, Quezon City serves only nominally as the capital, with government institutions firmly vested in Downtown Manila.

Around the 27-hectare (67-acre) **Quezon Memorial Circle ⑨** visitors will find an orchid farm, the Manila Seedling Bank, and the Ninoy Aquino Parks and Wildlife Center nearby. A 66-meter (215ft) -high tower in the circle, which offers broad views over Manila, honors late president Manuel Quezon. Northeast of the circle, closer to Katipunan Avenue in **Diliman**, is a university belt consisting of the University of the Philippines, Ateneo University, and Miriam College.

## North of the Pasig

North from Intramuros lie the districts of **Binondo** and **Tondo**, once villages that were contemporary with Sulayman's original Maynilad fortress in the 16th century. These areas, now heavily congested, are characterized by small shops and cramped residential quarters. Chinatown, which occupies most of Binondo, may be reached by crossing over Jones Bridge from Liwasang Bonifacio. At the foot of the bridge is a small street, Escolta, formerly Manila's major commercial street.

Thanks to their largely Chinese community and proximity to the river, Binondo and Santa Cruz became the city's richest mercantile borough at the height of the Manila–Acapulco treasure galleon run. Manila still has one of the world's major overseas Chinese populations, estimated at more than 1 million. Evidence of past grandeur may be seen in the old colonial houses that are now threatened by

*The 2,700-hectare (6,700-acre) city of Makati features more than half of Metro Manila's top restaurants, 200 high-rise office buildings and condominiums, 300 banks, 50 embassies and consulates, 25 airline offices, and at least 20 department stores.*

**BELOW:** fast-food store in Makati.

## Americans Return to Stay

American influence in the Philippines may have reached its peak in the days of General Douglas MacArthur, but since 1985, aggressive outreach by the Philippine Retirement Authority has reeled in nearly 1,000 Americans to spend their final decades in the country. Testifying to the popularity of retirement, condo projects expressly for foreign elders have opened on the main island Luzon, led by Manila and the city of Angeles near Clark and Subic.

Retirement visas are easy to get for those who are financially qualified. Businesses around the country have been enlisted by the government to offer foreign retiree discounts. Websites that advocate retirement say it's possible to live well on US$1,000 to US$1,500 a month.

Americans find the country appealing. Most Filipinos speak English, believe in a Christian faith, and harbor few obvious anti-foreigner sentiments. Land is cheap in much of the country, allowing expats to lease property for customized private mansions. Some retirees are former US servicemen who were once based in Asia. But there are drawbacks – as retirees themselves tell it, most of their ranks are single men. A percentage of those find themselves bored with their Philippine golden years, drink too much, and get into legal tangles with young local women who go after their money.

*Araneta Coliseum was host to the "Thrilla in Manila" – the 1974 heavyweight championship fight between Mohammed Ali and Joe Frasier. The mall next to the coliseum – Ali Mall – was named after the winner of that famous bout.*

**BELOW:** a boy searches through trash on Smokey Mountain.

the encroachment of modern concrete buildings. But within the decay a careful eye will pick out arched wooden windows, fancy wrought-iron grill-work on balconies, massive wooden doors, and brick walls.

As a result, Manila's **Chinatown** ❿ is a motley mix of influences. The traditional Chinese apothecary selling dried sea horses and ginseng tea huddles close to a modern bank outfitted with automatic doors and shotgun-toting guards. Chinese restaurants operate next to Italian furniture shops, while Chinese immigrants hawk cheap wares on the street. Down the choked grid of narrow streets still bearing Iberian names clip-clop the *calesas*, horse-drawn carriages preferred by some everyday citizens.

In traditional Chinese style, certain streets are known for selling a particular item. Ongpin Street is the king of gold and jade jewelry; Nueva Street vendors sell mainly office supplies. Head to Pinpin Street for furniture, and tiny Carvajal Street for the busy wet market and lunchtime *dim sum* with the locals.

Binondo is bounded on the north by Recto Avenue (Azacarraga), beyond which is Tondo, a district once the spawning ground of revolutionaries during Spanish times. Close to the harbor's piers, and densely populated, Tondo is among the largest slums in Southeast Asia. It's not the safest place in town.

## Divisoria

**Divisoria**, Manila's wild bargain basement, sprawls over several blocks between Tondo and San Nicolas. This flea market is an emporium for shoppers of all economic levels. Fruits, handicrafts, and hardware, too, are peddled in a thousand stalls, above which the drunken ghost of caveat emptor *(let the buyer beware)* hangs in a blissful state of abandon. Mall fans can visit the neoclassical Tutuban Center, founded in 1993 in the original Tutuban Railway Station, which was constructed in 1891 and closely linked to the activities of the revolutionary Katipunan.

Just north of Tutuban Center is the Philippine National Railway

## Smokey Mountain

The name may sound like something from a Country & Western tune, but Smokey Mountain of Manila is hardly the stuff of songs: the site also known as the Tondo Dumping Area is a garbage repository that has magnetized tens of thousands of poor Filipinos to scavenge in the trash for a living. The site, in the Vitas area north of Manila, attracts so many trash seekers that entire families have built shanties here. Motorists are warned to keep their windows shut to avoid having valuables stolen as they pause to take a look.

About 30,000 people live on the 2 million tons of trash, according to the Philippine-based Lopez Group Foundation. Children as young as age 3 scavenge for recyclables, which are sold cheaply to intermediaries who sell them onward. About 27 percent of the national population lives under the poverty line, the Asian Development Bank has found; 23 percent get by on less than US$1.25 per day. Elsewhere in Manila, shantytowns can be spotted along the Pasig River, and homeless families cook food on the curbs of Roxas Boulevard in upscale Ermita.

Philippine Christian Foundation CEO Jane Walker, the "Angel of Tondo," has built a school from cargo containers for 1,000 children. She hopes parents living near Smokey Mountain will send their kids to school instead of working the garbage.

Station. From here, one can take a train – though it's not generally recommended – south to Legaspi City in Albay Province.

An important, insanely busy thoroughfare, Recto Avenue, is usually jammed with jeepneys full of college students. The southern end is marked by a heavy concentration of movie theaters, department and hardware stores, magazine stands, and sidewalk vendors. Vendors hawk cheap clothing, toys, sunglasses, and watches. A few sell pornographic magazines.

## Quiapo

East, past Avenida Rizal, Recto Avenue is marked by a stretch of small shops selling new and second-hand books for the university belt extending from Recto Avenue's juncture with Quezon Boulevard. On Quezon is **Central Market**, a textile emporium. Turning right at Quezon Boulevard from Recto Avenue leads to **Quiapo Church ⑪**, at the foot of Quezon Bridge. The area beside the church is the terminus for most public road

traffic plying north–south routes in the city. A boisterous quarter of the city, it has long been considered the heart – some say armpit – of downtown Manila.

Quiapo Church, a landmark that makes this district famous, is home of the Black Nazarene, a life-sized Christ statue kneeling and bearing a huge cross on his shoulder. Every January 9, the image is borne forth in a frenzied all-male procession leading a massed throng of barefoot devotees down the backstreets of the district. It is believed that whoever touches the Christ image shall be purged of their sins.

Outside the church patio, Quiapo's fabled herb sellers push cures for everything from menstrual cramps to a lackluster love life. They peddle organic leaves, seeds, and oils from local plants. Some double as sellers of amulets, candles, religious calendars, and lottery tickets.

Around the corner stands a gem of a *bahay na bato* (stone house) on Bautista Street, the 1914 **Bahay Nakpil Bautista** (Mon–Fri

**BELOW:** Chinatown store.

9am–5pm, Sat 9am–noon; donations welcome), once home of four Filipino freedom fighters. In front of Quiapo Church is Plaza Miranda. Bounding this plaza are numerous markets, including one in the area under Quezon Bridge, where jeepneys heading northward make their U-turns. This cheap handicrafts market is known simply as **Ilalim ng Tulay** (Under the Bridge).

North along Quezon Boulevard towards Recto Avenue is another conglomeration of army surplus stores, pawnshops, restaurants, hole-in-the-wall astrologers, and movie houses. A right turn on Recto Avenue leads to the university belt, where colleges and universities disgorge tens of thousands of students to compound Manila's transportation problems. Near where Recto Avenue becomes Mendiola Street is **San Sebastian Church**, possibly the only prefabricated steel church in the world. Every piece of its structure was made in Belgium and shipped over for assembly at the end of the 19th century.

## Malacañang Palace

**Malacañang Palace ⓬**, the office-cum-residence of most Philippine presidents and previous rulers, gives tours by appointment of its **Malacañang Museum** (tel: 02-736-4662; www.op.gov.ph/museum; Mon–Fri 9am–4pm; charge). It showcases the memorabilia of past Philippines presidents.

Originally a country estate owned by a Spanish nobleman, Malacañang became the summer residence of Spanish governor-generals in the mid-1800s. Nineteen Spanish executives took turns ruling the country from Malacañang before it was turned over to the first of what would become 14 American governor-generals. Following Independence Day in 1946, nine Filipino chief executives set up shop in the Presidential Palace, the last being Ferdinand Marcos. Corazon Aquino broke with tradition by operating from the adjacent Guest House. North of Malacañang, at the corner of Lacson (Governor Forbes) and España, is the **University of Santo Tomas** (**UST**), founded by Dominicans in 1611 and the oldest university in Asia.

**BELOW:** Quiapo Church.

# Jeepneys

**Ingenuity meets art and convenience on board the long-bed, colorful, jeep-like vehicles that effectively take the place of public city buses in the Philippines.**

Garishly colored jeepneys are as essential and ubiquitous in the Philippines as double-decker buses are in London. Though a traveler may find the jeepney route system maddening enough to hop on a taxi instead, this form of public transportation continues to be de rigueur, as it has for more than half a century.

## Pop art decor

Jeepneys, which merge the words jeep with jitney, began as the sensible recycling of surplus US army jeeps left behind after World War II. They have grown into an institution of folk and pop art on wheels. No self-respecting jeepney driver would allow his beloved vehicle to crawl naked through the streets of Manila. The chrome bodies, either buffed to a shine or painted in vibrant colors, exhibit a wealth of brazen adornments, from small nickel stallions on the hood-and-chrome embellishments to non-functional antennae festooned with plastic streamers. Graffiti and religious slogans such "God Almighty" decorate the exterior, but jeepneys have yet to become popular as billboards for anything beyond their owners' whimsy.

Each one lists its destination (and sometimes the route) on the vehicle's front and side. To all intents and purposes, there are no rules dictating where the driver can and cannot stop. Tying up traffic in the middle of the road to pick up passengers is a simple fact of life, except in areas where traffic enforcement is taken seriously.

Depending on the driver, a strand of sweet-smelling sampaguita flowers may hang from the rearview mirror, while cartoon character effigies jangle above the dashboard, where a statue of the Virgin Mary or the Sto. Niño often occupies a place of importance to bless the trip.

## Prepare for the ride

The back of the jeepney – almost invariably open-air – extends longer than a normal jeep, with a row of padded seats on each side. Passengers crowd into the tight space, knees knocking, and ready handkerchiefs to shield nose and mouth from the diesel fumes. Outside, the jeepney's sleek rear end offers a glistening series of handrails and supports, for those who prefer to take their chances standing up. Such accoutrements are also necessary when the driver decides not to stop while picking up a passenger, and he must literally jump aboard.

Ever since the supply of surplus army jeeps ran out, the ingenious Filipinos have been building these machines from scratch. The metal body is hammered into shape; workers carefully pad seats with fiber from coconut husks; others prepare motors. Today, second-hand, reconditioned Japanese motors often keep jeepneys plying the streets. If government agencies some day get serious about enforcing the country's Clean Air Act, engine technology may need an update that doesn't foul the lungs of city dwellers. A World Bank report says pollution-belching jeepneys stay on the roads for lack of consistent pollution data and interdepartmental crackdown efforts.

Before riding a jeepney, ask a hotel clerk or airport information counter about routes. Prepare to pay about P7 or P10 for urban rides. Longer hauls may cost more.

**RIGHT:** garishly colored jeepneys are found everywhere in the Philippines.

# MANILA'S ENVIRONS

The ring of suburbs and countryside around Manila embodies a revolutionary past and teems with natural attractions, such as white-sand beaches and access to the spectacular, volatile Taal Volcano.

nside two hours' drive south from downtown Manila, it's possible to be standing on Tagaytay Ridge, looking across Taal Lake to a smoldering volcanic cone at its center, contemplating whether to take a boat and hike to the rim, conditions permitting. Alternatively, you could be savoring freshly caught fish on the shores of Lake Laguna, swimming in a sheltered cove off the coast at Nasugbu, or exploring the isolated islands off Quezon to the east.

Across the bay from Manila, Corregidor Island appeals to World War II historians, while divers and snorkelers will find pleasant sandy beaches in the province of Batangas a day-trip south of the capital. In Taal City, not far from the volcano of the same name, visitors will see an immaculately preserved Spanish-style architectural cluster.

Much of the capital's suburbia comprises an industrial zone linking Manila to ports for shipments of refinery products as well as food from farms. The Cavite-Laguna-Batangas-Aurora-Rizal-Quezon swathe south of Manila leads the Philippines in investment and employment. The region makes petrochemicals, mills flour, and grows coffee.

In the outer reaches of Manila's environs, isolated beaches, such as those in Quezon's Polillo islands, attract a steady stream of travelers making their way eastward along Luzon's south coast towards the Bicol region. Quezon National Park offers a simple hike to a low peak, plus the usual Philippine scenic duo of caves and waterfalls.

Transportation to most of the region is easy because of the short distance from Manila. A host of long-distance bus operators work the roads to Cavite, Taal, Batangas, and eastward toward Quezon.

**Main attractions**
CORREGIDOR ISLAND WAR MEMORIALS
TAAL CITY SPANISH ARCHITECTURE
BATANGAS WHITE-SAND BEACHES
PAGSANJAN FALLS RIVER TREKS
POLILLO ISLANDS
ANGONO ARTISTS' VILLAGE

**LEFT:** army barracks ruins in Corregidor Island. **RIGHT:** boats on Lake Taal.

*Because of their industriousness, the Spaniards called the Chinese seng-li, or sangley, meaning "business" or "trader" in the dialect of the Chinese from Fujian, who originally made up most of the Chinese immigrants. Sangley Point in Cavite was an important Chinese trading port in the 13th century.*

**BELOW:** Brothers in Arms statue, Corregidor Island.

Cavite Province, south of Manila, proved pivotal to the Philippine Revolution of 1896, and is a proud battleground. It first produced countless revolutionary heroes devoted to overthrowing three centuries of Spanish rule. Fifty years later, Filipino and American forces on Cavite's Corregidor Island battled to regain Philippine freedom from the Japanese.

## Corregidor Island

That famed sunset over Manila Bay does not always sink into a watery horizon. Rather, it may fall behind faint mountains. These vague, dull-blue contours outline the elongated peninsula of Bataan, an infamous World War II site. Off the southern tip is **Corregidor Island ❶**, a hallowed ground for war veterans.

A small rocky island 48km (30 miles) west of **Manila ❷**, at the mouth of Manila Bay, Corregidor has come a long way from the devastation of World War II. Today, ruined barracks and 100-year-old mortars peek out from a now forested

island. As its historical sites attest, Corregidor stands as a memorial to peace, valor, and international understanding, recalling the drama of World War II in the Pacific, when Filipino and American troops held their ground even as the US was unable to send help. Two monuments have been erected on the island. Through one, a domed white-marble memorial, the sun shines onto an altar built to honor those killed during the 1942 Japanese invasion. The second, an upward-reaching modern steel sculpture made from melted cannons, represents the flame of freedom.

Corregidor is one hour from downtown Manila, via jetboat (daily, 8am) from the CCP Complex on Roxas Boulevard. On the island, streetcars ferry visitors on a half-day, guided tour (charge). The tours include MacArthur's headquarters in Malinta Tunnel, the mile-long barracks, other military structures, and the Japanese Garden of Peace. A small museum displays photographs of prewar Corregidor, plus identification tags

and personal effects of those who died there.

## Las Piñas, Cavite, and Kawit

About 12km (8 miles) south from Manila Airport, visit **San Jose Church** in **Las Piñas** to see the world's only bamboo organ, built in 1821 and refurbished in 1975. Its pipes – 832 bamboo and 122 metal – reverberate each Sunday, and during February's Bamboo Organ Festival.

The crowded towns in northern Cavite – **Zapote** and **Bacoor** – seem an extension of Manila's traffic and chaos, littered by factories, refineries, and neon lights. Further south, beach resorts in one-time shipbuilding towns – Noveleta, Rosario, and Tanza – cater to Manileño weekenders, though their proximity to industry has made their waters less than inviting.

Cavite takes its name from the hook shape of its old population center – *kawit*, Tagalog for hook. At the hook's tip is **Cavite City**, until recently the provincial capital. Here the Spanish outfitted galleons for the Manila–Acapulco (Mexico) run, as well as small boats to fend off the marauding Moros from today's Mindanao Island. During a Dutch attack in 1647, a stone fort was damaged; its ruins still stand at Porta Vaga.

In the 1870s, a mutiny by Filipino dockworkers gave the Spanish government an excuse to punish the leaders of an increasingly incendiary movement. The ensuing martyrdom of three priests, surnamed Gornez, Burgos, and Zamora, ignited revolution. Emilio Aguinaldo, general of Cavite's revolutionary forces and president of the first but short-lived Philippine Republic, was born in the Cavite town of **Kawit ③**. Long after the revolution in Manila had collapsed from disorganization, Aguinaldo planned and implemented his strategy in Kawit, building a southern front to resist the

Spanish. On June 12, 1898 revolutionaries hoisted the Philippine flag from his house, to a battle hymn that eventually became the national anthem.

Though the revolution nearly succeeded, the US aborted the foundation of a new republic after winning the 1898 Spanish-American War. Cavite then housed a US colonial naval installation at Sangley Point until the late 1960s, at which time the Philippines Navy and Air Force took over the base.

Preserved as a shrine to the revolution is the **Aguinaldo Shrine and Museum** (Tue–Sun 8am–5pm; free), an architectural achievement of late colonial vintage, with an interpretive display of revolutionary Philippine history. The house, with its secret escape tunnels, is among the country's most elaborate older Spanish-style homes *(bahay na bato)*.

In General Trias, 25km (15 miles) south of Kawit, stands the **GBR Museum** (tel: 046-433-0313; www.gbr museum.com.ph; Wed–Sat, 9am–5pm, by appointment only; charge), so

**BELOW:** war memorial, Corregidor Island.

named for its owner, businessman Geronimo B. de los Reyes. The five galleries feature brilliant photographs of an almost unrecognizable Philippines from 1860–1930, archival photos of the Philippine-American War, a collection of rare books and maps, and a collection of Chinese imperial yellow Peking glassware.

Southwest along the coast, stop in **Maragondon** to see its church with an ornately carved door and rococo interior. Trumpeting angels on the altar and friezes on the pulpit conjure up images of the rattling swords and whizzing bullets of a revolution that overflowed into this church. Andres Bonifacio, head of the revolutionary Katipunan, was imprisoned here for trying to divide and rule the struggle in Cavite. He was later bludgeoned to death in the hills of Maragondon.

Fourteen different bus companies do the one-hour trip from Manila to Cavite, and Manila is due to extend its light rail into the suburban district where traffic snarls have made road transit increasingly intolerable.

## Tagaytay Ridge

South of Cavite, toward the Batangas border, is **Tagaytay Ridge**, with views over the Taal Volcano and its massive crater lake. Many Manileños escape the heat on weekends by heading to the cool of 600-meter (1,970ft) -high **Tagaytay City**, where pineapple, papaya, and other tropical fruits abound. There are a number of viewpoint restaurants on Aguinaldo Highway, along the ridge. The ruins of the Marcos mountaintop mansion anchors **People's Park**, a site 8km (5 miles) further east where visitors can enjoy mountain breezes and wide views.

Bus lines such as Crown and Celyrosa do routes from Manila to Tagaytay throughout the day. Drive time is about 1 hour 15 minutes.

## South to Batangas

Some of the oldest ancestors of Tagalog culture can be linked to Batangas Province, which the country today bills as a prime industrial area next to a deep port and a series of white-sand beaches.

**BELOW:** Aguinaldo Shrine and Museum.

Archeologists have traced human habitation in Batangas, around the southwestern coastline of Balayan Bay, to 250,000 years ago. Much later, fleeing Bornean chieftains came to the southern coast of Luzon, traversing the Pansipit River to settle on the shores of Lake Taal. They later controlled much of southern Luzon and Bicol. Archeological finds at graves in Calatagan and Lemery show that the people of this region, called Bombon, conducted a lively trade with Arab, Chinese, and Indian merchants over the centuries.

Upon the arrival of conquistadores Juan de Salcedo and Martin Goiti in 1570, the Bombon inhabitants were easily subdued. As Jose Rizal pointed out, "The people, accustomed to the yoke, did not defend their chiefs from the invader...The nobles, accustomed to tyrannize by force, had to accept foreign tyranny when it showed itself stronger than their own." Delighted by the rivers and "excellent meadows," the Spanish soon granted tracts of lands (*encomienda*) to individuals and used Catholicism to spread their cause. A century and a half would pass before the locals, annoyed that Augustinians and Jesuits had snatched their land, began taking up arms against the class-conscious Spaniards.

From the 18th century, Batangas enjoyed rapid economic growth, spurred on by the introduction of the coffee bean. Coffee thrived in the rich volcanic soil, fueling the rise of the Taaleño middle class and leading exports during the mid-19th century. However, a coffee blight destroyed plantations in the late 19th century, and the industry has never fully recovered. East of Taal lake, **Lipa City** has a collection of old ancestral homes, flower gardens, and coffee plantations. In the center of town sits **Casa de Segunda**, a typical Spanish-colonial *bahay na bato*, built in "stone house" style and lovingly restored to its original grandeur.

For visitors **Batangas Province** can be divided into two parts: around Lake Taal, and along the irregular coastline. The jagged coast of Batangas harbors a collection of bays, coves, and peninsulas. In the northwest, the towns of **Nasugbu**, **Lian**, and **Matabungkay** lead to beach strips with a range of beachfront accommodation, from bamboo cottages to upscale resorts. The **Calatagan Peninsula** in the southwest offers a relatively unspoiled strip of white-sand beach.

Buses and 10-person vans (called the "FX") connect Manila to Batangas, usually 90 minutes to about 2 hours. Major companies with air-con buses are ALPS, JAM, Tritran, and Batangas Express Liner.

## Lake Taal and Taal City

The 300-meter (1,000ft) -high **Taal Volcano ❹**, a crater within a lake, looms two hours' drive south from Manila. As one of the smallest, most active volcanoes in the world, it smolders and occasionally rumbles, always a dramatic sight. Since its first known eruption in 1572, Taal has spewed

**TIP**

Before climbing any volcano – especially unpredictable Taal – be sure to check conditions with the Philippine Institute of Volcanology and Seismology (tel: 02-426-1468; www. phivocs.dost.gov.ph).

**BELOW:** Taal volcano crater.

*A young girl awaits Holy Communion at the Basilica of St Martin de Tours.*

**BELOW:** tranquil Lake Taal.

over 40 times. A *banca* (pumpboat) can be hired from Talisay to cross the lake, leading to the trailhead for hiking up the crater. In 1999, the volcano churned ominously enough for geologists to warn against climbing it.

**Taal City** ❺, southwest of Taal lake and along the Pansipit River that flows into Balayan Bay, is one of the most faithfully preserved sites from the Spanish colonial era. The **Basilica of St Martin de Tours**, part of the Taal Heritage Village, draws visitors as one of the largest Catholic churches in Asia. From the belfry, take in the sweeping vista: waving fields of sugar cane, the meanderings of the Pansipit River, and present-day television antennae sprouting like a newly laid bamboo grove on the rooftops of century-old houses. Nearby stands the Shrine of Our Lady of Caysaysay, presumed to be miraculous for its supposed ability to return to this same spot even after being relocated.

Buses to Taal leave every 30 minutes from Cubao in Metro Manila, often en route to Nasugbu. Bus companies include Golden Dragon, Erjohn & Almark, and San Agustin. The trip takes two hours.

## Local specialties

Regional products include the Taal flip-open, butterfly knife (*balisong*) sold at roadsides. The *tawilis* and *maliputo*, two sardine-like species of fish found only in Taal lake, may end up on a visitor's plate. Drying in the sun in the public market are frames of bleached *piña, a fabric* woven from pineapple fibers, awaiting embroidery. A tradition of the provinces near Laguna de Bay, this detailed needlework distinguishes the *barong Tagalog*, or traditional Filipino man's dress shirt.

Perhaps it was needlework that gave Marcela Agoncillo of Taal a whole page of Philippine history – she sewed the first Filipino flag, which was unfurled from Aguinaldo's Kawit house in 1898. Learn more about this lady at the restored **Agoncillo Museum**, and take the opportunity of visiting a restored ancestral house at the **Leon Apacible Historical Landmark** (daily

8am–noon, 1–5pm; charge) on Taal's Marcela Agoncillo Street.

## Batangas dive sites and beaches

On the coastal side of Batangas, the small town of **Anilao** is a popular haven for scuba divers. Although the beaches are rocky and not particularly suited to swimming, Anilao offers some of the best macro diving in the Philippines, with close-up glimpses of a variety of tropical fish. Other dive sites, such as Bonito Island, are accessible via **Mabini**. Farther east, off Batangas Bay in the municipality of **Lobo**, isolated white-sand beaches can be found. Verde Island, best accessed from nearby Puerto Galera in Mindoro, is another top Batangas dive site.

Resorts along the Batangas coast include Matabungka Beach Resort & Hotel (tel: 0917-834-1269, www.matabungkay-batangas.com) and Verde Island Resort (tel: 043-723-2411; verde-island.resortsbatangas.com).

Although Batangas makes the Philippine government's honor roll as a leading area for heavy industry, with petrochemical plants close to Manila plus a deep port, the beaches sit apart from the wheels of production. A few spots on the coast fill with weekenders from Manila. But at most, the coves, white sands, and coral-enhanced waters stack up against beaches anywhere in the Philippines – ideal for Manila-based travelers with just a day or two to spend outside town.

## Laguna Province

Beyond Santa Rosa, home of the Enchanted Kingdom amusement park, the first town of interest to tourists in Laguna Province south of Manila is **Calamba ❻**, birthplace of Jose Rizal. The old Rizal house on the town's main street is now a national shrine, landscaped with fruit trees from around Asia. Visitors can wander this garden, fragrant with giant

*mabolo*, *santol*, and mango trees, and then stroll indoors to view the high-quality appointments of a home typical of Laguna gentry, a mix of conquistadores and insular Malay settlements. Inside the house, rice harvested from private fields was stored in huge grain baskets, coffee was ground in the kitchen, and reading was done by the light of kerosene lamps.

Los Baños, 19km (12 miles) beyond Calamba, is home to the **International Rice Research Institute** (IRRI), funded since 1960 by the Rockefeller and Ford foundations and dedicated to developing new varieties of rice to feed a growing world population. The **Riceworld Museum** (tel: 02-844-3351, 049-812-7686; Mon–Fri 8am–5pm; free) in the main complex offers an introduction to the history and the science of rice cultivation.

On the southern slope of extinct volcano Mt Makiling, beyond Los Baños, lies Hidden Valley Springs, in **Alaminos**. This mountain hideaway is a pleasant, albeit pricey, private resort where several springs are channeled into specially constructed bathing

*Anilao Beach has some of the best scuba diving in the Philippines.*

**BELOW:** a service at the Basilica of St Martin de Tours.

pools. Paths lead through a jungle of fruit trees, giant ferns, and wild orchids to the gurgling pools.

The stature of holy mountains Makiling and Banahaw dominates life in Laguna. On the periphery of these two extinct volcanoes, sulfur springs gush forth with a strength reminiscent of the old volcano from which they spurt.

**Mt Makiling** is said to be the home of goddess Maria, a guardian of the forest. To **Mt Banahaw**, her male counterpart, must the stout-of-heart travel to gain strength and wisdom. Nature lovers and birdwatchers alike take to the slopes of Makiling, while occult sects and faith healers live in the foothills of Banahaw. They claim to draw their insight and power from the towering mountain.

**San Pablo**, a major commercial center, is off to the east. An abundance of fish teem near the lakeshores in January – driven there by the rising sulfuric content of the waters from craters of extinct volcanoes. That means you should order a plate of fish if in San Pablo in the winter. From

San Pablo, the road leads southward to Quezon and Bicol.

Past San Pablo's seven lakes, in the east, lies **Nagcarlan**, a gem of history in Laguna Province, with its church and an oddly situated underground cemetery counted as national treasures. Baroque, Moorish, and Javanese styles add a mystifying touch to these two structures. Glazed blue ceramic tiles decorate parts of the church and a wall of the cemetery's underground crypt. On a landing leading to the underground tombs – now sealed off – are faded epigraphs in Spanish, too blurred to translate. In 1896, a cemetery crypt provided a clandestine meeting place for the Katipunan, the secret revolutionary society.

Nearby **Liliw** lies at the end of a road that seems to head straight into Mt Banahaw. This town is known for its high-quality, handmade footwear – though larger, Western sizes are often unavailable.

Out of Liliw, the road runs eastward to **Majayjay**, the oldest settlement in the area. It has a Brigadoon-like quality, laid over a series of small hills with

roads twisting and curving to reveal one colonial treasure after another. White-haired grandmothers contemplate travelers from the ground floors of squat stone houses, while children in the plaza may stop to stare. As elsewhere in the Philippines, everything converges on the church at the center of town, but there is added drama to Majayjay's elevated religious landmark, which has been reconstructed numerous times, with walls now three layers thick.

The church retains much of Majayjay's troubled history, marked by past tension between Franciscan missionaries and the locals forced for years to build it. The people of Majayjay had voted with their feet, erecting huts outside the town boundaries, only to have them torched by friars in need of labor to support their infrastructure.

Northeast in **Luisiana**, groves of giant pandanus trees grow thickly in the swampy soil along the road. Once the leaves are dried, they are woven into mats and bags, now the envy of fashion connoisseurs worldwide.

## Pagsanjan and points north

**Pagsanjan** ❼ (pronounced *pag-san-han*), along the Magdapio River, or Pagsanjan River, is known for whitewater experiences. At **Pagsanjan Falls**, visitors change into swimsuits or shorts and travel upriver in small *banca*. Often the boatman pushes, or lifts, the *banca* over shallows or other obstructions in the river. The return journey thrills those on board as boats negotiate the rapids.

Before coming to the falls, the *banca* slides into a picturesque gorge, glistening with small cascades, vibrant moss, and lichen. The walls rise nearly 100 meters (330ft), the air still and softly humming with forest sounds. At the second falls, passengers from the *banca* transfer onto bamboo rafts, guided by long ropes from the shore into the mouth of a cave beyond the falls,

drenching the visitor with refreshingly cool water. Francis Ford Coppola filmed this river for parts of his 1979 movie *Apocalypse Now*. By spending the night in Pagsanjan, visitors can make the most of their trip, waking early to be the first on the river. Weekdays are best, to avoid crowds. Long-distance buses run between Manila and Santa Cruz during the day, with jeepney rides of a few pesos per head to Pagsanjan. Resorts near the river offer overnight stays.

The provincial capital, **Santa Cruz,** dates back to 1688 and is laid out in grander colonial style than smaller settlements by the lake. Spanish-style houses can still be found in the town. Santa Cruz also makes *quesong puti*, an excellent white cheese from *carabao* (water buffalo) milk, and has cornered the market in antique Chinese pottery excavated from old graves in the surrounding coconut plantations. Those interested in the more scholarly value of these items can visit a small museum in **Pila**, south of Santa Cruz.

The road northeast of Pagsanjan heads into the hills to **Lake Caliraya,** a

**BELOW:** a scientist checks a GM crop at the International Rice Research Institute.

reservoir dug by the Americans in the 1930s far enough above sea level to be noticeably cooler than the lowlands. Facilities here are limited, though the lake is a haven for windsurfers escaping Manila for the weekend. The Lagos del Sol Resort (tel: 0919-540-0758; www.lagosdelsolresort.com) lets guests use a pool, sauna, and jacuzzi near the lake. Golfers can work the greens above the lake at the Caliraya Springs club (tel: 0917-857-8268; www.calirayasprings.com).

Further north, the communities of Paete, Pakil, and Pangil offer miniature snippets of colonial Spanish style. Their narrow streets and tiny houses, with carved balusters and scroll-worked eaves, take on an almost elfin quality compared to the highway. The exemplary churches in these towns are as tiny as they are exquisite, the most outstanding being the Santiago de Apostol Church in **Paete**, dating to 1645. A long woodcarving tradition is evident on its facade. That exterior depicts St James, the town's patron, as he rides off to battle the Moors, surrounded by a cornucopia of palms and blossoms characterizing Filipino Baroque. Likewise, a tradition of papier-mâché (*taka*) flourishes in Paete; wander the narrow streets to see rows of reindeer forms being prepared for export. **Pakil**, to the north, is noted for its delicate filigree wood-shaving art, *pahiyas tambag*. The toothpicks topped by fanned peacock's tails, butterflies or spiraling trees, found in Manila's hotels, come from Pakil. Ask for Ms Dominga Pasang on Gonzales Street to witness her filigree work.

At the northern boundary of Laguna Province is **Mabitac**, in the foothills of the Sierra Madre. Here stands a magnificent 17th-century church built on a hilltop to prevent mountain floodwaters pouring in.

## Quezon Province

This scenic but isolated area is normally left to farmers and nomadic peoples, but tourists with time to explore will find Spanish architecture, coastal islets, a national park, and everything they need to know about coconut cultivation.

## Splashing Out on Pagsanjan

Pagsanjan Falls is one of those frustrating places to visit, its spectacular scenery marred by overzealous boatmen and shockingly high, non-negotiable prices.

Visitors should arrange a trip to the falls through one of the hotels in Pagsanjan, where prices are fixed and journeys are guaranteed. The set rate is P580 a person, plus P100 for the mandatory life jacket and seat cushion. The minimum charge, however, is P1,160 per boat, with a maximum of three guests to any one boat. The price regime and over-charges by boat operators have held water because the 393-meter (1,290ft) -high falls lie just 60km (37 miles) from Manila, drawing weekenders who are willing to pay.

An increasing number of touts roam the streets outside city limits, stopping private cars and hustling unsuspecting tourists onto overpriced, unregulated boats. Resist these touts at all costs, as they will request additional fees halfway down the river, refusing to budge further. Be aware that boatmen may play on your good nature and con you into paying for additional items – a cold drink for such hard work, or a barbecued snack somewhere along the way.

The scenery is indeed beautiful, but, if you're not up to the haggling and the hassle, you may prefer to give Pagsanjan a miss.

Named after native son and former Commonwealth President Manuel L. Quezon and his First Lady, **Quezon Province** stretches like a narrow belt along the eastern coast of Luzon. People live concentrated along the western, sheltered side of the Sierra Madre and in secluded inland valleys. The small, relatively flat area to the south has an ample road network, while the mountainous four-fifths of northern Quezon remains practically inaccessible by land. Much of its forested terrain is home to nomadic people and wildlife, and, until tree felling was banned in 1999, also to loggers. East of the Sierra Madre, the flat coastline – in places falling sharply from 30-meter (100-ft) -high cliffs – supports a scattering of isolated villages that live off coastal waters.

Quezon witnessed bloody encounters between the Japanese and American forces during World War II. In fact, the entire history of Quezon is one of bombings and killings, of land problems and militarization, of the rebellion of its people in an attempt to right a wrong. In 1985, Marxist rebels in their heyday invited a photographer to take shots of a bloody daylight ambush in the municipality of Gumaca. That photo, splashed in newspapers around the world, introduced Quezon to global newsreaders as the impoverished host to a stubborn guerrilla force.

## Southwest Quezon

Coconut agriculture dominates the better-known, southern portion of Quezon, contributing substantial revenues. The strongly Hispanicized classes of yesteryear – horse-riding gentry resting secure on the income from their coconut plantations – have left tangible relics of their lifestyle throughout the area, beginning in **Tiaong** on Laguna's southwest boundary. Barely past the Art Deco angels gracing the arch of the provincial boundary marker lies **Villa Escudero**, a working coconut plantation of 800

hectares (2,000 acres). The plantation stands out as a self-contained community of some 300 interrelated families, many of them third-generation laborers. A lush resort on the plantation grounds includes a museum of ecclesiastical mementoes and other artifacts.

**Sariaya**, 12km (8 miles) east, is a prosperous trading town, where travelers can pick up heirloom pastries and fruit candies. Antique houses loom over narrow streets, the highest overlooking the dome of Sariaya's church, a hush of stained-glass windows displaying an unusually bloody, crucified Christ.

## Lucban and southeast Quezon

Southeast of Sariaya is **Lucena**, provincial capital of Quezon, and, to its north, the quiet, hilly town of Tayabas. It could have been only yesterday that the Spanish came and left **Lucban**, where isolation has ripened an exotic fruit to fullness. The church bells still peal at four in the morning, shaking the town's moss and mountain pools. To the northeast, along a rickety road,

*Quezon Province now aims to become the food basket of southern Luzon, pushing agriculture to the forefront and increasing milkfish production.*

**BELOW:** house decorations for the Pahiyas Festival, Lucban.

the scenery draws the odd visitor to coastal **Mauban**.

Come mid-May, Lucban springs alive to the festival of Pahiyas, when giant carabaos and scarecrows made of papier-mâché dance jubilantly past the courtyard of Lucban's 400-year-old church, all for the feast day of San Isidro Labrador, patron saint of the farmer and worker.

Quezon's coastline covers rich yet relatively untouched fishing waters. Those waters also lap up against beaches that will enchant a traveler who makes it that far. East of Lucena is the coastal town of Padre Burgos, a jumping-off point to **Pagbilao Grande** and **Pagbilao Chico** islands in Tayabas Bay. Connected by a sandy isthmus, these islands are actually a million-year-old coral reef, riddled with hundreds of coves and caves.

According to sentimental islanders, this Tayabas Bay topography is a result of the legend of Bulaklak and Hangin. In that story, the already-betrothed god Hangin (meaning *wind*) once wandered the earth. One day, his gaze fell upon Bulaklak (*flower*), a mortal

woman of haunting beauty. They fell in love, but torn by divine edict and mortal law, they were left no choice but suicide. Afterwards, their bodies were turned into the islands Pagbilao Grande and Pagbilao Chico, forever linked by a bridge of white sand. Local people say that on this sand each May, Bulaklak and Hangin cause a child to drown, joining them as offspring in the other world.

To relive the legend, visit Estamper Point, a cave lookout on the top of Pagbilao Chico. The two legendary lovers weren't the only ones to die there. From that peak, locals say, hundreds of Japanese sailors, whose ships had been sunk by American submarines, hurled themselves to death to avoid capture.

North of Pagbilao Grande, via the town of **Pagbilao**, lies the 9.83 million-hectare (24.3 million-acre) **Quezon National Park**, a short detour from the main highway. Check in with the park warden upon arrival. In two hours, a hiker can reach the 360-meter (1,180ft) -high peak through moist vegetation. Birds

**BELOW:** windsurfing at Anilao.

sing among large trees and writhing ancient vines. Doves, orioles, woodpeckers, and red-crested royal *kalaw* birds alight here in droves. Visitors can also wander into a maze of caves and stop along trails for views of waterfalls.

Plan ahead for this area; there is little in the way of accommodations in some parts.

## Northern Quezon

Terrain in this province is generally rugged to mountainous, with most of the *barangay* (the smallest socio-political unit) situated along the coastline. There is no pronounced dry season, and most rain falls October through January. People in the region live from farming, fishing, and logging. Two minority ethnic groups, the Dumagats and Negritos, live nomadically in the hinterlands of Infanta, General Nakar and other forested parts of the province. Most commerce takes place in town centers.

Northern Quezon is best accessed from Siniloan and Mabitac, on the northeast tip of Laguna de Bay. A winding road first reaches Real, then

Infanta. Though this area once saw a phenomenal amount of logging, government bans have at least slowed the felling of trees.

**Real ⑧**, a northern municipality with its coastline facing Lamon Bay, is bounded on the north by Infanta and General Nakar towns, on the south by Mauban and on the west by the Sierra Madre mountain range. A wealth of virgin natural areas in this district provides plenty of outdoor activity for nature lovers. Balgbag Falls in Barangay Mapalad spills water from 30 meters (100ft). Off the coast of Real, remote Baluti Island covers about 23 hectares (57 acres). A wide river separates the island from the mainland. It's mostly covered with pine trees instead of coconut trees. Swimmers will find gray sand and clear water.

A smooth drive from Real leads to **Infanta**, where the long, wide Libjo Beach invites travelers to picnic. Further on is the town of **General Nakar**, which has a few beaches with rock formations and a verdant forest. A cold spring is the draw at Pamplona Beach.

*Quezon Province now aims to become the food basket of Luzon, pushing agriculture to the forefront and increasing milkfish production.*

## Best Beaches Near Manila

Beaches line the coast about two hours' drive time south of Manila in Batangas Province. They're close enough to the capital for a day trip, though sometimes thick with city dwellers trying to escape town, especially at weekends.

In San Juan, white sand stretches for a kilometer at Hugon Beach, where snorkeling and swimming are common. In a cave not far off, white sand and living corals define Mahabang Buhangin Beach.

Gerthel Beach in the town of Lobo is also blessed with a 1km (0.5 miles) stretch of white-sand beach and a gradual drop into the sea for those who prefer wading to an all-out swim. And in the city of Nasugbu, Munting Buhangin, and Natipunan beaches harbor more stretches of white sand, this time sheltered in coves. Divers and snorkelers may proceed to Anilao for close-up views of fish off a rocky coastline.

Being close to Manila, unlike beaches elsewhere in the country, the ones near Batangas are seldom far from resorts, if not right in front of them. Buses from the capital run to Batangas, from which jeepneys, boats, and tricycle taxis take people onward to the sands. To reach additional beaches, take any of 15 ferries per day from Batangas to Puerto Galera. Trips take one to two hours. For more information, check the ferry schedule at puertogaleraferry.net.

## Polillo and Balesin islands

The ultimate nature treat for Northern Quezon is the **Polillo Islands** ❾. Polillo Coral Reef, measuring 5km (3 miles) long by 2km (1 mile) wide, near Polillo town, has gained a following among snorkelers and divers. Accommodations have followed up interest among tourists. One of the better-known stays is Isla Polillo Beach Resort (tel: 02-920-2903).

On the eastern coast, Bakaw-Bakaw Island in Burdeos is filled with mangrove trees and shrubs. The Burdeos Coral Area, one of the richest marine areas in Quezon, can be accessed there, as well. Also in the neighborhood, look for Binombombonan Island, an uninhabited white-sand islet that works for snorkeling and diving, and Ikulong Island, with a pearl farm run by a Japanese businessman. Anilon Island looks like a long sand bridge during low tide. The white sand of Minasawa, a game refuge and bird sanctuary, is covered with broken shells.

**Balesin Island** ❿, south of Polillo, is world class and idyllic, with resort facilities and spots to dive or snorkel in one of the richest yet least explored fishing grounds in the Philippines. For information on the island, see www.balesin.com.

## Rizal Province

Long before the Spanish laid eyes on **Laguna de Bay**, the archipelago's largest lake, the heart-shaped body of water already cradled a thriving community. The waters spread over 90,000 hectares (222,000 acres), with the Sierra Madre range to the east, and Mt Makiling and Mt Banahaw to the south. Farmers grew rice on the surrounding plain, fishermen harvested the abundant waters, and traders shipped goods to lakeside towns aboard gliding *bancas*. Large *cascos*, or barges, roofed with bamboo mats, sailed to Laguna's northwest shores and down Pasig River toward Manila. This 27km (16-mile) -long waterway, connecting the lake to Manila Bay, flowed heavy with goods for sale to the Tagalog people in old Maynilad.

Three routes lead from Manila to the Rizal countryside. The

**BELOW:** rice farm irrigation, Laguna de Bay.

northern road runs from Caloocan to Marikina; the middle route runs from EDSA to Pasig; and the southern road passes Parañaque. The road between Marikina and Pasig forks 20km (12 miles) from Manila. From the capital, jeepneys or FX vans leave from the SM Mega Mall in Mandaluyong City and in Cubao in Quezon City. City buses also travel to Rizal Province from Quiapo and Divisoria in Manila.

To the east lie **Cainta** and **Taytay**, both centers of creeping industrialization on the periphery of Manila. Just beyond Taytay lies hilly **Antipolo ⑪**, celebrated for pilgrimages to Our Lady of Peace and Good Voyage. She is enshrined atop a hill, surrounded by a bedlam of carnival crowds and peddlers of candles, medallions and *sampaguita* flowers.

## Angono Artists' Village

The **Angono Artists' Village** in Rizal Province has been noted as a top art center in the Philippines. Visit the **Nemiranda Arthouse** (tel: 02-451-1580; www.nemirandaarthouse. com; charge), featuring the whimsical sculptures and naked female forms favored by one of the top contemporary artists in the country. Down the street, the Balaw-Balaw Restaurant offers an eclectic collection of culinary treats, such as monitor lizard and wild boar, in addition to an art gallery that includes the town's papier-mâché *gigantes* used in festivals. The **Blanco Family Museum** (daily 9–11am, 1–5pm; charge), started in the mid-1960s, features hundreds of works by the family's nine artists.

Past Angono, along the lakeshore, sits the fishing town of **Cardona**, the balconies of its houses hanging over the lapping waters of the lake, where a milkfish industry prospers. Just beyond Cardona lies the old Spanish center of **Morong**. The ornate dome and belfry of its church rise over a sea of green fields. Continue along the lakeshore to **Tanay** and its waterfalls. From Tanay, a 20km (13-mile) stretch of winding mountain road runs through Pililla and on into Laguna Province.

**BELOW:** papier mâché *gigantes* at a festival in Angono.

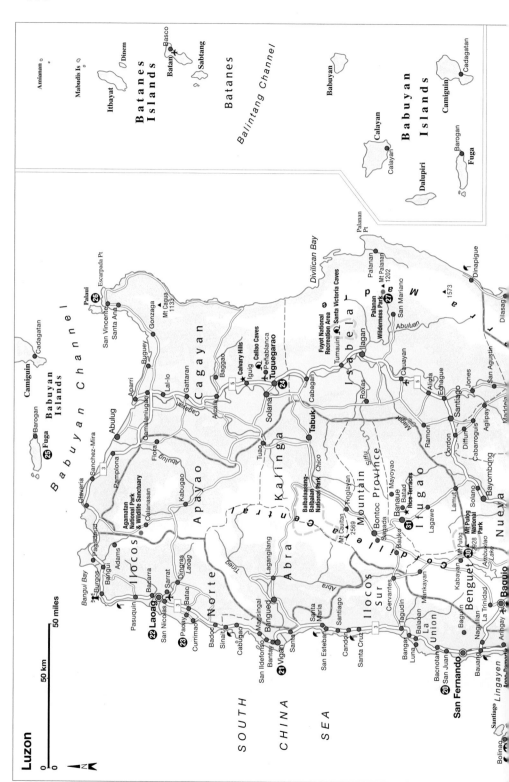

## Luzon

**SOUTH CHINA SEA**

*Bangui Bay*

*Babuyan Channel*

**Babuyan Islands**

Camiguin
Barogan
Fuga **25**

**Batanes Islands**

Amianan
Mabudis Is
Itbayat
Dinem
Batan **26**
Basco
Sabtang
*Balintang Channel*
**Batanes**

**Babuyan Islands**

Cadagatan
Calayan
Calayan
Dalupiri
Fuga
Barogan
Camiguin
Cadagatan

*Babuyan Channel*

Camiguin
Cadagatan
Barogan
Escarpada Pt
Palaui **26**
San Vincente
Santa Ana
Gonzaga
Mt Cagua 1133

Aparri
Abulug
Buguey
Lal-lo
Gattaran
Pamplona
Sanchez-Mira
Claveria
Pagudpud
Bangui
Adams
Burgos
Pasuquin
Bacarra
Laoag **22**
San Nicolas
Paoay **23**
Batac
Currimao
Badoc
Sinait
Cabugao
San Ildefonso
Bantay
Vigan **21**
Santa
Santa Maria
San Esteban
Santiago
Candon
Santa Cruz

Abulug
Camalaniugan
Alcala
Flora
Kabugao
Laganilang
Santiago
Santa Maria
Cervantes
Tagudin

**Apayao**
Agamatan National Park & Wildlife Sanctuary
Calanasan
**Ilocos Norte**
**Abra**
Bangued
Madsingal
Dingras

**Cagayan**
*Cagayan*
Baggao
Iguig
Calvary Hills
Callao Caves
Peñablanca
**Tuguegarao** **27**
Solana
**Tabuk**
Tuao
*Chico*
**Kalinga**
Balbalasang-Balbalan National Park
Tinglayan
Tabagan
Roxas

Divilican Bay
Palanan Pt
Palanan
Mt Palanay 1202
San Mariano
**Palanan Wilderness Park** **27**
Abuluan
Dinapigue
1573

Fuyot National Recreation Area
Tumauini
Santa Victoria Caves
Ilagan
**Isabela**
Cauayan
Alicia
Echague
Jones
San Agustin
Santiago
Aglipay
Cabarroguis
Diffun
Cordon
Ramon
Solano
Bayombong
Lamut
*Magat*
*Siffu*
Mayoyao
Banaue
Rice Terraces **31**
Batad
Lagawe
**Ifugao**
Mt Pulog National Park
Mt Pulog 2928 **30**
Ambuklao Lake
Kabayan
Baguio **29**
**Benguet**
La Trinidad
Kapangan
Mankayan
Bauang
San Fernando **20**
San Juan
**La Union**
Bacnotan
Luna
Balaoan
Bangar
Aringay
Agoo
Naguilian
Baguio
Arao-Damortis
*Lingayen Gulf*
Bolinao
Santiago

**Mountain Province**
Bontoc
Sadada
Balyko
Mt Cauitan 2569
**Central Cordillera**
**Nueva Vizcaya**

Roxas

Santa Ana
Escarpada Pt
Palaui

*50 km* / *50 miles*

N

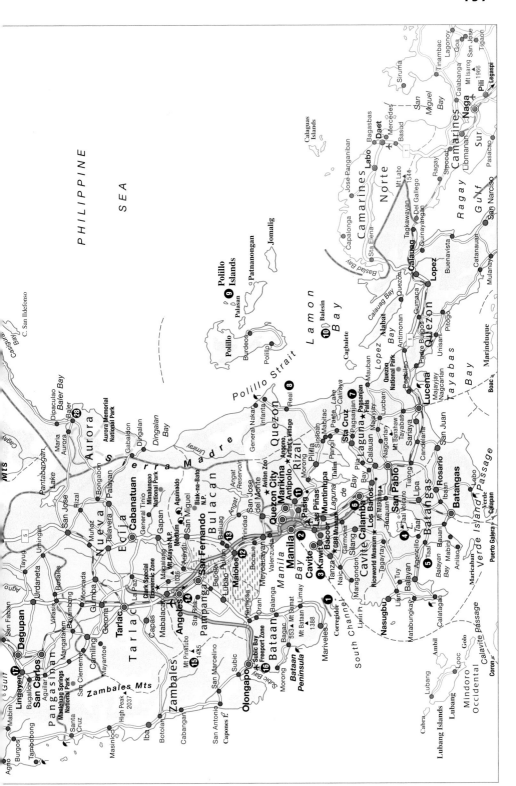

# THE CENTRAL PLAINS

**Manileños are wise to the proximity of the Central Plains north of the capital for weekend getaways, attracted by laid-back beaches, duty-free shopping, a frenzy of nightspots, and – beyond the flatlands – the mighty Mt Pinatubo.**

The sheltered agricultural and industrial region north of Manila holds a series of attractions. Travelers who know where to look can find historical monuments in Bulacan Province, a wild bar and restaurant scene in Angeles, and isolated beaches around Subic Bay. Seasonal festivals occur in San Fernando and Pulilan, and scholars of volcanic activity or wartime history will want to spend extra time here. An air-con bus ride just two hours from Manila leads straight into this heartland, making it oddly convenient.

An abundance of rich alluvial soil fed by rivers that have been swollen by monsoon rains gives the plains their agricultural legacy. North from the urban sprawl of Manila, the scene is nothing but rice fields – muddy during the dry season, and becoming green during the rainy season, when two crops are planted and harvested. Farther north, the rice gives way to vast fields of sugar cane, which in turn gives way to corn.

To the east, the Sierra Madre mountain range shelters the plains from fierce ocean typhoons whipping off the Philippine Sea. The Zambales range, to the west, cuts it off from the South China Sea, with the rugged Cordillera mountain range to the north. The Pan-Philippine Friendship Highway scoots traffic through this region. The tollway portion, which runs about 85km (50 miles) from Manila to Mabalacat in northern Pampanga, is known as the North Expressway or the National Highway.

## Bulacan

Urban Manila gives way to **Bulacan Province** in a continuous industrial sprawl of factories that make shoes, process food, or produce ceramic tiles. The first Bulacan town of **Valenzuela**, along the National Highway, is noted for its factories and the San Miguel Brewery.

**Main attractions**
ANGELES NIGHTLIFE
MT PINATUBO FLIGHT
OCEAN ADVENTURE, SUBIC BAY
BATAAN DEATH MARCH MEMORIAL
MARKERS

**LEFT:** hikers on Mount Pinatubo.
**RIGHT:** a scarecrow in a rice paddy.

*Bulacan derives its name from the kapuk tree – locally called bulak – which once grew profusely in the area, producing vast amounts of tradable kapok, or Java cotton.*

Fishing folk settled in Bulacan sometime before the 1st century. They initially lived along the shore of Manila Bay, but soon discovered the interior's rich soil and pushed inland to farm. The Bulacanos sided with their long-time trading partners in Maynilad against the invading Spanish, but were soundly defeated at the Battle of Bangkusay Channel in 1570. Writers from the province also developed a unique Spanish-Tagalog jargon that allowed them to flatter the Spanish on one hand while coyly criticizing them on the other.

Francisco "Balagtas" Baltazar was the foremost Bulacan wit in the late 1700s. Like other aspiring poets, Balagtas labored under strict friar supervision of his Spanish meter and metaphor, but he slipped Tagalog into his works to protest against Spanish tyranny. The friars thought that his celebrated poem *Florante at Laura* was about dueling Christians and Moors, but it really criticized Spanish forced labor, exorbitant taxes, and the capriciousness of the friars. The town of **Balagtas** (Bigaa) has a monument to

Baltazar, the father of Tagalog poetry. One of the oldest known tiled-roof houses in Bulacan stands in Balagtas: *Bahay na Tisa*, built in 1849.

Off the North Expressway, on the old highway, **Meycauayan** is famed for its leather crafts and **Marilao** is noted for its pig farms and poultry production. The tanning carabao hides and manure exacerbate the smell, so hold your nose. Bulacan is known further for producing jewelry, leather crafts, clothing, and furniture. As an agricultural region, it also spins off unusual foods. Look for the sweetened dairy product called *pastillas de leche* in San Miguel de Mayumo and the vinegar from Paombong.

In the provincial capital, **Malolos** ⑫, on September 15, 1898, Emilio Aguinaldo convened the first Filipino legislative assembly, the Malolos Congress, which framed the Malolos Constitution. This was the first democratic constitution ever undertaken by a former Spanish colonial subject, and unique for Asia in splitting the roles of Church and state. The Malolos Congress met in **Barasoain Church**,

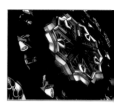

where former president Joseph Estrada took his oath of office in 1998. The **Barasoain Ecclesiastical Museum** (Mon–Fri 8am–3.30pm; free) stands on church grounds, showing antiques and local artifacts.

The revolutionary delegates' printing press stands along architecturally significant Parancillo Street. The historic town hall dates back to 1580, though the present structure was built around 1980. Around the corner is the private, ancestral Bautista House, with sculptures of Greek maidens on its facade.

On May 15, the town of **Pulilan**, 11km (7 miles) northeast of Malolos, beyond Plaridel, celebrates the Carabao Festival. Unlike other festivals in the region, this one stars the carabao (water buffalo). Thousands of carabao, adorned with flowers, parade to church where they kneel to be blessed.

A further 9km (6 miles) northeast is **Baliuag** (or Baliwag) **⓭**, a town once famous for its *buntal* (a type of reed) hats and furniture inlaid with carabao bone. Those interested in architecture and history may pass through **San Agustin Church**, a faithfully restored stone and brick structure, with a tall bell tower.

Thirty km (20 miles) north, **Madlum** and **Aguinaldo caves**, plus a mountain hideout, Biak-na-Bato, hid revolutionaries in the 1890s. Aguinaldo cave is known for cool, cold spring-infused breezes and an underground river, while pinnacle rocks put Madlum's caves on the map. Caves at Biak-na-Bato are filled with wildlife as well as stalactites. Guides on site lead cave tours. The nearby public springs at **Sibul** are famed for the medicinal effects of their clear waters. In the eastern portion of Bulacan stands the **Angat Reservoir**, providing approximately 80 percent of the water supply for Metropolitan Manila.

*San Fernando is known for its annual Christmas Lantern Festival.*

## Pampanga

This Central Plains province has edged its way onto people's travel plans as Clark Field's golf courses and duty-free shopping lure visitors, while Angeles makes a name for golf, gambling, and expat-driven nightlife.

**BELOW:** Clark Field and Mount Arayat.

On entering the province from Manila, you cannot help but notice the increasing prevalence of *lahar* (volcanic mud) – an ashen reminder of Mt Pinatubo's eruption in 1991. In Pampanga's low-lying areas, residents wage a constant battle against mudflows during the rainy season. Even the **FVR Megadike** – named for former president Fidel V. Ramos – despite its mighty name needs continual reconstruction in its efforts to contain *lahar* flows.

Local inhabitants, called Kapampangans, are not ethnically Tagalog like their neighbors. The first Pampanga settlers arrived in Manila Bay from Sumatra, Indonesia, around 1,700 years ago. Encountering an established population along the bay's shoreline, the Sumatrans moved up the Rio Grande de Pampanga and Rio Chico rivers to the plains. Soon, they had established large farming communities along the river banks. Spanish records attest to a tight Kapampangan community that met them with curiosity and great intelligence. Spanish firepower impressed the Kapampangan leaders, who, in exchange for privileges, chose to support the new leaders against the invading Chinese, Moros, Dutch, and British.

By the 18th century, a large *mestizo* Chinese community was well entrenched in Pampanga, descended from the Chinese who had fled the 17th-century massacres in Manila. The Chinese gradually took over large tracts of sugar cane and rice lands from the Kapampangan elite.

Pampanga's capital, **San Fernando**, noted in history as once being the country's capital, lies 66km (40 miles) north of Manila. Today, it is largely a commercial town, and one of three places where Chinese settled in large numbers. It is best visited during Christmas for the Lantern Festival: some lanterns are as large as 3 meters (10ft) in diameter.

**Bacolor**, temporary capital of the Philippines after the 1762 British invasion and devastated by Pinatubo's eruption, lies 9km (6 miles) southwest of San Fernando. Climb the Church of St William's belfry – half-buried by *lahar* – for a view of the ashen landscape. Along the Megadike is **Betis** and the beautiful

**BELOW:** a visitor to Clark Field poses for the camera.

interior of the Church of St James, reflecting the local Kapampangan woodcarving tradition. It is sometimes called the "Sistine Chapel of the Philippines" for its ceiling murals.

Fifteen kilometers (9 miles) northeast of San Fernando are Candaba and mountainous Arayat. **Candaba's swamps** are noted for their scenic beauty and the ducks from China that winter here. The 1,026-meter (3,366ft) **Mt Arayat** in Barrio Bano, 15 minutes from Angeles City, is 2km (1.2 miles) from **Arayat** proper. The national park offers swimming holes, and trekking and cycling trails, but there are no accommodations and some visitors have been put off by erosion and other evidence of logging.

## Angeles and Clark Field

West of Arayat, **Clark Field**, a major US military air base until its devastation by the eruption of Mt Pinatubo in 1991, has been transformed into the **Clark Special Economic Zone**. The US military left during the year of the volcanic eruption that also set back the whole region's economy.

Today the sedate American-designed former base is home to private resorts and golf courses, a casino, and giant duty-free stores that are more like malls. The duty-free shops sell everything from imported US grocery items to sporting goods. Former US military barracks and other installations used in part by the Philippine Air Force also occupy Clark. Texas Instruments and Yokohama Tires, among others, operate large plants here.

*Chess players on Angeles Field Avenue.*

**BELOW:** Angeles nightclub.

*Hot-air balloons at a festival in Angeles.*

**BELOW:** Lake Pinatubo crater lake.

chaotic main bar strip, Fields Avenue, sits right across a fence from the lush, quiet Clark development zone. The estimated 400 bars and restaurants in Angeles get much of their business now from Western expats, plus a growing number of South Koreans. Some long-stays have military backgrounds; others are tourists who never went home. Bars cover Old West themes such as Pony Tail and the Stampede as well as more suggestive names such as Bare Assets. On the quieter end of the strip and back one block, look to the Blue Boar Inn for beers, food, pool, and darts.

Restaurants in Angeles include two Thai eateries and a Japanese barbecue spot as well as countless places to fill up on Filipino chicken, fish, pork, and rice. A lavish Casino Filipino operates on the MacArthur Highway.

In stark contrast to all this revelry, the city is the venue for the unique, sombre and rather grisly **Seven Last Words Festival**. On Good Friday, performers clad in armor like Roman soldiers gather in Angeles City to re-enact Seven Last Words, a Christian

**Clark International Airport**, also called **Diosado Macapagal International Airport**, has become another entry-exit point into the northern Philippines for passengers seeking to bypass Manila. Flights from Clark go to foreign destinations such as Bangkok, Macau, Kuala Lumpur, and Seoul.

US military presence at Clark turned the Balibago district of the next-door city of **Angeles** ⑭ into a raging nightlife district. Balibago's

religious ritual involving Jesus Christ's final statements before death – and actual **crucifixion**. Ambulances wait on site to treat the devotees bleeding hands. The ritual is frowned on by the Vatican but relished by thousands of onlookers who share the passion. The city of Angeles also enthusiastically supports it as the event brings in media and gawkers from around the world. The half-century-old, annual ritual takes place around the same time elsewhere in Pampanga province.

The **Angeles City Flying Club** (tel: 045-865-1356; www.angelesflying. com) offers ultralight flights around Mt Arayat and Clark areas. Those who prefer thrills on the ground may end up at the amenities-loaded Mimosa Golf and Country Club (tel: 045-866-5143; www.mimosagolf-countryclub.com).

Victory Liner buses from Pasay in Manila to the Clark-Angeles complex stop at the Dau station after a two-hour drive. The same buses ply the highway to points further north, as well. Tricycle-taxis from the station ask as much as P100 more to reach Angeles proper. Be sure to haggle.

## Mt Pinatubo

Although 1,485-meter (4,872ft) **Mt Pinatubo** ⑮ stands on the eastern edge of Zambales Province, many treks and tours to the volcano originate in Angeles. Visitors can hike through the *lahar* (volcanic mud) areas or to the crater with a guide during the dry season, which is essentially the northern hemisphere's winter, or fly over the crater on clear days with Omni Aviation (tel: 045-892-6664, www.omniaviation.com).

Because of the unpredictability of flash floods and *lahar* flows, the military enforces a 16km (10-mile) off-limits area around Pinatubo during the wet season, which is from July to October. Check with the local tourism office (DOT Region III; tel: 045-961-2665/2612) before departing. Its eruption from June 1991 after a 600-year silence devastated farmland and left silt on offshore coral.

## Tarlac Province

A latecomer to the central plains, Tarlac was carved from Pampanga and Pangasinan in 1873, its population

**TIP**

One of the best ways to explore the stark moon-like volcanic terrain of Mt Pinatubo in Pampanga is from an ultralight (microlight) aircraft.

**BELOW:** Bataan Death March Monument.

## Death March Under the Sun

On the peninsula of Bataan, zero-point kilometer markers are found in the towns of Mariveles and Bagac, the starting points of the notorious Death March that took place during World War II.

In 1942, more than 75,000 Filipino and American prisoners – already weakened from lack of food and water – were forced to hike 100km (60 miles) up the peninsula to Japanese concentration camps in Tarlac. One tenth of the marchers perished along the road. Their route is now marked along Bataan's eastern coast. Outside Capas stands a monument to the fallen. Camp O'Donnell, 12km (7.5 miles) west of Capas, is the concentration camp that housed those who survived the ordeal.

being a cross section of Ilocanos, Pampangos, Pangasinenes, and Tagalogs. Although it is the region's major sugar-producing area, the province is best known for the infamous World War II Bataan Death March, which claimed the lives of thousands of Allied prisoners of war.

In Tarlac's upper reaches, those willing to find transportation can visit the 15-meter (50ft) -high Timangguyob Falls in San Clemente of Barangay Maasin, 40km (25 miles) north of Tarlac City. At just 6 meters (20ft) high, the Kiti-Calao waterfalls in the town of Mayantoc invite a 45-minute hike through a dense and diverse forest.

South of Tarlac City, near **Capas**, lies San Miguel, with Luisita Mall – a development by the family of former president Corazon Aquino. Here is the statue of Ninoy Aquino staggering on the airplane ladder (where he was shot) that used to be on Ayala Avenue in Makati.

**Nueva Ecija**, east of Tarlac, is the largest Central Plains province, and it's big on rice production. As

a tourist destination, Nueva Ecija offers little of interest except the pristine **Minalungao National Park** in General Tinio, 15km (9.3 miles) east of Barangay Pias. Parkland overlooks the narrow Penaranda River, which is lined with sheer limestone cliffs. Adventurers will also find dense forests and unexplored caves.

## Bataan and Zambales

**Mt Samat** on the Bataan Peninsula is the world-famous site of a fierce battle in 1942 before Filipino-American forces eventually surrendered to the Japanese. Near the summit stands a giant cross and the memorial Shrine of Valor. Several beach resorts are located between the communities of Orani and Mariveles.

Just north of **Olongapo City**, in Zambales Province, a road traveler will run into **Barrio Barretto**, where many of the retired US Navy veterans who once were stationed at Subic now run an eclectic batch of restaurants and seaside bars. A quiet strip of low-rises by day, these clubs roar to life after dark with dancing and drunken

madness. Check out the Mosquito bar and Night Riders.

Together with Bataan, Zambales was among the first provinces in Luzon to be brought under Spanish rule, when Juan de Salcedo plundered the region's western coast in 1572. He encountered a fierce and proud mountain people, the Zambal, who gave him such trouble that he mounted a punitive expedition to eradicate them. The indigenous Zambals have been pushed north, near Pangasinan.

## Subic Bay

The **Subic Bay Freeport Zone** ⓰, a former US Navy base, has been transformed into one of the country's most successful industrial and tourism centers. International charter flights bring in foreign tourists who mingle comfortably with the carloads of people from Manila who visit on the weekends.

The Freeport, accessible from Manila by modern highways, offers jungle tours, secure beaches, a casino, duty-free shopping, and the **Ocean Adventure** marine theme park (tel: 047-252-9000; www.oceanadventure.

com.ph; daily 9am–6pm; charge). Three types of dolphins, false killer whales, and sea lions inhabit the park. Offshore, local authorities are pursuing ecotourism in the bay's protected waters. Nearby Grande and Chiquita islands shelter the highest coral concentration in the bay, which is home to 75 species of fish. There is a resort on Grande Island, which is accessible by pumpboat. Divers in the bay will find up to six World War II shipwrecks.

Drive around the Binictican housing area to see a replica of a suburban American neighborhood built by the US Navy to house the families of sailors. It is now home to many expat investors. Or hike the Apaliin Trail to see the jungle plus a sea view from a lookout point. Visitors can get back to central Subic by boat. Out at night? Scout the sky for bats.

Driving west to San Marcelino and San Antonio, visitors may stop at Pundaquit, a jump-off point for tiny Capones Island, known for green waters and an old lighthouse. Northward, beach resorts dot the coastline.

*Magsaysay Avenue, the road into Olongapo City from the Subic Freeport, was lined with nightclubs during the days of the US Navy. Today, it is home to restaurants, money-changers, and shops selling navy mementoes.*

# ILOCOS REGION

Squeezed between the sea and the central
mountains, the Ilocos region has plenty to
interest the traveller. The wild coastline vies
for attention with the Spanish colonial
treasures of Vigan and the Unesco World
Heritage-listed Paoay church.

Manila

Perched on a narrow ledge along the rugged northwestern coast of Luzon is Ilocos, a wild place with many intimate charms. The coast rises from the South China Sea to rocky bluffs and rolling sand dunes. Here lie three coastal provinces once known for gold but now driven by farms and fisheries.

Adventurers will find understated resorts tucked away along broad South China Sea beaches where high waves have attracted surfers. Among the most accessible, most developed beaches around Ilocos are San Juan and Bauang in La Union Province, Hundred Islands in Pangasinan, Cabugao in Ilocos Sur, and Pagudpud on Bangui Bay in Ilocos Norte. Others are further from highways or lack places to stay the night. The coastline west of Laoag, for example, is one wide swathe of sand with virtually nothing built alongside.

Sometime after the 1st century, waves of migration swelled from Borneo to the northern Philippine coast. The seafarers flooded the coves, around which they built their communities (*ylocos*). With superior numbers and metal weapons, the immigrants soon pushed local tribes, such as the Tingguian (Itneg) headhunters, high into the bordering mountains. When the Spanish explorer Don Juan de Salcedo arrived in Vigan in 1572, he would have found thriving towns and an active trading economy run by Malay, Chinese, and Japanese settlers.

## Exploring Pangasinan

Three rivers flow west from the Cordillera, a Spanish term for mountain range, bringing water to the rice, tobacco, and sugar-cane fields of **Pangasinan** Province north of Manila along Luzon's west coast. The province is known best among tourists for its Hundred Islands national park,

**Main attractions**

HUNDRED ISLANDS
SAN JUAN SURFING
VIGAN SPANISH ARCHITECTURE
LA PAZ SAND DUNES
PAOAY CHURCH
MARCOS MEMORIAL MUSEUM
ADAMS WATERFALLS
BATANES ISLANDS

**LEFT:** Laoag River.
**RIGHT:** *burnay* pottery, Vigan.

islets off the coast popular with campers and birdwatchers. There are also a number of historic churches and a highway linking Manila to attractions farther north.

The first Pangasinan settlements developed along the coastline thousands of years ago. Inhabitants would catch pangasinan *bangus* (milkfish), putting it on menus throughout the country. The province is also rich in rice fields, and a chief industry is solar evaporation of salt from seawater.

Pangasinan's Lingayen Gulf has stood as a regional trading center since earliest times. Tattooed Zambal people and mountain Igorots came to barter gold nuggets for pigs, carabao (water buffalo), and rice. Ilocanos gradually came from the northern coast to trade, and finally settle, in Pangasinan. Later, the Chinese and Japanese arrived, exchanging silk, metals, ceramics, and mirrors for local indigo, fibers, sugar cane, beeswax, deerskin, and civet musk.

In the late 16th century, the Chinese corsair Limahong made his way to

Pangasinan, followed shortly by the Spanish conquistadors. The locals fought with the Spaniards against the Chinese, but once the alliance ended the natives of Pangasinan fled into the mountains to escape the clenched fist of Spanish rule. The Spaniards mounted expeditions against the escapees, with gold-hungry soldiers raping and looting as they progressed.

## Urdaneta and Lingayen

The National Highway passes through **Urdaneta**, which has a strip of fast-food eateries and is known for producing much of the nation's dried fish. *Bagoong* is also sold here – the muddy-colored, pungent Pinoy version of caviar that lends its flavor to most Ilocano dishes. Beyond Urdaneta, a turn-off leads 12km (7.5 miles) toward the coast, to the Shrine of Our Lady of Manaoag. Faith healing is heavily practiced there.

Along the Romulo Highway, just past the Tarlac town of **San Clemente**, and near the Pangasinan community of Mangatarem is the **Manleluag Springs National Park**, with a hot

spring nestled in the foothills of the Zambales Mountains.

A road from Bugallon leads to **Lingayen ⑰**, a sprawling old capital by the sea, with two distinct sections. The older section, built inland by the Spanish in their particular style, has all buildings facing the town plaza. Market day is a portrait in small-town trade, with some hard bargaining among the vendors under their large *buri* fans, which are used as sunscreens. The Americans built the newer part of Lingayen by the sea. Today, although this section is a bit down-at-the-heel, its spread of wide-crowned flame trees can be a startling first sight. The provincial capital building is modeled on early American colonial architecture, with marble columns and a golden eagle.

Between Lingayen and **Dagupan**, to the east, lie many World War II battle-scene beaches, with memorials recording where the Japanese landed in December 1941, and where Americans came ashore in January 1945. From Lingayen, a 40km (25-mile) coast road leads west to **Alaminos**.

## Hundred Islands

At Alaminos, signs lead to Lucap, where numerous motorized *banca* wait at the pier to ferry travelers to the **Hundred Islands National Recreation Area ⑱** (also a national park comprising 124 volcanic islands). **Quezon Island**, the largest, has a beach, pavilions, toilets, and viewing decks, while Children's Island is for campers. **Governor's Island** is more secluded, particularly the small beach at the back. With a little urging, boat operators also offer tours of the lesser-known islands, such as the one named after former first lady Imelda Marcos. There are no diving facilities on the islands, and some underwater explorers bring their own equipment. Camping, fishing, and birdwatching are common activities.

Few venture beyond Alaminos to **Bolinao ⑲**, just an hour away. It is regrettable, because the old town and its *barangay* and islands are where Pangasinan's heritage maintains its ancient patterns. Scenic Cape Bolinao is an emerging beach area with a string of comfortable resorts along

**TIP**

If visiting one of the isolated beaches in the Hundred Islands, be sure to pack lunch for lack of food for sale. Bring plenty of drinking water (it can get hot) and shoes or slippers to wear in the water to avoid getting cut by the sharp coral.

**BELOW:** Hundred Islands.

the coast. The **Bolinao Museum** (Mon–Sat 9am–4.30pm; donation) stands as the cultural link, displaying some important archeological finds from backyards and beaches, including gold bracelets from under coconut trees and ceramic shards washed up by floods. Treasure-seekers have turned up Tang, Song, and Ming porcelain, as well as skeletal remains adorned with gold earrings and necklaces. All of these are considered significant links in 7th–15th-century Philippine history, though many of the finds have ended up in private collections.

One Bolinao treasure that has not lent itself to cultural piracy is the **Church of St James**, in the center of town. Niches on both sides of the facade still have ancient wooden *santos*, aged by wind and sun, their features blurred by time. Generations of people from Bolinao have lived unchanged lifestyles in this quiet spot, still speaking a dialect distinct from their Pangasinan neighbors.

To the port of Bolinao, and the surrounding islands of Silaqui, Santiago, and Dewey, have come Chinese corsairs, English and Dutch freebooters, and Moro pirates. **Santiago Island** has been home to more than its share of fugitives, many of them escaped slaves. Today, Santiago is a haven for scuba divers and features coral-laden Fourteen-Mile Reef.

Bolinao also berths the country's second-highest lighthouse and a University of the Philippines effort to save near extinct marine species by cultivating the same.

To the south, Dendro Beach is a golden-sand beach near the Piedra Point lighthouse. In Agno, umbrella rocks dot the mouth of the Balincaguing River, looking more like toadstools than umbrellas. Farther south, **Tambobong**'s White Beach is accessible through Burgos. In the center of the Cape Bolinao peninsula, **Bani** and **Mabini** offer excellent cave exploring. Those near Mabini in the dry season can enter Cacupangan Cave to see its underground river.

## La Union Province

Just north of Pangasinan lies La Union, a coastal province founded in 1854 that today serves as an administrative center of the Ilocos region. Travelers seek out La Union mainly for its surfer-friendly beaches, San Juan most noted among them, along its lengthy north–south South China Sea coastline.

If traveling on a Partas or Maria de Leon bus bound for the provincial capital, be sure to request San Fernando, La Union, not San Fernando, Pampanga. **San Fernando** bursts into colorful life on market day. A dragon-encrusted Chinese temple called Macho overlooks the city.

The La Union town of **Rosario** stands out for roadside stalls selling dried fish 24 hours a day. **Santo Tomas** claims to sell the freshest, cheapest oysters in the country. A woodcarving trade also thrives along the highway. The **Agoo-Damortis National Seashore Park** sits on a hooking point in Lingayen Gulf, near **Agoo**. The

*Vigan school children take part in a Valentine's Day Parade.*

**BELOW:** San Juan surfer.

Shrine of Our Lady of Charity in the Baroque-styled Agoo Basilica attracts visitors on Good Friday, when patron saints are paraded through the city's streets. The adjacent **Museo de Iloko** (Mon–Fri 9am–4.30pm; donation) houses artifacts of Ilocos culture.

Further north, 10km-long (6-mile) **Bauang Beach**, with fine grayish sand, is one long strip of resorts. Water sports, mountain-biking, cultural events, and a water parade cap the Rambak Festival here on Easter Sunday. Along the road, stalls sell sweet green grapes. Just inland is **Naguilian**, the *basi*-making capital of the Ilocos region.

## Seafood and surf

The **La Union Botanical Gardens** lie 8km (5 miles) east of San Fernando, and the region's best medical facility, Lorma Hospital, is just north of town. Out on the nearby beach are quieter cottages and small resorts. While here, try the fresh seafood, including a dish known as Jumping Salad – chunks of raw fish cured in a light vinegar, spiced with garlic and chilies.

Six kilometers (4 miles) north of San Fernando, along Monaliza Beach in **San Juan** ⓴, novice surfers can try the sandy beach break fronting La Union Surf Resort. The more experienced can handle a rockier point in front of Monaliza. The best season is November–February, when competitions are held; by July, typhoon swells are bringing in the waves. Beyond its regionally famous surfing attraction, San Juan is a pottery-making town, with a century-old church.

In **Bacnotan**, watch local silk production at the Don Mariano Marcos Memorial State University. In the mountains to the east, around **Bagulin**, trails along the Bagulin-Naguilian River offer limited trekking, although hiking is better in the Cordillera Mountains.

**Balaoan**, along the National Highway, features a sprawling treehouse that can be seen from the main road. The church of St Catherine, in **Luna**, houses an image of Our Lady of Namacpacan, patroness of Ilocano travelers, while **Bangar**, just before the Ilocos Sur border, is a known center

**DRINK**

Basi, the local Ilocano wine, is a fermented sugar-cane concoction colored with duhat bark. It is quite good, sometimes tasting like port. But the taste differs from maker to maker, so sample first.

**BELOW:** harvesting tobacco leaves in Candon.

*Vigan Heritage Village.*

nearly reaching the water's edge in some places. Like La Union to the south, Ilocos Sur's quiet, sparsely developed beaches draw surfers, but its main attraction is the immaculately preserved Spanish-style city of Vigan.

Principal crops in this farming-heavy province are tobacco, rice, and corn. To overcome deficiencies of the sandy soil, most Ilocanos have turned to trade and handicrafts. Towns along the coast extract salt from seawater. In San Esteban, locals quarry rock to make mortars and grindstones. San Vicente, Vigan, and San Ildefonso specialize in woodcarving, importing raw materials from mountainous provinces. Skilled silversmiths work in Bantay. Other towns make saddles, harnesses, slippers, mats, brooms, and hats.

for making native *bolo* knives and the labor-intensive weaving of wide blankets. Those venturing offshore to Research Reef near San Fernando (10 minutes by boat from the Ocean Deep Resort in Barangay Canaoay) will find an intricate cave with tunnels, sand, and lobsters.

## Ilocos Sur Province

**BELOW:** antique store, Vigan Heritage Village.

The province of **Ilocos Sur** twists along the coast as the narrowest Ilocano province, with the Cordilleras

In the town of **Tagudin**, a functioning sundial built by the Spanish in 1848 sits in front of the Municipal Hall. **Candon** has a beach complex with a huge swimming pool, and a thriving nightlife. Just beyond Candon, roadside stalls sell *itak*, the local *bolo* knife.

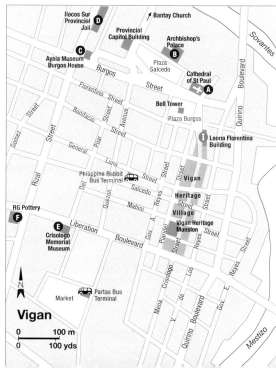

**Vigan**

0   100 m
0   100 yds

**Santiago** has a short stretch of golden sand, while in the next town, **San Esteban**, rocky Apatot Beach and a Spanish stone tower built to keep watch for marauding Moro pirates bring in travelers. Now a national landmark, a centuries-old church that served as a fortress during the 1986 revolution stands in **Santa Maria**. Near Santa Maria is **Pinsal Falls**, a setting for many films, and home of the footprints of the Ilocano legendary giant, Angalo.

*Carabao* (water buffaloes) wander on the beach, and fishermen drag their nets in waist-deep water by the shoreline. Farther north, the elevated **Santa Maria Church** in the town of **Bantay** is one of four Baroque churches in the country designated as Unesco World Heritage Sites, offers a good view of the area. The nearby bell tower was built in part as a lookout for Moro pirates.

## Vigan sights

**Vigan ㉑**, the provincial capital of Ilocos Sur, was built by the Spaniards in 1572, their third settlement on the islands after Cebu and Intramuros in modern-day Manila. It remains everything that Intramuros should be: a living, breathing repository of Spanish architecture and Filipino culture, all within a pedestrian-friendly central district.

The **Cathedral of St Paul Ⓐ**, built in 1641, stands in the center of Vigan. In 1758, a royal decree transferred the northern Luzon Diocese of Nueva Segovia to St Paul's, making it the ecclesiastical center of the whole area. This grandiose stone structure is 86 meters (280ft) long, and supported by buttresses. Stretching out in front of St Paul's is the elliptical **Plaza Salcedo**, with a bell tower separate from the church, as is the style in earthquake country. Revolutionary Gabriela Silang, the first woman to lead a revolt against the Spanish, was hanged in the plaza in 1763.

North of Plaza Salcedo is the **Archbishop's Palace Ⓑ** (Mon–Fri by appointment; free), displaying sliding *capiz* shell windows, floral motifs, gardens, and a priceless

**BELOW:** a café in the Vigan Heritage Village.

## Vigan's Architectural Heritage

Followers of European architecture will lose themselves in Vigan, a compact city that has vigorously fought to keep its Spanish-style buildings alive. In the late 16th century, Don Juan de Salcedo entered the town to convince the Ilocanos that a Spanish garrison might be useful against the headhunting neighbors they had earlier displaced. Before long, the Spanish introduced corn, cocoa, tobacco, and Christianity to the area. They built churches, fortifications, and schools. A Spanish friar was appointed as the agricultural officer, financial adviser, teacher, and architect.

Compulsory native labor and hired Chinese artisans produced Spain's most lasting landmarks, including the grand cathedral. To help withstand earthquakes, masons concocted a durable mix of coral, limestone, and sugar for the bricks used for the cathedral and outlying churches. The 17th and 18th centuries saw a flowering of European Baroque in the Philippines, now most evident in Vigan's grandiloquent plastered brick houses, complete with hardwood floors, *capiz*-shell windows, and intricate grille work. These are now the ancestral homes of once-wealthy Chinese, Spanish, and *mestizo* merchants and artisans. In recent years, some of the two- and three-story buildings have been refashioned into cafés and boutique hotels.

collection of ecclesiastical artifacts. It served as a garrison for US forces in 1899.

### Vigan museum and jail

West of the plaza stands **Ayala Museum**  (Tue–Sat 8.30–11.30am and 1.30–4.30pm; charge), also called Burgos House, the birthplace of martyr Father Jose Burgos and the best repository of Ilocano culture in the region. The well-maintained house features a fine collection of antiques, icons, and a library of English-language books that visitors can read while on site.

The **Ilocos Sur Provincial Jail** ①, to the north of Burgos House, directly behind the Provincial Capitol Building, is open to visitors. It dates from 1855 in present form, although a jail was first built on this site in 1657. The open atmosphere of the prison is a refreshing change. Few are confined to solitary cells, families live inside the walls on weekends, and inmates make handicrafts, and take classes. Former Philippine president Elpidio

Quirino was born in the small room up the wooden stairway on November 16, 1890, when his father was warden of the prison.

### Vigan Heritage Village

Looping back to the south of Plaza Salcedo and St Paul's, one finds the best street food in town – crispy empanadas dipped in *basi* vinegar – around **Plaza Burgos**. From here, the cobblestoned Mena Crisologo Street stretches southward along Vigan's most famous attraction, the old ancestral houses of the former Mestizo District, now called the **Vigan Heritage Village**. The well-ventilated brick structures, with red-tiled roofs and *capiz* shell windows, served as homes to the wealthy, who made money trading indigo dyes, *abel* (woven) fabrics, gold, and tobacco.

Today, horse-drawn carriages ferry visitors for P50 per ride through the lovingly preserved area that now houses antique shops, bakeries, craft shops, hotels, and a few funeral parlors with impressive, antique hearses.

**BELOW:** horse-drawn carriages, Vigan Heritage Village.

Unesco has contributed funds to maintain and renovate the village. Vendors sell basketry, furniture, and locally made Basi Revolt-brand plum wines.

Much of the old architecture that catches the eye now houses cafés, restaurants, and boutique hotels charging P1,500 to upwards of P3,000 per night. Visitors to the restored Vigan Heritage Mansion may order from a rooftop bar and sip away in a *nipa* hut with views of the mountains.

Other Vigan attractions include the **Crisologo Memorial Museum** **E** (tel: 077-722-8520; Sun–Fri 8.30–11.30am, 1.30–4.30pm; free), on Liberation Boulevard. Upstairs, original furnishings of a typical ancestral home are on show. The first floor features family memorabilia of Congressman Floro Crisologo who was assassinated in Vigan Cathedral in 1970. Don't miss **RG Pottery** **F** at the western end of Liberation Boulevard, where the famous Ilocano jars are made for storing vinegar, *bagoong* (local fermented fish paste), and the local wine. Built by the owner's grandfather, a model

dragon kiln on the site attests to Chinese influences in Ilocos.

The local fiesta falls on January 25, honoring the conversion of St Paul. Viva Vigan, a cultural festival, occurs during the first week in May. This is a good chance to see Ilocano culture on parade, in song, dance, and drama. For more information, visit the tourist office in the historic **Leona Florentina Building**, at the northern end of Mena Crisologo Street.

North of Vigan in **Magsingal**, the **Museum of Ilocano Culture and Artifacts** has a collection of early trade porcelains, Neolithic tools, weaponry, baskets, agricultural implements, and old Ilocano beadwear.

A guesthouse and picnic huts can be found along the white sands of Pug-os Beach, in **Cabugao**, a 30–45-minute drive north of Vigan. Warm-water waves at this cove welcome swimmers and snorkelers, but they leave a wide beach even at high tide. The one Cabugao resort rents beachside rooms next to a pool and

**BELOW:** Vigan potter.

**TIP**

Take an air-con long-distance bus from Vigan to the Partas terminal in Laoag (15-minute walk from Downtown) to see snippets of the coastline, industry, and scenery that make Ilocos unique. Buses leave once an hour.

a restaurant-bar, but in some seasons the whole compound comes alive with stinging red ants. Further north, the town of **Sinait** has a century-old church where a Black Nazarene, found floating in a casket off the coast in the 17th century, is enshrined and fêted in early May.

Inland, look for the **Cervantes Eco-Trail**, a route through verdant mountains punctuated by pines, orchids, and more than a dozen waterfalls.

## Ilocos Norte

This northern province has drawn travelers lately for sand-dune surfing in **La Paz** and Paoay, as well as remote coves along a rocky coast, plus hikes amid the waterfalls of Adams. Most visitors pass through the laid-back capital, Laoag.

Ilocos Norte is rich in timber, minerals, fisheries, and agriculture. Garlic, the principal cash crop, gives parts of the province a peculiar aroma. It is also noted as the home province of the Philippines' longest-serving president, Ferdinand Marcos.

## Laoag

The provincial capital, **Laoag** ㉒ is a friendly, inexpensive, agricultural hub, nearly two hours' drive north of Vigan.

In the city center look for **St William's Cathedral**, an example of Spanish-style earthquake-proof Baroque architecture dating from the 16th century. Outside the cathedral's quiet, breezy cavern of pews stands the Sinking Bell Tower, so mired in the sandy soil that, if it weren't for the do-not-enter signs, you would have to stoop to pass through the doorway.

In the center of the nearby city plaza, the **Tobacco Monopoly Monument** commemorates the lifting in 1881 of the century-long Spanish tobacco monopoly, which forced locals to grow tobacco solely for delivery to the government. The **Ilocos Norte Museum** at General Luna and Llanes streets (tel: 077-770-3836, www.museoilocosnorte.com; charge) showcases the region's economic, ethnic, and historical trends. In Aurora Park, the fountain sculpture shows the Ilocano ideal of the perfect woman: her arms draped in garlic bulbs and tobacco leaves – presumably grown in the province. In the quiet residential streets outside Downtown, scout for ancestral homes where caretakers may allow free entrance for small fees.

Some international tourists visit Laoag especially for its 77-hectare (190-acre), beach-side, Spanish-style Fort Ilocandia Resort and Casino (www.fortilocandia.com.ph).

Near Laoag, surfers who prefer land to water have discovered the **La Paz Sand Dunes,** a 45-hectare (110-acre) geological monument located about 6km (4 miles) from Laoag. The hummocks of 10–30 meters (33–100ft) high form a part of the Ilocos Norte Sand Dunes that extend some 52km (32 miles) from the town of Currimao south of Laoag to Pasuquin north of Laoag. Ask in Laoag about 4X4 rentals. Also near the provincial capital is **Bacarra**, one of two places in the country where 17-stringed wooden

**BELOW:** Cathedral of St Paul, Vigan.

harps are made. Bacarra is also known for its quake-damaged bell tower.

## From Badoc to Sarrat

In the province's southerly town of **Badoc,** reproductions of works by 19th-century master Filipino painter Juan Luna are exhibited at **Luna House** (Tue–Sat 9am–5pm; donation). The Badoc Church also warrants a visit, with its wooden image of La Virgen Milagrosa, patroness of the Catholic Diocese of Laoag. Visitors may hop 15km (9 miles) north from here to **Currimao**, once host to a thriving tobacco monopoly. Today, tourists to the Spanish-designed town of brick buildings enjoy its beach, which has jagged outcrops of coral formations

From Currimao, a side road leads 10km (6 miles) to **Paoay** ㉓. A Unesco World Heritage Site, Paoay Church combines the features of earthquake-proof Baroque – such as massive lateral buttresses – with an Asian quality reminiscent of Javanese temples. Built of coral blocks at the turn of the 18th century, its bell tower served as an observation post during the Philippine revolution and was occupied by guerrillas under Japanese occupation.

Just north of the town is **Paoay Lake National Park,** site of a 400-hectare (988-acre) body of water that was likely formed by an earthquake. Ferdinand Marcos once made himself at home at **Balay Ti Amianan** (now a museum called Malacañang of the North; Tue–Sat 9am–5pm; free), built overlooking the lake in 1976 as a 60th birthday present from his wife, Imelda. A short drive east is the Marcos Mausoleum in **Batac.** Loom-weaving is a major activity of the area, producing textiles with ethnic Ilocano designs.

**San Nicolas**, on the south bank of the Laoag River, is the pottery capital of the Ilocos and here, the first church in the region, made of stone and brick, was built in 1591. Today, the town functions as the province's industrial center.

## Marcos Museum

The embattled Ferdinand Marcos was born in **Sarrat**, home to the **Marcos**

*The stones in the Bacarra River reputedly possess healing powers. Do not be alarmed to see older people rubbing them onto their skins.*

**LEFT:** Sinking Bell Tower, Laoag.
**BELOW:** La Paz sand dunes.

*Most visitors to the Marcos Mausoleum in Batac think the waxy body on display of the former president looks too perfect to be real. To this day, it is unclear where exactly Imelda has laid her late husband's body to rest.*

**Museum** (Mon–Sat 8am–noon, 2–5pm; free). The museum houses family memorabilia, including the grand four-poster bed in which the man was born, the clock beside it set to the time of his birth. His only son, Ferdinand "Bongbong" Marcos Jr, formerly served as the Ilocos Norte governor, and his daughter Imee has held the job since 2010.

Sarrat's **Santa Monica Church and Convent**, which are connected by a massive bridge-staircase across a river, are well-preserved specimens of colonial architecture. Further inland, in **Dingras**, are some church ruins and an old Spanish well.

## North from Laoag

Salt-making prevails in **Pasuquin**, north of Laoag, not far from the phonetically inviting Seksi Beach. Cape Bojeador lighthouse, near **Burgos**, the tallest in the country, rewards a climb up a narrow, iron spiral staircase with a dramatic view of the northern coast. A short drive east, the visitor can enjoy an even loftier view from the observation deck in

**Bangui** where coves and golden-sand beaches of Bangui Bay spread out on the vista.

**Pagudpud** on Bangui Bay is known for its fresh lobsters and has excellent coral reefs and beaches. The reef off Mayraira Beach is virtually untouched. From here, there is a sweeping ocean vista along the Patapat Viaduct, a bridge at the foot of a cliff in the north Cordillera mountain range.

Also on the northwest coast, local tourism officials are pushing visits to the hard-to-reach, untouched white sands of the Malingay Cove blue lagoon as well as Saud White Sand Beach (a resort operates there; see Travel Tips Accommodations). Transportation to points further north can be tough, as one must ride the back of a motorcycle-taxi from the highway. Those who go that far often make guided treks of 40 minutes to 12 hours among the 14 documented waterfalls near the town of **Adams**, inland from Luzon's northernmost coast. The tourist office in Laoag (tel: 077-771-1473; dotlaoag@digitelone.com) can recommend guides.

**BELOW:** San Agustin Church, Paoay.
**RIGHT:** Marcos Museum, Sarrat.

# Remote Batanes

**These wind-beaten, mountainous northernmost islands in the Philippines have few signature attractions, but visitors may see the small, intimate population at work building boats.**

Beyond the northern tip of Luzon is the country's smallest province, mountainous **Batanes**. The Ivatan people, of Malay stock, and émigré Ilocanos inhabit these 10 isolated islands, 160km (100 miles) north of Luzon and 190km (120 miles) south of Taiwan.

The islands came under Spanish control only in 1788, when the locals were persuaded (under threat of force) to move to the lowlands and adopt Western dress and Christianity. The US took over from the Spanish in 1899, introducing a public school and improving local infrastructure. Today, the 230-sq-km (90-sq-mile) islands are noted for their unspoiled marine environment, natural beauty compared to that of New Zealand, and the signature all-weather headgear of the Ivatans, known as *vakul*. Batanes is also known for nearly impenetrable stone and limestone block buildings and churches, with thick walls and thatched roofs to withstand typhoons.

To survive, the Ivatans must be self-sufficient, farming the green hills. Garlic, the leading export, is harvested from February to April. Schoolchildren lead the family's livestock out to graze early in the morning, spend the day at school, and later fetch the animals in the evening. The Ivatans further keep busy building new rounded-bottom boats to replace those lost to the rough seas.

## Island-hopping

The capital, Basco, is a one-hour flight from Laoag or Tuguegarao. The dry season is from April to June, when the winds are calm and the sea smooth. Typhoon season follows. From December to February the islands get rain and temperatures in the teens. Transportation and communications are generally unreliable, so visitors should be adventurous without a tight schedule. A few jeepneys ply the island roads, with *carabao* (water buffalo) carriages heading into the farmlands. Boat *travel* can be canceled altogether in rough weather.

**ABOVE:** typical Batanes house. **RIGHT:** Sabtang Island.

Batan, Sabtang, and Itbayat are the main islands, with a commuter flight reaching Itbayat. Their towns are anchored by Catholic churches, about 200 years old. Local cottage industries include making ropes, doormats, baskets, hats, and fishing nets. Specific attractions on these main islands include Chadpidan and White beaches, plus a third, Nakaboang, that features a cave. Inland look for the prehistoric burial caves in the town of Itbayat.

## Open doors

Few people live on the islands of Dequey, Siayan, Mabudis, Ibuhos, Diogo, North, or Y'ami. Batanes has a population of only 18,000. That means no need for formality – most inhabitants leave their doors and windows wide open.

For more information on travel in the islands, contact Batanes Eco-cultural Tourism Cooperative (tel: 0919-369-5341; michaeladalla@yahoo.com).

# NORTHEAST LUZON

Luzon's isolated rural provinces straddling the towering Sierra Madre mountains, the remote Cagayan Valley, and offshore islands are gaining a name for caving, trekking, and surfing.

**E**co-adventure is scrawled across this landmass in the far north of the Philippines. Though linked to Manila by road, the region still stands out for its relatively isolated mountain forests and undeveloped wind-sculpted beaches. Travelers also go to see a series of deep caves, through which rivers may run. Almost the entire northeast of Luzon Island is characterized by rolling hills, secret beaches, wide vistas, and dramatic drops into the rolling Pacific Ocean.

The Cagayan valley is a structural depression, located between tributaries of the Cagayan River flowing from the Cordillera Central mountains in the west, the thickly forested Sierra Madre mountains towering over the Philippine Sea in the east, and the Caraballo mountains in the south. Such isolation has kept the region rural and disconnected from goings-on elsewhere in the country.

Like much of the Philippines, the far northeast leans largely on farming. Growers have historically prized the region for tobacco, and tilapia fish aquaculture has been added to the cornucopia. Tourism is starting to peek through as a money-maker as visitors try beaches and mountain treks.

Cebu Pacific flies from Manila to the northeast's regional hubs of

Cauayan and Tuguegarao. Dalin Bus (tel: 02-722-7999) runs coaches from Manila to Tuguegarao. Local buses, jeepneys, and tricycles handle shorter trips within the region. Private pump-boats link mainland Luzon to its islets.

## Cagayan

Through this province flows the country's longest river, and within it dwells one of the richest archeological sites in the Philippines. At one time Pleistocene elephants and rhinos roamed the region, while seafaring

**Main attractions**
CALLAO CAVES
PALAUI ISLAND
PALANAN WILDERNESS AREA
SIERRA MADRE TREKKING
BALER SURFING

**LEFT:** white-water rafting on the Cagayan River. **RIGHT:** local transportation, Tuguegarao.

*Busy downtown street in Tuguegarao.*

**BELOW:** St Peter's Cathedral.

For a one-stop lesson on the province's history, visit the **Cagayan Museum and Historical Research Center** (tel: 078-446-1574; Mon–Fri 8am–noon, 1–5pm; free). Look for the extensive collection of fossils, Iron-Age pottery, and china from the Ming and Song dynasties. To see Cagayan's modern grandeur, go to the Provincial Capitol Compound for a view of rolling hills, the Cagayan River, and Sierra Madre mountains.

St Peter's Cathedral, built in 1761, offers the usual evidence of Cagayan's link with Spain. Nearby, San Jacinto Chapel was the first chapel in Tuguegarao, built in 1724. The Tuguegarao Horno, where old Spanish kiln bricks were baked for building the cathedral and chapel, still lies at the south end of town.

Neolithic Ybanag villagers dominated the human landscape. Cagayan also has the Philippines' largest remaining lowland forest and its longest cave system. Economically, it thrives on agricultural and mineral resources.

**Tuguegarao** ㉔, the capital of Cagayan, is an hour's flight from Manila. Bus lines also ply the Manila–Tuguegarao route. Tricycles and jeepneys move people around town, which is also walkable. There are a few modest places to stay.

## Callao Caves

The **Callao Caves** are the longest and second deepest in the Philippines. While no one knows the exact number of caves, best estimates top 300, only 30 of which have been mapped. The village of Callao, in Peñablanca

municipality, serves as the gateway to these underground treasures.

Caving here caters for all levels of ability. For the novice, easy passages lead to rock formations, stalagmites, and stalactites. For the hardcore caver, rarer gems such as calcite rafts, crystalline waterfalls, and gypsum formations await after hours of negotiating subterranean rivers, plus rappel drops.

Inside the Callao Caves Park is a spot called Mororan, known for its continuous self-generated rain shower. In the same complex, jump off the natural limestone diving boards and swim the clear waters flowing from the Pinacanauan River. Peñablanca municipality also holds the underground treasures of Sierra Cave and the Odessa Cave System, the technically challenging Lhoret Cave, and Don Don, with its roller-coaster crawls.

Since Callao Caves are protected, permission from the Department of Environment and Natural Resources (tel: 078-844-1621) is required. It is best to hire an accredited guide who will arrange the permit and serve as an escort. Guides are found at the park entrance.

## Rio Grande de Cagayan

**Rio Grande de Cagayan**, the longest river in the Philippines, bisects Cagayan Valley from north to south. It is home to various fish, including *lurung*, considered the rarest in the country. Bunton Bridge – the second longest in the Philippines – crosses the Rio Grande de Cagayan.

On 11 hectares (27 acres) of rolling terrain overlooking the river can be found **Iguig Calvary Hills**. Arranged across the undulating site are life-sized concrete structures depicting Christ and the Fourteen Stations of the Cross amid a cluster of Spanish relics such as a brick stairway, a three-centuries-old well, and Dominican convent ruins.

## North to Aparri and Fuga Island

At the northern end of the valley, past **Gattaran**, site of Tanlagan Falls, lies **Camalaniugan**, where the aptly named Bell of Antiquity is located. It dates back to 1595.

*The first known cave-diving expedition to the Callao Caves took place only in 1997. It discovered cave formations in still pristine condition.*

**BELOW:** Callao Caves.

*Don Hermanas Islands, in legend, were two sisters who bade goodbye to their husbands and were left waiting hundreds of years for their return.*

On the coast, **Aparri** has a following for marlin and sailfish fishing. Around town, the coastline spreads out into a run of beaches, tangled estuaries, and swamps. Here, ancient tribes once wove cloth, baked clay, and fashioned fishing and hunting implements from the bamboo that grew in their forests. If in Aparri, look for the Hotel Aparri (tel: 078-888-2850) on Rizal Street.

**In Buguey**, east of Aparri and the oldest Spanish foothold on this coast, visitors may still hear older people playing 19th-century wooden harps, unusual any place else in the country. West of Aparri, bamboo craftwork thrives in **Sanchez-Mira**.

Also on the north coast, check out **Fuga Island** ㉕, northwest of Aparri. Some of its beaches glow pink with pulverized coral and attract visitors for scuba diving or snorkeling. Wild honey gathered from the interior forests and an ancient church in the old town are the fringe benefits of a trip to Fuga.

### Palaui Island

White herons that flock to the rice fields near towns along the northern coast of Cagayan may keep travelers company on the 1.5-hour drive from Aparri to the northeastern tip of the province at Port San Vicente.

Off this coast is **Palaui Island** ㉖. Its white beaches, steep, rugged cliffs, and the surrounding Babuyan Channel are enticingly remote. Wave-polished corals, seashells, and rock formations sprouting like mushrooms make the waters ideal for diving, snorkeling, or swimming. Every year, national and international game-fishing competitions are held on the island. Climb up the old Spanish lighthouse to take in the unlimited view of the **Don Hermanas Islands**, jutting out of the South China Sea.

Among the north-coast destinations, the relatively large island of Palaui is most accessible. Jotay Resort (tel: 078-372-0560; www.jotayresort.com) organizes boat trips in conjunction with a local operator.

### Isabela

Isabela Province offers one of the easiest gateways into the Sierra Madre, in addition to caves and a mega resort-casino.

**BELOW:** a peaceful stretch of the Cagayan River.

The rich mountain soil of **Isabela**'s grassy plains and forests grows tobacco as well as rice. Passers-by may also see cows grazing on the plains. **Ilagan**, the capital, is accessible by land and air from Manila. Modest hotels and pension houses can be found around town.

Travelers use Ilagan to launch a journey toward **Santa Victoria Caves**, located at Fuyot National Recreation Area. The multi-chambered cave shelters a natural swimming pool that's ideal for caving and birdwatching.

North of Ilagan in **Tumauini**, the century-old church has a round bell tower with decorated friezes. Southeast of the capital in **San Mariano**, hike toward the gateway to the 200,000-hectare (500,000-acre) **Palanan Wilderness Area** ㉗. Palanan's forests, which are about the most accessible part of the giant Sierra Madre range, make up 10 percent of the country's remaining primary rainforest. Inside the biologically diverse park, visitors may spot a Philippine eagle and numerous native species of flora and fauna. Palanan and the

surrounding area are some of the last places where the Agta Negritoes still follow traditional lifestyles. Boats and small planes also reach the wilderness area from other parts of the northeast.

The town of **Cauayan** houses the Isabela Hotel and Resort, site of the only Casino Filipino in the region. This resort, grander than its peers elsewhere in the country, features water slides, horseback riding, cycling, and roller-skating lanes. Short flights to Palanan use the airstrip here. At the southern entrance of **Santiago**, to the southwest, look for a picturesque view of rice fields against an urban backdrop of buildings and housing.

Elsewhere in Isabela, the beach of **Dinapigue** is popular for its white sands and crystal waters. It is not far from the **Sierra Madre National Park**.

## Quirino

Adventure travel is the byword for this province of jagged Sierra Madre peaks. In the upper Cagayan River Basin, **Quirino** stands ringed by the peaks of the Sierra Madre and Mamparang

*Unlike the churches of Cagayan, which were built in the earlier colonial Baroque style, Isabela's, strung out in squat dignity along the National Highway, show a simpler antique Spanish architecture, with unrestored red brickwork.*

**BELOW:** lush Cagayan valley scenery.

*Sabang Beach is a popular surf spot.*

**BELOW:** boats moored on Sabang Beach.
**RIGHT:** underground river, near Sabang Beach.

ranges. Generally mountainous and agricultural, like most of the region, the landscapes are largely pristine. Populated by waves of people drawn here by its vast natural resources, the province was until the 20th century occupied mostly by Dumagats or Negritos, the aboriginal inhabitants of the Philippines. Some still live in the Sierra Madre.

A traveler can see right away how remote it is: **Cabarroguis**, the provincial capital, is accessible via a seven-hour bus journey from Manila to Santiago in neighboring Isabela Province, from where jeepneys run to the town.

Cool yourself at the forested **Bisangal Falls**, some 35km (21 miles) from Cabarroguis. Nearby **Aglipay Caves**, a series of 38 inter-linking caves, features well-preserved stalagmites and stalactites. **Maddela**, accessible from San Agustin in southern Isabela Province, offers some of the best whitewater in the archipelago.

**Governor Rapids** has a gigantic perpendicular wall and deep bluish water.

## Nueva Vizcaya

Approaching **Santa Fe** from Manila, the entry into Nueva Vizcaya is marked by a gradual ascent into the brown foothills of the Caraballo Mountains. On a zigzagging road through the 915-meter (3,000ft) -high **Dalton Pass**, history recorded a long, bloody battle between Philippine-American troops and the rear guard of the Japanese army toward the end of World War II. A memorial now sits on a hill at the pass.

At **Aritao**, St Dominic Cathedral shows vestiges of the grandeur of this old town, but there is little else to see. Beyond it lies **Bambang**, a dusty 15km (9 miles) with a geographical curiosity – the snow-like hill at Salinas Salt Springs, which spews salty water into the mountain air.

In the same area look for Villa Margarita Mountain Resort, with spring-fed pools set in a citrus plantation (tel: 078-326-5501). **Bayombong**, the provincial capital, lies just beyond.

In August, native Aeta people come down from the nearby mountains to dance in front of a century-old church. While in town, try crossing the **Hanging Footbridge of Ambaguio**, an 80-meter (260ft) -long, 20-meter (65ft) -high span made of wood, vine, and rope.

## Aurora

The coastal province of **Aurora** is all but synonymous with its capital, **Baler ㉘**. The centuries-old **Baler Catholic Church**, with its simple, plain facade, stood witness to the last Spanish garrison of four officers and 50 men captured by Filipino insurgents. The La Campana de Baler, a quality ancient bell, is stored as a relic at the church.

Most people go to the town to take on its heavy surf. Outside the town proper, numerous white-sand beaches are adorned with sea shells, corals and rock formations. Some swim, snorkel, or dive. But the beaches transform themselves into surfing areas during the northeast monsoon, October through March.

**Sabang Beach** is the most popular surf spot, while Charlie's Point, 10 minutes' drive north, also swells during typhoons. Francis Ford Coppola filmed the "Charlie don't surf" scene of the movie *Apocalypse Now* at Charlie's Point.

Reaching Baler usually requires a trip along the cement-constructed Baler–Bongabon Road, which zigzags through mountains prone to landslides and fast oncoming trucks. The provincial government suggests grabbing a Genesis Transport Bus from Pasay City in Manila rather than using a private vehicle. The trip takes about five hours. Boats to outlying stretches of coast near Baler dock along the banks of a river next to a bridge at Barangay Sabang. Water transit south of Baler is possible only by private pumpboat.

Elsewhere in Aurora Province, primordial forest cover and wild rivers await those who figure out how to get there. Among the interior highlights are Ditumabo Falls, Banyu Springs, Cunayan Falls, Dibut Bay, Dilasag Coast, and Lamao Caves.

**TIP**

The coasts stretching in either direction from Baler offer a variety of waves accessible by road or by boat. The friendly local surfers, known as the "Baler Boys," might just share their secret wave-riding spots with you, if you charm them enough.

**BELOW:** hiking towards the Sierra Madre mountains.

## The Sierra Madre

The 1.7-million-hectare (4.2-million) main mountain range of northeast Luzon has remained unspoiled because of its relatively hard-to-reach location. Some 335 species of plants have been identified in the dense, unbroken forests, among them orchids and unusual ferns. There are 240 kinds of birds as well as barely documented species of frogs.

Environmentalists, in-country and overseas, have protested against persistent, illegal logging in the mountains. The government has declared the partly coastal, partly inland Northern Sierra Madre Natural Park a protected area.

As with most mountains in the Philippines, the Sierra Madre can be trekked by people with precise directions, perseverance, and a guide. Visitors usually reach the mountains through the Palanan Wilderness Park in Isabela Province. Take a Florida-Liner bus past Cauayan, past the junction to San Mariano, and then catch a jeepney to central San Mariano. Ask there about guides and supplies for the trip. Villages near San Mariano are jumping-off points for treks along the most often traveled trails: Aguinaldo, Bisag, and Carabao.

Natural scenery aside, trekkers may best remember the sometimes incessant rain, high rivers, slips on rocks, and many moments of being saved by paid native guides. Treks may last four to five days.

# CENTRAL CORDILLERA

**Luzon's mountainous land-locked provinces are home to various ethnic groups, practicing ancient rituals and farming the astonishingly spectacular, contour-hugging rice terraces.**

Manila

This mountainous, forested, and oddly cool region of the usually sweltering Philippines draws travelers most often for its terraced rice fields, step after green step of hillside carved out by indigenous tribespeople. So remarkable are the hundreds of hectares of terraces near Banuae that in 1995 Unesco listed it as a cultural heritage site. But six years later the same agency declared the same site in danger, a result of deterioration and lack of conservation work.

Also in these higher elevations, sheltered by pines in some parts and known by the Spanish word "cordillera" for mountain range, visitors can see how indigenous people have lived almost untouched by three centuries of fiercely opposed Spanish rule. In one town, Sagada, travelers have made a growing impact as they go there to see native architecture located near caves that are both scenic and celebrated as burial grounds.

A typical vista might unfold like this: a morning mist hangs low over a tightly knit community of 30 small huts, made of cogon grass thatch. An older man from the tribe winds his way through the vegetable beds tucked around the village (*ili*), stopping at the council house (*ato*), where his peers are waiting. Dressed scantily,

despite the cold mountain air, the men squat around a low fire, puffing on tiny pipes of carved hardwood and cast bronze. The council house is made of pine, blackened by age and soot. Its roof is a bulky, round thatch of cogon; the spirits of visiting forefathers would not appreciate an iron roof resounding under the rain. An approaching storm threatens the rice harvest: to placate the gods, a chicken is being sacrificed at the sacred tree, which, with the *ato*, is the center of life in the highland community.

**Main attractions**
BAGUIO CITY MARKET
TAM-AWAN IFUGAO ARTISTS' VILLAGE, BAGUIO
SAGADA CAVES AND FOREST HIKES
BANAUE TERRACED RICE PADDIES

**LEFT:** Banaue rice terraces.
**RIGHT:** an Ifugao elder.

**TIP**

Roads throughout the Cordillera are necessarily rugged, but gratifyingly scenic. Be sure to bring a heavy sweater or coat, as frosty air might seep through the open-sided jeepney at higher elevations.

Perhaps, one day, this will be a rare scene in the **Cordillera Administration Region**, encompassing all the land-locked provinces of the Cordillera mountains of northern Luzon Island. The highlands account for 7 percent of the total land area of the Philippines, though they are home to less than 2 percent of the country's population.

Three main roads lead from the lowlands to the Cordillera. The Kennon Road, built by the Americans in 1903, zigzags north from Sison, Pangasinan, to Baguio. From La Union Province, the Marcos Highway branches off from the National Highway in Agoo, reaching Baguio in less than two hours. Quirino Highway (Naguilian Road) leads in from Naguilian, further north.

## Ethnic groups

*Igorot*, literally "people of the mountains," is a blanket term invented by the Spanish. The people of the region prefer to be called by the name of their own distinct ethnic groups: the Kankanaey and Ibaloi of Benguet;

the Ifugao of Ifugao Province; the Kalinga and the Isneg of Apayao; and the Bontoc, Balangao, Gaddang, and Bayyo of Mountain Province.

The Bontoc are the proudest and most warlike, whose men maintain a deep territorial imperative. Codes of conduct and legal matters are associated with the hard-working Ifugao, who also take their rituals seriously, employing as many as 15 priests for a ceremony. For the Kalinga, the major preoccupations are oratory skills and a unique system of peace pacts that culminate in grand celebrations.

The Spanish, whose occupation of the lowlands involved only a modicum of effort, once encountered stiff opposition in the mountains from these "restless and warlike tribes." Spanish missions failed in these mountains. Headhunting by certain tribes particularly infuriated the colonists, who mounted many punitive expeditions but never pacified the mountain peoples. It was not until American occupation and the opening of the highlands by army engineers that the tribes finally

**BELOW:** Igorot tribeswoman displays her tattoos.

accepted colonists, including religious missions.

Today, Christianity is well established in the region, with mission schools omnipresent and English usage widespread. Many of the mountain people have adopted Christian first names – Clifford and Kathleen, for instance – while retaining tribal surnames such as Kinaw-od and Killip. Yet many still cling to ancient tribal customs, as at a highland funeral. On such an occasion, a feast lasts for three days. The deceased sits strapped to a wooden chair in the center of the house, as though surveying the time-honored proceedings. Animal sacrifices are made and the meat passed around to the entire gathering. Bronze gongs clang deep into the night, while the people dance in a circle with fluttering, bird-like motions. Rice wine is served from centuries-old jars traded from some Chinese junk, ladled with aged coconut shells. Invocations are said to a pantheon of spirits, including Kabunyian, the creator, and Lumawig, a folklore hero.

## Baguio

The road to the highlands from Manila usually runs through **Baguio** ㉙, a six-hour bus drive from Manila (four hours by private car). Nestled aloft a 1,500-meter (4,900ft) -high plateau in the Cordilleras, Baguio's cool climate and pine-clad hills have

*Shopping mall in Baguio.*

**BELOW:** Baguio Cathedral.

**TIP**

If you don't mind having stuffed animal heads stare at you, try staying at the Safari Lodge in Baguio (tel: 074-442-2419).

consistently lured visitors to the sprawling city of 302,000 people. The city shows little evidence today of an earthquake that caused severe damage in 1990, as domestic tourism and a concentration of colleges keep the economy running.

Baguio is best known for the leisure and relaxation offered by its forested hills. The city serves as a summer getaway from the crowds and heat of Manila, refreshingly averaging 18°C (64°F) throughout the year. Baguio seduces visitors also with clean parks, lovely gardens, quaint churches, and a variety of restaurants and hotels. Accommodations are easily available in Baguio, except during Holy Week. Maps and information on lodgings are available free at the **Department of Tourism** Ⓐ office on Governor Pack Road.

A highlight in Baguio is the month-long **Baguio Flower Festival**, or **Panagbenga**, which means the "season for blossoming" in the Kankanaey dialect. It is held every February, with parades of floral floats, marching bands, and dance troupes.

Getting around Baguio is easy. Jeepneys congregate at the northern end of Session Road and follow regular routes. However, with rates low, taxis are sensible for extended trips through the city. Try taking a cab down Naguilian Road for a view of the sunset over the Ilocos coastline or up to Mt Santo Tomas for a view of the South China Sea.

## Head for the market

Long walks have become a source of recreation in Baguio, the time-honored route being up and down **Session Road.** The strip stands out for its bookstores, bakeries, Chinese restaurants, coffeehouses, pizza parlors, and movie theaters. At the northern end of Session Road, opposite the jeepney terminus, is **Baguio City Market** Ⓑ. Vendors in the well-stocked market sell produce from both highland and lowland farms, from Spanish tomatoes and yams to blueberries. Some peddle sausages, woven bags, baskets, woodcarvings, jewelry, clothing, or kitschy souvenirs.

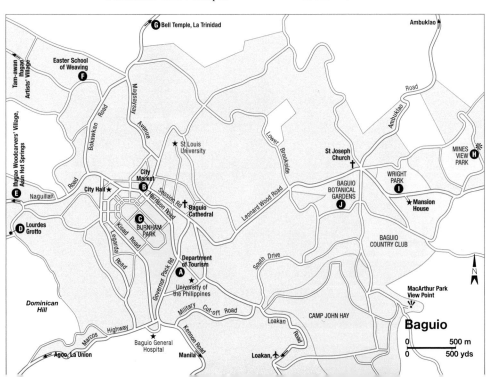

**Burnham Park** , containing a manmade lake, sports ground, and orchidarium, stands at the center of Baguio, south of Session Road. Between far-flung Naguilian Road and Mt Santo Tomas sits **Lourdes Grotto** , where devotees climb 252 steps to the Lady of Lourdes shrine and a good view of the city. From Lourdes, head west 5km (3 miles) to the **Ifugao Woodcarvers' Village** , where prices on crafts run lower than those in town. The **Asin Hot Springs**, with lush vegetation and hanging bridges, lies 16km (10 miles) northwest of Baguio.

Also north of the city center is the **Easter School of Weaving** , where export-quality native cloth and curio items sell for bargain prices. Local weavers using backstrap-looms are the main attraction. Go downstairs to watch them make the cloth. Some 10 minutes' drive from Downtown up Magsaysay Avenue, look for the **Bell Temple** . At this collection of temples bedecked with dragons and Chinese ornamentation, monks or priests practice a blend of Buddhism, Taoism, Confucianism, and Christianity. They may try to tell your fortune.

Not too much farther west is the **Tam-awan Ifugao Artists' Village** (tel: 047-446-2949; tam-awanvillage. com/index.php). The park-like village was built in the style of native Ifugao houses and opened in 1996 to help foster a deeper understanding of the culture of the Cordillera people for visitors without time to penetrate farther into the mountains. In the village are huts typical of 10 native Cordilleran tribes. Guests can overnight in the huts for P500 to P1,000 per night.

In the northeastern part of the city, **Mines View Park**  affords a view of a so-called mineral bowl, a hole in the earth where gold and silver have been mined. Gold mining continues today, but in limited quantities. From there, take Leonard Wood Road to **Wright Park** , where children can take pony rides. Opposite the park is the **Mansion House**, summer residence of Philippine presidents. Further down Leonard

**TIP**

North of Baguio is the Mountain Trail, or "Halsema Highway" – rough, partially paved, and often washed out in the rainy season – running to Bontoc. Although Bontoc, Banaue, and points south to Baguio are accessible by bus, other towns here have only a limited service.

**BELOW:** Baguio City Market.

*Waterfall, Asin Hot Springs.*

**BELOW:** Asin Hot Springs, Baguio.

Wood Road is the **Baguio Botanical Gardens** . South of Mansion House are **Baguio Country Club** and **Camp John Hay**, once an American military retreat and now housing a resort called The Manor at John Hay.

## Beyond Baguio

The province surrounding Baguio leads past strawberry vendors to mountain treks and 500-year-old mummies. **La Trinidad**, the capital of Benguet Province, stands just north of Baguio. It's an ideal place to load up on fresh strawberries. From there, a partly paved road winds northward to Bontoc. At the 52km marker on the Mountain Trail, near the Natubleng Vegetable Terraces in

Buguias, follow the right fork south to Kabayan town, four hours from Baguio and the base for trekking **Mt Pulog** ❸. The second-highest peak in the country – and the highest in Luzon – towers 2,928 meters (9,606ft) above sea level. For climbers, a ranger station is located on the main Kabayan road.

Trekking Mt Pulog (sometimes spelled Pulag) is best from February to April; allow at least three days to reach the peak for a view of the **Cagayan Valley** and **Sierra Madre** range, and the Philippine Sea in the distance. Pine stands give way to oak forests, then alpine and bamboo grass-covered slopes, which thin out towards the peak, explaining Pulog's name, meaning "bald." Mt Pulog also has three mountain lakes – Tabeyo, Incolos, and Bulalakaw – and several unexplored caves around its base. Treks take two days, and with guide service they cost around P3,350 per head. Call Pulog Climb for guides (tel: 02-392-2006).

Towering **Tinongchol Burial Rock**, once home to the mummified

remains of Ibaloi ancestors, awaits near Kabayan. Many of the remains have been stolen, however. Nearby, on **Mt Timbac**, are more burial caves, with mummies that are at least 500 years old. Unlike wrapped Egyptian mummies, these are naked and with tattoo marks of geometric patterns still visible. They lie in the fetal position, in wooden coffins carved from tree trunks. Some of these mummies are displayed at a museum by the Kabayan town hall.

## Mountain Province

Some of the terraced rice paddies and burials that make the Cordillera stand out on the tour map can be found in this aptly named part of the country. Mountain Province was created in 1907, during American rule, and included most of the Cordillera highlands as well as a predominantly indigenous population.

Toward the 90km Mountain Trail marker, near Sabangan, a road to the left ascends to **Bauko**, an eerily quiet logging center that may be shrouded in mountain mist. Visitors may take

hikes through pine forests and are advised to spend the night rather than pushing on toward further-flung places after dark. Try the Mt Data Lodge (tel: 0918-199-1901). It has a restaurant, bar, plenty of woodwork, and a huge fireplace for cold nights.

## Rice terraces and burial caves

An hour's drive north from Bauko, the road descends to the Chico River, running parallel with it to Bontoc and beyond. **Bontoc** itself offers not much more than gas and provisions. But traveling by bus usually means staying the night at one of Bontoc's comfortable and cheap lodges.

Hikes outside Bontoc provide a good survey of how traditional rice terraces are maintained. These terraces are unlike the more famous ones in Banaue. Here, the walls are made from rocks instead of mud. Locals say that their terraces, though smaller than the massive spread in Banaue, are more difficult to construct and therefore more picturesque. A visit to the **Bontoc Museum**

*The forests of Kabayan are mired in a controversy about patents on certain native herbal medicines. A local medicine man supposedly gave information on local herbs to US pharmaceutical companies, which now stand to profit from the development of life-saving drugs.*

**BELOW:** an artist at work in the Tamawan Ifugao Artists' Village.

*Rice bundles are often used as payment among the Ifugao people.*

**BELOW:** working the rice fields, Banaue.

(daily 8am–noon, 1–5pm; charge) is a must for insight into Cordilleran culture.

Much of the charm and coziness lacking in Bontoc, with its harsh trading-post atmosphere, can be found in **Sagada**, an indigenous town one hour away by bus or jeep. It has become increasingly popular among travelers, evidenced by the numerous inns and hotels that some have criticized as over-development.

Hiking is again the order of the day in this upland valley, which has lime and shale formations, plus a labyrinthine series of burial caves. Wooden coffins are stacked together at the mouths of several caves a short walk from town. Others, called "hanging coffins," dangle over cliff edges, as Sagadans are traditionally "buried"

with full exposure to sunshine, wind, and rain. Many of the trails to the caves are poorly maintained; hire a guide to maximize your visit. For more information on Sagada, including lodging and cave access details, visit: www.travel-philippines.com/locations/central-luzon/4-sagada.htm.

A number of attractions are within an hour's hike of town: an underground river; the Kitongan bottomless pit that supposedly remains unfathomed; and the tiny Bokong Waterfall, with a swimming hole.

## Banaue rice terraces

The Unesco-blessed rice terraces, which have been sculpted by indigenous farmers for about 2,000 years, fan across the mountains near Banaue, in **Ifugao Province**, to give the Cordillera global fame among travelers.

A bus leaves Bontoc in the morning on the two-hour drive to **Banaue** ㉛, 50km (31 miles) southeast over the Mt Polis highway. Terraced fields with spiral beds, oak trees gnarled to perfection, and mountain orchids

are fascinating sidelights along the highway. Banaue and surroundings remain the best sight in the Cordilleras (see The Fabled Rice Terraces of Ifugao, page 202).

The massive expanse of rice terraces covering entire mountainsides is bound to awe even the most jaded traveler. Built 2,000 years ago, the terraces cover more than 260 sq km (100 sq miles) of steep mountains. People elsewhere in Asia terrace rice fields, but the expanse in Ifugao stands out for the extensive latticework of stone and mud walls blending naturally into contours of the steep mountainsides, all built by the engineering-savvy local Ifugao people before modern machinery. There is also a pre-modern but highly effective irrigation system (aided now by a hydropower project). It took the Ifugao population as a whole to make the terraces work. As Unesco puts it, the terraces depict an "absolute blending of the physical, socio-cultural, economic, religious, and political environment" of Ifugao people.

Banaue sits in the heart of Ifugao country. The word "*ifugao*" simply means hill – and for the Ifugao people, the "hill" means everything. An extensive social system exists here. Those who own the lower, larger terraces are the wealthy elite. The peasants till the upper, narrower terraces.

Today, Philippine officials are working to get the rice terraces removed from Unesco's sites-in-danger list. The UN agency says government efforts aimed at improving local economic conditions offer hope that the terraces can return to normal status. It also notes local programs to ensure "landscape restoration" and a revival of "traditional practices" that once helped blend the people with the terraces.

The Banaue Hotel and Youth Hostel (tel: 074-386-4087) frequently offers cultural dance performances in the evenings for a modest fee, as well as accommodations with a view – but the same can be said of many cheaper lodging places in this dedicated backpacker town that has sprung up around terrace-based

**TIP**

To view inscriptions on Sagada's hanging coffins, be sure to bring along a pair of powerful binoculars.

**BELOW:** steep terracing, Banaue.

## Hydropower Conservation

As the Ifugao rice terraces of the Philippines Cordillera, dubbed by some the eighth world wonder, face deterioration, a foreign organization has stepped in to save them.

In January 2010 the Canadian NGO Global Sustainable Electricity Partnership opened its 200-kilowatt Ifugao-Ambangal Mini-hydro project along a mountain river to generate 18 percent of the province's energy demand. The US$1 million project, built by hand due to its location, supports local efforts to water the terraces while developing sustainable mini-hydro power resources for the people living nearby.

Power sales to an electricity distribution cooperative will secure US$70,000 annually for the conservation fund charged with running the hydro plant.

tourism. Behind the Banaue Hotel, 240 steep steps lead down to **Tam-an village**, where Ifugao people tend rice terraces and produce woodcarvings and beadwork to supplement their income. Heading north along the road by jeepney or pedicab, you reach the Banaue Viewpoint, where handicraft stalls line the path that leads to a full-blown vista of the rice terraces. Ifugao elders in full tribal dress will pose for pictures – for a small fee.

In Banaue, be sure to check out the small museum (open on request) at the Banaue View Inn (tel: 074-386-4078). The hotel is run by the family of H. Ottley Beyer, an American anthropologist who studied the Ifugao, eventually taking a native wife and dying here.

## The farms

Reached by a series of steps from the road below Banaue center, the community of **Bocos** has some interesting sights. The huts are adorned with the skulls of buffaloes and wild pigs, which indicate the status of the families. Villagers keep their most sacred idol, *bulol*, or rice god, in the granary. It comes out only at harvest time to be bathed in the blood of sacrificed animals.

A footpath leads to **Poitan**, a village with a collection of houses roofed with both traditional cogon grass and sheets of galvanized iron. Here you can get a good view of the stone post protected and idolized by the Ifugao, and the stone-lined pit where elders gather to discuss serious affairs.

Some 4km (2.5 miles) from Banaue lies an ideal spot for a picnic, where a small waterfall tumbles into a natural pool in a community called Guihob. Take a dip in the crystal-clear waters and gaze at the surrounding rice terraces. The pool is a 4km (2.5-mile) private vehicle ride from the Banaue Hotel or about 45 minutes by foot from Banaue town center (not recommended for people who get tired easily). **Hapao**, 16km (10 miles) southwest of Banaue, offers one of the most beautiful, stone-lined rice terraces

**BELOW:** Ifugao totems.

in the mountains. Other terraces in **Banga-an**, 14km (9 miles) from Banaue, are accessible by climbing steep stone steps.

The spectacular, amphitheater-like terraces of **Batad**, 16km (10 miles) east from Banaue, are reached by a 4km (2.5-mile) footpath from the road. Here tattooed men and women work the fields. For a truly memorable journey, hire a guide to Batad, but first spend the night in Cambulo, where you can cool off by swimming in the rushing river. About an hour beyond Batad, by difficult footpath, cascades Tappiya Falls, with its enormous natural swimming basin.

**Mayoyao**, 44km (27 miles) northeast of Banaue, offers a breathtaking view of rice terraces. From Banaue, backtrack to Bontoc and Baguio, or descend to the lowlands and the National Highway through **Lagawe**, Ifugao Province's capital city. In Lagawe, visitors can explore the Bintakan and Nah-toban caves, and a fine museum of Ifugao culture.

## Kalinga, Apayao, and Abra provinces

The remaining Cordillera is more remote, best suited for trekkers, white-water rafters, and travelers keen to understand indigenous cultures.

From Bontoc, the adventurous can proceed directly to **Kalinga Province**, one of the most rugged in the Cordillera region and home of the Kalinga people. The Kalinga-Bontoc Road runs 130km (80 miles) to Tuao on the Cagayan-Apayao border. From Tuao, a spur road (210km/130 miles) leads all the way to the South China Sea in Laoag, Ilocos Norte.

In Tinglayan, two hours' drive north of Bontoc, you can join a tour offered by Chico River Quest (www. chicoriverquest.com), an ecotourism operator set up by local guides and an American rafting company. Its trips cover cultural tours and trekking to traditional villages and rice terraces in the area. Several hours

to the north from Tinglayan is **Balbalaasang-Balbalan National Park**, known for its unspoiled, natural beauty and sweet, locally grown oranges.

**Apayao Province**, to the north of Kalinga, is named for its main river, the Apayao. It is noted for clear waters, wildlife, and old-growth forest. The river is accessible through Kabugao, 70km (43 miles) from Tuao, where motorized boats can be hired. Among the provincial highlights is the **Agamatan National Park and Wildlife Sanctuary**, located by the Ilocos Norte border, in Calanasan. Waterfalls abound in this province, including some of the tallest in the country. Be prepared for multi-day hikes to see them.

**Abra Province** is usually accessed by road from Ilocos Sur. The 47,000-population provincal capital, **Bangued**, stands out for handicrafts, such as sturdy baskets and woven garments. The capital serves as a good jump-off point for exploring the seldom-visited hinterlands of Abra, such as the Abra River.

**TIP**

For a more romantic view of the Ifugao Rice Terraces, hire a guide to take you further afield. Vertigo sufferers beware! The terrace edges are steep.

**BELOW:** Ifugao women sorting coffee beans, Tulgao village.

# The Fabled Rice Terraces of Ifugao

**The hardworking Ifugao people tend to their rice terraces, hewn from the steep hillsides, as their ancestors have done for the past 2,000 years.**

Spread throughout the province of Ifugao, but seen by most people at Banaue, the rice terraces are a testimony to the early technological advancement of the Ifugao people. Constructed 2,000 years ago, employing simple tools and backbreaking labor, the exquisitely sculpted terraces are a distinctive trademark of Ifugao culture. An ingeniously designed irrigation system directs water through sluices, delivering the right amount to the young rice shoots.

In Ifugao, the most mountainous part of the Philippine Cordillera, rice is king, and the coarse, homegrown variety is preferred to store-bought rice. Sweet potatoes are grown in forest clearings, but only rice appears during celebratory feasts – alongside chickens, pigs, ducks, and the occasional water buffalo, or carabao.

## Changing times

Although the Ifugao covet mountain-grown rice, today, few families can claim self-subsistence from the terraces. Over time, the terraces require extensive repairs, and the irrigation system must be dredged to maintain water flow. A growing population dictates that each child inherits an increasingly smaller plot of land. Sadly, most of the younger generation is reluctant to undertake the laborious chore of rice farming. To combat further deterioration and create funds for conservation, a Canadian NGO has stepped in to provide a mini-hydro project (see page 199).

**Above:** In the remote hills around Banaue, age-old tribal customs survive.

**Below:** An Ifugao woman plays a traditional wooden flute.

**Left:** Rice field markers, used by the Ifugao to mark territorial divisions.

**ABOVE:** An Ifugao man with a rice god carved from local narra wood.

## MUCH-REVERED RICE GOD

Holding a special place in the Ifugao pantheon is the *bulul*, or rice god. Standing watch over each family's granary is a pair of *bulul* figures, carved from narra wood. During ceremonial rituals, Ifugao elders will slaughter chickens, recite divine incantations, and pour the sacrificial blood of chickens over the head of the *bulul*. In turn, it is believed that the *bulul* will watch over the rice, and also help increase the yield of the coming harvest. Although the tradition of honoring the *bulul* persists, it is increasingly difficult to find a finely carved old rice god *in situ*, strapped to the wall of an Ifugao house. Antique collectors offer princely sums of cash to families willing to part with such treasures. These include not only the *bulul*, but also the structures integral to an Ifugao house: the pine posts flanking the doorway and the support beams.

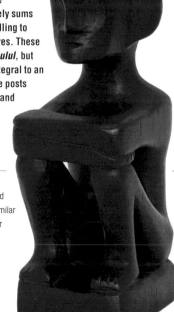

**RIGHT:** A traditional-seated rice god figurine. Items similar to this are sold in souvenir shops in the region.

**ABOVE:** Hiking along the precipitous rice terraces offers panoramic views. Little wonder that Unesco has recognized the rice terraces as a World Heritage Site.

**BELOW:** Animal skulls on the exterior of an Ifugao home indicate the relative wealth of the family. Carabao skulls are scarce, as it's difficult to bring the water buffalo up to these heights.

# BICOL PENINSULA

This dense farming region of Luzon island, east of Manila, stands out for active volcanoes, thrilling Pacific surf, undeveloped beaches, and the opportunity to swim with gentle whale sharks.

I n a lake near one of the world's most perfectly shaped volcanoes swim the world's tiniest freshwater fish. Steam drifts through the palm trees where geothermal power is tapped for electricity. Bold hikers on organized treks can be found pushing up the same cones, namely the mossy forests of Mt Isarog near the hub city of Naga or the rocky scrambles of Mt Mayon, which is closer to Legazpi city. And should the volcanoes be too steep, some of the flattest land lies also on this peninsula, allowing for extensive agriculture and some industry.

The Bicol Peninsula, the far south of Luzon, is a vivid place. Offshore are islands with some of the whitest sand beaches and clearest coral-reefed waters one is ever likely to see. Water-skiers and wake-boarders test their skills at the booming Camsur Watersports Complex.

This densely populated area has its fair share of challenges. In the later months of the year, powerful typhoons sweep in from the Pacific to batter the region. And every decade or so one of Bicol's volcanoes spews deadly lava. A road system that extends to Manila, plus ferries and pumpboats, link up much of Bicol, making travel easier than in less developed areas.

**LEFT:** Mayon Volcano. **RIGHT:** the seas off Bicol teem with fish.

## Camarines Norte

Surfing and remote beaches define for the tourist this province built largely on farming. The rice granaries of Camarines Norte caught the attention of a Spanish mission in 1569. In 1929, the province of rich mineral and agricultural resources known simply as Camarines – derived from the Spanish word for granary – was divided into Camarines Norte and Camarines Sur.

**Camarines Norte** occupies the northwestern portion of the Bicol region, with a Pacific Ocean coastline.

**Main attractions**
CAMSUR WATERSPORTS COMPLEX
MT ISAROG TREKS
MOUNT MAYON CLIMBING
CAMALIG WHISTLING CAVES
DONSOL'S WHALE SHARKS
CATANDUANES ISLAND SURFING

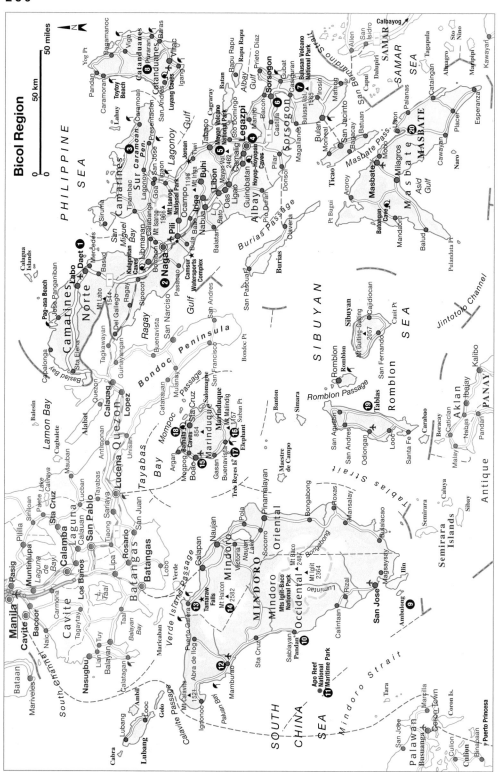

## Bicol Region

50 miles
50 km

**PHILIPPINE SEA**

**SOUTH CHINA SEA**

**SIBUYAN SEA**

**SAMAR SEA**

**Manila**
Cavite
Bacoor
Pasig
Muntinlupa
Pililla
Sta Cruz
Calamba
Los Baños
San Pablo
Laguna
Laguna de Bay
Nasugbu
Balayan
Lipa
Rosario
Batangas
Calatagan
Lobo

Mariveles
Bataan

Lubang
Cabra
Looc
Golo
Ambil

Calavite Passage
Verde Island Passage

Puerto Galera
Tamaraw Falls
Mt Halcon 2582
Mts Iglit-Baco National Park
Mt Baco 2364
Mt Iglit 2487

**MINDORO**
Mindoro Occidental
Mindoro Oriental
Calapan
Naujan
Naujan Lake
Victoria
Socorro
Pola
Pinamalayan
Bongabong
Mansalay
Bulalacao
Magsaysay
Ilin
**San Jose**
Sablayan
Sta Cruz
Calintaan
Rizal

Apo Reef National Maritime Park

**Palawan**
Culion
Busuanga
Coron Is
Coron Town
Binalbagan
San Jose

**Puerto Princesa**

**Lucena**
**Quezon**
Lopez
Calauag
Alabat
Mauban
Atimonan
Unisan
Catanauan
Mulanay
San Francisco
Bondoc Pt

**Bondoc Peninsula**

**Tayabas Bay**
**Lamon Bay**
**Mompoc Pass**

**Marinduque**
Boac
Gasan
Buenavista
Sta Cruz
Santa Cruz
Mt Malindig 1157
Tres Reyes Is
Elephant I
Suban Pt

**ROMBLON SEA**
**Romblon Passage**
**Tablas Strait**

**Romblon**
Tablas
Sibuyan
Mt Guiting-Guiting 2057
San Fernando
San Agustin
San Andres
Odiongan
Looc
Santa Fe
Carabao
Simara
Banton
Maestre de Campo

**Semirara Islands**
Caluya
Sibay
Semirara

**PANAY**
**Aklan**
Kalibo
Ibajay
Nabas
Pandan
Malay
Caticlan
Boracay
**Antique**

**Masbate**
**MASBATE**
Aroroy
Mandaon
Milagros
Mobo
Baleno
Balud
Cawayan
Placer
Esperanza
Cataingan
Palanas
Dimasalang
Uson
Batuan

**Ticao**
**Burias**

**Camarines Norte**
**Daet**
Labo
Mt Labo 1544
Jose Panganiban
Pag-asa Beach
Calaguaa Islands

**Camarines Sur**
**Naga**
Pili
Mt Isarog 1966
Mt Isarog National Park
Iriga
Nabua
Bula
Balatan
Pasacao
Bato
Buhi
Libmanan
Cabusao
Sipocot
Ragay
Del Gallego
Lupi

**Camsur Watersports Complex**
**Kulapnitan Caves**

**San Miguel Bay**
**Ragay Gulf**

**Caramoan Pen.**
Caramoan
Presentacion
San Jose
Goa
Lagonoy
Tigaon
Sangay
Tinambac
Siruma

**Lagonoy Gulf**

**Catanduanes**
**Virac**
Bato
Baras
Bagamanoc
Viga
Pandan
Caramoran
Gigmoto
San Andres
Igang
**Toytoy Beach**
**Luyang Caves**

**Albay**
**Legazpi**
**Mayon Volcano National Park**
Mt Mayon 2462
Daraga
Camalig
Guinobatan
Ligao
Oas
Polangui
Libon
Tabaco
Malinao
Tiwi
Malilipot
Bacacay
Sto Domingo
Manito
Rapu Rapu

**Hoyop-Hoyopan Caves**

**Sorsogon**
**Sorsogon**
Gubat
Bulusan
Barcelona
Casiguran
Juban
Magallanes
Castilla
Irosin
Prieto Diaz
Bulan
Matnog
Donsol
Pilar

**Bulusan Volcano National Park**
Bulusan Vol 1565

**Burias Pass**
**Burias Passage**
**Ticao Pass**
**San Bernardino Strait**

**SAMAR**
**Calbayog**
Allen
San Isidro
Dalupiri
Capul
Sto Niño
Tagapula
Maripipi
Almagro

**Jintotolo Channel**
**Asid Gulf**

① **Daet**
② **Naga**
③ ④ ⑤ ⑥ ⑦ ⑧ ⑨ ⑩ ⑪ ⑫ ⑬ ⑭ ⑮ ⑯ ⑰ ⑱ ⑲ ⑳

Daet ❶, the provincial capital, is known as the most accessible surf site along the Philippines' east coast, reached by a 45-minute flight, or eight-hour bus ride, from Manila. Its historical landmark is the country's first Rizal monument, built in 1898, in front of the Municipal Hall. Nearby is the 1544-meter (5066ft) Mt Labo, Bicol's northernmost volcano.

While not quite like the monster waves of Catanduanes or Siargao, the province's beach break surf sites are suitable for novice surfers. For instance, the white-sand **Bagasbas Beach**, 5km (3 miles) from Daet, has relatively small breaks that are easier to ride. More experienced surfers head straight for the picturesque fishing village of **Mercedes**. It has a 2km (1.2-mile) gray-sand beach, and 1–1.5-meter (3–5ft) waves on ordinary days, which swell to 2–3 meters (6–10ft) during typhoons. The adrenaline and brine of the surf can be washed away at the natural hot spring of nearby Lanot Beach, and then Mercedes' underwater **Canton Cave** can be explored at low tide.

## Camarines Sur

A one-of-a-kind water-sports park, the extinct Mt Isarog volcano, and a cave dominated by bats are among the attractions of Camarines Sur, a province that lives off of rice, bananas, and coconuts. Mining, fishing, and bamboo craft-making also lead the provincial economy.

The high point of the year for the province's largest city of **Naga** ❷ is September's water parade in honor of the Virgin of Peñafrancia, housed at the **Peñafrancia Basilica**. The statue is carried on a great barge, or *casco*, which starts its colorful voyage from near the market (see Fiesta Fantastica, page 73).

To learn more of the region's history, visit the **Naga Metropolitan Cathedral**, built in 1578, and look at the centuries-old San Francisco Church, the province's first, where

a Spanish governor surrendered to Filipino revolutionaries toward the end of colonial rule. Don't miss the Quince Martires monument, built in honor of the 15 Filipino martyrs who were executed by the Spaniards. Nearby is the sprawling 1873 Holy Rosary Minor Seminary, one of the oldest seminaries in the country. The well-preserved Colegio de Santa Isabel, founded in 1868, was the first school for girls in the Philippines. Within the city is the sprawling **Provincial Capitol Complex**, which has a children's park, a modern amphitheater, and a jungle garden for relaxing promenades.

The province has moved up on tourist destination charts because of its **Camsur Watersports Complex** (tel: 054-477-3344; villadelreyreservation@gmail.com; daily 8.30am–9.30pm; charge). The 6-hectare (15-acre) provincial government-run complex in Pili, near Naga, features the largest cable-pulled wake-boarding center in Asia, options to "cable ski" 8–12 meters (26–40ft) above water, and the distinct sport of knee-boarding. The

*When the Bicolano is not enjoying mundane life to the hilt, he may be contemplating it in the church or seminary, for many Filipino priests come from the Bicol region.*

**BELOW:** Rizal Monument, Daet.

*Diving off a bridge in Naga.*

**BELOW:** Peñafrancia Basilica, Naga.

park holds regular dragon-boat races, which are usually associated with Chinese rather than Filipino communities. A range of lodging lies just outside the center.

At night, Naga's Magsaysay Street comes to life with bars, cafés, and restaurants. Try The Clubhouse and the Happy Ending Bar.

## Around Naga

Travelers can hang with bats at the **Kulapnitan Caves of Libmanan**, an hour's drive north from Naga. The site is named for the thousands of *kulapnit* or cave bats that hang on its gold-crusted ceilings, a spectacle of limestone formations. Continuing along Quirino Highway is the Villa Esperanza Resort in **Sipocot**, a modern resort in a tropical setting. **Del Gallego** houses the PNR Marker Park, where the late President Manuel L. Quezon drove a golden nail during the inauguration of the north- and south-bound railroad tracks, which finally linked Manila and Legazpi.

Back in Naga, take a jeepney east to *barangay* **Panicuason**, home to the 13-meter (43ft) Malabsay Falls and Nabontolan Spring, located near the edge of a ravine. Past these falls is Mt Isarog. Along a rough road south of Mt Isarog at **Tigaon** is Consorcep Resthouse, 550 meters (1,800ft) above sea level.

About 15km (9 miles) north from Naga toward San Miguel Bay is the **Leaning Tower of Bombon**, the local counterpart of Pisa's famous landmark. In the neighboring town of Calabanga stands the brick-made

**Ladrillo Church of Quipayo**, built in 1616. Rare artifacts excavated in this church are displayed in a museum behind the altar.

Toward the Caramoan Peninsula, **Lagonoy** has the twin attractions of Bolanogan Falls, located in a lush forest setting, and Adiangao Cave, whose underground marvels have attracted many cavers. Sabang Beach in **San Jose** features crystal-clear waters and powdery sands, as does its undeveloped, under-explored peer **Atulayan Island**. This environmentally protected islet can be reached from the fishing village of Nato, in the town of Sagnay, which is an hour's ride from Naga or Pili. After arrival, look for vast beaches between undisturbed green jungles and aquamarine waters.

## Caramoan Peninsula

Off the eastern coast of San Jose is the ultimate adventure destination of **Caramoan Peninsula ❸**. With a feast of bays, islands, islets, protruding rocks, brooding limestone cliffs, and heavily forested highlands that are home to abundant wildlife, Caramoan has all the attributes of a prime ecotourism destination. Rent a bike and cycle to **Gota Beach**. Nearby are numerous white-sand islets, surrounded by caves accessible by foot. Caramoan is ideal for island-hopping, sea-kayaking, scuba diving, snorkeling, and hiking, but infrastructure is minimal, so arrange plans before heading to the area.

## South to Iriga

About 15km (9 miles) southeast of Naga is the city of **Pili**, named for the pili nut, one of Bicol's more popular exports. The nearby town of **Bula** has the milky-white Nalalata Falls and an 18th-century church. Continuing south on the highway, **Nabua**'s main tourist claim is Lake Bato, an inland lake habitat of wild ducks.

Sheltering in the shadow of the 1,196-meter (3,924-ft) Mt Iriga, also known as Mt Asog, is **Iriga City**, thought to be the youngest city in Bicol. The volcanic mountain is popular for its relatively easy trails and the spectacular view from its peak.

*Naga's Metropolitan Cathedral has led a highly eventful life: destroyed by fire in 1768, rebuilt by 1843, damaged by a typhoon in 1856, restored again by 1879, once more damaged by an earthquake in 1887, and rebuilt in 1890.*

**BELOW:** wakeboarding at the Camsur Watersports Complex.

*Panicuason hot springs.*

**BELOW:** Kulapnitan Caves of Libmanan.

The neighboring town of **Buhi** is home to numerous waterfalls, spring-resorts, and little lakes. **Lake Buhi** is also the habitat of *tabios*, the world's smallest freshwater fish, locally known as *sinarapan*, and measuring about 3–4mm (0.2ins). The *sinarapan* once formed part of a substantial fishing industry, but the introduction of predatory species and overfishing has endangered the tiny creatures. **Roca Encantada**, an island in the middle of the lake, is popular for picnics and strolls.

## Albay Province

South from the Camarines is the province of **Albay**. Volcanoes and rolling hills covered with coconut plantations, rice fields, and patches of forests dominate the farming-rich terrain. The provincial capital **Legazpi** ❹ is a bustling commercial center. It sits in the shadow of the perfectly cone-shaped Mayon Volcano. Visit in October to see the week-long Ibalong Festival, a blaze of costumes, ranging from the beautiful to the bizarre, and a riot of music, both traditional and modern, all to honor local people's pre-colonial resilience in the face of typhoons. **Legazpi City Museum** (Mon–Fri 8am–noon, 1–5pm; free) showcases old photographs, documents, religious and cultural objects of local importance. World War II remembrances can also be found in Legazpi, one being a tunnel used as an arsenal by the Japanese. Joggers often take to Legazpi Boulevard along the coast.

There are daily flights from Manila to **Legazpi** and various bus services on the Legazpi–Manila route.

## Mayon Volcano

**Mayon Volcano** ❺ takes its name from *magayon*, the word for beautiful

in the Bicolano dialect. It first erupted for European eyes in 1616, when a passing Dutch ship witnessed its explosive abilities. Since then, Mayon has erupted over 50 times. In August 2006, lava burst out of the mountain, and a typhoon in December that year set off mudslides that killed hundreds. Ash and lava also pushed through the mountainside in 2009. Weak volcanic activity was recorded on Mayon in 2011.

Those events hardly overshadow 1814, when Mayon erupted with brief but massive violence, burying the settlements of Cagsawa and Buiao in the town of **Daraga**. Local inhabitants ran for shelter to Cagsawa Church, but a tide of lava flowed right into it, killing at least 1,200 people. Today, **Cagsawa Ruins**, mostly submerged 40 meters (130ft) below the ground, remind visitors of that eruption, considered to be Mayon's worst. On a hilltop overlooking the town, 5km (3 miles) away from Mayon, stands the overgrown **Daraga Church**, which locals built after the 1814 eruption. Mayon

is still considered the most active volcano in the Philippines, erupting every 8 to 10 years.

The 2,462-meter (8,077-ft) **volcano** covers 465 hectares (1,150 acres) and was proclaimed a national park in 1938. Its ecosystem is home to endemic and endangered flora and fauna such as bleeding heart pigeons – so-called for the red marking on their breasts. At the foot of Mayon's slopes, farms take advantage of the rich volcanic soil.

Guide services offer three-day treks to the Mayon summit. Groups usually stay at two established campsites along the way. Views from the top take in Mount Isarog and the seas on either side of the Bicol peninsula. Treks may be suspended after eruptions.

Those who want to take it easier can sign up for half-day tours of the mountainside flora or butterflies. Nestling right on the volcano, at an altitude of 760 meters (2,500ft), is **Mayon Skyline Hotel and Convention Center**, formerly the Mayon Resthouse. The resort offers an exhilarating view of

**TIP**

Like most of the country, the Bicol peninsula is well supplied with untamed beaches, many on outlying islands. Most are undeveloped save for a handful of cottage resorts, if that. Check with tourism authorities before planning an overnight trip to make sure there's a place to stay.

**BELOW:** verdant forest.

**TIP**

To see the wriggly *sinarapan* – the world's smallest freshwater fish – swimming, visit Buhi Freshwater Demonstration Fish Farm, or the Municipal Aquarium at Buhi Town Hall. Visitors to Lake Buhi can stay at the Magindara Resort.

**BELOW:** Mount Isarog National Park.

the Pacific Ocean and Eastern Albay. On the same site is the **Holy Rosary Mountain**, whose giant rosary beads garland a huge cross on a slope right above the hotel.

The neighboring mountains of Masaraga, Malinao, and Catbuwaran also welcome trekkers. The undeveloped islands of San Miguel, Cagraray, Batan, Rapu-Rapu, and Buhatan – off the eastern coast of Legazpi – have several dive spots.

## Camalig's whistling caves

In the Albay city of **Camalig**, 15km (9 miles) northwest of Legazpi, are the **Hoyop-Hoyopan Caves** (literally "blow-blow" – derived from the sound of the wind whistling through the main entrance), part of an extensive series of limestone caves tunneling through a mountain. Carrying a smoky flare, the guide leads visitors down a twisting subterranean path that eventually ends on the other side of the mountain. A steep climb up the hill arrives at another entrance and then dives back underground. A fourth access point offers a magnificent vista

of green coconut plantations, with Mayon towering above them. Finally, the hike re-emerges at the original entry point.

**Calabidong Caves**, 2km (1.5 miles) distant, have a small underground stream and a dense population of bats. Altogether, over a dozen caves have been discovered within an 8km (5-mile) radius of the main caverns.

North of Legazpi, at the town of **Sto Domingo**, is Mayon Spring Resort, well equipped with facilities and dotted with pine trees. The next town of **Bacagay** has almost unspoiled **Sogod Beach**, known for its clean, black sand. Its coconut palms and lush vegetation provide cool shade. Continue north along the coast to **Malilipot** where the 245-meter (800ft) Busay Falls have seven tiers of white foam cascading down to a major basin that branches out into several smaller ones. The next town, **Tabaco**, is known for its Buang Spring Resort with a natural spring-fed swimming pool. Off the coast of Tabaco is the quiet green

## Mt Isarog Trek

The 1,966-meter (6,450-ft) **Mt Isarog**, a dormant volcano in Camarines Sur near Naga, draws hikers to its verdant forests punctuated by waterfalls and sulfur springs. Virgin rainforests shelter a variety of rare flora and fauna. Trekking trails, while long, are not too technical. Inside the volcano's crater appear Magragobdob Falls, small at just 40 meters (131ft) but undeniably picturesque.

Organized multi-day volcano treks originate from Manila or Naga. Trekkers headed straight for the summit, an 8–10-hour climb, normally start from Barangay Penicuason. The trail, about half an hour's drive from Naga, links several campsites on the mountainside. A second trail, the Patag-Patag, starts from Tigaon.

There are waterfalls and springs at lower elevations. Within the Mt Isarog National Park (charge), Malabsay Waterfalls are near the entrance, inviting visitors to swim. Not far off is Nabuntulan Spring. Hikers may also run into a butterfly farm and a deer farm. Hotels and restaurants cluster near the park entrance.

Isarog is at its best between January and April. Lower elevations are warm, but temperatures cool quickly as one climbs toward the crater. (For trekking details, call the Department of Environment and Natural Resources, tel: 054-473-1617).

island of **San Miguel**, home to the white-sand, clear-water Punta Beach. Beyond Tabaco, Amater Resort in **Malinao** has a natural spring-fed swimming pool.

Beach-lovers could also seek out the white-sand beach along the southern tip of Cagraray Island, a 45-minute drive from Legazpi, plus a 5-minute boat ride. You land at the 20-hectare (49-acre) Misibis Resorts, Estates & Spa.

In **Tiwi**, 20km (12 miles) north of Tabaco, the surging ocean comes upon Putsan Beach. Jet-black sands here used to make the region's ancient ceramics. Every third Saturday in August, thousands of devotees flock to small *barangay* **Joroan** in Tiwi to pay homage to the miraculous image of Nuestra Señora de Salvacion, patroness of Albay. The event, popularly known as the Pilgrimage to Joroan, features a procession carrying the saint down to the beach. Along Tiwi's highway are steep cliffs. Strategically placed rest areas reward travelers with Pacific Ocean views.

## Sorsogon Province

A fine drive along a coastal, cliffside road south of Legazpi loops across mountain ridges that plummet straight to the sea. This takes you to **Sorsogon Province**, the southernmost in Bicol and known for a spot where people can swim with gentle whale sharks. At least 10 buses (involving 13 hours of travel) from Manila reach the capital city, **Sorsogon ❻**. Or you can fly to Legazpi, then take a jeepney. At the center of Sorsogon is the attractive Provincial Capitol Building, while Sorsogon National High School is considered one of the most ornate high-school buildings in the country.

Just 7km (4 miles) north is a white-sand beach in **Bacon**, with cottages and picnic huts. Twenty kilometers (12 miles) east is Rizal Beach in **Gubat**, a long, crescent-shaped strip of white sand, ideal for boating, swimming, and beachcombing. A little way south is **Barcelona**, noted for its church and fortress ruins.

Farther south is **Lake Bulusan**. It sits at 600 meters (1,970 ft) above sea level inside the 3,670-hectare

**TIP**

Mt Mayon erupts on a regular basis, each time forcing the evacuation of hundreds of surrounding villages. Anyone planning a climb should check first with the Philvolcs office in Legazpi, or call the local tourism office to ask whether any guides are leading treks during a given timeframe.

**BELOW:** Lahuy Island.

**TIP**

To arrange for a trekking guide on Mayon Volcano, call the Albay Tourism Office (tel: 052-820-6314 or 052-820-6316). For more information: www.pinoymountaineer.com/2008/10/mayon-volcano-2462.html

(9,070-acre) **Bulusan Volcano National Park** . A 2km (1.5-mile) hiking trail winds around the lake and up to the 1,565-meter (5,130ft) **Bulusan Volcano**, home to more than a hundred kinds of plants and flowers. At its foot is San Benon Spring, which has a mixture of sulfuric, steaming, lukewarm, and cool waters. Just 7km (4 miles) away is **Masacrot Spring**, a man-made pool with bubbling, cool, and natural soda water.

North of the park, Namuat Falls in **Casiguran** is surrounded by a variety of flowering plants, and to the south, Bulus Spring of **Irosin** has clear and cool water springing out from obscure fissures. Falling water from the nearby scenic Mapaso Spring emits a fine spray. Along Sorsogon Bay is Pepita Park, complete with rest houses, cemented walks, beaches, a children's playground, and lush greenery.

Sorsogon's current crowd-puller is the town of **Donsol**, off which the gentle *butanding* or whale sharks are spotted seasonally. The best time to go is between February and May, when officers from the municipality guide boat-loads of people to swim and interact with the gentle giants – an opportunity seldom found anywhere else in the world. The polka-dotted fish, the world's largest, are gentle enough to cavort alongside human swimmers. Still they measure up to 12.2 meters (40ft) long (for more information, visit www.sorsogontourism.com/whale_shark_interaction_guide.htm).

## Catanduanes

A flight northeast from Legazpi leads to Catanduanes, an island endorsed by surfers. The 15,110-sq km (5,830-sq mile) island province of **Catanduanes** is a huge mountain mass with thick forests of hardwoods, one of the main sources of Philippine mahogany. Called "Land of the Howling Winds," Catanduanes lies east of Luzon and bears the first impact of the typhoons that regularly strike the area. The same late-year storms excite surfers, who see Catanduanes as home to a fickle surf break called Majestics. When that is not pushing swells toward the coast,

**BELOW:** jeepney outside a mall in Legazpi.

surfers proceed to Coconut Point, Twin Rocks, Morning Point, Rocky Point, and Bintikayan.

As the island slowly gains interest as a surfing destination, **Toytoy Beach** and **Igang Beach**, previously enjoyed only by locals, are becoming modestly developed. Toytoy has a clean, white beach and underwater coral formations; the white-sanded Igang Beach sits close to caves and more coral.

Around town there are a couple of hotels and restaurants, providing a base, when the weather is good, for exploring more of the island. Puraran Beach is clean, white, and invigorating, with a dining hall and surfing area. Mamangal Beach is lined with trees with picnic sites and drop-off points for scuba divers keen on its reefs swarming with colorful fish. A commercial complex called Catanduanes Island Resort has white and brilliantly clean beaches ideal for surfing, skindiving, and sports fishing, as well as an 18-hole golf course.

Lush vegetation, forests, and wildlife provide an excellent backdrop for hiking and climbing around **Nahulugan Falls**. The scenic **Binanuahan Waterfalls** has picnic grounds and sheds for overnight stays, and is good for swimming, diving, and hiking. **Luyang Caves** feature a grotto-like limestone formation.

*Swimming with whale sharks, Donsol.*

**BELOW:** zip-wire at Lignon Hill.

# LUZON'S ISLANDS

A scattering of islands off Luzon's south coast, including Mindoro, Marinduque, Romblon, and Masbate, offers virgin forests, mysterious caverns, soothing hot springs, untouched beaches, and camping beneath the stars.

string of large islands south of Luzon leads intrepid travelers to the coastal and underwater scenery for which the Philippines is known worldwide. But due to the lack of infrastructure on many of those islands, it takes patience or a bit of roughing it to reach some of the better spots. Roads may be patchy, taking jeepneys half a day to get somewhere, or requiring a bit of money for a private pumpboat ride. Unlike the more developed regions of the country, many of the white-sand beaches lack any kind of resort or diving facilities.

Most tourists to this region go to Mindoro, the largest and most rugged of the island chain. Puerto Galera in Mindoro's north draws a regular beach crowd, as it's an easy ferry ride from Luzon, while the more remote Apo Reef in the south pulls in hard-core divers. Inexpensive resorts along a public beach near the major southern city San Jose may be perfect for swimmers. San Jose is also a hired boat jumping-off point for offshore islets, such as Ambulong, that are popular with divers and cavers. Travelers in the right parts of Mindoro may meet some of the indigenous Mangyan people, a nomadic tribe whose land has been hollowed out by ranching and farming.

East of Mindoro lies the island of Marinduque, where the foremost attractions are the Bathala Caves complex in Santa Cruz and the Mainit Hot Springs, as well as the annual Moriones pre-Easter festival. Southeast from here, the three-island province of Romblon features a series of beaches, and on the island of Masbate further east, Talisay Beach has grown into a booming resort area with a reputation for its diving board-like rocks. Visitors to Ubo Falls, also in Masbate, will get the scenery

**Main attractions**
APO REEF DIVING
PUERTO GALERA RESORTS
MARINDUQUE'S MORIONES FESTIVAL
TRES REYES ISLANDS' CAVES AND REEFS
ROMBLON'S WATERFALLS

**LEFT:** Tamaraw Falls.
**RIGHT:** Puerto Galera.

**TIP**

Watch the tide when visiting Ilin Island. Some of its beaches are fringed with reefs, making passage difficult during low water.

of other Philippine waterfalls without the annoyances of crowds. Day-trippers from Masbate can boat out to Ticao Island or Burias Island for even more further-flung beaches, as well as a manta ray gathering point popular with divers.

Locals to these islands live largely off fishing and farming. Boats from Batangas near Manila serve Puerto Galera on Mindoro, and daily flights from Manila reach San Jose on the island's south coast.

## Mindoro

Lying just south of Manila is the large island of **Mindoro**. Its name comes from Spanish, *mina de oro*, meaning gold mine, though no major gold deposits were discovered here at any time. Today, as in much of the Philippines, extensive fruit farming and fishing anchor the economy, with logging and beach tourism right behind those income sources. The island is divided by the Mindoro Mountains into Mindoro Oriental, on the eastern side, and Mindoro Occidental, to the west. Most travelers

**BELOW:** Mangyan family.

to the islands just south of Luzon pick Mindoro first for its Puerto Galera beach complex or its less developed places to dive, snorkel, and look for members of the dwindling Mangyan tribe.

## Mindoro Occidental

**Mindoro Occidental** is endowed with numerous natural attractions, many of them pristine for lack of commercialization. These include virgin forests and white-sand beaches as well as offshore islands rich in marine life, coral gardens, caves, and waterfalls. The offshore waters are rich in tuna, marlin, and swordfish.

There are cheap accommodations throughout the province, some without electricity. But who cares when you're trekking the interior of the mountains, visiting indigenous Mangyan settlements, or trying to steal a glimpse of the wild *tamaraw* (wild upland dwarf buffalo)?

There are regular flights to the province's two major cities, Mamburao and San Jose, from Manila. Boats and fast ferries depart every hour from

## The Mangyans of Mindoro

T he indigenous mountain-dwelling Mangyan people, who resemble the darker-skinned Austronesian people of the South Pacific, settled on Mindoro about 3,000 years ago, but have dwindled as more recent arrivals drive them away from traditional land. An estimated 100,000 live in Mindoro today.

Taditionally living off hunting, fruit-gathering, or subsistence farming, their languages differ from those dominant in the Philippines, and even from one another as some tribes remain completely isolated. Some have their own writing systems, which pre-date the arrival of the Spanish. They live in villages comprising houses made of palm wood and covered with palm straw. Some dress only in native g-strings, others in Western clothes; Hanunoo men wear a loincloth and shirt, the women an indigo-dyed skirt and embroidered blouse. Accessories for both males and females may include beaded bracelets, necklaces, and chokers.

Illegal loggers, Christian settlers, and ranchers have ousted the Mangyans from the land they once occupied. Elusive and shy, these people have retreated deeper into the mountains, many deliberately avoiding contact with outsiders as they struggle to preserve an identity and hold onto precious land.

Batangas to Calapan. Buses ply the off-again, on-again highways that circle the island.

On the southwest coast of Mindoro Occidental is the city of **San Jose.** San Jose's airport is just 3km (2 miles) from Downtown, connected by a road that parallels a wide beach popular with everyday water frolickers. There are daily flights to and from Manila just 40 minutes away. The tree-shaded Sitakuna Beach Hotel (tel: 043-491-4108) along the beach, just five minutes by tricycle-taxi from the airport, can serve as a launch pad for outlying islands, as pumpboats leave from the beach just outside. The next-door White House Beach Resort (tel: 043-490-1656) offers more luxurious, more expensive rooms right next to where pumpboats begin trips to smaller isles.

Off San Jose sits the 3,000-hectare (7,400-acre) **Ambulong Island ⑨**. White beaches, cliffs, and underwater caves characterize the island. There is a fishing village on the sheltered side, and coral gardens and tropical fish in numerous coves. Dive spots, such

as Iling Point, Baniaga Reef, Ambulong Bank, Dungan Reef, Sardines Reef, Manadi Island, and Apo Reef, are accessible from San Jose.

To reach Ambulong, hire a public pumpboat from a beach behind the ragtag San Jose wet market. Some travelers pick up another boat from Ambulong to Grace Island, home to a resort by the same name (www.graceislandresort.com). When crossing to San Jose from Ambulong, stop off at **Ilin Island** for a glimpse into life in a Philippine fishing village.

Boats from San Jose also do day trips to the uninhabited White Island atoll. Trees, *nipa* huts, shells, and coral cover the islet; calm, clear shallow waters next to it invite snorkeling or swimming among tiny blue fish. Marine turtles occasionally bury their eggs in the sand there.

*Tropical vegetation on Mindoro.*

**BELOW:** scuba diver, Apo Reef National Park.

Off the west coast of Mindoro, **North Pandan Island** , is ideal for snorkeling, fishing, boating, and swimming sites, as well as rock formations. When all accommodations in Mindoro are fully booked, especially during Holy Week, North Pandan Island offers a paradisiacal slice of tropicana to visitors looking to dodge the crowds. Camping here is a nice option for those so inclined; otherwise, Pandan Island Resort (tel: 0919-305-7821; www.pandan.com) offers bungalows.

## Apo Reef

North Pandan Island is the major gateway to **Apo Island**. Located on this island is the **Apo Reef National Park** , acclaimed as one of the best dive sites in the Philippines. Apo itself is less than 1km (0.5 miles) long, but the reef holds enough underwater interest to keep divers busy for a week. Some 400–500 coral species live in the waters around the island, and its Shark Ridge presents the best underwater adventure on the reef. The best time to visit Apo is March through early June,

between the monsoons and when the seas are calmer.

In the heart of Mindoro is the 75,450-hectare (186,400-acre) **Mt Iglit-Baco National Park**, home to the last significant population of *tamaraw* and the endangered Mindoro imperial pigeon. To search for these endangered beasts, hire a guide at the Tamaraw Conservation Project. As activists try to save the *tamaraw* from total wipe-out, the local tourism office in San Jose runs one-hour van trips to the *tamaraw* reserve.

Tayamaan Beach in **Mamburao** is a 1-hectare (2.5-acre) strip of sand lined with coconut trees and native cottages. The secluded 14-hectare (35-acre) Mamburao Beach Resort, has a 4km (2.5-mile) light gray sand beach, ideal for swimming, scuba diving, windsurfing, snorkeling, deep-sea fishing, and water-skiing. Glass-bottomed boats, speedboats, and outrigger boats are also available.

## Caving challenges

Unexplored caves dot the mountains of Mindoro. Experienced cavers may

**BELOW:** idyllic beach, Puerto Galera.

want to take the challenge of **Luyang Baga** (Lung Cave) in Cabacao, Abra de Ilog. Getting to the cave, however, is tough. After a jeepney ride from Mamburao to Abra de Ilog, hire an indigenous Mangyan guide from the settlements near Cabacao to take you to the entrance. Be prepared with everything as supplies in town are sparse.

From Cabacao the trek takes eight hours, and involves 21 river crossings in chest-deep water. Once in the caves, visitors can marvel at the white crystalline floors and walls and deep pools of gin-clear water. Consult with your guide to make sure you are adequately equipped to tackle the more difficult passages.

Northward is **Ambil Island**, a favorite fishing ground for sports enthusiasts. On Ambil is the Besay Falls, consisting of a series of waterfalls each cascading into a crystal-clear basin about 5 meters (16ft) in diameter. A 30-minute pumpboat ride northwest of Lubang lies **Cabra Island**. Generally flat, Cabra has golden-hued sandy beaches in the southwest and rock formations along its east coast. It's also known for sports fishing.

## Mindoro Oriental

In a sheltered inlet sits the island's main destination, **Puerto Galera** (PG) ⑬ ("Port of Galleons"). Today, the resort magnet of six decades, which is ominously accessible by ferry from Manila, marks its days with the comings and goings of increasing numbers of visitors. Some of the beaches along this particularly scenic bay on the north Mindoro coast are developed wall-to-wall, right down to the sand, with resorts and restaurants. Some argue that it has become overdeveloped, though some like the party atmosphere. The farther-out beaches retain their isolated charm, while the mountains above are ripe for hiking and overnight camping.

Although Puerto Galera's **Sabang Beach** was once described as "Little Ermita," a reference to Manila's

entertainment district, the number of bars has decreased. It has also been a target for police busts against selling *shabu*, the local word for methamphetamines.

There are plenty of peaceful, pleasant spots along the coast for water-skiing, kayaking, scuba diving, snorkeling, sunbathing, and swimming. Despite a coral blanching incident in 1998, the colorful undersea life forms have grown back, stunning divers with their diversity. Small **La Laguna Beach** has coral reefs, good for snorkeling and scuba diving. **Talipanan Beach** and **Punta Guarda Beach** are perfect for swimming. **White Beach** has swim beaches and entertainment facilities. **Aninvan Beach** is close enough to White Beach to walk to, but far enough from the noisy nightlife. If you want a patch of sand all to yourself, hire a boat to take you to **Bikini Beach**.

Inside the Roman Catholic convent is **Puerto Galera Museum** (Mon–Fri 8am–5pm; free), exhibiting valuable artifacts dating from Spanish and pre-Spanish times. The **Marble Cross**

**TIP**

To reach Puerto Galera, take the ferry from Batangas, which passes through the swirling waters of the Verde Passage. Batangas is about three hours by bus from Manila.

**BELOW:** essential beachwear.

*Inter-island transport.*

**BELOW:** one of
Puerto Galera's
popular beaches.

alongside the roadside 15km (9 miles) southeast of Puerto Galera and has a natural swimming pool at its base. Hire a jeepney to get here.

Further southeast of Puerto Galera, **Calapan** lies in the shadow of 2,582-meter (8,471ft) **Mt Halcon** , the highest mountain in Mindoro, and the Philippines' fourth highest. Considered one of the country's finest trekking peaks, it has several rivers and rock formations and is a haven for wildlife. If considering a climb, for safety's sake get a guide.

Continuing southeast, **Naujan Lake**, the largest freshwater lake in the province, is home to freshwater species that enter the lake to feed before going to the open sea to spawn. Adjacent is the volcanic **Pungaw Hot Springs**, located among large boulders. Go to the nearby Dome Hill for views of the lake, a vast agricultural plain, and the Butas and Lumangbayan rivers.

at Muelle commemorates the crew of the Spanish warship *Canonero Mariveles*, which sank during a storm on November 18, 1879.

**Ponderosa**, an exclusive 9-hole golf club sitting on an 800-meter (2,600ft) elevation, offers Puerto Galera's shimmering beauty on one side, and mist caressing the deep-green mountains on the other. The 130-meter (430ft)-high **Tamaraw Falls** is located

## Marinduque

An isolated volcanic mass surrounded by coral reefs, **Marinduque** lies between Mindoro Island and Quezon

Province's Bondoc Peninsula, where it serves as a coconut growing center for the Philippines. The relatively undeveloped island's main tourist attraction is the week-long **Moriones Festival**, celebrated in the towns of Boac, Mogpog, and Gasan every week before Easter. This religious event re-enacts the story of Longinus, a Roman army officer who was blind in one eye. In Marinduque, men wearing masks (*moriones*) and colorfully dressed as Roman soldiers roam about scaring children or doing other stunts to get attention. Some of the wooden masks are sold to tourists after the festival (see Fiesta Fantastica, page 70). Diving, caves, and a hot spring draw other visitors to Marinduque.

**Boac** ⑮, the provincial capital and a seat of commerce on the west coast, is best accessed by sea from Lucena, Quezon. There is also a 40-minute flight from Manila. The town's 18th-century **Boac Cathedral** features Filipino-Hispanic Gothic architecture, with much of the original structure faithfully preserved – the facade and main body, the belfry, and the altar.

The **Battle of Pulang Lupa,** now the subject of a landmark, two hours' drive time from Boac, was the first known major battle won by the Filipinos over the Americans, on July 31, 1900. Despite having inferior weaponry, the group of Filipino soldiers overcame their American enemies, thereby forever earning their place in Philippine history books. A marker stands at the site, which is now surrounded by dense vegetation.

**Mainit Hot Springs**, in Boac, a flowing brook of hot water, is Marinduque's version of a hot spa.

Dominating the south of Marinduque is **Mt Malindig** ⑯, an inactive volcano that rises 1157 meters (3,800ft) above the sea and is accessible from Santa Cruz. Dense forest covers its upper half, but the rest is nearly deforested due to slash-and-burn farming. Fortunately, this does not affect the mountain's reputation as an excellent place for climbing, camping, and birdwatching. At the volcano's base, the warm waters of **Malbog Sulfur Springs** offer relaxing baths to visitors.

*In 1981, a sunken galleon was found between the waters of Gaspar and the mainland, yielding millions of pesos worth of artifacts and treasures, mostly porcelain.*

**BELOW:** men dressed as Roman soldiers at the Moriones Festival, Marinduque Island.

From Gasan you can take a 30-minute ride by motorized outrigger to **Tres Reyes Islands** (Three Kings Islands). The largest of the three, and closest to Marinduque's southwest coast, is Gaspar Island, with Melchor Island and Baltazar Island beyond.

These islands are ideal for fishing, swimming, and snorkeling, with their precipitous shore cliffs and underwater caves and reefs. Marine species such as grouper, snapper, mackerel, and sweetlip swim in these waters, and coconut crabs called *igod* are frequently found on the beach.

Off the coast of Buenavista town are sheer cliffs, with a lengthy beach of white sand and crushed corals surrounding **Elephant Island**.

In the Marinduque town of Santa Cruz is the mysterious **Bathala Caves** complex. One cave is called the Simbahan (church), owing to its cathedral-like interior where stalagmites form a rough likeness to an altar, a bell, and a silhouette of the Virgin Mary carrying the Child. The second cave is darker and deeper. The third has an underground river, and the fourth harbors human bones, thought to be the remains of World War II soldiers.

Off the coast of Santa Cruz are the islets of Polo, Mompong, and Maniwaya, characterized by white-sand beaches and sandy cliffs. The nearby, privately owned **Salomague Island** has a long white beach of sand and crushed corals.

On the northwestern tip of Marinduque is scuba-diving haven **Natangco Islet**, an 8-hectare (20-acre) islet with a short stretch of powdery white sand that gradually slopes into the sea, filled with corals and aquatic life. Coasta Celina, another diving favorite, further south in Torrijos town, is flanked by cliffs with an undersea wall that is rich in marine flora and fauna.

## Romblon

Southeast of Marinduque is the province of **Romblon**: three major islands and several islets. The biggest island is **Tablas** , where the provincial airport is located. The province is surrounded by deep waters between Masbate and

**BELOW:** Cooling off at the Tamaraw Falls.

Mindoro. There are several 45-minute flights a week, and also twice-a-week, 14-hour boat trips, from Manila.

Romblon features topography that is rich in marble and other rock types, all of which supply materials for sculpture and building. Places of interest include Bonbon Beach, Cambon Beach, Bita Falls, Tinagon Dagat (Hidden Lake), and waterfalls in San Andres and Odiongan towns.

**Romblon Cathedral** features a Byzantine altar and several icons and paintings. Nearby on the seafront are two old forts, **Fort Santiago** and **Fort Andres**, that were once used as lookouts for pirates during the Spanish regime.

## Masbate

The name **Masbate** ⑳, like others in the Philippines, was born out of a miscommunication. A squad of Spanish soldiers saw a couple here preparing beverages out of cocoa. One of them asked the locals the name of the region. Thinking that the soldier had asked what she was doing, the woman answered "Masa bati, masa bati," which literally meant to mix and beat more and more. Today it is known as the country's cattle country for its abundant grazing pasture land. The complex of largely undeveloped islands is accessible by plane from Manila or by boat from both Manila and Bicol.

Beaches, springs, caves, and waterfalls dominate Masbate's natural scenery. On the northwest tip, limestone cliffs rise almost perpendicular along the Sibuyan Sea. Dacu Beach in Mobo town is a favorite site for picnics, coconut-lined Aroroy Beach is popular for excursions, and Talisay Beach is famous for its "diving board" rocks. There are also **Ubo Falls**, scenery without the hassles of touts, and the 18-meter (60ft) **Tagoron Falls**, which plays host to a variety of colored fish near its base.

Just 1.5km (1 mile) from the national road at **Batongan** is a cave with three openings. One, at the base, is very wide and has a church-like formation, giving an eerie yet religious atmosphere. Another is at the center, and the third is found at the top of the cave. Inside is a large tunnel, connecting to another cave in **Zapatos Island** in Balud town. About 120 meters (390 ft) from the cave is the cool and fresh **Batongan Underground River**, ideal for dips. Not far away is the **Matang Tubig Spring,** where surrounding giant trees and rich vegetation makes it popular with budding artists and poets seeking inspiration.

**Ticao Island** and **Burias Island,** known for out-of-the-way beaches and fishing villages, can be done as day trips away from Masbate. For those into island hopping, boats connect Claveria, on Burias, with Donsol, Sorsogon. The latter is the home of a huge cave discovered in 1999, which had a trove of prehistoric gravestones and Ming dynasty porcelain. Offshore, 10km (6 miles) from Ticao Island, is Ticao Pass, where giant manta rays have been known to gather en masse, giving divers quite a treat.

*Masbate cowboys compete in the annual Rodeo Masbateño, usually held in May, June, or July.*

**BELOW:** fisherman's boat and tools, Romblon Province.

# VISAYAS

**A group of large islands between Luzon and Mindanao makes up the Visayas, known for their spectacular beaches and marine life. Among them are Cebu, Bohol, and tiny Boracay.**

Strung like a necklace of uneven beads, held together by seas, straits, and gulfs, the Visayas are home to the Philippines' premier tourist attractions. The six major landmasses and fringe groups of isles between Luzon and Mindanao parade calm waters, shimmering coves, and palm-fringed beaches. Seafood is enviably fresh in the region dominated economically by hauls from under the ocean.

Visayan labels the people and dominant language of the region, though three distinct cultural-linguistic groups live on the islands that span Leyte in the east to Panay in the west. Most people farm or fish, with rural poverty widespread.

The most popular Visayan island is tiny Boracay, where 3km (2-mile) -long White Beach rocks to the beat from scores of noisy resorts. It's a teaser for more pristine coastlines elsewhere that are just as popular with divers and snorkelers. Bohol's Alona Beach caters to diving, and more sedate Moalboal on Cebu Island and tiny Apo Island off Negros see more scuba traffic. After toweling off, tour Fort San Pedro in Cebu city or grab beers in one of the city's bar districts.

Jet planes whisk travelers from Manila to Cebu and most other Visayan capitals in under an hour, but the best way to see the Visayas up close is by boat. It takes 20 hours by sea from Manila to the Visayas. Far shorter routes from Cebu reach Bohol, Negros, and Samar.

One guy who should have avoided boating in the Visayas is Portuguese sailor Ferdinand Magellan. The trip started well on March 16, 1521, when he anchored in Leyte Gulf. Enrique de Molucca, Magellan's Malaysian slave, hailed a small boat of eight natives from the rail of their ship the *Trinidad*. The natives understood him perfectly, meaning the world had been circled linguistically. Enrique de Molucca became the first known person to circumnavigate the globe.

Six weeks later, Magellan had sailed north to Cebu to "Christianize" the rajah and 500 followers. Lapu Lapu, a minor rajah of Mactan – a muddy coral island where Cebu's international airport now stands – was less accommodating. He defended his island with some 2,000 warriors against 48 armor-clad Spaniards, the battle claiming Magellan's life. A white obelisk on Mactan today marks where Magellan fell.

**PRECEDING PAGES:** dusk at Alona Beach. **LEFT:** Alona Beach, Panglao Island.
**ABOVE, FROM LEFT:** house in Tacloban; Cebu Ciay.

# EASTERN VISAYAS

The two large islands of Samar and Leyte are best known for the brutal battles of World War II which took place here, but also host seldom trodden tropical beaches, mountains, and caves.

Manila

**Main attractions**
WORLD WAR II MONUMENTS, LEYTE
LEYTE MOUNTAIN TRAIL
BILIRAN ISLAND
SOHOTON NATIONAL PARK, SAMAR

The eastern part of the Visayas is the least prosperous, and the least developed for tourism. Be advised that typhoons often batter this Pacific Ocean-facing region with their full force before weakening over other parts of the country. There is plenty to explore and the off-the-beaten track feel of this far-flung region appeals to adventurers.

Samar and Leyte cradle some of the country's lushest forests and pristine shores, offering ample opportunities for action sports, historical tours, and scenic leisure strolls. Venues abound for surfing, trekking, and rock climbing.

Locals live largely off rice and coconut farming, with the usual Philippine staple of fishing ever in the economic picture. A geothermal plant in Leyte gives the island an unusual natural resource advantage over other regions. So poor is Samar that government officials have targeted it as a development priority.

## Natural wealth

Owing to its rich ecosystems, most of the region's people are engaged in farming and fishing. Its plains and valleys are fertile, producing hemp, copra, corn, rice, tobacco, bananas, papayas, and pineapple. The swamps teem with *nipa* and mangrove, while rattan and timber grow thick in the mountains. Thousands of hectares of virgin forests still survive. The driest months are April to August, with November to January the rainiest. Typhoons from the Pacific usually hit Eastern Samar, sparing most of the region from the calamity as the force of the storms generated by low pressure over the Pacific Ocean reduces after reaching land.

The eastern Visayas abound in ritual. During the cropping season, farmers perform ceremonies invoking nature

**LEFT:** farmland in rural Leyte.
**RIGHT:** Sangyaw Festival, Tacloban.

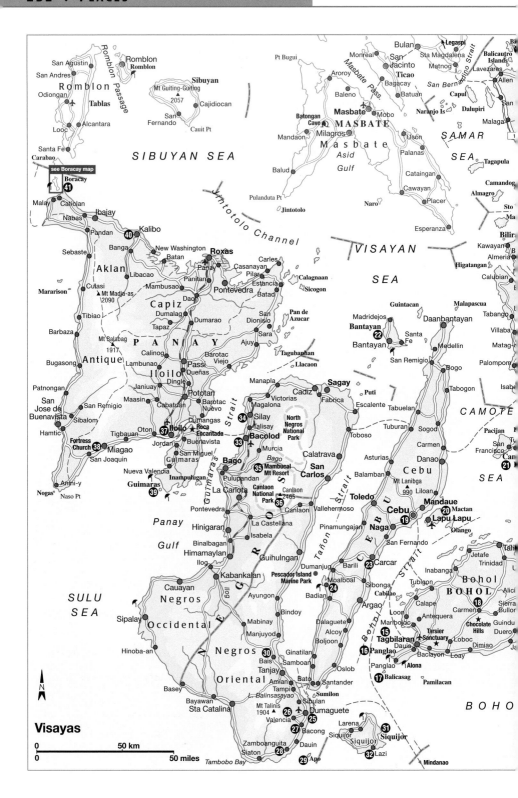

Visayas

0           50 km

0           50 miles

and ancestral spirits for a good harvest. This is complemented by Christian customs such as the recitation of a *novena*, a nine-day prayer of devotion among Catholics. Fisherfolk, likewise, ask permission from the water spirits for safety at sea and a good catch. Fiestas are celebrated with prayer, food and drink, dance and music. June is party time. The Pintados Festival revives a tradition of painting the body and dancing to the rhythm of bamboo sticks. Fishermen in the coastal villages of the region celebrate the Subiran Regatta, an annual race for locally designed sailboats.

## For travelers

The region has an array of lodgings, ranging from luxurious to smaller hotels and pension houses. Cozy, native huts and cottages are also available. Most people speak the Leyte-Samar dialect, Waray, although some are also conversant in Cebuano, Filipino, and English. Those wanting to learn more of the local culture can get information on home-stay programs through the local tourist office. Note that power supply is erratic in some towns, and rain is the most common source of drinking water among rural households. In contrast, facilities for ballroom and disco dancing may turn heads.

The most favored destination in the region is Tacloban, served daily by one-hour flights from Manila and a half-hour flight from Cebu. Several bus companies ply the Manila–Quezon–Bicol–Samar–Leyte route via the Maharlika Highway (plus a ferry link); the estimated travel time is 24 hours. A good road network connects the region's municipalities and villages, which are accessible by bus, jeepney, and private vehicles.

Shipping lines offer regular trips to the region's major ports. There are three round trips per week on the Manila–Tacloban route. High-speed ferries by Supercat and Waterjet take passengers to closer ports. Ferries also cross the Surigao Strait from Maasin south to Lipata Point, in Surigao del Norte, where a highway proceeds across Mindanao. Outlying islands can be reached by pumpboat.

## LEYTE

Leyte, poorer and less developed than other large Philippine islands, draws travelers seeking to keep away from the crowds. Some

*Religious icons in Tacloban. Most Visayans are Roman Catholic due to the fact that the first churches in the Philippines were established in the region.*

**BELOW:** Leyte Provincial Capitol.

visitors also come to see war sites and monuments, as Leyte was a massive battleground during World War II.

The capital of both Leyte Province and the region of Eastern Visayas is **Tacloban City ❶**. It became a vital trading point in the region as early as the 16th century because of its strategic location, but it wasn't until June 12, 1952, that it received chartered city status.

At the corner of Magsaysay Boulevard and Sen. Eñage Street are the Tacloban City Park and Playground and Plaza Libertad, where a Filipino version of the Statue of Liberty stands. In front is the **Leyte Provincial Capitol**, once the seat of the Philippine Commonwealth Government under President Sergio Osmeña Sr. Visit the Leyte SME Assistance and Trade Center for a glimpse of local culture and art. Just off Magsaysay Boulevard, look for **Leyte Park Resort**, a tourism and convention complex built by former first lady Imelda Marcos on 6 hectares (15 acres) overlooking San Pedro Bay and Mt Danglay on the island of Samar.

Farther along to the right is the **Maria Kannon Garden**, with the first of numerous war monuments: a statue of an Asian madonna donated by the Japanese people as a symbol of peace following the atrocities of World War II. Adjacent is the Philippine-Japan Peace Commemoration Statue and Park. On a hilltop in the next compound sprawls the Tacloban City Hall and Park, with the **Balyuan Tower/Mini Amphitheater** below with a panoramic view of Kankabatok Bay.

## Wartime reminders

To start a tour of World War II sites in Tacloban, look for the **CAP Building** (formerly Price Mansion; Mon–Fri 8am–noon, 1–5pm; free). It was the official headquarters of General Douglas MacArthur during the liberation of Leyte in 1944. The MacArthur Room is preserved for public viewing.

One block southeast, on the corner of T. Claudio and Sen. Eñage streets, is the **Redoña House**, residence of President Osmeña during the same liberation. Along Avenida Veteranos Extension, towards Serin district, stand the **Stations of the Cross**: 2-meter (7ft) -tall concrete statues of Jesus and other biblical characters. On top of the most obvious hill sits the 5.5-meter (18ft) Sacred Heart monument.

Japanese pillboxes are still preserved in **Dio Resort** (also known as Baluarte San Jose). The city's Daniel Z. Romualdez Airport served as a battle stage during World War II, as well.

In front of the Coca-Cola Bottling Company is the **Boy Scout Monument**, erected in 1941. From here, turn left to the national highway.

At Pawing, just before the Leyte Government Center, stands the **Monument of the Filipino Soldier**, a tribute to the Filipino World War II veterans. Not too far from these grim reminders of some of the worst fighting of the 1940s sits the 9-hole golf course and driving range at the foot of the city's most prominent peak, **San Gerardo Heights**.

At Red Beach, Candahug, in **Palo ②**, the **Leyte Landing Memorial** shows where MacArthur came ashore in 1944 with his Allied Liberation Forces to fulfill a famous "I shall return" promise to the Filipinos and oust the Japanese invaders. Bronze statues, at one-and-a-half times bigger than life size, mark the site of the landing. Close by is the 50th Leyte Landing Commemorative Rock Garden, and in the adjacent MacArthur Beach Resort you can view

*Monument of the Filipino Soldier, Tacloban.*

**BELOW:** Leyte Landing Memorial.

*San Juanico Strait is the narrowest navigable strait in the world. Its islets hold firm against whirlpools and rushing water.*

enlarged photographs of MacArthur during the liberation days.

**Palo Metropolitan Cathedral**, a local landmark built in 1596 by Augustinian friars, was converted into an evacuation hospital for the Americans, and served as a refuge for Filipino civilians during the war. Nearby are La Purisima Shrine, an image of the Virgin Mary dating back to Spanish times, and **Hill 522**, a battle area during World War II.

## Santo Niño Shrine and Heritage Museum

Along Tacloban's Real Street is **Santo Niño Shrine and Heritage Museum** (daily 8–11am, 1–4pm; charge), a once-sumptuous presidential rest-house built by Ferdinand Marcos and sequestered during the Aquino presidency. Imelda Marcos' collection of statues of the infant Jesus and other artifacts are on show. Guests would have danced in the spacious ballroom and have occupied bedrooms decorated with Filipino motifs.

Adjacent is the **People's Center and Library** (daily 8–11am, 1–4pm;

**BELOW:** Santo Niño Shrine and Heritage Museum, Tacloban.

charge), equipped with a social hall, gymnasium, and a reading room. The centre holds 82 ethnic tribe dioramas, historical documents, and books on humanities. From there, visitors can take a left to Avenida Veteranos, then go right, passing Rizal Avenue, to shop for souvenirs and local delicacies. Specialties include pineapples and sticky rice with chocolate, all wrapped in banana leaves.

Close to MacArthur's former headquarters, the **San Juanico Bridge** crosses San Juanico Strait to Samar. At 2.2km (1.25 miles) long, it claims to be Southeast Asia's longest bridge.

A short day trip west of the Palo Metropolitan Cathedral lies **Jaro's Mt Kankahanay**. It's known as a hunter's paradise because of its virgin forests and cool sub-alpine climate at 1,230 meters (4,000ft) above sea level. To the north is the town of **Barugo**, site of the battle between Filipino guerrillas and Japanese Imperial forces in August 1944. The site is significant for the lack of Filipino casualties; all the Japanese except one were killed. A monument made up of three stairs, fenced by silver-colored chains and flagpoles that resemble bayonets, commemorates the battle.

The nearby town of **Carigara** has made a name for Sunduan Ha Carigara, an annual Easter Sunday celebration of cultural and religious activities, such as a float parade contest, cockfighting and dances. **Break Neck Ridge**, to the west in the city of Capoocan, was the site of one of the bloodiest scenes in the battle to free the Philippines from Japanese occupation.

## Leyte Mountain Trail

On Leyte's western coast, thousands of Japanese and American soldiers died in Buga-Buga Hills in **Villaba**, during Japan's assault to capture this area during World War II. Inland, the **Leyte Mountain Trail** runs 40km (25 miles) from Tong-onan to Lake Danao, continuing southeast to Mahagnao National

Park. Ideal for trekking, the trail winds through rainforests, skirts lakes, passes Guinaniban Falls, and touches the Amandiwing mountain range.

North of **Ormoc City** look for **Tongonan Hot Springs National Park**. The springs are known for curative powers and have become a vital geothermal power source in the lush surrounding forest. Geothermal power needs are driving development around the park, adding conveniences for travelers. Just southeast sits the violin-shaped **Lake Danao**, 640 meters (2,100ft) above sea level and hemmed by cloud-capped mountain ranges and forests.

From Lake Danao the Leyte Mountain Trail continues, wending its way to temperate **Mahagnao National Park ❸**. Scout the park for craters, hot springs, and lakes of multicolored mud and rocks. They rest in a virgin forest with giant ferns and orchids. The park's Facebook page gives details on specific sights and directions. Nearby, one can ride **Daguitan Rapids** in makeshift rafts of banana trunks, or steadier rubber tires fashioned into rafts, for a different

way to see the countryside. From Lake Mahagnao, hike north to the town of **Buraguen**, where horses can be rented to explore the surrounding area.

South from Ormoc is the town of **Baybay**, home to Visayas State College of Agriculture, situated on the foothills of the Baybay mountains. Further south is **Hilongos**, where Hilongos Bell Tower, the highest existing bell built during the Spanish era, is located. **Kaupnit Balinsasayaw Park**, situated along the Baybay-Mahaplag road, is a favorite stopover and campsite for travelers.

A road from Baybay follows the west coast to **Maasin ❹**, provincial capital of Southern Leyte. Attractions here include the Esfa Beach Resort and the Busay Falls. **Maasin Cathedral** holds images and saints dating back to the Spanish era. Off the southern tip of Leyte is historic **Limasawa Island ❺**, where one of the country's first Catholic Masses was celebrated. Northeast is **Panaon Island**, where the popular Bitu-on and Maamo beaches can be found. Remote beauty is the key; travelers go for scuba diving

*The Japanese invasion in 1942 marked the onset of the darkest period in the history of Tacloban. The Battle of Leyte Gulf is one of the biggest naval battles in modern Philippine history.*

**BELOW:** Bas-relief depicting General MacArthur's Landing, Leyte Provincial Capitol.

## World War II Battleground

US military strategists sent troops to the island of Leyte in October 1944 in the first stage of an attempt to end the almost three-year occupation of the Philippines by Imperial Japanese forces. Japan already had a grip on the larger Luzon Island, but the US landing in Leyte compelled it to divide its forces.

On October 20, US troops established beachheads around Tacloban. Despite weak initial opposition from the Japanese, the Imperial forces moved their air and sea power to Leyte to counter the threat. The Japanese soon had an upper hand, leading to large losses of life during the ensuing battles.

A series of skirmishes in the same October almost completely wiped out Japan's naval power, giving the US side crucial control over the nearby seas. After two months of ground-fighting in Leyte, American troops had secured parts of the island for logistics bases, on their way toward broader control. In addition to the enemy, they also had to contend with difficult, muddy terrain. In December 1944 General Douglas MacArthur announced that the US Eighth Army would take control over the Leyte battle lines. Fighting, though brief, grew intense enough to leave behind a series of World War II markers that give visitors a keen sense of what Leyte was like in late 1944.

**TIP**

When trekking, refresh yourself with young coconut juice (*buko*), readily and cheaply available. Just ask the owner of the coconut grove. For a few pesos, he'll probably climb up the tree and pick the *buko* and cut it open for you.

and whale watching, but compared to other Visayan beaches there are few amenities on Panaon.

## Biliran Island

Connected to Leyte's northern coast by a bridge lies the picturesque **Biliran Island** ❻, a 55,540-hectare (137,200-acre) province. Its busy main port, which is crowded with rows of buses and jeepneys, belies the highly rural nature of the province. Outside town, Biliran abounds with waterfalls, countless streams, hot springs, and fine sand beaches. The most notable sites on the coast are Agta Beach in Almeria and Banderrahan Beach in Naval. Biliran's highest peaks, **Tres Marias** (Three Marias), form a trio of seemingly equidistant mountain tops, a favorite for local climbers and the pristine, heavily forested home of the Philippine spitting cobra. Two-day trekking tours can be arranged in Tacloban (contact local guide Rene Galleros, tel: 0910-698-9517).

Located on the island's eastern coast is the town of **Caibiran**, which has the spring-fed San Bernardo Swimming Pool and Tomalistis Falls, both known for oddly sweet-tasting water. The hot sulfur springs of Mainit and Libtong can be found off Caibiran.

Smaller islands near Biliran include pristine **Maripipi Island**, **Higatangan Island**, and **Sambauan Island**. For the more physically inclined, mountain biking on the National Cross Country Highway reveals a full, if humid, panorama of beaches, forests, and dense vegetation.

If you missed the Ifugao rice terraces of Luzon, Biliran offers its own version. The comparative lack of level ground here compels farmers to build hillside mud terraces, which are nourished by the province's numerous streams. The **Iyusan Rice Terraces** in Almeria are just one example.

## SAMAR

A poor island, without the tourist development of the Visayan islands further to the west, Samar draws visitors largely to the caves and limestone cathedrals or Sohoton National Park and the festivities every September in the city of Basey. Reminders of World

**BELOW:** Religious markers placed by Japanese veterans at Break Neck Ridge.

War II, Magellan's first landing, and other fragments of history also occur on the island. The adventure seeker will find rewards in remote beaches and a hard-to-scale X-shaped offshore rock.

The Samar city of **Basey ❼** is the launch pad for **Sohoton National Park.** The 840-hectare (2,075-acre) park stands out for its four distinct complexes of limestone walls, arches, and caves, all swathed in verdant vegetation. Visit caves overhanging the clear river waters on board a locally made outrigger, a 1¾-hour ride. The boat also eases past small, picturesque villages along the **Basey Golden River**. Rawis, a barrio near the river, houses the seldom-explored **Rawis Cave**. The park is about two hours by water from Basey.

In town, the **Church of Basey** was built in 1864, and features a watch-tower built a decade earlier. Every year, on September 29, the town suddenly comes to life as it celebrates the feast of St Michael, the town's patron saint. The outlandish partying lasts an entire week. The most-awaited festival, how-ever, is the Banigan-Kawayan Festival,

a cultural street-dancing showcase of props and traditional attire made of bamboo and mats. It takes place around the same time as the feast of St Michael.

To the southeast is the town of **Marabut ❽**, where the Marabut Marine Park encompasses 15 tower-ing rock islands with secluded beach coves and coral gardens, perfect for sea kayaking. Guests at the anchor business, the Marabut Marine Park Beach Resort (tel: 053-325-6000), can get easy access to snorkeling and scuba diving. **Malatindok**, a 21-meter (70ft) X-shaped rock formation jutting out of the sea off Calabuso Beach, has challenged countless rock climbers, few of whom have been successful in conquering its low but daunting peak.

The extreme topography of Eastern Samar makes it a challenge to access. The village of **Balangiga ❾** was the site of a controversial incident between the Philippines and the United States. After locals launched a surprise attack on American soldiers on September 28, 1901, the American military retali-ated by killing thousands of Filipinos

**TIP**

Mobility at the Sohoton National Park is partly limited by tidal shifts, so bring a packed lunch and start the tour early in the morning.

**BELOW:** Break Neck Ridge, Capoocan.

*limestone cave, Sohoton National Park.*

the first Filipinos made contact with Magellan's Spanish colonizers. Not coincidentally, the town's **Church of the Immaculate Conception** is a beautifully preserved 16th-century structure with hand-carved altars and doors.

The **Guiuan War Memorial Complex** includes the Guiuan World War II Operating Base, a 3km (1.5-mile) runway which was constructed by American Seabees, for the B-29s that dropped the atomic bombs on Japan. Sulang Beach attracts a trickle of travelers for deep-sea fishing and scuba diving; multicolored schools of fish are a common sight.

Off the southernmost tip of Guiuan town is **Homonhon Island**  where Magellan's fleet first landed in 1521. The United States ran its **Navy 3149 Base** here as one of the biggest American patrol torpedo boat bases of World War II, with over 300 boats and 150,000 American soldiers. The base commands a view of the Pacific Ocean, where Samar's typhoons originate before slamming into shore.

and removing the town's church bells, which were used as a signal during the raid. The incident was dubbed the "Balangiga Massacre" by the American press, and to this day the two countries are in dispute over the ownership of the bells, which are on display on an airbase in Wyoming, USA.

## Guiuan and Homonhon islands

**Guiuan ⓾**, a city near Suluan Island, goes down in history as the spot where

## Northern Samar

The east-coast town of **Maydolong** houses Menasnge Park and its awesome natural rock formations. **Borongan** ⓬, the provincial capital of Eastern Samar, is noted for cattle and swine breeding. Its attractions include the stone-walled Hamorawon Spring, Guintagican Beach, San Julian Beach, and the Santa Monica Caves.

To the south, Canhugas Beach in **Hernani** town stands out for its 200-meter (650ft) footbridge from the reef to the sea. There is also a rock formation that looks like man-made steps, the waters slamming against it flowing down through the steps like a waterfall.

Northern Samar is so remote that locals find it odd to see foreigners. East of Catarman, aim for the raging **Pinipisikan Falls**. Off the western tip of the province, **Biri Island** ⓭ brings in travelers for its corals, shells, and rare tropical fish, as well as the flattish, wave-chiseled Magasang boulders.

North of Catarman, **Ojay Beach** has a scimitar-like shape alongside blue waters accessible to swimmers and surfers. The wave-battered Pacific Ocean beach is lined with swaying coconut trees and formulates a piece of scenery not often found in the Philippines. On the west coast, traveling south, **Calbayog** is the site of two historic cathedrals and an airport connecting the region to Manila; **Catbalogan** is the provincial capital. In between is Gandara, with its Blanca Aurora Falls. In **Calbiga** ⓮, spelunkers can enjoy the karst **Gobingob-Lanugan Cave**.

*sixteenth-century Church of the Immaculate Conception, Guiuan.*

# CENTRAL VISAYAS

Cebu, Bohol, and their outlying, reef-fringed islands encompass emerald coves and white-sand beaches aplenty, plus diving just offshore, and cosmopolitan Cebu City for shopping and entertainment.

The Philippines' third largest city Cebu fans out past historic Fort San Pedro through several night-life districts to Mactan Island, where Magellan was slain and luxury hotels now make a killing on beachgoers. Diving resorts known for sea turtles and broad coral reefs are scattered across other parts of Cebu Island and around the coast of Bohol. Where there's diving there are sandy beaches for swimming and resorts decked out in tropical flora.

The usual entry point to Central Visayas is Cebu City. From here one may take plane hops to the capital cities of neighboring islands, board fast ferries to some destinations, or travel by slow boat to others. The island of Bohol, known also for its dark-colored rolling Chocolate Hills, is most easily reached via its chief city Tagbilaran by air from Manila or ferry from Cebu. Negros–Cebu ferries take four hours and leave daily. Ferries dock at Dumaguete and also just north of Dumaguete at Sibulan, which is the closest point to Santander at the southern tip of Cebu Island.

## BOHOL ISLAND

Miguel Lopez de Legazpi, the Spanish colonizer who became the first governor-general of the Philippines,

anchored briefly at Bohol Island in 1563, sealing a blood pact with a chief-tain, Sikatuna. Today divers anchor at Atona Beach and just about every-one ventures inland to the unusually shaped, rolling Chocolate Hills. Keep an eye out for tiny tarsiers in the trees, or replicated in gift shops.

Boholanos are known to be clan-nish and industrious, though casual tourists will find little difference between those and other Filipinos. The province is one of the largest coconut-growing areas in the country,

**Main attractions**

ALONA BEACH DIVING, PANGLAO ISLAND
PHILIPPINE TARSIER SANCTUARY, BOHOL ISLAND
CHOCOLATE HILLS, BOHOL ISLAND
FORT SAN PEDRO AND COLON STREET, CEBU CITY
MAGELLAN MARKER, MACTAN ISLAND
MALAPUSCUA
DIVING AND MOUNTAIN BIKING, MOALBOAL, CEBU ISLAND

**LEFT:** Bohol's Chocolate Hills are best seen in summer. **RIGHT:** fruit stall, Tagbilaran.

while cottage industries continue production of delicacies and handicrafts sold from the Visayas to Luzon.

Notable among the Boholano weaver's products are mats and sacks made of *saguran* fibers, Antequera baskets combining bamboo and nito, and items woven out of local grasses and reeds. Antique wooden furniture and *santos* (saints) – now fashionable decorative items in Manila – are often sourced from Bohol's far-flung towns.

## Tagbilaran and beyond

The Boholano capital Tagbilaran sits on the west end of a reliable road system that follows the 160km (100-mile) island circumference. **Tagbilaran** ⓖ is Bohol's main port of entry. Ferries do the two-hour trip throughout the day from Cebu City. Ferry ticket lines can be long, so book ahead if possible.

At the **Mangga public market** in the northern outskirts, look for the day's catch usually sold late in the afternoon. For a small charge, you may take your selection to the back of the market, have it cooked Boholano style, then gorge on your choices right on the spot, where there are tables and benches. A selection of handicrafts and delicacies is available at the centrally located **Torralba market**. While there, try the purple yam called *kinampay*.

Also in the buzzing Bohol capital, rest in the cool, white stone **St Joseph's Cathedral** or visit the **Old West Museum** (9am–10pm) above the Garden Café, a diner with more American West decor but full Filipino meals. A signboard inside the café and geared toward foreigners posts real-estate ads and notices about transportation around Bohol.

Accommodations in the capital range from budget inns to high-end hotels. Tagbilaran has two major bus terminals, with information on fares and schedules announced on prominent whiteboards. The buses – regular and mini – link the capital to all the main towns. Jeepneys ply the same routes but on shorter hops, as well as more rugged roads leading to the forested interior. Flights operate between Tagbilaran and Manila.

**BELOW:** dining on Alona Beach, Panglao Island.

Touts at the ferry pier channel tourists into the capital's distinctive, heavily built tricycles. Their unusually sturdy metal frames ply the streets for P20–50 under icons to Jesus Christ or quotations from the Bible.

Some of the best-preserved Spanish churches, watchtowers, and fortifications in the country are found in Bohol. Compare the lavishly painted church ceilings and ornate decor of these colonial architectural samples found in the towns of Baclayon, Dauis, Panglao, Loay, Loboc, Dimiao, Jagna, Cortes, Balilihan, Maribojoc, Loon, and Calape.

Some 7km (4 miles) east of Tagbilaran is **Baclayon Church**, one of the country's oldest, built by the Jesuits in 1727. It was converted into an L-shaped convent in 1872, connecting the already fortified church with a bastion that has been overgrown with shrubbery and now lies hidden behind a grotto of the Virgin of Lourdes. A church museum houses a rich collection of religious relics, ecclesiastical vestments, and old librettos of church music in Latin inscribed

on animal skins. Both the church and museum are open daily during daylight hours.

Close by is the **Blood Compact Marker**, commemorating the historic agreement between former Boholano ruler Rajah Sikatuna and the Spanish expeditionary leader Legazpi.

## Panglao Island

Welcome to one of the country's top coastal tourism magnets. About 10km (6 miles) south of the capital is the town of **Dauis** on tiny **Panglao Island** ⑯, linked to Tagbilaran on Bohol Island by two short causeways. Here a concentration of dive camps and budget cottages has turned Panglao's main commercial hub, **Alona Beach**, into Bohol's primary area for tourist accommodations. The beach is said to have remained nameless until Alona Alegre, a buxom movie star from Manila, on a location shoot in the 1970s, regaled locals and backpackers alike by showing off the first bikini ever worn in Bohol. Today fully, fashionably clad visitors from Europe, China, and South

*In the 16th century, Rajah Sikatuna and Spanish explorer Legazpi are said to have slashed their arms and allowed their blood to mix in a historical act of bonding.*

**BELOW:** scuba diving off Alona Beach.

## Adventure off Bohol

**T**hose who find Panglao Island too busy can make a side trip to less-explored islets near Bohol.

Guarded by a lighthouse, **Cabilao Island**, off the western coast of Bohol and accessible from Loon or Calape, features a mangrove-studded lagoon and reefs for the intrepid diver. A major tenant here is Polaris Beach Dive Resort (www.polaris-dive.com). The island of 3,500 people, many of whom have left to work elsewhere in Bohol, lets visitors walk around to witness what remains of the fishing and farming community.

Nearby is **Sandingan Island**, which is linked to the mainland of Bohol by a bridge. Off the northwestern town of Tubigon is **Inanoran Island**, with dense mangrove. Here, an Australian has established a small resort.

More appealing to private atoll seekers might be the islet of **Pungtud**, off Panglao town, lying in the middle of a great lagoon at just 250 meters (800ft) in length at high tide. Its core attraction is a dive wall at 33–65 meters (108–213ft) below the water's surface, a site described as a coral garden. Pungtud also suits snorkelers when the water is calm.

The islet can be reached in 20 minutes by pumpboat from Panglao Island, making it ideal for a day trip. An alternative is the overnight sea-kayak camping trip on Panglao offered by Bohol Xtreme (tel: 0919-479-2809).

Korea delight in the white sands of Alona's chief public beach at the end of a main road lined by guesthouses and restaurants. Swimmers compete with diving boats for space at the water's edge.

Jeepneys from central Tagbilaran leave every half-hour and take about one hour, or you can choose a costlier private tricycle-taxi from the Tagbilaran pier.

Long **Dolho Beach**, close to the town of Panglao, reveals a sand flat at low tide where locals comb the tidal pools for edible crustaceans. Particularly succulent is sea urchin roe, locally called *swaki*, which is collected in small bottles by elderly women, dipped in vinegar and *calamansi* juice, and peddled as an aphrodisiac. **Momo Beach**, on the west side of Panglao, is a quiet cove, with accommodations provided by rustic cottages at the jungle's edge. Popular among locals for weekend picnics is **Dumaluan Beach**.

On another fine stretch of white sand is the Bohol Beach Club (tel: 038-522-4162; www.boholbeachclub.com.

ph), a luxury resort with a pool, sauna, jacuzzi, tennis courts, the works. The Beach Club has scores of resort competitors, from the low-rent but cozy Citadel Alona to the more lavish ChART Resort Alona Beach (tel: 038-502-9095; www.charts-alona.com) across the street with a bar, garden, and pool. Smaller resorts with *nipa* hut-style rooms, swimming pools, and terraced cafés line the beach. Many of the resorts house diving shops that lead expeditions from 6.30am.

If you tire of these amenities, there are always the blue starfish which gather by the hundreds close to the shore.

Other attractions on Panglao Island include **Dauis Church**, built by the Recollects in 1784, beside which is a hexagonal watchtower erected a decade earlier that features delicate carvings on its limestone blocks; the four-story, octagonal **Panglao Watchtower**, the country's tallest coastal tower, which stands behind the seaside ruins of a Baroque church; and **Hinagdanan Cave** with its underground bathing pool half-lit by a pair of natural skylights. To get to these sites around the island, keep a tricycle-taxi driver's number handy or rent your own motor scooter in Alona Beach.

## Diver's haven

Some 35 diving schools operate near Alona Beach, up from fewer than 20 in 2009. They charge upwards of P8,000 per head for licenses and have little trouble filling boats as foreigners are so keen on diving that some stay in Panglao up to six months. Among the instructors are Sun Divers (tel: 920-523-8513; www.sun-divers.net) and the Bohol Divers Club Dive Center (tel: 038-502-9050; www.bohol-diversclub.com).

Panglao also serves as the access point for reef-fringed **Balicasag Island** ⓱, a diver's haven with well-appointed cottages, and for pumpboat cruises for whale- and dolphin-watching off

**BELOW:** a tarsier at the Philippine Tarsier Sanctuary.

**Pamilacan Island**. Balicasag's marine sanctuary, protected by its own community, is well known as one of the country's top diving sites. Among its highlights is the Black Forest, a gradual slope of black coral on the island's northeastern side. For those who don't scuba dive, the snorkeling can also open views onto the turtles, barracuda, and jack fish that make the area famous. The Philippine Tourism Authority (PTA) maintains the Balicasag Island Dive Resort, with comfortable accommodations. A service boat ferries guests to and from Tagbilaran.

On **Pamilacan Island**, nearly an hour's ride by pumpboat from Baclayon or Tagbilaran, locals guide ecotourists seeking dolphins and whales to give visitors an insight into their former prey. Simple cottages are available for overnight stays.

## Bohol interior

Northeast from Tagbilaran and through the hinterland of Bohol is **Corella**, home of the **Philippine Tarsier Sanctuary** (www.tarsierfoundation.org) where you can trek through a 6-hectare (15-acre) mahogany forest and look at the Philippine tarsier, one of the smallest primates in the world. Among other forest wildlife are the flying lemur, grass owl, and a species of hornbill.

A further 19km (12 miles) from Tagbilaran is the town of **Loboc**, where you may visit an old stone church or embark on a scenic river cruise that wends past lush greenery and women washing clothes along the river banks. After 7km (4 miles), the meandering route ends at a modest waterfall, where you can bathe with the playful locals, mostly young boys, before the trip back. Some cruise operators use large bamboo rafts outfitted with palm-weave roofs and tables for a pleasant picnic lunch.

A short distance north of Tagbilaran is **Maribojoc**, with the much-visited **Punta Cruz Watchtower**, a two-story,

triangular fortification built by the Jesuits in 1796. The landmark stands within a park, overlooking the Cebu Strait. Northeast of Maribojoc is the mountain town of **Antequera**, where a legion of visitors converges daily, but especially on Sundays, for woven baskets and other bargain handicrafts.

## Chocolate Hills

What remains Bohol's most famous attraction is a unique panorama in the vicinity of **Carmen ⓭**, a town 55km (34 miles) northeast of Tagbilaran. Here, 1,268 hills – formed by limestone, shale, and sandstone, in an area once covered by ocean – rise 30 meters (100ft) above the flat terrain. They are called the **Chocolate Hills**, for the confectionery-like spectacle they present in summer, when their sparse grass cover turns dry and brown. Two of the highest hills have been developed, offering a hostel, restaurant, swimming pool, and observation deck. Buses from Tagbilaran to the Chocolate Hills take two-and-a-half hours.

On more remote parts of the coastal road one must be prepared to lodge

**BELOW:** the Chocolate Hills of Bohol Island.

*"Bai" (pronounced "buy") is the familiar term of endearment used by Cebuanos to address all males, just like "man" or "guy." "Day" (pronounced "dye") is used to address females.*

in modest surroundings or rely on the kindness of strangers. A counter-clockwise course is recommended, passing first through the towns on the southern and eastern coasts. Among these towns is **Anda**, a two-hour drive from Tagbilaran with low-key beachside accommodation.

The next stop from Jagna is the sleepy town of **Duero**, from where a 26km (16-mile) drive inland leads to a valley where the Eskaya tribe has drawn anthropological attention for adhering strictly to traditions. These include forbidding both marriage to anyone not of the village, and the wearing of trousers by females. Most curious is the continued use of an ancient script and dialect distinct from any spoken on the rest of the island. The Eskaya have been Christianized to some extent, but believe that Christ was originally a Boholano born in Dauis on Panglao Island.

## CEBU ISLAND

Cebu has become a model for tourism development. With its deep-water port and growing international airport, the city and province of the same name are magnets for investment, both Filipino and foreign. In the tourist portfolio, they are investing in massive resorts, beach amenities, and even mountain bike treks. Divers will find space on the reefs, gamblers in a casino, and history followers in the old Spanish quarter.

The city of **Cebu** ⑲ is the oldest in the Philippines, the commercial and education center of the Visayas, and the hub of air and sea travel throughout the south. Before booming into the country's second metropolis with 823,000 people, the original settlement of Sugbu was an important trading community even before the arrival of the Spanish. Ships from the East Indies, Siam, and China paid tribute to the local chief for the right to berth here and barter. Legazpi began the Spanish colonization in 1565, making Cebu the capital until the takeover of Manila six years later. It's now a hub for agriculture-related industries, the fish trade, and ship-building enterprises, with software and telecom bubbling up behind

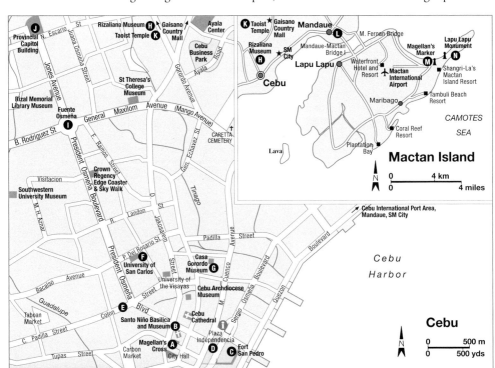

those in the Asiatown Information Technology (IT) Park.

A large wooden crucifix that was left by Magellan in 1521 commemorates the archipelago's first encounter with the West. **Magellan's Cross** , at upper Magallanes Street, is Cebu's most important historical landmark. Its supposed remnants are encased in a black cross of *tindalo* wood and housed in a kiosk (to stop people from taking home pieces as souvenirs), which also serves as a shrine commemorating the initial conversion of the islanders to Christianity. It's unsure whether the original cross has survived, but what is known is that Legazpi replaced that original cross of evangelization four decades later. Cebuano devotees may be seen visiting the shrine, pausing for prayer, lighting candles, or dropping coins into the alms box.

Nearby, off Osmeña Boulevard, is the **Santo Niño Basilica and Museum**  (open on request; free), formerly known as San Agustin Church, which was built in 1565 to house the country's oldest religious relic, the Image of the Holy Child Jesus. This was presented by Magellan to Queen Juana of Cebu on her conversion to Christianity. One of Legazpi's men found the image intact 44 years later, when Spain resumed its colonization of the Philippines. It has since survived fires and earthquakes.

In January, also known as the "Santo Niño month," the area around the church swarms with pilgrims from all over the country. Religious fervor reaches a peak with the staging of the Sinulog Festival in the third week of January, with thousands of revelers shouting, parading, and dancing with organized, wildly costumed groups up and down the streets of downtown Cebu, to the frenzied beat of drums and the toot of whistles (see Fiesta Fantastica, page 69).

As the oldest Spanish settlement in the country, Cebu has numerous sites that depict its rich colonial heritage. The foremost is the Fuerza de San Pedro or **Fort San Pedro**  (daily 7am–10pm; charge), a Spanish fort built in the 17th century and reinforced in 1738 to repel attacks by Muslim or European raiders. It is a triangular fort with bastions at each point, and an earth embankment. The walls are 6 meters (20ft) high and 18 meters (60ft) thick, with the bastions rising some 9 meters (30ft). Two of its sides face the sea, with a 15th-century gun emplacement still in place. Other, smaller Spanish cannons are similarly preserved. It has a total floor area of 2,025 sq meters (21,800 sq ft). The largest building, called "Cuerpo de Guardia," used to house the fort's defenders, while an adjacent structure called "Viviendo del Teniente" served as living quarters for the highest official. The fort has since been used as a prison for Cebuano rebels during the Spanish era, a military outpost by the Americans, and a prisoner of war camp during the Japanese occupation. Its main building now houses a museum.

Across Fort San Pedro is **Plaza Independencia** , formerly Plaza

*Queen Juana of Cebu was formerly called Rani Humamay; Magellan may have played an esoteric joke by renaming her after Spain's mad queen, Juana la Loca.*

**BELOW:** Magellan's Cross, Cebu City.

*The 17th-century Fort San Pedro.*

**BELOW:** Santo Niño Basilica, Cebu.

Libertad, a tree-shaded promenade square where stands an obelisk honoring Legazpi. Nearby is the Department of Tourism office.

## Colon Street, Cebu

A few blocks away are the **Cebu Cathedral** and **Cebu Archdiocese Museum** (Mon–Fri 9am–5pm; free). Farther up is **Colon Street ❸**, named after Christopher Columbus.

Colon used to be Cebu City's main street, where all the moviehouses and ritzy shops were found, and all jeepney routes began and ended. A business address in Colon once meant that your restaurant, shop, or office was in the very heart of the capital, but other commercial centers have edged out Colon's prestige. Today, Colon is usually so crowded it has become off-limits to most jeepneys. Shoe and watch repair stalls stand alongside an eclectic mix of hardware, machine, electrical, and noodle shops.

A block north of Colon is the **University of San Carlos ❺**, on the site of the oldest college in the country, first built in 1595. It has a

biology and anthropology museum and the Cebuano Studies Center. Several streets eastward is **Casa Gorordo Museum ❼** (tel: 032-418-7234; usually open daily 10am–6pm; charge), a century-old residence turned into a private museum displaying artifacts and memorabilia related to Cebu's traditional lifestyle. The museum had been the residence of the first Filipino bishop of Cebu, who was descended from the wealthy Gorordo family.

## Cebu's museums

Near the **Cebu Country Club and Golf Course** may be found the **Sian Tian Temple** on Archbishop Reyes Avenue, further evidence of Chinese presence and influence in the capital.

Off Salinas Drive nearby is the **University of Southern Philippines' Rizaliana Museum ❽** (tel: 032-232-5932; Mon–Fri 9am–5pm; free), which exhibits a collection of memorabilia of national hero Dr Jose Rizal. Here are some of his first literary writings, articles of clothing, etchings, and personal letters to his family, and the oil lamp used inside his cell at Fort Santiago when he wrote his valedictory poem, *Mi Ultimo Adios*.

Closer to the city center, visitors will find three more small museums maintained by educational institutions: **St Theresa's College Museum** on E. Pond Extension, the **Rizal Memorial Library Museum** on Osmena Boulevard, and the **Southwestern University Museum** (all open Mon–Fri 9am–5pm; free) in the Sambag II district.

For a full list of city museums and contact details, visit www.cebucity.gov.ph/tourist-information/local-attractions/museums.

### Shopping and entertainment

One of Cebu City's newest attractions is the Crown Regency (tel: 032-418-8888), a 38-story hotel complex where thrill-seekers can ride an Edge Coaster

or go for a Sky Walk on the building's exterior. These adventures stay open until at least midnight. Inside the complex, look for restaurants and a 4D theater.

Directly north of the **Cebu International Port Area** are two of the capital's enormous malls, **SM City** and **Ayala Center**. **Gaisano Country Mall** is further north in the Banilad district, which also has Banilad Town Center and Crossroads. These major shopping malls compete as consumerist delights, landmarks of cosmopolitanism, local hangouts, and leisure and activity centers. At night they teem with moneyed Filipinos who go to eat or tip back a few bottles.

A nightlife district with a seedier edge lines **Mango Avenue**, also in central Cebu City. Customers can tell what it's all about by reading the neon names hung from these windowless vaults: Love City, Pussycat, and Red Lips, to name a few. Dancing girls emerge – and retire – late. Customers are urged to stay just as long, buying drinks for the decked-out women as well as for themselves.

**Fuente Osmeña**  (Osmeña Circle), a roundabout that is virtually at the center of the city, spins off shopping arcades, midtown hotels, nightspots, restaurants, beer houses, and barbecue stalls that thrive mainly after dusk. A fountain is situated in this circular park that connects the **Avenue of Nations**, flanked by narra trees that blossom into a shower of gold in summer, and **President Osmeña Boulevard**. The park and the boulevard are named after Cebu's "Grand Old Man of politics," Sergio Osmeña Sr, who served as the country's third president during turbulent times, 1944–6. The late president's descendants are still prominent nationally, as well as locally.

Of pre-war vintage, the **Provincial Capitol Building** – seat of the provincial government – is unrivalled in grandeur throughout the country, with a backdrop of undulating hills highlighting its dome.

Northward is the posh residential enclave of **Beverly Hills**, atop which is the much visited **Taoist Temple**. Devotees engage in traditional rites on

*Cebu City, the commercial hub of the Visayas.*

**BELOW:** Ayala shopping center, Cebu.

Wednesday and Sunday, visitors can go any day to scan the city sprawl below and Mactan Island across the narrow channel. Nearby is **Nivel Hill**, revealing more views of the city, especially at night.

First-class to mid-priced hotels in the city center can be found mostly around Fuente Osmeña. Any number of pensions and budget inns dot Downtown Cebu, most in the bustling streets off Fuente Osmeña. Another concentration of economy lodging places is near Ayala Center at the Business Park. The Marriott is the business park area's chief high-end hotel.

Next to the city core, **Mandaue City** **L** is a bustling industrial site with one attraction, the centuries-old **St Joseph Church**, commonly called the Church of the Last Supper for its life-sized statues of Jesus and the Apostles, all handcarved during Spanish times. The *Pasyon sa Mandaue*, a dramatic 24-hour presentation, here re-enacts the death of Jesus.

A historical relic that has been overwhelmed by urban blight is the **Mandaue Watchtower**, a cylindrical rubble tower built in the 19th century, when raiders shifted their seasonal attacks from Cebu's well-defended southern parts to the northern towns of the island. It may still be glimpsed from the Mandaue-Mactan Bridge I across a landscape of shanties and gasoline depots.

## Mactan Island

For many visitors, Cebu means handcrafted guitars and ukuleles made of soft jackfruit wood. The guitar-making industry is centered on **Mactan Island** **⑳** just off Cebu City. Visitors can watch the local craftsmen at work or be entertained by a quality-control expert trying out a freshly completed guitar.

Mactan is most famous for **Magellan's Marker** **M**, which was erected in 1886 where he was slain on the island's shore. The **Lapu Lapu Monument** **N** stands just a lance's throw away. The latter portrays the Mactan chieftain with his *kampilan* (a machete-like weapon) raised above his head, ready to strike, although his back is diplomatically turned to the old foe Magellan's marker. Additional Lapu Lapu statues stand at city hall in Lapu Lapu town and at Punta Engaño, near the **Mactan Tourist Souvenir Shop**. All three statues are bronze-hued, if not actually made of bronze, and all of them glint golden in the sun. On April 27 every year, history comes to life at the **Kadaugan sa Mactan Festival** with the re-enactment of Magellan's fatal encounter with Lapu Lapu.

Cebu is well known for its sundrenched, white-sand beaches and year-round tropical climate. Beach resorts from mid-priced to posh have clustered on Mactan Island near Cebu airport, making it an inviting destination for visitors who fly in directly for weekends without having to pass through Manila or even central Cebu. About 20 hotels, mostly higher-end, operate on Mactan. The Waterfront Hotel & Casino (tel: 032-232-6888;

**BELOW:** guitar craftsman, Mactan Island.

www.waterfronthotels.com.ph) is a headliner with its 200 slot machines and a baccarat hall. There is also the Bluewater Maribago resort (tel: 032-492-0100; www.bluewater.com.ph) and Plantation Bay (tel: 032-505-9800; plantationbay.com).

Some resorts specialize in seafood or massages. The swankier Mactan hotels staff booths in the airport to arrange stays for arriving passengers. Hotels begin to appear just across the street from the international terminal. Flights connect Cebu to Seoul, Taipei, and the Middle East.

Gaisano Mall and other shopping centers in Lapu Lapu City and Maribago, both districts of Mactan Island, can satisfy consumerist or souvenir needs. Outside the resort areas, the island of Mactan is still a piece of uncongested countryside.

## Transit hub

Cebu is a ferry hub for the Visayas. From Manila, the WG&A Super Ferry sails daily and reaches Cebu City in 21 hours, with accommodations ranging from luxury cabins to economy class. Other inter-island shipping lines, some of them with rather decrepit vessels, ply the same route, and onwards to Mindanao. Ferries run throughout the day from Cebu City's terminal just outside Fort San Pedro to Bohol, Dumaguete, Siquijor, and ports in northern Mindanao. Get there early as lines form fast and service is slow. A metered taxi ride from the Mactan Island airport to the ferry terminals takes about 30 minutes. Buses also leave regularly from Cebu City to northern and southern parts of the island.

## Northern Cebu

Undeveloped white beaches, islets for the crowd-averse, and jungle trekking for the intrepid invite travelers to venture north of Cebu City. Past the town of **Sogod**, some 60km (40 miles) north of the city, lies Allegre Beach Resort, which has its own private stretch of white sand, luxury cottage accommodations, and restaurant facilities.

Off Sogod are the **Camotes Islands** ㉑, in the middle of the Camotes Sea below Leyte. The slow ferry ride to these unfrequented but charming islands can take as much as four hours from Cebu City to the town of Poro in Poro Island. The three large islands, each about the size of Mactan, come with white-sand beaches and wildly colorful flora.

A 33km (20-mile) drive north of Cebu City is newly industrialized **Danao City**. It's known for native cheeses and an assortment of snake-skin bags and shoes. An hour-long pumpboat ride reaches **Gato Island**, where Japanese fishermen discovered a bounty of sea snakes in the 1930s. This led to a sea snake industry in Barrio Tapilon of Danao, where the reptiles are sold not only for their hide but as main courses.

Off the northwestern tip of Cebu Island, **Bantayan Island** ㉒ is becoming popular among beach fanciers with a taste for soft-shell crabs. For information on cottages, restaurants,

*Renowned Cebuano painter Dr Julian Jumalon uses an unusual medium for his works, creating "lepidomosaics" by arranging butterfly wings into mosaic designs. They include a nearly life-sized portrait of Charles Darwin.*

**BELOW:** Lapu Lapu Monument, Mactan Island.

**BELOW:** Cebu–Bohol ferry, Tagbilaran.

and beaches, check wowbantayan.com/wowhome or www.bantayan-island.net. Ferryboats operate daily to the island, since the fishing grounds off Bantayan are a major source of Cebu City's seafood. In the towns of **Santa Fe** and **Madridejos** are the remains of small stone forts built *c.*1790.

**Malapascua**, a small island off the northern tip of Cebu, has earned itself an enviable reputation of late as one of the most rewarding places to dive in the country, thanks to a healthy population of thresher sharks, dolphins, manta rays, the occasional whale shark, and other marine life. Thresher sharks are not usually found at such shallow depths in other parts of the world. The island, just 3km (2 miles) long and 1km (0.5 miles), wide is accessible via a half-hour boat trip from the main Cebu Island town of Maya. Tourists and the infrastructure that comes quick on their tails have sprung up in the last few years here. Examples are the Exotic Island Dive Resort (tel: 032-406-5428) and the Tepanee Beach Resort (tel: 935-982-7844).

The Cebu Island interior is rugged yet mostly farmed. The local government has protected the 504-hectare (1,245-acre) Cantilpa Forest and hikers are welcome to slip into the untouched jungle, but they must trek some four hours from the 27km marker (Sitio Catalpa, Barangay Tabunan) on the trans-central highway to reach it.

## Southern Cebu

An hour's drive south of Cebu City is the idyllic and upscale Japanese-owned Pulchra Resort (tel: 032-232-0823; www.pulchra.co.jp) in **San Fernando**. The next big town is **Carcar ㉓**, which is worth a visit for its array of well-preserved Antillan houses, a few of which are open for an intimate look at well-maintained period appointments. Farther on is **Argao**, with another old stone church and the Casay Beach Resort.

The road leading south from Cebu City along the eastern coast is a scenic drive, with Mediterranean-like views when it ascends cliffside turns bringing into view emerald waters

shimmering in small coves a sheer drop below. As in Bohol, the southern part of Cebu Island is studded with towns that formed part of the Spanish defense perimeter against marauding pirates. The stone fortifications and watchtowers remain particularly impressive in the towns of Argao, Dalaguete, Obong, Coro, Alcoy, Boljoon, Caceres, Oslob, and Looc. The southernmost town is **Santander**, where flame trees line the coastal road, an unusual sight when abloom in summer. A short trek from Santander leads to **Pontong Lake**, the reputed habitat of a rare species of bird with the ability to go under water for much of the day. Regular ferries from Santander cross to Negros Island, which is in easy view, and buses link the opposite pier to Dumaguete.

## Moalboal

Moalboal ㉔, three hours southwest of Cebu City, is another one of the area's renowned dive spots. Blessed with three marine reserves – Tonggo Island, Ronda Island, and Pescador Island – the area teems with corals, fish, and, frequently, dolphins and whale sharks. Divers can ply the waters year-round, and beginners can explore in the friendlier waters.

The diving legacy has made Moalboal a magnet for long-stay expats, as the town has remained smaller and calmer than Boracay or Alona Beach in Bohol. At least a dozen dive shops operate in Moalboal, many run by Germans or Koreans in honor of the clientele's nationalities (www. dive-moalboal.com).

The hub of activity around Moalboal is **Panagsama Beach**, which is a dense collection of restaurants, dive shops, and lodgings. A huge typhoon washed the beach away in 1984, but it has recovered much of its past glory. The adjacent **White Beach** is an alternative, with its quiet, expansive stretches of sand that invite sunbathers and strollers to visit. Everything shuts down here

earlier, however, so check with your resort beforehand if you need anything after 7pm.

For those who prefer inland sports, the Planet Action Adventure Company sets up mountain-biking trips near Moalboal. It also rents rooms by the ocean at its Tipolo Resort on Panagsama Beach (tel: 032-474-3016; www.tipoloresort.com).

North of Moalboal and closer to Cebu City, **Barili**, with the Barili Hot Springs, is a top choice among city folk who want to camp out for the weekend. South of Moalboal, about 17km (11 miles) away, or a 30-minute ride on a bumpy road, is **Badian**, known for **Kawasan Falls** with three natural pools.

Nearby is the upscale Badian Island Resort & Spa (tel: 032-475-1102; http://badianhotel.com) on **Badian Island**, a 10-minute pumpboat ride from the main island of Cebu. Certified honeymooners are treated to a special tree-planting ceremony in the resort's back garden. As the couple plant their love tree, they are serenaded by staff with a love song of their choice.

**TIP**

President Osmeña Boulevard is also often marked as Jones Avenue, which leads to some confusion for those poring over a city map.

**BELOW:** one of Moalboal's beautiful beaches.

# WESTERN VISAYAS

Stunning natural beauty and powerful cultural and spiritual traditions merge on the islands and islets of Negros, Panay, and Boracay, attracting water-sports enthusiasts, history lovers, and fans of fiestas.

Manila

This region of the Philippines harbors some of the country's best beaches amid stiff nationwide competition, as well as the complementary development not always found on ideal coastlines elsewhere. At the top of just about any Philippines itinerary is Boracay, a 7km (4-mile) -long island at Panay's northerly tip, dominated by White Beach, with resorts that extend all the way down through the coconut palms almost to the water's edge. Just south of Negros, the tiny islet of Apo draws divers to its abundance of coral reefs and marine sanctuary.

Across Negros and Panay, the two largest islands of the Western Visayas, there are tree-shaded towns, markets brimming with local delicacies, and local festivals such as the much-imitated Ati-Atihan in Kalibo, which fills the streets with dancers. Negros is known for its mountain resorts and the Canlaon Volcano, which draws hikers to its slopes and hot springs. Panay, to the west, offers scuba diving, whitewater kayaking, and even mountain biking. Tropical Baroque-style churches can be found in its easterly towns, and Iloilo City has retained its Spanish and Art Deco architecture.

For caves and relatively undiscovered beaches, southerly Guimaras Island is the place to go. If shamanism draws your curiosity, Siquijor Island, east of Negros, is known for its sorcerer-healers.

## NEGROS
### Negros Oriental

Reef diving, snorkeling, and lakes in the high mountains have made this large province across the sea from Bohol a growing destination for tourists. It's anchored by the provincial capital **Dumaguete** ㉕, a port town built around the Protestant-run Silliman University.

**Main attractions**
RIZAL BOULEVARD, DUMAGUETE
APO ISLAND DIVING
CANLAON VOLCANO, NEGROS ISLAND
WHITE BEACH, BORACAY ISLAND

**LEFT:** Boracay Island. **RIGHT:** scuba divers, White Beach, Boracay Island.

Island-hopping from Cebu City to Negros Island may be done by fast ferry, a two- to three-hour trip by air-conditioned hovercraft to Dumaguete City, by ship (about six hours), or by bus down Cebu Island to Santander and then by slow ferry across Tañon Strait to Sibulan and a jeepney ride to Dumaguete.

**BELOW:** Silliman University Anthropological Museum.

The university sprawls over a good portion of the city, its central quadrangle bordered by old acacia trees presenting a "groves of academe" postcard view. On one end is a Protestant chapel; on the other the **Silliman University Anthropological Museum** (Mon–Fri 9am–noon, 1–5pm; free), housed in a period wooden structure with notable filigreed eaves. Among the items on display are instruments of sorcery from neighboring Siquijor Island, including ritual candles and voodoo dolls.

Beyond the museum may be glimpsed an occasional ship gliding on Tañon Strait. This seafront end of the campus calls for a lingering visit. **Rizal Boulevard**, an esplanade that stretches along the sea wall from the wharf, is an ideal promenade area at all hours, especially at sunset, as shell and seaweed gatherers roaming the tidal flats call it a day. Makeshift beer-and-barbecue stalls sprout for an alfresco treat, rivaling the seafront row of cafés and restaurants that have become popular with an expat crowd living in the compact city ringed by modest, quiet detached houses.

Downtown in the city of few traffic lights, the omnipresent tricycle creates a perennial buzz. Jeepneys and mini-buses are taken only for longer out-of-town routes, so tricycles do all in-town trips. The main street is chock-a-block with banks, student canteens, cinemas, and a department store with the only escalator in town – always a hit with the local children. The **Ninoy Aquino Freedom Park** faces the centuries-old **Dumaguete Cathedral**, its vine-grown belfry once used as a lookout for marauders, whose seasonal attempts at pillage gave Dumaguete its name – from *dumaguit*, which means "to swoop down."

Inland to the southwest is the garden town of **Valencia** ㉖, where *suman budbod kabog* (a steamed delicacy wrapped in banana leaves) and thick native chocolate make inexpensive treats at the market. A tricycle ride from here leads to **Camp Look-out** in the foothills of Mt Talinis, also known as Cuernos de Negros (Horns of Negros) for its twin peaks. This setting offers a commanding view of Negros' southern portion, the islands

of Siquijor, Cebu, and Bohol across the strait, and, on a clear day, the northern coast of Mindanao.

Also accessible from Valencia is the towering **Casiroro Falls**, which may be reached by riding up a dirt road, trekking down a gully, and following a boulder-strewn stream. Closer to town is the **Banica River Resort** with freshwater pools, bathing streams, and picnic settings.

## Dauin-Zamboanguita

On the highway leading south from Dumaguete, the first town is **Bacong** 27, a 20-minute drive. Its old church fronts the sea, while close by is a weaving room and stonecraft shop for souvenirs. The town park has modest monuments to Dr Jose Rizal and local hero Pantaleon Villegas, a revolutionary general also known as Leon Kilat.

Kilat's amulets and acrobatic prowess apparently helped him rise quickly up the Katipunan ranks in the south to seek an overthrow of rule by Spain. He led Cebuano forces in laying seige to the Spanish defenders of Fort San Pedro, but he was assassinated after making a retreat. The close relations between Cebu and Negros Oriental, both of which speak the Cebuano language, are reflected in this historic episode.

Further south, is the clean, sedate town of **Dauin**. A walk from the highway past the church and along shady residential streets leads to a thin line of sand, white in some places, that fronts on a marine sanctuary. Three major resorts (a number sure to grow as coconut farmers sell land to developers) lead dive expeditions or rent snorkeling gear for close-up looks at schools of brightly colored fish among growths of coral in the Dauin Marine Sanctuary. The high-end Bahura Resort & Spa (tel: 035-400-5254; www.bahura.com) teaches diving lessons, as well.

South of Dauin, stop in **Zamboanguita** 28. The coastal hamlet is home to the **Zoo Paradise World**

**and World Peace Museum**, maintained by a religious sect called the Lamplighters, who still walk barefoot and sport very long hair. Resorts have also proliferated along Zamboanguita's coast as divers ply the ocean or rent pumpboats bound for Apo Island. **Malatapay**, near Zamboanguita, comes alive every Wednesday with a colorful open-air market, offering anything from livestock to seafood and handicrafts. Pumpboats may be hired from the market for the 45-minute crossing to Apo Island.

**Apo Island** 29 is a hilly islet that has become increasingly famous among international divers for its marine sanctuary. Fishing is illegal (though still practiced on the sly) and just 15 divers are allowed at any one time, following payment of a fee to reach the islet. Divers will find whale sharks as well as 15 species of clownfish. On the island, visitors can stay at the Apo Island Beach Resort (tel: 035-225-5490; apoislandresort.com) and a few smaller guesthouses along a forested path behind the pumpboat pier. For more

**BELOW:** Dumaguete seafront.

*Dumaguete's easy pace is confirmed by the rare sight of a tartanilla – a horse-drawn carriage. The pedicab and motorized tricycle have nearly rendered the tartanilla a vanished breed, but a few holdovers are subsidized by the regional tourism office.*

**BELOW:**
Zamboanguita market.

information, visit www.dumagueteinfo. com/apo-island-marine-sanctuary.php.

Farther southwest along the Negros mainland coast is the agricultural hub city **Siaton**, off which is **Tambobo Bay**, today a marina established by retired expats who recognized the boat-building skills of the locals.

North of Dumaguete are several interesting towns, beginning with **Amlan**, from where you can hike (or hire a roadside motorcycle) up to the twin crater lakes of **Balinsasayao** and **Danao**. Before Amlan is a beach hotel called Wuthering Heights, appropriating the name of the former picnic area lorded over by a grassy promontory. The three-story hotel at sea's edge leaves little room for a pocket beach below, but its rooftop restaurant and open terrace offer a panoramic view of the strait between Negros and Cebu, as well as coconut plantations and the misty peaks of Mt Talinis. North of Amlan is **Tanjay**, which has a colonial-era church beside a plaza that lights up on weekends with open-air ballroom dancing. With its well-trained choirs and generations of musicians,

the town prides itself as the "Music Capital of Negros."

## Bais City

An hour's ride north on the coastal highway from Dumaguete is **Bais City** ❸⓪, where tourists flock, especially during the hot months, for its main attraction of whale- and dolphin-spotting cruises on Tañon Strait, home to 9 of the 23 marine mammals found in the Philippines. Bahia de Bais, a hilltop hostel run by the Philippine Tourism Authority (PTA), offers modest rooms, a small restaurant, and a terrace with views of Bais Bay and the surrounding lowlands. The PTA regulates the popular cruises in coordination with the Coast Guard. The full-day tour first proceeds to a mangrove swamp where an extended boardwalk has been laid out. Other stops include a sandbar for swimming and an islet for a picnic lunch in between the morning and afternoon sessions of cetacean spotting. To book a trip, call the city government, tel: 035-402-8174 or 035-402-8040.

Bais is identified with an influential *mestizo* community descended from

early Spanish settlers. On a stretch of highway leading to the city, century-old trees form a thick canopy, alongside which stand vintage wooden residences where local sugar-mill officials were once housed, a testament to the Negros economic staple. Antillan houses made of stone still stand in the city. Near Bais travelers can find swimming and snorkeling beaches, such as the white sands of Tag-It, or hike over a bamboo boardwalk in Talabong Mangrove Park to see a nesting place for birds and other wildlife.

Another three hours of traveling northwestward, through Negros Island's mid-section, leads to Bacolod City. The route passes close to **Canlaon National Park**, where Negros's last forest stands atop a volcano. Nearby is the upland **Canlaon City**, Negros Oriental's "summer capital."

## SIQUIJOR ISLAND

**Siquijor Island** ③ has earned a name as the center of sorcery in the southern Philippines. Some 50 or so of the 100,000 islanders are *mananambals*, or folk healer-sorcerers. They are classified as either "white" or "black" sorcerers, depending on the nature of their abilities. Some heal, while others bring harm.

A one-hour fast ferry from Dumaguete berths at the capital town of **Siquijor**, near where the barrio of Siquijor San Antonio serves as the center for shamanistic activities. Here, *mananambals* from all over the Visayas and Mindanao gather during Holy Week for a ritual called *tang-alap*. Medicinal plants and various elements from surrounding forests, caves, and cemeteries are gathered and put into piles from which the sorcerers distribute samples at dawn.

Local transportation leads smoothly to **Larena** and **Lazi** ②. The former is the island's main port, and the latter known for its centuries-old church with a pink-colored facade, and, across the street, a massive but deserted two-story convent with hardwood plank flooring, capacious interiors, with period furniture, and colored glass windows. Along the route one will find the customary Philippine white-sand beaches, some of which

**BELOW:** Dauin Marine Sanctuary.

*The Zoo Paradise World and World Peace Museum in Zamboanguita is run by a religious cum environmental section called the Lamplighters.*

**BELOW:** a sorcerer conducts a black magic ritual in a cave on Siquijor Island.

are attended by modest resorts such as Sandugan and Palaton.

## Negros Occidental

This province in the northwest of Negros Island gets visitors mainly for its mountain resorts, access to a volcano, and urban sights that describe the region's bittersweet sugar industry.

Sugar still dominates the economy despite ups and downs that have seen their share of social struggle, as well. The industry started with *hacienderos*, landowners who can usually trace their lineage to early Spanish settlers. They were often regarded as an idle and profligate group with strong political clout. From the time commercial sugar production on Negros Island had its beginnings in the late 19th century, they lorded it over migrant workers called *sacadas*, who streamed seasonally into Negros from the rest of the Visayas. The fall in sugar prices in the 1980s delivered a relative comeuppance, forcing the gentry to shift to other, less

profitable crops, or try their hand at new industries. But the attempts to diversify the economy into shrimp breeding, corn, rice, and native crafts have since regressed, owing to a recent, if temporary, resurgence in the sugar industry.

## Bacolod

The capital of Negros Occidental (Western Negros) Province, **Bacolod** ㉝, is a relatively new city that has flourished somewhat haphazardly from the rise and fall of sugar profitability. It has experienced several decades of lean years after fat ones, when, for a time, it ranked second only to Manila in the number of registered motor vehicles. But urban development continues unabated in terms of commercial centers, and Bacolod remains the most financially advanced and modernized city on Negros Island.

Sprawling over 2 hectares (5 acres) of manicured lawns is the **Provincial Capitol Park**, bounded by Gatuslao Street, North Capitol Road, and South Capitol Road. It

## Sorcery and Special Powers

The story is still told of how an old lady named Mameng – the most powerful white sorcerer in the 1970s and 1980s – was once summoned to call on Imelda Marcos, who was said to have been stricken by a strange skin disease that dermatological experts couldn't treat.

The tale goes on to recount how Mameng diagnosed the affliction to be the result of a curse placed on the First Lady by mermen who had been injured during the construction of San Juanico Bridge linking Samar and Leyte islands. Mameng was supposed to have counseled Imelda to make a conciliatory offering, which she did by the base of the "love bridge" that had been built in honor of the First Lady by Ferdinand Marcos. Her skin disease disappeared, and Mameng was amply rewarded.

Siquijor's star attraction in recent years has not exactly been a sorcerer, but a man with unusual kinetic powers. Just ask to be taken to Jess, who will accommodate anyone with a demonstration of his special skills.

Jess cuts out a pair of figures from cigarette cartons, goes into trance, and starts dancing. He has been well documented on video and film by visiting academicians, documentarists, and incredulous foreigners seriously into psychic research.

includes a large lagoon and central fountains fronting the capitol building. More popular for promenaders is the **Bacolod City Plaza**, similarly endowed with trees, park benches, concrete gazebos, and water fountains that are colorfully lit in the evenings. Cultural programs are staged regularly there on weekends, with orchestral bands and smaller musical groups alternating in providing free entertainment to park visitors.

The **Bacolod Cathedral** stands across one side of the plaza, which is also flanked by the Central Public Market, Seabreeze Hotel, and the City Hall.

Not far from the city plaza is the **Negros Occidental Provincial Museum** (Mon–Sat 9am–6pm; free; tel: 034-434-5552), also known as the "Sugar Museum" for its display of facets of sugar technology. On nearby Lacson Street is the **Negros Showroom**, featuring regular handicraft exhibits. Bacolod teems with restaurants, movie theaters, and shopping malls, as well as an upscale concentration of nightspots and girlie bars called Golden Fields, where the Casino Filipino is also located.

A 35-minute drive north is **Silay ㉞**, a town with old houses recalling the Castilian past, when it was a regional center for culture. At 21 de Noviembre Street look for the **Hofileña Art Collection**. It includes works by Picasso and Goya as well as paintings by Philippine masters such as Juan Luna. Another common stop is Ideal Bakery, a byword for its Castilian delicacies, such as *hojas, pan de ara,* and *pio nono* (a sugared roll commemorating Pope Pius IX).

Further north is the massive **Victorias Milling Company**. Within the "Vicmico" compound is **St Joseph the Worker Chapel**, with an awesome mural in full technicolor depicting a furious Jesus and his disciples. Scout this chapel also for saints shown with Filipino features and garb and a psychedelic mosaic made of broken soda bottles.

## Around Bacolod

Off **Cadiz City** at the province's northern tip, 64km (40 miles) north of Bacolod, is **Llacaon Island**, 9 hectares (22 acres) of gleaming white-sand beaches fringed by coral reefs. On the northeastern tip, 94km (60 miles) from Bacolod, **Escalante** has several resorts, such as Jomabo Paradise and Northwind Beach, that face the Tañon Strait, where visitors can dive, windsurf, or explore caves. A 10-minute pumpboat ride will take you to **Isla Puti** (White Island), and Bag-ong Banwa Island is also close to the town.

Some 45 minutes' drive southeast of Bacolod, through **Murcia** town, is **Mambucal Mountain Resort ㉟** (tel: 0947-324-1969; www.mambukalhaven. com/murcia_history.html), with a tourist lodge, several cottages, camping grounds, swimming pools, and seven waterfalls, three of which are easily accessible along concrete pathways. The resort features a bathhouse, where, for a minimal fee, one can soak in hot sulfurous water.

Mountain climbers might attempt an ascent of **Canlaon Volcano ㊱**,

**TIP**

Among the dive operators in Negros Oriental are Heinz Spalthoff (tel: 0912-359-4040; www.apodiver. com) and the shop at Mike's Dauin Beach Resort (tel: 0916-754-8823; www.mikes-beach resort.com/scuba-diving.php).

**BELOW:** shell jewelry for sale in Zamboanguita.

**TIP**

On the approach to Bais, check out the antiquated steam locomotive on the roadside as you come within sight of the sugar mill, which has towering, cylindrical chimneys.

which rises 2,465 meters (8,087ft) to a summit of twin craters, one extinct and the other active. The usual starting point for the climb is Canlaon, 100km (60 miles) from Bacolod and 170km (100 miles) from Dumaguete. Some of the Negros Occidental towns at the volcano's foothills also serve as jump-off bases. One trail starts near Ara-al, a *barangay* of **La Carlota** where hot springs abound, while another one that is better marked and easier to follow ascends the southwest side, starting near Biak-na-Bato. **Hacienda Montealegre** has become the starting point for an organized trek led by the local guides. Ideal visit times are the dry season from February to May.

A night is usually spent halfway up at a surprising 2-hectare (5-acre) stretch of white sand called **Margaha Valley**. A second night may be spent by leisurely climbers at the volcano's shoulder, some 600 meters (1,970ft) below the craters. From the summit, one can peer into the 100-meter (330ft)-wide active crater, which descends to a depth of 250 meters

(820ft). Many tours run for four days, starting with breakfast in Bacolod and ending with a hotel shower. In between, hikers will pass Makawiwili Peak, watch a sunrise, and stop at a lagoon to restock water supplies. For more information, visit www.aenet.org/canlaon/canclimb.htm.

**Sipalay**, 160km (100 miles) south of Bacolod, is known best for the Tinagong Dagat (Hidden Sea), accessible through a narrow channel between Dinosaur Island and the Negros mainland. Corals and tropical fish teem in this seaside lake. Nearby, Maricalum Bay has similarly abundant marine life, and attracts deep-sea anglers with varieties of mackerel, barracuda, grouper, and tuna.

## PANAY

On this large Visayan island, look for Spanish as well as Art Deco architecture in the city of Iloilo and a string of remote beaches along the boundless coastline. Panay's cities of Kalibo and Caticlan are gateways to the resort island of Boracay for those who arrive by air.

**BELOW:** villagers at a rice mill in Negros Oriental.

## Iloilo

**Iloilo City ㊲**, an urban hub of Panay, blends Castilian heritage with that of the local Ilongo population. It's also the most important port in the region, having been open to international shipping since 1855. Hearing of Iloilo's excellent harbor, the Spanish conquistador Legazpi came from Cebu in 1569 and subsequently made Iloilo his base for explorations northward to Manila.

By the river's mouth is **Fort San Pedro**. Originally constructed in 1616 with earthworks and wooden palisades, it was transformed in 1738 into a stone fort, quadrilateral in shape with a bastion at each corner, and defended by 50 guns. In 1937, Fort San Pedro became the quarters for the Philippine Army. The barracks was eventually removed and the fort turned into a promenade area, popular in the early evening hours.

Look for the Chinese restaurants on the main street, J.M. Basa, as well as department stores, and movie houses that have taken over the old shells of Art Deco buildings.

The **Museo ng Iloilo** (Iloilo Museum: Mon–Fri 9am–noon, 1–5pm; charge) on Bonifacio Drive showcases prehistoric artifacts from the many burial sites dug up on Panay Island, including gold-leaf masks for the dead, seashell jewelry, and other ornaments worn by pre-Spanish islanders. Also of note is an exhibit of the cargo recovered from a British ship that sank off Guimaras Island in the 19th century: Victorian chinaware, port wine, and Glasgow beer are among the shipwreck's treasures.

Speaking of food and drink, Iloilo's Molo district has become famous outside Panay for a noodle dish known as *pancit Molo*. La Paz, another Iloilo district, is the home of the original La Paz *batchoy*. Both are variations of Chinese noodles and regularly appear on menus in the Western Visayas. Panaderia de Molo (Molo Bakery), among the oldest bakeries in the south, is another favorite spot to eat or gift shop for foodie friends back home.

**Jaro** district, also part of Iloilo, stands out as a traditional center for loom-weaving and hand embroidery

**EAT**

While in Bacolod, treat yourself to the locally made but nationally known chicken *inasal* (barbecued chicken with lemongrass) found on sidewalk stalls, or at Manukan Country, a concentration of barbecue stalls by the reclamation area, popular among budget diners.

**BELOW:** sugar plantation.

**TIP**

For a good look at the culture and a peek into lives during Silay's glorious days, visit Balay Negrense in Silay. Owned by the Jalandoni family, the residence has been turned into a private museum.

of *piña* and *jusi*, delicate fabrics used for the Filipino *barong tagalog* (traditional shirt). **Arevalo** district has generated an industry out of producing leis, bouquets, and wreaths. In the 16th century, Arevalo was a shipbuilding center and a supply base for Spanish expeditions to Muslim Mindanao and the Moluccas.

From Bacolod, it is a leisurely two-hour ferry ride across Guimaras Strait to Iloilo City. Negros Navigation provides daily ferry services.

## Religious fortitude

The presence of many old churches underscores the high regard the Spanish colonizers had for Iloilo Province as a religious and commercial center for the region. Some 13km (8 miles) north of Iloilo lies the Renaissance-inspired **Pavia Church**, with red brick walls and window frames of coral rock. The neoclassical **Santa Barbara Church**, where Ilonggos first gathered to declare the revolution against the Spanish rulers, is also found in this region. At kilometer 25 on the same northward road is

**Cabatuan Church**, also of neoclassical style and built in the early 1880s.

Westward from Iloilo, along the southern coast, a more frequented road runs past beach resorts and Iloilo's more distinctive old churches. At kilometer 22 is the coastal town of **Tigbauan**, worth a stop for its Baroque church, sadly ruined by an earthquake in 1948, like so many of the country's churches.

At kilometer 40 is the **Miagao Fortress Church** ㊳, built in 1786 as a place of worship, as well as an impregnable fortress. The most impressive among Iloilo's formidable array of centuries-old churches, its facade features a bas-relief of intricate botanical motifs reminiscent of Aztec art. Largely because it best exemplifies what is called the tropical Baroque style of architecture, the church has been declared a world heritage and conservation site by Unesco.

## Outer islands

Fifteen minutes by pumpboat from Iloilo is the island province of **Guimaras** ㊴, the site of the

**BELOW:** nineteenth-century mansion, Iloilo.

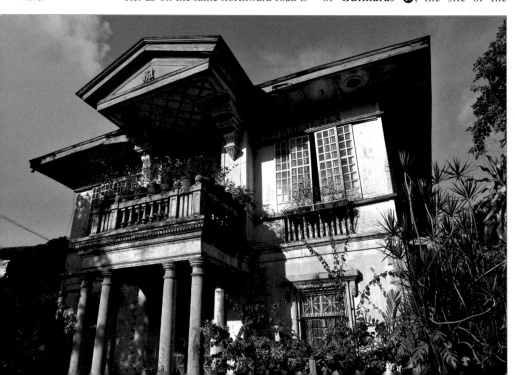

much-admired **Roca Encantada** (Enchanted Rock), summer house of the distinguished Lopez family. Perched on a promontory overlooking Guimaras Strait, it is visible on the ferry ride to or from Bacolod. Some visitors to Guimaras also visit the Oro Verde mango farm, as it's open to the public, or go find a remote beach.

**Inampulugan Island** is entirely taken over by a first-class resort named Costa Aguada. In **Santa Ana Bay**, which is 45 minutes by pumpboat from Fort San Pedro pier in Iloilo, is Isla Naburot Resort (tel: 0918-909-8500; facebook.com/IslaNaburot). Lovingly created by the Saldaña family, this resort lures guests with its unusual features, such as antique wooden doors that double as windows.

If in the town of **Nueva Valencia**, look for **Catilaran Cave**, where Ming jars have been unearthed. At times hundreds of devotees recite Latin prayers while crawling through the 500-meter (1,640ft) cave, believing they will acquire supernatural powers, useful against countering evil spirits. Nearby, **Tatlong Pulo** (Three Islets) offers smaller caves, plus excellent swimming, snorkeling, and island-hopping. Bus and boat combo trips to the undeveloped, relatively undiscovered Tatlong Pulo beaches can take 90 minutes. Some pitch tents to spend the night.

**San Joaquin** is the southernmost town of Iloilo Province. San Joaquin Church, dating back to 1869, stands out for its gleaming white coral and facade depicting the historic Battle of Tetuan, where Spanish forces routed the Moors in Morocco in 1859.

More untapped islands lie off the northeastern coast of Panay, amid the rich fishing grounds of the Visayan Sea. From **Ajuy**, one can proceed northward to **Estancia**, a fishing town dubbed by local geography books as the "Alaska of the Philippines" for its marine resources. There is little evidence of tourist attractions in this area.

## Antique and Aklan provinces

**Antique Province** hugs the west coast of Panay. A high, rugged range of mountains runs parallel to this coast, lending the province an isolated character underscored by roads that have only been paved in recent years. The province also has its share of unexplored beaches.

**San Jose de Buenavista**, the capital, is 100km (60 miles) from Iloilo. Several beach resorts are found in the *barangay* of San Jose. Close by is Hamtik, the site of the landing of the 10 Bornean Datuks, or princes, in 1212, which is the beginning of the timeline for Malay people in the Philippines. Off Anini-y, which is one hour's drive to the south, is **Nogas Island**, which has a white-sand beach that is an ideal launch for scuba diving and snorkeling. The island, requiring private pumpboat hire, lacks development and has no roads in places, beckoning travelers to overnight under the stars. Located in *Barangay* Dapog of Anini-y, the government-run **Sira-an Hot Springs**

*In Manapla, northern Negros, a chapel has earned the distinction of being "the most Filipino" of all places of worship. The Hacienda Rosalia Chapel is in the shape of a stylized native hat called the salakot, its walls composed of traditional carabao cartwheels.*

**BELOW:** Miagao Fortress Church, Panay Island.

lets visitors soak in sulfurous water and take in sea views.

North of San Jose de Buenavista, in the town of **Tibiao**, whitewater kayaking is organized by the Kayak Inn, likewise hikes up the seven-tiered Bugtong Batao Waterfalls. Further up the coast is **Culasi**, off which is coral-ringed **Mararison Island**. Rising 2,090 meters (6,857ft) is the extinct **Mt Madja-as**.

The volcanic area, accessible by pumpboat, supports several upland lakes and a proliferation of waterfalls. Deer and wild boar still roam the island, and local hunters still make it a practice to bag a trophy or two as prized game meat during fiestas. The big festival in Antique is the Binirayan Festival, which takes place for three days at year end.

North of Culasi, cross over into **Aklan Province**, located near Panay's northwestern tip. The port town of **New Washington** handles inter-island shipping connections. Those who have failed to make early plane or ship reservations for nearby Boracay can fly or take the ship to

Roxas instead, then travel by bus to **Kalibo** ⑳, the oldest town in Aklan and home of the famous **Ati-Atihan festival** in January. The festival's success has led to replication of the street dancing in various other cities in the Visayas and northern Mindanao, where local versions are staged in honor of historic episodes or favorite religious icons (see Fiesta Fantastica, page 69).

## Capiz Province

Anglers will find the Capiz Province coastline of Panay a rich fishing ground. **Napti Island**, off nearby **Panay** town, offers great varieties of seafood and isolated beaches. Capiz's thriving fishing industry is known to supply many of Manila's restaurants with quality seafood, from oysters and bamboo clams to the largest, freshest groupers, marlin, jacks, squid, octopus, and prawns. **Roxas City** is the capital of Capiz.

**Panay Church** has a marble floor and 3-meter (10ft) -thick walls of white coral. The interior is decorated with *retablos* (altar pieces) of silver

and hardwood. **Baybay Beach** has modest tourist accommodations in addition to nightlife, and on nearby **Olutayan Island**, the surrounding waters will thrill the angler as well as the swimmer and snorkeler. The **Ivisan Coves** in the barrios of Basiao and Bataring are known for natural bathing pools.

Over an hour's drive south from the capital leads to **Dumalag Church**, which was built in the 1800s. Nearby is another attraction, Suhot Cave. East of Roxas, some 45km (30 miles), is Casanayan Beach.

## BORACAY ISLAND

This island of **Boracay** ❹ is synonymous with Philippine beach tourism and has become a fabled paradise for both budget and posh resort travelers because of its long white-sand beach with coral gardens just offshore, plus diving tours that leave each morning just hours after the last resort party ends. Boracay was first "discovered" off the northeastern tip of Panay in the 1960s, when beachcombers went looking for its rare *puka* shells. By the 1970s, the island was on the hit list of every intrepid adventurer in Asia. They came in small numbers at first, staying in the *nipa* huts along White Beach, the long sandy one, for a couple of dollars a night. As word spread, by the 1980s adventurers had become hordes, and boutique resorts sprang up all along White Beach.

Today resorts are packed in wall-to-wall, vying for a piece of the oceanfront along with dive shops, Western restaurants, and open-air massage parlors. Mobile touts sell sunglasses and souvenirs on the sand, while swimmers mix with bancas in the light-blue waters offshore. The south end of White Beach is generally less crowded and more laid-back than the central sands. A 15-minute walk eastward from White Beach leads to the less scenic, wind-whipped "back beach" (Bulabog Beach and surroundings), where a few resorts have opened for travelers who are weary of commotion elsewhere on Boracay.

In the morning, before headcounts thicken, the sight greeting arrivals can hardly avoid being photographed: a

**TIP**

Stay in Roxas City at Plaza Central (www.plazacentralinn.com) and use it as a base to search out food.

**BELOW:** the wind-whipped "back beach," just east of White Beach, on Boracay Island, is popular with kite-surfers.

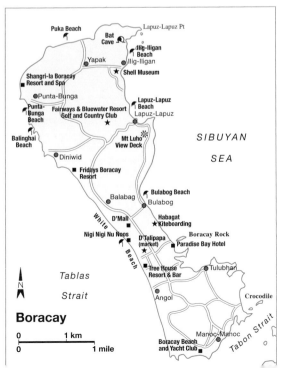

Boracay map

Puka Beach
Bat Cave
Lapuz-Lapuz Pt
Ilig-Iligan Beach
Yapak
Ilig-Iligan
Shell Museum
Shangri-la Boracay Resort and Spa
Punta-Bunga
Punta-Bunga Beach
Fairways & Bluewater Resort Golf and Country Club
Lapuz-Lapuz Beach
Lapuz-Lapuz
Balinghai Beach
Mt Luho View Deck
SIBUYAN
Diniwid
SEA
Fridays Boracay Resort
Balabag
Bulabog Beach
Bulabog
D'Mall
Habagat Kiteboarding
Nigi Nigi Nu Noos
Boracay Rock
D'Talipapa (market)
Paradise Bay Hotel
Tree House Resort & Bar
Tulubhan
Tablas
Angol
Crocodile
Strait
Boracay
0     1 km
0     1 mile
Manoc-Manoc
Boracay Beach and Yacht Club
Tabon Strait

gentle sea, the whitest of white beaches, tall coconut palms swaying in the breeze. For an arresting view of Boracay and its surrounds, head up to the **Mt Luho View Deck**. Or ask resorts about island-hopping tours that hit Crystal Cove Island, where visitors can swim in the caves.

About 100 hotels operate in Boracay, and the constant sound of drilling on vacant lots proves that the boom is hardly over. Names range from the sprawling, party-hardy Nigi Nigi Nu Noos to the much quieter, mostly wooden Tree House Resort & Bar (www.boracaytreehouse. com). The Paradise Bay resort has two dozen quiet rooms facing the water on back beach. For a list of hotels, visit www.hotelclub.com/Philippines/ Boracay-Aklan-hotels/List-of-Hotels.

Lower-end guesthouses are springing up behind the frontlines in the jungles between White Beach and a highway that runs the island's full length. Even during peak periods, a drop-in traveler can usually find a simple room just by knocking on enough office doors. Some of those rooms lack air-con, and don't expect in-room wi-fi even along the beach.

Travelers normally fly from Manila to Caticlan via turbo-prop flights operated by Cebu Pacific, among other carriers, and take the 15-minute pumpboat crossing to the island. You can also take the more regular jet flight to Kalibo, and ride a jeepney or van (two to three hours) to Caticlan for the crossing. Banca boats, which take visitors from the port in Caticlan to the boat jetty in Boracay, start up around dawn and stop service at sunset. Visitors are levied a pier-usage fee and an environmental impact fee, in addition to the banca ticket.

## Full-blown vacation

Since the mid-1980s Boracay has moved way upmarket, attracting the well-heeled of Europe, America, and Asia, as well as vacationing Filipinos, who have begun to outnumber foreign visitors.

Visitors can hire sailboats, kiteboards, and windsurfers at any of the score of rental shops along White

**BELOW:** Boracay Island's rapid development has attracted global brands.

## Growing Pains

**B**oracay has now become a firm player in Asian tourism, despite a rough beginning during which uncontrolled growth led to severe environmental issues. A short-lived health scare in 1997 was a wake-up call: tourism officials met with the island's proprietors for lessons in environmental management. Thereafter, sewage and water pipes were laid to the mainland, and a new jetty was built to make the Caticlan embarkation process a smoother affair. These days, change is still in high gear, and visitors will notice one or two resorts that look more like roadside motels than tropical beach getaways. There's even a hotel at the Boracay pier and a couple in tiny Caticlan.

Now there is another problem as development presses ahead. Boracay's sand, cool to the sole even at noon, comes from finely crushed calcareous materials, in other words corals and seashells that have expired in the course of time. Marine biologists warn that if the reefs fringing the island are left unprotected, the sand will not be replenished. Eventual erosion would see the white beaches diminishing in size, which they are already doing as human-made seawalls push the sand back out to sea. Environmentalists, together with tourism, health, and science officials, face the task of figuring out a long-term program for conserving the island's natural assets.

Beach. Other shops equip travelers for jet-skiing, parasailing, and scuba diving in the coral just offshore. Among the scores of dive guides and gear rentals are Dive Gurus (tel: 036-288-5486; www.divegurusboracay.com) and WaterColors (tel: 036-288-6745). Some Boracay dives take just three hours and do not require certification.

Bicycles are available for exploring the tiny island, which is only 7km long by 3km wide (6 miles by 2 miles). A bike rider might end up at Yapak village, on the northern end of the island, once a public pit of *puka* shells. Shells still cover the beach, but a scavenger might have better luck with *pukas* at a souvenir shop than on the beach, as collectors have picked it over. The beach has remained free of the crowds and resorts that dominate other parts of Boracay.

Boracay dining, which was once simple and based on good island fare, now ranges from haute Filipino to haute French, with Indonesian, Thai, Italian, Chinese, Swiss, and English available. Some restaurants offer dancing on the beach beneath the stars.

There are still some basic *nipa* huts, such as at the Angol Point guesthouse, which rents them out by the night, but mostly more modern resorts populate the beach now.

An uproar was caused in the late 1990s with the establishment of the posh Fairways & Bluewater Resort Golf and Country Club, which takes up 118 hectares (292 acres) in otherwise pristine Yapak. But the proprietors of the world-class leisure hub eventually overcame concerns about overtaxing the island's water supply and other natural resources.

The Resorts World casino operator in Manila hopes to open a high-end gambling complex in Boracay, though the country's gaming regulator says it's too early to say whether the project will be allowed.

Locals can't complain about the influx of tourists, since they enhance employment and business opportunities. Poorer folk living in shacks can still be spotted around the island's interior, another clue that development hasn't penetrated all the way into the heart of Boracay.

**TIP**

Don't worry about dressing for dinner on Boracay. The island's undressed code (bare feet and bikini) is acceptable even in the smarter joints. Sandals are recommended, though, in case of occasional objects in the sand.

**BELOW:** White Beach, Boracay Island.

# LIVING SEAS: SOURCE OF LIFE AND PLEASURE

**Whether for recreation or sustenance, the abundant marine resources of the Philippines continue to serve both tourists and locals.**

With more coastline than the continental USA fringing the 7,107 islands and islets of the Philippines, and 1.7 million sq km (656,375 sq miles) of territorial waters, the country was once considered a repository of one of the world's richest fishery resources. Islanders have been living off this life-giving abundance throughout recorded history. One-tenth of the world's 20,000 fish species are found here, and in 2011 the value of the local fishing industry was calculated at US$5.2 billion, with more than 2 million people involved in fishing and its related service industries.

Sadly, report after report from NGOs shows the country's marine environment has deteriorated to crisis levels. Illegal fishing through the use of dynamite and cyanide, likewise turtle egg collection, are destroying the seas. Scuba-divers wax lyrical over the fabulous coral reefs and gin-clear waters, but the coral, and the marine life it supports, has dwindled . The seas face threats from poaching, water pollution, and everyday collection of shells from beaches. Policing is notoriously fishy despite a list of strongly worded environmental laws. The Sulu Sea, a coral hotbed, and the passage between Batangas and Puerto Galera, known for its rich variety of marine life, have raised particular concern. But local officials have set up sanctuaries, replanted mangroves, and monitored shifts in the numbers of protected species. NGOs have meanwhile put the word out about the urgency of saving marine species as activists comment on blogs or sign online government petitions to keep the issue above water. (See page 24 for more on environmental issues.)

**ABOVE:** Fishing continues to account for a significant proportion of the Philippines' economy.
**LEFT:** A stilt fishing village in the Sulu archipelago off the souhwest coast of Mindanao. The Moken sea gypsies of this area make their living from the rich bounty of the seas.

**ABOVE:** The best-known resort in the Philippines, Boracay is a major center for water sports.

**Above:** Protected mangrove forest in a marine reserve off the coast at Zamboanga, Mindanao.

**Above:** Scuba diving off Apo Island.

## Ski Set

At tourist beaches, jet-skiing is a popular option for those who like to stay above water. It is an expensive sport, though.

There's a very good reason why people get easily hooked on diving in the Philippines. Its warm tropical waters teem with an astounding variety of marine life – including the largest ever-recorded gathering of whale sharks in the world – and extensive reefs. For divers, this is a watery nirvana as they plunge into its clear waters to suss out its more than 488 of the world's 500 species of coral and over 1,000 fish species.

Among the more intriguing species are sharks and giant turtles. Shark sightings are rare, but divers occasionally glimpse large, long-tailed threshers or white tips. According to the International Shark Attack File run by the Florida (US) Museum of Natural History, none of the 75 unprovoked shark attacks on humans from 2011 occurred in the Philippines. Five species of endangered sea turtles may also swim past. They are the green sea, hawksbill, leatherback, loggerhead, and olive ridley turtles. Turtles are quite timid and often dive deep to flee approaching divers.

For more information on Philippine diving, check out www.philippine diving.com, scubadive philippines.com, or www. divephil.com. (See also Diver's Haven, page 97.)

**Right:** The coral reefs around the Philippines' myriad islands offer some of the world's most spectacular diving.

# PALAWAN

**Caves, waterfalls, unpopulated beaches, and a marine park centered on a reef in the Sulu Sea reward the intrepid traveler to the islands of Palawan.**

The elongated island province of **Palawan** points like a *keris* (a Malay wavy short sword) towards northern Borneo in the southwest part of the Philippine archipelago. A quarter of the country's islands are found in the Palawan group, but their geography meant virtual isolation until natural gas, then tourism, came along.

Palawan's isolation means more natural scenery for the traveler. Protected reefs in the far south attract divers, beaches below vertical cliffs have driven a resort boom around El Nido in the north. Jungle trekkers explore the main island's center, running into barely touched indigenous tribes. Around the coast, clear, calm waters – ideal for snorkeling – fringe mangrove-shaded beaches.

Before the year 1000 the Chinese called the island Palao-Yu, or "land of beautiful safe harbor." It was then inhabited by settlers of proto-Malay stock, whose descendants still exist today as the Batak, Pala'wan, and Tagbanua. In the 13th century, more settlers filtered in from the Majapahit empire of Java. The sultans of Jolo and Borneo controlled Palawan when the Spanish arrived. Spain gained a foothold relatively late in the 19th century in the town that was later to be called Puerto Princesa and is now the provincial capital.

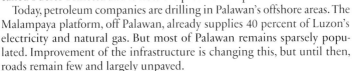

Today, petroleum companies are drilling in Palawan's offshore areas. The Malampaya platform, off Palawan, already supplies 40 percent of Luzon's electricity and natural gas. But most of Palawan remains sparsely populated. Improvement of the infrastructure is changing this, but until then, roads remain few and largely unpaved.

For travelers seeking fringe locations, Palawan's rough going yields rewards of considerable merit. Visitors come to watch birds'-nest gatherers at work, scaling cliffs for the prized nest of swiftlets that will make its way to some Chinese restaurant. They might journey up the Puerto Princesa Underground River to marvel at limestone cathedrals, or visit caves containing important archeological finds. Divers who venture down to Tubbataha Reef Natural Park will be treated to undersea views of the Unesco World Heritage Site.

**PRECEDING PAGES:** bancas moored near El Nido. **LEFT:** an idyllic spot on Coron Island. **ABOVE, FROM LEFT:** traditional dance; tropical birds.

# NORTHERN PALAWAN

The northern half of Palawan is a land of white beaches and abrupt cliffs backed by mountains that shelter caves and an underground river. All are a magnet to travelers prepared for a little rough going.

**N**orthern Palawan refers to the long main island from its capital Puerto Princesa to El Nido and on into the outlying islets anchored by Coron. This landmass is not just another cluster of white-sand beaches. The sparsely developed, staunchly preserved region is a prime tourist draw for its unusual scenic features, on shore and off. Travelers brave Palawan's spotty infrastructure to see the mighty Underground River near Puerto Princesa, remote yet exclusive resorts beside the coastal cliffs of El Nido, and the quiet beach hamlet of Port Barton.

Divers head for Coron Bay in the outlying islands, while birdwatchers follow the main island's South China Sea coast to pick out unusual migratory species. Honda Bay in Puerto Princesa invites snorkelers and boat tours that hop from one tiny islet to the next. Attractively tree-lined, litter-free streets make the compact urban core of Puerto Princesa, the island's only real city, something of a novelty. You may encounter the indigenous Bataks, who live in native villages and look strikingly different from other Filipinos.

The economy of Palawan depends on fishing, coconut products, and offshore gas-drilling, as well as tourism.

Airports in Coron, El Nido, and Puerto Princesa handle regular flights from Manila, which is about an hour away by air and 24 hours by ferry.

Northern Palawan, particularly around Puerto Princesa, has more infrastructure than the south, including a two-lane highway that goes most of the way from Puerto to El Nido. But further-flung destinations, such as Port Barton, are hard to reach without private boats or private all-terrain vehicles. Travelers are advised to leave plenty of time to complete

**Main attractions**
PUERTO PRINCESA
HONDA BAY
EL NIDO
BARRACUDA LAKE, CORON
ST PAULS SUBTERRANEAN RIVER
PORT BARTON

**LEFT:** Lake Cayangan on Coron Island is believed by locals to be sacred.
**RIGHT:** Sabang Beach.

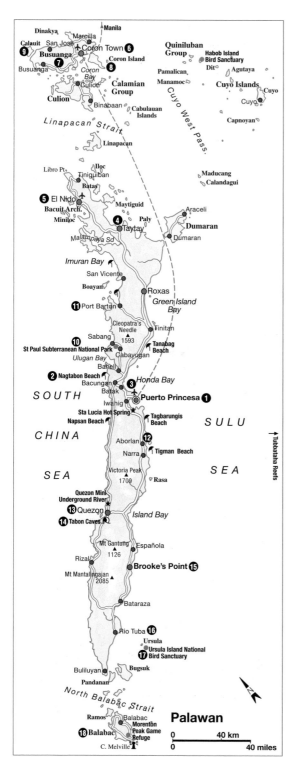

Palawan

0    40 km

0    40 miles

the highlights of this region and still may end up hiring pricey private vans or taking full-day boat rides to reach some spots.

## Puerto Princesa

Situated near the middle of the eastern coast of Palawan Island, the environmentally progressive city of **Puerto Princesa** ❶ works well as a base for exploring beaches, bays, caves, and inland jungles. Several airlines operate daily flights from Manila.

The early Spanish colonizers regarded the bay as "a princess of ports," thus giving the name to what was just a small coastal settlement. Puerto Princesa was slowly developed into a base for naval operations, until it became a town with a dozen roads and a hospital by 1883. A precursor to the city's reputation today, a government report from 1884 said: "It had orderly streets, buildings and houses, and the community kept it clean."

Puerto Princesa has gained the distinction of being a model city and an ecotourism haven. It has perennially set the standard for environmental awareness, and has the country's most acclaimed local government unit.

## City sights and entertainment

Close to the city is the **Palawan Wildlife Rescue and Conservation Center**, where visitors often stop for an educational tour and souvenir buys of sundry items made of crocodile skin, such as bags and shoes. There is also a mini-zoo featuring a few of Palawan's uncommon fauna. The **Children's Park** and **Immaculate Conception Cathedral** are found close to Rizal Park near the seaport. Also in the central city look for Mendoza Park and the **Palawan Museum** (tel: 048-433-2963; thepalawanmuseum. wordpress.com), which is open during regular office hours.

Along the axial J. Rizal Avenue, there are several pensions and mid-priced hotels, the most popular of which are **Badjao Inn** and **Casa Linda Inn**. Both have a small stage by the bar and dining area where folk singers are nightly attractions for the NGO crowd, a discernible population in Puerto Princesa, as well as expats who work as foreign consultants. Many more budget inns are found toward the parallel main street of Manalo Extension and Abad Santos Extension south of J. Rizal Avenue.

A couple of large, three-star hotels are located north of the airport and along the dense mangrove stands of Puerto Princesa Bay. Near the airport terminal numerous resorts and restaurants do brisk business. Among the hotter nightspots are the **Salo Bar** inside the Legend Hotel and the **Scenario Bar** in the Asturias Hotel. A popular hangout for the culturally inclined is **Kamaricutan Café & Galeri**, which is intricately designed with bamboo and other indigenous materials. For a massive

Filipino feast, try **KaLui** at 369 Rizal Avenue, about 1km (less than a mile) from the airport.

A favorite hangout in Puerto Princesa is Kalui Touro-Touro, a café with New Wave music and a mini-library.

## South from Puerto Princesa

Traveling southeast, 16km (10 miles) from the city, is the unique "prison without walls." At the **Iwahig Prison and Penal Farm**, most prisoners roam freely within the reservation's 37,000 hectares (90,000 acres) of beautiful undulating rice fields and orchards. Handcarved items of *kamagong* (ebony) and mother-of-pearl inlay work are among the best of the handicrafts produced by the inmates.

A little farther south on the provincial road is Sta Lucia Hot Spring.

*Puerto Princesa, the self-proclaimed ecotourism capital of the Philippines.*

**BELOW:** Puerto Princesa Mayor Edward Hagedorn watches as endangered green turtles are released into Honda Bay.

## Clean, Green Puerto Princesa

Puerto Princesa's urban core stands out in the Philippines for its tree-lined streets and lack of litter. Credited with the inspiration behind the city's unusual order is former criminal and long-reigning mayor Edward Hagedorn.

Hagedorn's dramatic conversion from street-gang leader to city official has resulted in two feature-length movies based on his life. He left the mayor's post in 2001, after first being elected in 1992, due to term limits. When the city began to degenerate, district leaders in Puerto Princesa demanded him back and won a Supreme Court ruling to let him run again in 2002. The 65-year-old was still mayor in 2012.

The journey into town from the airport passes columns of roadside trees. Urban Puerto Princesa is on the move, with new hotels and a new mall. But Hagedorn has saved the vast tracts of mountains and beaches surrounding the urban core from illegal logging, mining, and cyanide fishing. They are likely to withstand the pressure for development and remain appealing to eco-travelers in Palawan.

These successes can be traced to partnerships with non-governmental organizations. As a result of their and Hagedorn's work, Puerto Princesa has earned awards for environmental conservation and public education.

**EAT**

Ask a tricycle driver to take you to Puerto Princesa's Vietnamese Village, where restaurants serve their native cuisine. It's on the highway leading north out of town.

**BELOW:** the harbor at Puerto Princesa.

This road continues southward until it reaches the eastern coast near **Turtle Bay**, a destination for snorkeling or kayaking amid mangrove thickets and rich marine life. Beyond, **Tagbarungis Beach** is serviced by the Blue Sky Sport & Beach Resort (tel: 048-433-9490; also on Facebook).

The provincial road eventually crosses over to the South China Sea side of the island at **Napsan Beach**, known for pure waters and coastal rock formations. Nearby, yet a bit of a trek, are the **Salakot Waterfalls** and deep pools that invite a cold plunge. A rougher road from Napsan leads to **Santa Lourdes Hot Spring**.

From the Bacungan junction, a secondary road leads back west to Nagtabon Cove. Here the 1km (0.6-mile) -long **Nagtabon Beach** ②, some 45km (30 miles) or over an hour's drive from Puerto Princesa, offers a stretch of beige-colored sand, lapped by clear turquoise waters. Two small resorts – Pablico's and Georg's Place – are situated at either end of the placid strip, flanked by undulating hills and green cliffs.

## North of Puerto Princesa

The islands in **Honda Bay** ③, on the southeast-facing coast of Palawan, have become popular frolicking grounds for beach fanciers and water-sports enthusiasts. Here one can select any offshore islets for a day trip and overnight at resorts such as Villa Leonora (tel: 0999-413-3247) on the main island.

Honda Bay's island-hopping is recommended, and resorts nearby can set up boat trips. Travelers may also snorkel or scuba dive into the bay's coral and look for eels and turtles among the tropical fish. Bigger islets offering facilities for water sports, restaurants, and accommodations include Starfish, Meara, Fondeado, Cowrie, Snake, Buguias, and Arrecife. The northeast coast, some 50km (30 miles) from the central city, has excellent beaches.

Trekkers in this part of Palawan can also ask their resort operator about cross-country jungle expeditions that may take them all the way to **Cleopatra's Needle**, a rugged mountain with a sharp peak that rises

to 1,593 meters (5,226 ft). The **Tarau Caves** just 30 minutes by foot loom right behind the beach at kilometer 60 (guide service recommended). A further 12km along the highway there is an active indigenous **Batak village** (open business hours, donation requested). Walk through an amphitheater, peek into the classroom, study the homes on stilts, and browse a gift shop selling handmade baskets, mugs, and musical instruments.

North along the coast from Honda Bay, divers and sea kayakers may stop for a stay at the beachside bungalows of Modessa Island Resort (formerly Coco Loco Beach Resort, tel: 048-434-1584; www.modessaisland.com) near the highway town of Roxas.

Close to the northern tip of Palawan is the old town of **Taytay** ❹, one of the first Spanish fortifications to be built on the island. It was founded in 1622. Nearby is the island of **Paly**, with waterfalls and white-sand beaches, where giant sea turtles lay eggs in November and December. Off Taytay is **Malampaya Sound**, an angler's paradise.

## El Nido and the Bacuit Archipelago

Northwest of Taytay, 50km (30 miles) away, is **El Nido** ❺, where towering black marble cliffs provide swiftlets with enough nooks and crannies in which to build their nests, which are popular in soups throughout the Chinese world. Gatherers clamber up rickety bamboo scaffolding to collect the nests from crags and deep caves in the cliffs.

The small town of El Nido can be reached via dodgy roads after a rough full day's travel from Puerto Princesa, or by plane from Manila. Alternatively, from Sabang on the west coast hire a pumpboat for the seven-hour trip.

Nest gathering, though anachronistic given the region's ecotourism push, won't interfere with a holiday alongside nature. El Nido is the base for excursions to the surrounding limestone islands of the **Bacuit Archipelago**. Stay at one of the far-flung but upmarket resorts, such as Club Noah Isabelle on **Apulit Island** in Taytay Bay or El Nido Resort on

**TIP**

Cheap cottages are available in El Nido, a sleepy town of some 27,000 residents, where the houses bear a personal touch: instead of numbers, signs announce the names of the owners.

**Lagen Island** and **Miniloc Island**. These are also havens for divers and lovers of aquatic sports – and of El Nido's fabled shrimp-lobster hybrid dinners.

El Nido Resorts (tel: 02-813-0000; www.elnidoresorts.com) opened with its Miniloc operations in 1982 and soon drew attention as an environmentally friendly outfit. Some of its native cottages stand on stilts right over the edge of a cove. Guests can feed wild fish, which gobble offerings from your hand. Offshore, there is a small lagoon and coral formations accessible to the snorkeler. The lagoon is land-locked but for a narrow passage at low tide, and swimming amid the unspoiled jungle setting can be a memorable experience.

As El Nido grew in popularity, Club Noah Isabelle (tel: 0918-909-5583) and El Nido Lagen opened with more lavish facilities than the Miniloc resort. The Department of Environment and Natural Resources allows a maximum of only three resorts on El Nido's 45 islands. The third is a health spa, the Malapacap Island Resort (tel: 0917-896-3406; www.malapacao.com), on **Malapacao Island**.

**Pangulasian** is 40 minutes by pumpboat from El Nido village. The Robinson Crusoe-type island, with its long stretch of paradisiacal beach and trails snaking off into the hibiscus jungle, can be visited on day trips from other resorts. Other islands in the Bacuit Archipelago worth visiting include **Pinasil**, with Cathedral Cave which is big enough to drive a motorboat into.

## Coron island complex

Boats run from Manila to Puerto Princesa city in Central Palawan, stopping halfway at **Coron Town** ❻, on **Busuanga Island** ❼ in the Calamian group, north of Palawan's main island. For details or bookings, visit the WG&A Superferry website at www.superferry.com.ph. Chances are that you will have enough time during the boat's layover to wander about the old town for handicraft buys, wild honey, and dried sea cucumbers sunning on a pavement fronting a Chinese store.

**BELOW:** aerial view of Coron Island.

Daily flights from Manila now land in Coron airport in Busuanga Island. Busuanga, together with **Coron Island ❽** (not to be confused with Coron Town), have by word of mouth built a reputation as an adventurer's delight. Numerous destinations are within reach of Coron Town by pumpboat or rickety bus.

**Maquinit Hot Springs**, accessible by road or a 20-minute pumpboat ride from Coron, lets travelers bathe in hot sulfuric water in twin waist-deep pools by a mangrove stand, and flanked by a Virgin Mary grotto.

Cross over from Coron Town and scale trails past limestone cliffs for an hour or so to **Barracuda Lake** (Lake Cayangan), a basin of emerald water trapped in a virtual circle of tropical verdure and karst formations. It is home to a giant barracuda, which frequently shows up during lake dives – hence the site's more common name. Calm and quiet, the lake is perfect for kayaking. Another upland lake, **Cabugao**, is larger but farther off and requires longer than a day trip out of Coron Town. This land is the first in

the country to be returned to the control of a tribal people, the Tagbanua. Check accessibility, fees, and other rules such as camping and kayaking parameters, before visiting the beaches, lakes, and other attractions in this area.

All around **Coron Bay**, south of Busuanga Island, are dive sites popular enough to lure dive operators with equipment and services. Divers may spot the wrecks of Japanese ships and planes that went down during World War II. The wrecks have become historical underwater landmarks, particularly near Sangat Island. Dive Link Resort (tel: 0918-959-2604; www.divelink.com.ph) on **Uson Island**, barely 10 minutes by pumpboat from Coron, is a good jumping off point for underwater adventure, with a dozen Japanese wrecks at depths of 20–40 meters (65–130ft). The resort also provides leisure for non-divers.

Off the northern tip of Busuanga Island sits the **Calauit National Wildlife Sanctuary** on **Calauit Island ❾**. Giraffes, elands, zebras,

**BELOW:** Maquinit Hot Springs, Coron Island.

*Dive in Lake Cayangan (better known as Barracuda Lake) to meet the fish that give the lake its alternate name. Local dive operators take a banca to a crack in the limestone wall, where divers must scale 25 meters (80ft) of razor-sharp coral, in full dive gear. A descent into the warm lake leads to a zone where visibility drops to zero.*

**BELOW:** Rufous-headed hornbill.

bushbacks, impalas, gazelles, and waterbucks were shipped here in 1977 from Africa. The Conservation and Resource Management Foundation (CRMF), tasked to oversee the sanctuary, has done well enough, despite poaching, and the African animals have prospered, attracting photographers to the island.

To get to Calauit, take the pumpboat from Buluang, the end town of the provincial road, or make arrangements with any of the few resorts in the area. Two of these, Las Perlas and Las Hamacas Beach Resort (tel: 0921-412-8208), are found close to **Old Busuanga** town, while the upscale Club Paradise (tel: 0918-912-7106; www.clubparadisepalawan.com) occupies **Dinakya Island** off San Jose. Another resort close by is Maricaban Bay Resort (www.sailing.org.ph/maricaban_bay_res.html). Resort-bound tourists can take a pumpboat ride around the coast from Coron.

The Quiniluban and Cuyo Islands, southeast of Culion, may be reached in good weather in about half a day by motorized outrigger. There are

well-preserved Spanish forts on both **Agutaya Island** in the Quiniluban island group and **Cuyo Island**. Beaches include Caymanis Beach on the southern part of Cuyo, and Matarawis Beach in Agutaya. At the northern end of the Quiniluban islands is the **Halob Island Bird Sanctuary**, while the exclusive Amanpulo Resort (tel: 02-976-5200; www.amanresorts.com/amanpulo/home.aspx) occupies all of **Pamalican Island**.

## St Paul Underground River

The Underground River in **St Paul Subterranean National Park** ❿ (also known as the Puerto Princesa Underground River), a landmark of international acclaim, is the premier attraction of northern Palawan.

Pumpboats take visitors into St Paul cavern through a subterranean world of cathedrals with massive stalactites, icy lagoons where the eerie quiet is occasionally pierced by shrill cries of swooshing bats, and cave wall formations that resemble a George Lucas film set. High-powered lamps

### Bats to Badgers

**P**alawan, being largely off-limits for development, nurtures a rich range of tropical plants and animals, many not seen elsewhere in the Philippines. Tiny Palawan peacock pheasant roam the interior along with the 30cm (1ft) -tall mousedeer (*chevrotain*). They share space with the monkey-eating eagle and its prey. There is also the tabon bird, whose large eggs are collected to make a prized omelet.

Other species include hornbills, bearcats, civets, stink badgers, scaly anteaters, porcupines, flying squirrels, and the Palawan mongoose. The giant sea turtle lays its eggs on certain beaches at the end of the year. At dusk giant bats fly along the coast en masse to look for fruit by night.

handled by expert guides illuminate these attractions.

Exploration takes one to five hours. If you wish to tarry longer in the area you may register with the park wardens for overnight camping at any of the white-sand beaches clustered at the entrance to the subterranean river or check in at a nearby resort if rooms are available. Boats and vans run passengers from central Puerto Princesa to St Paul. As transportation has recently been upgraded, ask your hotel about the best way to get there.

Not far from the Underground River, the unspoiled town of **Sabang** displays a selection of empty beaches and limestone cliffs jutting from the ocean. Laid-back, low-end lodging is nearby. Nine kilometers (6 miles) inland from there, look for **Cabayugan**, home of cone-shaped cliffs interwoven with rice paddies. Adventurers can try the nearby **Kawaili and Lion caves**.

## Port Barton

On Palawan's South China Sea coast travelers find solace in the sands, dive sites, and interior island hiking of **Port Barton** ⑪. Here, you can sail or take pump-boats to other parts of Palawan. This quiet, non-commercialized town on Pagdanan Bay features a long stretch of beach where several budget hotels have opened. One such choice is Summer Homes (tel: 0920-969-9768; www.portbarton.info/summerhomes). A more upscale option is Greenview Resorts (tel: 0929-268-5333; www.palawan-greenviews.com). Visitors from Puerto can take a rough jeepney ride for four hours to reach Port Barton, but should check schedules in advance as departures are infrequent. Private vans take three hours.

*Northern Palawan boasts some dramatic scenery.*

**BELOW:** St Paul Underground River.

# SOUTHERN PALAWAN

Rough roads lead south through a largely untouched landscape, where birds patrol the skies, evidence of Stone Age man has been uncovered, and the surrounding seas harbor fabulous marine life.

Travelers with the time for challenging road trips and long pumpboat rides will find scenic riches in this part of the Philippines that has largely been left alone because it is so far from everything else. South Palawan's attractions are mostly natural, such as the Tabon Caves, which have yielded evidence of early human habitation. Inland areas are largely protected by the government. People seen en route may belong to indigenous tribes or work as merchants who trade along historic sea routes to the nearby Muslim world.

To make the most of a limited time, newcomers to Palawan are advised to book everything in advance. Few resorts operate in the region; towns are isolated and small.

## South of Puerto Princesa

On the road south from Puerto Princesa, at kilometer 69, about two hours' drive along the east coast, the municipality of **Aborlan** ⑫ is an agricultural town where a reservation has been set aside for ethnic minority groups. Princesa Holiday Beach resort and Camille del Sol are the prime attractions, along with **Tigman Beach.**

Some 30km (18 miles) farther south is the town of **Narra**, near which is an interesting inlet called **Tinagong**

**Dagat**, or Hidden Sea. **Rasa Island**, offshore from Narra, is a bird sanctuary and an ecotourism destination. Inland from Narra, a rugged mountain called **Victoria Peak**, with **Estrella Waterfalls** on its northern slopes, invites trekkers – with guides to make sure no one gets lost. King's Paradise Island Bay resort lies another 30km (18 miles) south of Narra.

### Tabon Caves

About 155km (100 miles) southwest of Puerto Princesa – four hours

**Main attractions**
VICTORIA PEAK, ESTRELLA
  WATERFALLS
QUEZON MINI UNDERGROUND RIVER
TABON CAVES
BALABAC ISLAND
TUBBATAHA REEFS NATIONAL PARK

**LEFT:** Tabon Caves.
**RIGHT:** green turtle, Tubbataha Reefs National Park.

by bus or jeepney – is the town of **Quezon** ⑬, from where one may take a half-hour boat ride to **Tabon Caves** ⑭. Tabon features a huge complex of some 200 caves, of which only 30 or so have been explored. Here, human remains were found and carbon-dated to 22,000–24,000 years ago, the oldest traces of *Homo sapiens* in the Philippine archipelago. Cave visitors should get entry permits from the tourism office in Quezon.

With the Tabon relics were found Stone Age implements and artifacts of later eras, including burial jars and kitchen utensils. Overlooking a bay studded with small islands, the entrance to Tabon Caves is situated about 30 meters (100ft) above sea level, on a promontory facing the South China Sea. The large mouth leads to an equally imposing dome-shaped chamber, beyond which are numerous sections where archeological work is still being carried out. From anywhere within Quezon town, ask a tricycle driver to take you to the **Tabon Museum**, which exhibits

artifacts and reading material on the archeological story behind the caves.

Close to Quezon, along Kanalong Bay in **Tarampitao**, runs a 10km (6-mile) stretch of white-sand beach that is ideal for swimming and watching sunsets. Also close by is the **Quezon Mini Underground River**, not quite as extensive as St Paul's near Puerto Princesa but also worth a few hours' exploration.

Further south, the east-coast highway is in very poor condition, mercifully ending before it reaches the southernmost tip of the mainland. Travelers usually reach the tip from Quezon via the town of **Española**.

## Muslim traders

Lying 150km (90 miles) south from Puerto Princesa, and reached only over very rough roads that make the drive painfully slow, is **Brooke's Point** ⑮. Here you may note the sudden preponderance of Muslim traders, who are not seen much in central and northern Palawan. The old trading and migratory routes that had established a bond between the southernmost part of mainland Palawan and the islands south of Mindanao, to the southeast, as well as the northernmost islets of Malaysia directly south, are still serviceable for maritime people whose mental and cultural maps transcend notions of political boundaries.

Check out **Port Miller & Lighthouse Tower**, which has long served as a beacon for seafarers and shoreline communities. From Brooke's Point, accessible by way of determined trekking, are **Mainit Falls**, reachable from the village of Mainit, and **Sabsaban Waterfalls**, further northeast, on the foothills of Mt Gantung.

Still further south, more easily reached by sea, are the predominantly Muslim communities of **Bataraza** and **Rio Tuba** ⑯. Rio Tuba has been thriving of late, thanks to a large copper mining company that provides

**BELOW:** great horned owl.

employment. But the mine also chokes the town in red dust stirred up at the pits.

A tribe distinct from the Batak and Tagbanua of the north used to enjoy pre-eminence in this area, calling themselves, simply, Pala'wan. But the inroads made by mining firms and both Christian and Muslim settlers have encroached on their territory. They are known for their age-old mystic practices in communion with revered spirits. To contact those spirits, tribe members chant and play traditional string or wind instruments, until some go into a trance and start dancing in the middle of the enchanted circle.

Video film-makers from Manila, one of whom traces his roots to the tribe, have helped them stage a waterborne protest against the activities of a pearl farm operator who had cordoned off a sandbar where the indigenous people used to gather clams and other marine delicacies. The documentary was shown on local television, though little has changed for the dwindling tribe.

## Nearby islands

Some 5km (3 miles) off Rio Tuba sits the **Ursula Island National Bird Sanctuary** ⓱. At one time the area was hit by a plague of rats and most of the birds moved to far-off **Tubbataha Reefs** in the middle of the Sulu Sea (see panel). Since the establishment of the Ursula Island sanctuary in 1960, some of the birds have returned. Migratory birds from China and Siberia also roost here from November to February. The sanctuary can be reached by a five-hour pump-boat ride from Brooke's Point. For more information, visit www.pcsd.ph/protected_areas/ursula.htm.

Off the southern tip of Palawan Island are **Bugsuk Island** and, close to the endpoint of Palawan Province, **Balabac Island** ⓲, famous for its rare seashells. Other interesting features of this island are **Basay Waterfalls** close to Balabac town, the **Morenton Peak Game Refuge**, and **Melville Lighthouse**, overlooking the strait that separates the Philippine archipelago from Malaysia.

*The world's largest pearl, the "Pearl of Lao-tze," was found in the shell of a giant clam off Palawan in 1934. It weighed in at 6.6kg (15lbs) and measured 24.2cm (9.5ins) long and 14cm (5.5ins) in diameter. Valued at more than US$40 million, it is kept in a San Francisco bank.*

**BELOW:** brightly colored gorgonian, Tubbataha Reefs National Park.

## Tubbataha Reefs

Lying remote in the Sulu Sea, Tubbataha Reefs is a large expanse of diverse corals, serving as a rich habitat for tropical fish, marine mammals, birds, and marine invertebrates – an abundance and diversity virtually unparalleled anywhere else in Asia. Large marine life is often present, including whales, sharks, and manta rays. Four species of dolphins and two species of marine turtles also inhabit the surrounding waters. The small sand cays in the area offer breeding grounds for several species of seabirds, including the critically endangered Christmas Island frigatebird and the colorful red-footed booby.

The only purely marine World Heritage Site in Southeast Asia allows diving by permit into waters with 30 to 45 meters (100–150ft) of visibility along a pristine coral reef with a 100-meter (330ft) perpendicular wall and two coral islands. Visitors must pre-arrange boat trips from mainland Palawan to the reefs. Boats from Puerto Princesa take about five hours. For more information, tel: 048-434-5759 or visit www.tub-batahareef.org. The website links to a list of diving operators.

The Reefs, however, have fallen prey to extensive dynamite and cyanide fishing. Since there are neither sizeable islands nor fresh water to support human habitation of any sort, the Philippine Navy can only send intermittent patrols..

# MINDANAO

**Mindanao, the major island of the southern Philippines, claims the country's highest mountain and tallest waterfall, and is home to many ethnic minorities.**

**T**he mention of this 94,630 sq km (36,530 sq mile) island might immediately conjure up images of insurgency, but much of that activity has been pushed to the western extremes of Mindanao, an island that is second in area in the Philippines only to Luzon. Those who stick to the safer parts will see Mt Apo, the highest peak in the country, the tropical beaches of Samal Island near Davao, and the towering Aliwagwag waterfall – just the top of a long to-do travel list.

The region is also home to the world's largest eagle, the world's most expensive shells, the world's richest nickel deposits, and some of the world's deepest water. The island teems with hiking and trekking, scuba diving and white-water action not far from the booming city of Davao.

Indigenous tribes range across Mindanao, occupying huts that stand on stilts above the ground, where wild animals may otherwise attack, or over the water in seafaring regions. Some indigenous groups follow Islam, and mosques may outnumber Catholic churches in southwestern towns as locals adhere to the religion introduced about 800 years ago, before the Spanish arrived.

Sub-groups on Basilan Island, in the Sulu Islands and near Cotabato still do war with the government over what they perceive as ongoing, illegitimate land grabs. Anyone traveling to western Mindanao should check conditions with embassies and local officials, as some parts remain volatile and kidnappings have occurred. Seeking to make the region safer, the government of President Benigno Aquino III met for the first time with a major rebel leader in 2011.

Plan trips to the interior mountains or waterfalls judiciously, with time to spare. And while most of Mindanao's rich natural resources remain untapped, those already exploited – by illegal logging and rampant gold mining, for instance – have experienced serious environmental degradation.

---

**PRECEDING PAGE:** Kadayawan Festival, Davao City. **LEFT:** Maria Cristina Falls.
**ABOVE, FROM LEFT:** the Philippine eagle – most commonly found in Mindanao; Mindanao tribespeople.

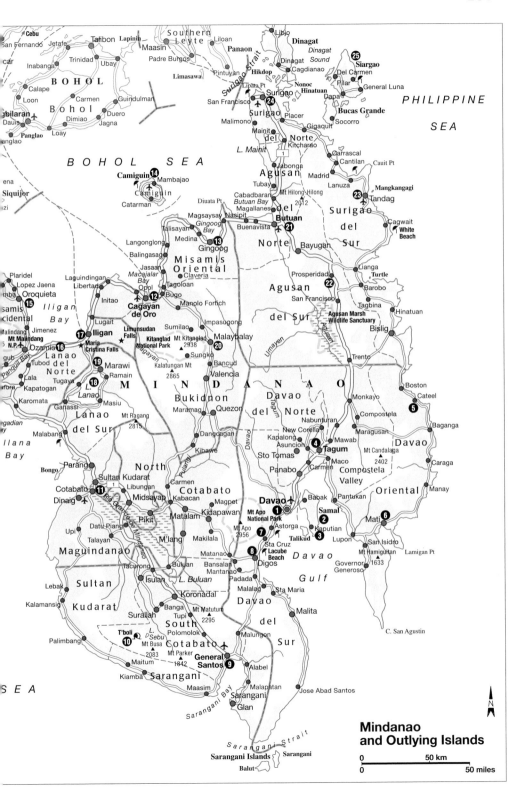

## Mindanao
## and Outlying Islands

| 0 | | 50 km |
|---|---|---|
| 0 | | 50 miles |

# SOUTHERN AND CENTRAL MINDANAO

The Philippines' highest peak, jungle waterfalls, misty lakes, and the fast modernizing regional capital, Davao, are among the attractions awaiting visitors to this less-traveled island.

**W**ith calm mostly restored to Mindanao's south-central provinces, travelers are venturing further afield to explore the island's remarkable natural beauty, flora and fauna.

A growing number of tour operators now lead treks and white-water rafting expeditions. The adventurous can set off on a four-day expedition to scale Mt Apo, the nation's highest peak, while others may relish the thrill of white-water tubing at Sibulan River Rapids. Those with their own transport can find obscure white-sand beaches along the east coast, visit an offshore island pearl farm, or travel inland to the towering Aliwagwag Falls and the chance to see native T'boli tribespeople.

Davao, the nation's second-largest city, is growing fast as its progressive mayor tries to boost tourism, conferences, and commerce while keeping the place relatively clean – not easy for a large conurbation in the Philippines.

## Davao

Change has certainly found its way to **Davao City ❶**, a flagship for the massive, scenic, and embattled island of Mindanao. On the 30-minute cab ride downtown from the airport, looking at mom-and-pop

dinettes and watching children run off to school, you would never think Davao had been a "laboratory" of urban death squads, led by guerrillas operating with impunity in the early 1980s.

Nowadays, the city of 1.5 million people, in the northernmost part of Davao del Sur Province, is booming with hotels, malls, and housing projects. Many of those are under construction at Davao's otherwise scrappy fringes, and some extend into the jungles beyond as the local

**Main attractions**
DAVAO CROCODILE PARK
PEARL FARM RESORT STILT HOUSES
ALIWAGWAG FALLS
MT APO TREKKING
T'BOLI, SANTA CRUZ MISSION

**LEFT:** a weaver at work at the T'boli Weaving Center. **RIGHT:** Davao street stall.

*With 18 colleges and four universities, Davao has the most universities in the Philippines outside of Manila.*

government seeks to bring in international conferences and foreign tourists who normally shy away from anything under the heading of Mindanao.

Davao has been kept especially safe under the past two mayors, a father and daughter surnamed Duterte. The city may have the crumbling infrastructure and smelly vehicular exhaust found elsewhere in the country, but litter is oddly missing. And as of 2012 Davao was on a campaign – unusual for the Philippines – to stop smoking in public places.

As a testament to its cleaner image, the city has picked up flights from Singapore, Indonesia, Palau, and throughout the Philippines. Commercial jets start buzzing into the airport around sunrise and continue throughout the day.

## Central Davao

Downtown Davao, compact compared to its peers Manila and Cebu, is a pedestrian-friendly mix of malls, university buildings, and streetside diners. Those grazing for street food will find pancakes, waffles, and cooked bananas; fried chicken jumps out of every fourth or fifth doorway. When out for a stroll, you may pass bookstores packed with English-language titles for the numerous university students in town. Along **Quimpo Boulevard** you will see a mosque and a sample of the city's low-rise, riverside slums.

Among the downtown attractions is **St Peter's Cathedral Ⓐ** on San Pedro Street. The oldest church in the city, it exhibits a blend of Muslim and Christian architecture.

The **Museo Dabawenyo** on Recto at Pinchon streets (tel: 082-222-6011; Mon–Sat 9am–noon, 1–6pm) gives a snapshot of the region's numerous indigenous tribes, including replicas of their bamboo homes built on stilts to keep away ocean water or wild animals. Artwork displayed in the museum uses unusual media such as bamboo (in place of canvas), a broken wine bottle (instead of paint), and durian rinds. The museum's historical exhibits explain the era around 1900 when Americans

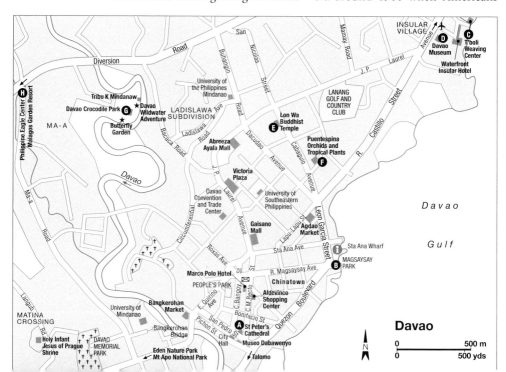

Davao

made a mark trying to develop the region.

A walk through town should take in **People's Park** on Camus Street. It's known for manmade waterfalls and a dancing fountain that comes to life at night. The **University Mall** on Ramon Magsaysay Avenue is filled with internet cafés. Nearby is the Marco Polo, Davao's tallest luxury hotel, and across from that, the **Aldevinco Shopping Center** has a compact nest of shops with good selections of Muslim brass and tribal artifacts from around Mindanao.

Just outside downtown lies **Magsaysay Park** Ⓑ, named to honor the third president of the Philippines (1950s). The park, popular with locals escaping the gritty streets, features a durian statue – a monument for the strong-scented tropical fruit grown around the island – and the shaded Fishcado Grill with bamboo seating, and a palm-lined promenade along the sea. **Santa Ana Wharf** next door is the most common take-off point for diving around the islands and reefs in the Davao Gulf.

Outside the park is the red gate to a once sprawling **Chinatown**, which today appears not obviously different from the rest of town, selling imports from shops owned by Chinese.

North of the town center, on J. P. Laurel Avenue, is **Gaisano Mall**, and the sprawling **Abreeza Ayala Mall** that opened in 2011 with 300

*The Arch of Unity marks one of the entrances to Davao's Chinatown.*

**BELOW:** a display of tribal art at the Museo Dabawenyo.

Matina Town Square on MacArthur Highway is a live music venue.

**BELOW:** woven fabrics at the T'boli Weaving Center.

commercial spaces. Abreeza's swanky stores include top foreign-brand clothes, and restaurants here range from intensely local to obviously foreign.

Along the lengthy J. P. Laurel Avenue, **Insular Village** is the site of the Waterfront Insular Century Hotel, occupying immaculately kept grounds. On the same grounds is the **T'boli Weaving Center ⓒ**, where tribal women in native attire weave *dagmay*, a fabric made from *abaca* fibers. Insular Village Phase I contains the **Davao Museum ⓓ** (tel: 082-300-8046; Mon–Sat 9am–noon, 1–5pm; charge), featuring ethnological maps, dioramas, photographs, and displays of tribal artifacts.

## Davao's suburban sights

**Lon Wa Buddhist Temple ⓔ**, the biggest Buddhist temple in Mindanao, stands in a setting of candle trees and bamboo not far from the city center. The temple features Italian marble slabs, a Buddha statue, carved wood ornamentation, carp-filled lily ponds, and high-ceilinged halls. Also within easy taxi distance is **Puentespina Orchids and Tropical Plants ⓕ**, a garden featuring several varieties of native orchids, including Mindanao's signature *waling-waling*.

In the verdant low hills, just 15 minutes from town, lurks the regionally famous **Davao Crocodile Park ⓖ** (tel: 082-286-8883; www.davao-crocodilepark.com; daily 8am–6pm; charge). Several sizeable enclosures

show the reptile in different stages of growth, including dozens of 60cm (2ft) -long juveniles sunning themselves en masse in the heavily fenced compound replete with a variety of palms offering cool shade. Pangil, a 6-meter (19ft) -long crocodile, is the star of the mini zoo that also comes with tigers, toucans, native deer, and a civet. Buloy, a 3.3-meter (11ft) -long albino Indian python, is tame enough to put on one's shoulders for photographs.

Admission to the park also allows entry to a neighboring **butterfly garden**, so full of its celebrated winged insects that one's camera lens can capture multiple species with minimal effort. Look for the **Davao Walk 'N Waterball** pond next to the garden, where visitors float in giant transparent plastic bubbles over a pool of water. Also here is **Tribu K. Mindanaw**, a riverside showcase of bamboo stilt homes similar to those used by some of the 25 indigenous tribes in Mindanao. A restaurant inside Tribu K serves traditional dishes and drinks, including coffee from

beans grown around Mt Apo. Tribu K puts on a "fire show" from Friday through Sunday, 5.45–6.30pm.

The Riverwalk Exotic Resto-Grill next door serves crocodile meat. The whole compound is flush with coconut palms and other jungle vegetation that provide relief from urban Davao.

Located in the back of the Davao Crocodile Park is **Davao Wildwater Adventure** (tel: 082-286-1055 or 0920-954-6898; www.psdgroupph.com; 8.30am–4.30pm). The boat operator uses a nearby river with waterfalls to offer white-water rafting trips, from easy to medium grade.

## Eagle center

A 35km (22-mile) drive northwest of town is the **Philippine Eagle Center** Ⓗ in **Malagos**, Calinan, a sanctuary for the monkey-eating raptor also known as the *haribon*. Other bird species, wild deer, tarsier, and a python can be seen here. En route to the sanctuary, stop briefly at **Sul Orchids**, a 2-hectare (5-acre) orchid farm where a variety of crossbreeds are grown to perfection.

**TIP**

There are numerous fruit and flower plantations just outside Davao. Although most welcome visitors, it's best to check with the local tourist office at City Hall (tel: 082-222-1956) for opening hours before proceeding.

**BELOW:** a resident of the Davao Crocodile Park.

The **Malagos Garden Resort** in Calinan hosts the best works of National Artist awardee Napoleon Abueva, a sculptor. About one-and-a-half hour's drive to the south, in **Toril District**, a road leads to **Eden Nature Park**, a hilltop garden resort with views of the city.

## Samal Island

Stretches of white sand, clear blue waters, mangroves, coral reefs, rolling hills, and caves in **Samal Island** ❷, 7km (4 miles) offshore from Davao, await the visitor who wants to relax or pursue adventure. Samal is a 28,000-hectare (69,000-acre) archipelago of nine islands, accessible via a five-minute *banca* ride from Buhangin town in Davao. The world-class 11-hectare (27-acre) **Pearl Farm Resort**, in a secluded cove in the town of **Kaputian** ❸, is Samal's most popular attraction. It was once a pearl farm, where Sulu Sea oysters were cultivated for their pink, white, and gold pearls. It features stilt houses, and visitors can watch tiny fish frolicking between the sturdy poles that anchor them. The

resort can arrange transportation from Davao airport.

Water sports are the main reasons to visit Samal. Kaputian, for instance, has two sunken World War II Japanese vessels. The land-based adventurer will also find Samal good for trekking, mountain biking, and caving. **Mt Puting Bato**, the main hiking destination, offers a superb view of Davao City, Davao Gulf, and the surrounding islands at sunrise and sunset, from its peak. Caliclic Cave in **Babak** features four rooms with skeletal remains, believed to be those of the Kalagan tribes.

On the coasts of mainland Mindanao outside central Davao, motorists will see the beaches of Talomo, Talisay, Salokot, and Guino-o, to name a few, which are interesting for their proximity to fishing villages. **Talomo**, on the south side of the city, was the scene of a World War II Japanese landing in 1942 and an American landing in 1945. Coastal resorts are sparse here as beaches lack the white sand and clear waters sought after by tourists.

**BELOW:** Philippine eagle.

## Davao del Norte

A 77km (48-mile) drive north of central Davao lies the town of **Talaingod**, a 65,000-hectare (161,000-acre) settlement of a tribal group by the same name. The town has rich natural resources, including a 6,000-hectare (14,830-acre) virgin forest. The town hall, built on a mountain top, overlooks the village of a people plagued by inter-tribal friction and poor infrastructure, though in recent years the area has become more attractive to visitors.

**Tagum ❹**, the provincial capital of Davao del Norte, features **Mainit Springs**, composed of a cold and hot spring that meet in a river. White-sand **Tagnanan Beach**, 45km (28 miles) southeast of Tagum, offers a haven to swim, hunt shells, fish, and scuba dive.

Explore the cave of **Mawab**, 865 meters (2,835ft) long, with curtain-shaped stalactites and huge calcite pillars. A small subterranean waterfall tumbles into a lake. The 345-meter (1,130-ft) -long **Tuburan Cave** in Monkayo, however, requires technical skill and climbing equipment because of the 15-meter (50ft) pit inside. A potable spring and crystal-clear underground river await the diver, and the fish and crab catcher. Contact Tagum City Hall (tel: 084 218-1957) for details on guided tours.

Visitors to nearby Compostela Valley Province, best known for gold mining and a fabled wild-west spirit, may trek up **Mt Candalaga**. Treks can be arranged with the town of Maragusan, or through the Regional DOT in Davao City (tel: 082-221-6955). Over the three-hour trip, hikers will see more than 30 waterfalls and 100 cold springs, thick primary rainforest and wildlife of startling variety. Other eco-tours are being offered to the Nabunturan caves and the Malumagpak waterfall.

## Davao Oriental

East of Monkayo is **Davao Oriental Province**'s town of **Cateel ❺**, site of the towering **Aliwagwag Falls**. At 340 meters (1,110ft) high and 20 meters (65ft) wide, these are the highest falls in the country, comprising a series of

*A jar of water (banga) and a coconut-shell dipper are placed near the entrance to each house for the guests to wash away the sand after a day of bare-footing it on the beach. In local custom, this gesture symbolizes the cleansing of the spirit.*

**BELOW:** Sambuokan Festival, Mati.

*The T'boli women are known for their intricately woven fabrics.*

pumpboat from Mati.

For the really adventurous traveler, San Isidro town, an hour southwest of Mati, is the starting point for a trek on **Mt Hamiguitan**, whose narrow, leech-infested, and slippery trails run across steep, unforgiving slopes. The most difficult ascent is a 60-degree climb of about 350 meters (1,150ft). Climbers will eventually reach the uninhabited **Tinagong Dagat** (Hidden Sea), situated 300 meters (975ft) above sea level, in the midst of a virgin forest.

Further south, near Governor Generoso, accessible by a 30-minute *banca* ride, is white-sand **Sigaboy Island**.

## South of Davao City

Southward from Davao City, in the town of **Santa Cruz** ❼, the **Sibulan River Rapids** is the venue for an adrenaline-pumping craze known to adventure buffs as white-water tubing. Similar to white-water rafting, tubing involves riding atop an inflated rubber tube – usually the interior of a truck tire – and being carried downstream by the current.

84 falls appearing like a stairway, with each step ranging from 2–34 meters (6–110ft).

**Mati** ❻, the provincial capital, teems with beach resorts and is home to the 250-hectare (620-acre) Menzi Citrus Plantation where guests can stay in a refurbished Castilian-style house replete with a pool. Scuba dive on the 155-hectare (385-acre) white-sand **Pujada Island**, one hour by

In the same region, visitors can rappel down the 90-meter (300-ft) Tudaya Falls, just below the foot of **Mt Apo** (see page 309).

**Digos ❽**, the provincial capital of Davao del Sur, is built on seven hills surrounded by rice fields. Its features include forested **Sinawilan Hot Spring**, 4km (2.5 miles) away, and places to spot bats along a gray-sand beach in **Talucanga**, 6km (4 miles) from town. Holiday Beach Resort in *barangay* Dawis puts people up in cottages and has water-sports facilities.

Trudge an hour on rough but picturesque roads to experience the colorful culture of the B'laan tribe at the **Bolon Sabak B'laan Village** in Matanao. Piapi Beach in **Malalag** is dotted with picnic huts and offers panoramic views of Malalag and the nearby wharf. In the next town of **Malita** go shipwreck-diving or deer-watching. Off the southern tip of San Jose town are the **Sarangani Islands**. On **Ballestic Island**, look for the fortress remnants of the late Roy Lopez Villalobos, a Spanish explorer.

## South Cotabato

The farming-reliant region of South Cotabato grows pineapples, bananas, coffee, rice, corn, and asparagus. Beaches, natural spring resorts, caves, and a rich culture are its major attractions.

Perched on **Sarangani Bay**, on the southern tip of Mindanao, is **General Santos City ❾**, or "Gensan," transformed from a backwater into a boomtown by US$270 million in foreign aid and private investment. There are an increasing number of flights between General Santos and Manila and Cebu. **Makar Wharf**, Gensan's international seaport, is one of the most modern installations in the country. Visitors can walk through the Gensan Fish Port Complex in the morning to see the range of fish hauled in from nearby seas.

In **Polomolok**, 20km (12 miles) northwest of Gensan, cavers can explore the stalactites and stalagmites of **Salkak Cave**, where a series of chambers leads to an underground river. Trekkers can climb the 2,295-meter (7,515-ft) **Mt Matutum** through dense forests and the B'laan

*The Mandaya, Mansaka, and Dibabawon are the three most prominent ethnic groups in Davao. The Mandaya settle in areas close to rivers; the Mansaka in upland areas; the Dibabawon are mostly nomadic. All three groups are renowned for their silver-smithing.*

**BELOW:** cattle herder on Mt Apo.

tribal highlands, with chances to see monkeys, birds, wild pigs, and deer. The **Dole Philippines** clubhouse is the usual base for climbing; overnight stays can be arranged through the company's personnel department.

The ultimate caving challenge is to the west at **T'boli Cave** , in T'boli town, where only the first 250 meters (810ft) of calcite pillars and crystalline formations have so far been explored. Be technically prepared.

Mindanao is known for its multiple ethnic minorities. Ethnic T'boli women often wear an *abaca* turban, a colorfully ornate, broad and round hat. *T'nalak* cloth, made from pounded bark, is the tribe's famous weave. The T'boli also create intricate beadwork, basketry, and traditional brass ornaments. The local **Santa Cruz Mission** runs 27 schools, including a college, in T'boli territory, and sells traditional artwork. The annual September T'boli Festival, a tribal thanksgiving, is celebrated with horse fights, traditional dances, and games. From

Kabacan in North Cotabato, the national highway heads west to Midsayap, Libungan, and finally **Sultan Kudarat**, the provincial capital of **Maguindanao** Province. North of this point is the former territory of the Muslim revolutionary group known as the Moro Islamic Liberation Front (see page 329). Much of the area, including the revolutionaries' headquarters, **Camp Abubakar**, was retaken by the Philippine military under the Estrada administration. The area remains unsafe for tourists.

## Cotabato City

**Cotabato City** is accessible by land from Kidapawan and by air from Manila. Here, the **Autonomous Region in Muslim Mindanao (ARMM) Compound** showcases an unusual blend of modern and Muslim architecture. Inside are the Shariff Kabungsuan Cultural Center, Regional Museum (Mon–Fri 8–11.30am, 1.30–5pm; free), and Regional Library. The museum's collection includes artifacts of the Maguindanao, Maranao, and Tiruray tribes of Muslim Mindanao.

**P.C. Hill**, a towering 28-meter (90-ft) stone fort, which now houses the City Internal Defense Command, is Cotabato City's landmark and a former watchtower to detect assaults during World War II. For pure fun while in Cotabato, go to **Kiwa**, an adventure park with a swimming pool and a zipline.

South of Maguindanao is the province of **Sultan Kudarat**, whose soil is one of the richest and most fertile in the Philippines. Buluan Lake and the *waling-waling* orchid are its main tourist attractions, though it is unsafe to visit. Beaches to the south in **Sarangani** are mostly undeveloped. The province has lost much of its marine resources to destructive fishing practices, but the tide seems to have turned with a rebound in fish and corals.

**BELOW:** T'Boli man, Lake Sebu.

# Mount Apo

**Hikers with three to four days can hire guides to take them past lakes and waterfalls, sighting eagles and monkeys, to the peak that crowns Mindanao**

From the depths of Mindanao soars Mount Apo, the highest Philippine peak, challenging outdoor enthusiasts to scale its full 2,956 meters (9,698ft).

The name Apo, which means "Lord," came from the Bagobo tribespeople living on its slopes. They believe that the "Garden of Eden" had its beginning in the tropical rainforest around Lake Venado. Now a national park, Mt Apo encompasses a 72,800-hectare (180,000-acre) base of lush tropical rainforest, boiling mineral springs, sulfur vents, lakes, and waterfalls. The only recorded eruption was in 1640. All physical indications, however, point to continuing volcanic activity deep below.

## On the trail

A traveler might first spot the peak from an airplane window while flying into Davao. Buses from Cotabato and Davao approach the mountain via Kidapawan. From here take a tricycle to the Kidapawan Tourism Council office to get a climbing permit. Buses and jeepneys proceed to the Lake Agko staging area.

A trail from the launch point follows the Marbel River canyon, crossing the water 13 times. Trekkers have a chance of seeing monkeys, wild pigs, and the endangered Philippine eagle as they hike through the jungles past legendary Lake Venado. Another route, the Kidapawan Trail, jumps off at the continuously boiling Lake Agco, passing through a part of the Marbel River, the Mainit Hot Spring, and Malou Shi Waterfalls. Atop awaits an unobstructed panoramic view of the whole of Mindanao.

## Mountain guides

Paid guides are required. The guides, who may also work as porters, run three-day and four-day trips from Davao to the summit. Trekkers – or their outfitters – should bring tents, stoves, and hiking poles. For more information, visit Tours by Locals

www.toursbylocals.com/mtapo to book a trip in advance, or reocities.com/Yosemite//3712/gapo.html for tips on how to book on arrival. National Department of Tourism offices (DTO) can also link tourists to organized climbs. The Mt Apo Climbers Association organizes regular trekking events, and can be contacted through the DTO.

Vandalism has become rampant along the trails, as some visitors have etched or spray-painted their names on trees or rocks, catalyzing a push for more security as tourism officers and mountaineering clubs try to prevent further deterioration.

To take it easier, try one of the three official hiking trails on the mountain, each with unusual features. Check with the regional tourism office in Davao about which trails are open. There is also a 400-meter (1,312ft) zipline at Camp Sabros, a side trip in the Mt Apo environs.

**ABOVE:** at the summit of Mt Apo. **RIGHT:** Mt Apo is a good place for spotting the endangered Philippine eagle.

# NORTHERN MINDANAO AND CARAGA

**This region is home to a variety of cultures and an abundance of wilderness scenery, accessible from busy, industrialized cities.**

A trip through Mindanao's extensive northern reaches takes travelers to the waterfalls of Iligan, the fast-developing beaches of Opol near Cagayan de Oro, and the peaceful, tourist-friendly Islamic city of Marawi. Throughout the region visitors with the time to explore will find obscure lakes, protected forests, and tribes who have lived there for thousands of years. One of the top draws is the Surigao area, where surfers seek the perfect swell and everyday beachgoers enjoy white sands in a relatively undeveloped location.

The region where agriculture makes up a third of the economy thrives largely on its signature crop, pineapple, with forestry and fishing playing big supporting roles. Industry gives Northern Mindanao another third of its income, and services, including tourism, make up the rest.

Though not pressed for infrastructure like some parts of the country, Northern Mindanao poses the usual challenges in getting around outside cities. Travelers should use the usual artful patience in linking buses, jeepneys, tricycle-taxis, and pumpboats to reach far-flung destinations.

## Misamis Oriental

**Misamis Oriental**, on the central north coast, is the export manufacturing and processing center of Northern Mindanao, with a land area of 3,570 sq km (1,380 sq miles) and a long, sheltered coastline with deep, natural harbors. Rivers traverse its rugged mountain ranges and lush valleys, flowing past 173,945 hectares (429,820 acres) of fertile cropland and 168,850 hectares (417,220 acres) of forest.

Travelers to this area should check with tourism authorities about any lingering impacts of Tropical Storm Sendong, which wiped out several villages in 2011. Floodwaters killed 500

**Main attractions**

OPOL BEACH, CAGAYAN DE ORO
CAMIGUIN ISLAND
ILIGAN'S 20-PLUS WATERFALLS
ISLAMIC CITY OF MARAWI
SURIGAO REGION BEACH SPORTS

**LEFT:** Talaandig woman at the Talaandig Center for Living Traditions. **RIGHT:** pineapple plantation, Bukidnon Province.

people and raised fears about a slow-down in travel – once a growing business – to the areas around Cagayan de Oro.

**Cagayan de Oro City** ⑫ (CDO) is the regional capital and main entry point to the broader region. Cebu Pacific flights reach CDO from Manila and Cebu, while ferries reach the city from Manila, Cebu, and other ports. From the city, one can go to any point of Mindanao by land, taking advantage of a well-paved road network.

CDO is highly urbanized, with a wide range of lodgings, restaurants, markets, and shopping centers. Jeepneys and *motorela*, six-person motor scooters in front of a chassis, ply the streets. The Cagayan River bisects the city. On its eastern side, visit Gaston Park and inside the park **San Agustin Cathedral**, with an unusual water tower. On Corrales Avenue sits Xavier University, housing the **Museo de Oro** (tel: 088-857-4472; Mon–Fri 8am–noon, 1–5pm; free). It displays archeological finds, Hispanic antiquities, and tribal artifacts, as well as

memorabilia from the Philippine-American war. It operates alongside the Santillano Shell Museum, exhibiting over 1,000 priceless shells from around the world. On weekend evenings, check out the night market near Divisoria for food, bargain buys and occasional performances.

CDO's best beach is 9km (6 miles) west of the city in **Opol**. A cluster of resorts operate on the sandy seashore. There is an aviary and a mini-zoo in the city that is growing quickly as a suburb of CDO. In nearby **Laguindingan**, check out Cueva Con Agua, where water drips from a cave roof. Past Gitagum and Libertad is **Initao** and Initao Cave, home to unusual bats with cauliflower-like noses. **Macahambus Cave**, where in 1899 Filipino revolutionaries scored a major upset over American forces, sits some 14km (9 miles) southeast of CDO. Walk through the cave to emerge among gigantic rocks and savage-looking trees overlooking Cagayan River.

From Opol, a road inland at **Cugman** leads to the small but scenic Catanico Falls, with a swimming hole and picnic area. Continuing 7km (4 miles) onward is *barangay* **Bugo**, site of the Del Monte Philippines cannery plant (tours by appointment, 8am–2pm).

From Bugo, a steep, twisting road proceeds inland, offering views of **Macajalar Bay.** This bay, with its 175km (110-mile) -long shoreline, is ideal for windsurfing and jet-skiing. On a hill overlooking the bay is the 200-hectare (495-acre) eco-village of **Malasag**. The village features "tribal houses," where various ethnic groups from Mindanao are authentically represented. Guesthouses let visitors stay the night.

Northeast of CDO, in **Claveria**, try the Noslek Canopy Walk. Its hanging bridges and viewing decks perch as high as 18 meters (60ft) in the trees, affording views of lush virgin forests.

**BELOW:** giant clams.

## Coastal towns

In the town of **Lagonglong**, north of CDO, travelers often spend time at the clear, cool Sapong Spring. Farther on, at **Talisayan**, is the government-run Calamcan Beach. The next town, **Medina**, has several white-sand beaches, with the cool Alibwag Spring nearby. **Duca** has gained a name for its good dive site, with underwater gardens. Thirty minutes away by pumpboat are **Pampangon**'s sunken pontoons, overgrown with marine life.

The next stopover, **Gingoog City** ⓭, leads visitors to Libon-Lawit, Tiklas, and Odiongan waterfalls. Badiangon Beach and Spring, also in the area, has two known caves, Agayayan Sunog and Tinuluyan. Here the Don Paquito Lopez Pass, or **Kisoong Ridge**, stands 1,280 meters (4,200ft) above sea level. An underwater hill, sitting atop a plateau dotted with caverns and abundant marine growth, sits unperturbed in **Gingoog Bay**. In **Magsaysay** farther east, travelers often make a point of seeing Punta Diuata, a series of 13 connecting caves.

## Camiguin

Off the coast of CDO, the island province of **Camiguin** ⓮ forms an idyllic pear-shaped island with steep volcanoes, jungles, waterfalls, white-sand beaches, and natural springs both hot and cold. At its heart is the **Ardent Hot Springs** mineral pool, fed by the active **Hibok-Hibok Volcano** (1,330 meters/4,370ft). Picnic here, under a canopy of trees, or cool off in springs of varying degrees of heat. Alternatively, swim at the isolated sandbar called **White Island**, which can be accessed from Paras Beach Resort (tel: 088-856-8563; www.parasbeachresort.com) in **Barangay Yumbing**.

Head south along the highway to see the ruins of **Gui-ob Church**. Loll about on the grassy area where the church pews would have been: thick stone walls are now all that remains after a powerful volcanic eruption in 1871.

Toward the eastern side of Camiguin is pretty **Mantigue Island**. For a small fee, partake of the daily catch while learning about the life for the local

**TIP**

Jetfoils and ferries depart for Camiguin from Cagayan de Oro. Once on the island, consider rentomg a motorcycle or scooter. The 64km (40-mile) loop road and all of the roads that lead off it offer unlimited potential for exploring an area with the highest number of volcanoes per square kilometer of any island on the planet.

**BELOW:** Camiguin Island.

*Mountains around Mt Malindang were probably formed through a series of volcanic activities, Unesco believes. One indicator is the contour or Lake Duminagat, which means Crater Lake.*

fishing community. It is also possible to head out to **Kabila Beach**, where rare *taklobo* (giant clams) are being bred. Ask local private boat operators about rates and schedules.

To cool off, rappel down the 76-meter (250ft) **Katibawasan Falls** to a pool surrounded by orchids and ferns, or trek along a rocky river bank to reach **Tuasan Falls**.

## Misamis Occidental

Surrounded on three sides by water, the province of **Misamis Occidental** features fisheries packed with marine life. Rolling hills characterize the inland terrain, which becomes particularly rugged toward the western border. Industry revolves around coconut processing and fishing.

But visitors do not go to Misamis Occidental for comfort or luxury. Tourism in the province is associated more with abundant seafood, a little history, mountaineering, and beach life. Inexpensive hotels and pensions or family-run rooms supply accommodations, with travel provided by either tricycle or jeepney.

**BELOW:** Mount Malindang.

Oroquieta City ⓖ, the provincial capital, is accessible via a seven-hour Cagayan de Oro–Pagadian–Dipolog bus ride. At its heart is the **Provincial Capitol**, replete with flower gardens, fountains, and a children's park. **Camp Ceniza**, 2km (1.2 miles) away, leads travelers to scenic views, trees, and a floating pavilion. El Truinfo Beach is lined with shades and cottages for picnickers, while up-close looks at natural ecology and wildlife have put the **Oroquieta Agro-Industrial School Mini-Park** on regional travel itineraries.

North of the city, beaches in the Biasong and Peneil villages of the town of **Lopez Jaena** are shaping up as potential tourist spots. Farther on in **Plaridel**, commoners built Nazareno Dam, an old irrigation canal considered among the best in the country, without the aid of sophisticated machinery.

## Wildlife watershed

Visitors setting priorities for this part of the Philippines should leave time for **Mt Malindang**, a 53,000-hectare (130,960-acre) national park and wildlife sanctuary south of Oroquieta. The Malindang Range is a watershed of over 20 rivers, and home to a variety of wildlife such as the Philippine eagle, a giant bat, a python, and a rodent species called the Malindang rat. **Lake Duminagat** spans 4 hectares (10 acres) of the park. The protected park has received P800 million from an ecological work fund, most of which comes from foreign donors. Preserved locally since 1971, the park was submitted in 2006 to Unesco for consideration as a World Heritage Site.

The town of **Panaon** has several beaches and the 2-meter (6ft) -high Imeldanita Fall, framed by green trees and boulders. Farther south, **Ozamis City** ⓰ holds the province's cultural treasures. Near the wharf is **Fort Santiago**, also called Kota, a Spanish fortress built in 1707 to protect the region from pirates. At the **Immaculate Concepcion Cathedral** there is a pipe organ from Germany, while **Doña Prospera Park** is a pleasant open space next to the City Hall complex.

**Regina Swimming Pool**, a natural pool fed by cold springs, is 3km (2 miles) from Ozamis. **Tangub City**, or the "City of Fish Traps", along **Panguil Bay** exports tiger shrimp from the bay to Japan.

## Lanao del Norte

Southeast of Misamis Occidental, the province of **Lanao del Norte** stands out mostly for its waterfalls, high and low, accessible and remote. The province is best reached from Cagayan de Oro City via a two-hour bus trip to **Iligan City** ⓱. It is highly industrialized – and some say poorly planned. Shopping malls, restaurants, and small hotels abound.

Fast boats and ferries ply the waters to Iligan from Cebu and Manila. Its deep harbor is home to National Power Corporation (NAPCOR) among other large corporations. The 98-meter (320ft) **Maria Cristina Falls**, fed by the Agus River, has supplied most of Mindanao's electricity since

being harnessed for hydroelectric power in 1952. The Mabuhay Vinyl Corporation Park and Lagoon, on top of a hill within the plant, has grown to where it operates a small park along the lagoon. Iligan City Hall stands atop **Buhanginan Hill**, 45 meters (150ft) above sea level and in clear view of sunsets. **Iligan Museum** (tel: 063-881-3426; Mon–Fri 8–11am, 1–5pm; free) is located in an old residential house along Badelles Street.

Just 54km (34 miles) from the city the two-tiered **Limunsudan Falls** in *barangay* Rogongon ranks as one of the country's highest falls at 265 meters (870ft). Deeper into the forest awaits the three-chambered Sadyaan Cave with stalactites and stalagmites that may look ominous to strangers but are sacred to natives.

Also in the waterfall department, the 27-meter (90ft) -high Mimbalut Falls in *barangay* Buru-un is the most accessible of Iligan's 20-plus cascades, just 11km (7 miles) from downtown. Nearby Tinago Falls is hidden in a deep ravine and forms a calm, deep pool that allows swimmers.

**WHERE**

The National Power Corporation (NAPCOR; www.napocor.gov.ph) complex at Iligan has an underground plant which can be viewed by prior arrangement. Visitors can ask to have the water to the majestic Maria Cristina Falls switched on.

**BELOW:** Maria Cristina Falls.

*The Maria Cristina Falls are an attractive Mindanao landmark, as well as providing hydro-electric power for Iligan City.*

**BELOW:** Muslims perform their ablutions in Lake Lanao.

Also in the province, Cathedral Falls, with a natural swimming pool at the base, can be found in *barangay* Kapatagan at **Tubod**, the otherwise uneventful provincial capital.

## Lanao del Sur

Travel through **Lanao del Sur** Province signals that the traveler has entered Muslim country. The first town south of Lanao del Norte, **Balo-i**, shows more crescent moons than Christian crosses. Some of the town's innumerable mosques are brilliantly painted in reds, yellows, and greens. Truck bumpers are blazoned with *Trust in Allah* rather than *Trust in Jesus*, and women wear step-in *malongs* rather than skirts.

In the green corn-growing countryside just 40km (25 miles) outside leaving Iligan, **Lake Lanao** ⑱, Mindanao's largest lake, comes into view. Down the road, the Islamic City of **Marawi** ⑲ has produced 65 mosques, the most of any Philippine city. Marawi is an easy 30-minute ride from Iligan, along a well-paved and checkpoint-studded national highway. West of Quezon Boulevard, across the bridge over the Agus River from Marawi, is the 40-meter (130ft) **Signal Hill.** On this hill, battle signals were sent to Camp Vicar and Camp Overton during World War II. In the same province, check out **Dayawan** for its hand weaving and ornate designs by the ethnic Maranao, who are often described as "people of the lake." **Tugaya** is the local brassware capital.

**Mindanao State University**, the country's second-largest public university, is based in this province. Students of different ethnic origins are housed

in the same dormitories to further cultural understanding, an antidote to decades of fighting between religious groups that are determined largely by ethnicity. The **King Faisal Mosque** and **Institute of Islamic and Arabic Studies** stand just within the university gates of the massive 1,000-hectare (2,500-acre) campus.

For a place to stay or eat, visit the Marawi Resort Hotel and its complex of bamboo cottages. And for a historical look back at the region, check out the **Aga Khan Museum** (Mon–Fri 8–11.30am, 1–5pm; free), at the crown of the campus, featuring Maranao and Moro artifacts.

## Bukidnon

Bukidnon Province, in the heart of Mindanao, is a land of pineapple plantations and coffee fields, extensive forests, lofty mountains, and deep canyons. Buses ply the Cagayan de Oro–Bukidnon–Davao route, and public utility jeeps service commuters to and from the different municipalities. **Malaybalay** ❷⓪, the provincial capital, is a two-hour ride from CDO.

The **Pines View Park**, also called "Little Baguio" for its abundant pine trees, stands at the back of the Provincial Capitol. This popular camping destination also hosts the **Kaamulan festival** in February or March, where local tribes decked in colorful costumes gather to sing and dance, compete in indigenous games, and perform rituals. Farther on, toward **Bancud**, is Matin-Ao Spring and the extra-verdant, almost navigable Nasuli Spring.

About 90 minutes' drive along an unpaved road from Malaybalay, near Nasuli Spring, is the village of **Sungko**. Children from the local Talaandig tribe learn traditions from the **Talaandig Center for Living Traditions** in a two-story *nipa* and bamboo house. Not far away, national artist Leandro Locsin designed the **Monastery of the Transfiguration**.

**Kitanglad National Park** (31,300 hectares/77,350 acres) in North Central Bukidnon (more information on the provincial website at www.bukidnon.gov.ph) consists of more

**TIP**

Watch sunrise from the highest point of the golf course facing Lake Lanao and admire the calm, deep-blue waters, and the "Sleeping Lady" mountain – so called for its human form – in the background, capped with thick fog.

**BELOW:** Talaandig women in traditional dress.

*Pottery for sale in Malaybalay.*

**BELOW:** Sierra Madre view.

than a dozen peaks. Vanilla, which is technically a type of orchid, grows here in the wild environs. Inside the park, towering Mt Kitanglad (2,938 meter/5,639ft) has been held sacred by many tribes since pre-Hispanic times as well as by modern-day climbers who plod through forests for five hours to reach its summit.

To the north, in San Roque in Sumilao, stands the 2,745-meter (9,000ft) **Palaopao Hill**. Its sides contain caves, rock shelters, and wooden artifacts.

In the town of Manolo Fortich, wind on up the zigzag road through **Mangima Canyon**, home of the Mangima Challenge, an annual contest for off-road monster-truck and four-wheel-drive enthusiasts. The contest, launched in 1998 and also known as Maximum Underdrive, takes place in April. In the same town, an elliptical **Stone Marker of Yoshitois Grave** bears two sets of inscriptions for high-ranking Japanese officials killed during World War II. In nearby **Valencia**, travelers often stop at the clean, green 25-hectare (60-acre) Apo Lake for boating and fishing.

## Agusan del Norte

Around 250km (155 miles) north of Davao, **Butuan City ㉑** is the provincial capital and the region's major jump-off point, served by daily flights from Manila. The city is known for antiques and archeological finds, has three museums: **Balanghai Shrine Museum** showcases skulls and burial coffins from the prehistoric age; **Butuan Regional Museum** has a huge repository of artifacts that

depict the city's once thriving pre-Hispanic existence; and the **Diocesan Ecclesiastical Museum** houses a prized collection of religious artifacts (all Mon–Fri 8am–noon, 1–5pm; free).

A historic marker commemorating the first Mass in Mindanao stands in **Magallanes**, a town north of Butuan. Also in Magallanes check out the century-old *bitaug* tree lit by thousands of fireflies at night. Visitors with an interest in the economy will find in the same town Phimco, the only match factory in Mindanao, and Santa Ines Plywood Corporation, a wood-processing complex.

Not far off, the undiscovered jungle passages of 2,012-meter (6,601ft) **Mt Hilong-hilong**, in the town of Remedios T. Romualdez, challenge climbers seeking its waterfalls and lake. A road leads to Cabadbaran, the starting point for **Mas-ai Peak**, an obscure trekking spot.

Back on the coast, the **Tubay Mountain Beach Resort,** secluded between Tubay forest and Butuan Bay, has artfully sandwiched a swimming pool between the two topographic extremes. From the national highway, one can bike a 5km (3-mile) road through panoramic forest to the pick-up point, from where a covered motorized *banca* takes visitors to the resort. For more information, see http://caraganon.com/2006/11/tubay-mountain-beach-resort-above-sea.html.

## Agusan del Sur

To the south of Butuan is **Agusan del Sur**, the country's most thinly populated province. In the capital **Prosperidad** ㉒ the main attraction is Binataba Falls, believed to be linked to an underground stream. The other attraction is people.

The Manobo, who have settlements in **Bayugan**, are known for planting and harvesting rituals as well as traditional wedding ceremonies. Another ethnic group, the Higaonon, live in high, swaying treehouses that consist of small family rooms linked by gangplanks to a central communal area.

The 68,000-hectare (168,000-acre) **Agusan Marsh Wildlife Sanctuary** is both the largest freshwater and

*The 50,000-strong Bukidnon people of east Lanao are a tribe of fiercely independent highland dwellers.*

the largest mangrove swamp in the Philippines. Between the river and the coast runs the rugged, twisting **Sierra Madre of Mindanao**.

## Surigao del Sur

On Mindanao's northeastern coast the provincial capital, **Tandag** ㉓, is evolving into a backwoods surfing paradise with white-sand beaches and wild swells, an undisclosed twin sister of not-far-off Siargao Island. Among the most popular breaks are Big Star, Moshi-Moshi, and Glenda. Just 3km (2 miles) off Tandag, **Mangkangagi Island** has gained attention for its three guano-filled caves and a series of white-sand beaches. Hire a boat to get there.

Northwards, the town of **Lanuza** presents a laid-back ambiance as well as some of the best longboard surf waves in the country, alongside a boardwalk that is just as competitive. Farther up the highway in **Cantilan**, Maletangtang Cave is known for its boat-like shape and cool springs. White sands of Malinawa Beach are also located in Cantilan.

South of Tandag lies the famous white-sand beach in **Cagwait**. **Turtle Island** in nearby Barobo has an 8-hectare (20-acre) white-sand beach where a multicolored coral reef adds to its attraction.

Inside **Picop Plantation**, one of the biggest pulp and paper companies in the Far East, visitors may find Nyholm and Borboanon Falls. From Mangagoy wharf in **Bislig**, pumpboats go to black-sand Barcelona Beach and Hagonoy Island, a scuba-diving site.

## Surigao del Norte

On the northernmost part of Mindanao, **Surigao del Norte** attracts travelers for kayaking, caving, snorkeling, diving, and swimming. **Casa Real** in the provincial capital **Surigao City** ㉔ is the residence of a former Spanish governor. Outside town look for Sabang Beach, with a long black sandy shore, Ipil Beach with white pebbles, and Mabua Beach with rock formations that serve as natural diving boards. **Day-asan Floating Village** features houses built over shallow water and canals for boats. Snorkelers

**BELOW:** students from the Maranao tribe, Mindanao State University.

## People of the Lake

Islam, a hallmark of Mindanao, goes back to the earliest days of the religion for the people who live at Lake Lanao. The tribe whose name means "people of the lake" say that the body of water high above sea level was created when angels carried humans to the site on Allah's wishes and filled a hole with blue water.

Today the Maranao aim to hold on to their estimated 5,000 years of tradition without succumbing to lowland lifestyles. Keeping that spirit alive, tribe members tend to specialize in their own distinctive styles of weaving, brass-making, or woodcarving, among other crafts. Highly stylized floral motifs called okir are used to decorate homes, boats, and even domestic utensils.

and divers can get directions and gear from the Punta Bilar dive shop. At night, try dancing at Club Alcatraz.

The province is also a source of mineral deposits as well as native basketry, locally made hats and embroidery.

Transportation in and out of Surigao del Norte is easy. The provincial capital is accessible via fast Supercat ferry from Cebu. Buses also leave from here for the major Mindanao city of Davao. Cebu Pacific flies to Surigao City from Manila.

## Gulf islands

In the gulf between Surigao City and Siargao Island, Rocky **Raza Island** makes the odd claim of low tide on one side at the same time high tide hits on the other. **Sibaldo Island** is home to the 10-meter (33ft) -high Zaragaza Rock Formation and the solitary rock islet known as Tamulayag, where trees grow without soil, giving it the look of a huge floating flower vase.

**Hikdop Island** in the same complex of odd rocky islets has a white beach rich in rare seashells. On its northeast side, Punta Kalabera looms as a naturally sculptured stone formation that looks like a human skull from a distance. **Bayagnan Island** stands out in the complex for its offshore whirlpools that appear and disappear with the tides, an effect of converging currents in the area. Also worth visiting is the longish **Cantiasay Foot Bridge** joining the islands of San Jose and Cantiasay. Snorkeling sites give local fame to nearby **Dinagat Island.**

Moving inland, **Lake Bababu** rests beneath steep inclines and lush vegetation. Rock formations on the neighboring islets of San Roque and Hagakgak are said to resemble a duck, turtle, ship, eagle, and candle. **Desolation Point**, on the northern tip, was where American troops first landed on October 17, 1944, to help the Philippines fight the Japanese. Farther on is the 10-hectare (25-acre), 20-meter (65ft) -deep **Tambongan Lagoon** in the town of Tubajon.

One hour's fast ferry from Surigao City is **Siargao Island** ㉕, famous for **Cloud 9**, a world-class reef break off **General Luna** town, or "GL." Westward, huge tracts of mangroves, rugged forested foothills, and unusual rock formations bring visitors to **Del Carmen**. **Bucas Grande Island** has become famous for **Sohoton Lagoon**. Explorers there can experience an eerie passage through a cave at low tide, into a lagoon of countless islets, or scuba dive in the waters around the town of Socorro. A natural swimming pool at **Magpupungko**, off the town of **Pilar,** appears at low water levels, when it is cut off from the ocean. Dako and **Guyam Islands** make for a day boat trip, the latter being a tiny speck of trees and sand. Off the beach, look for Ocean 101, a gazebo overlooking the water.

Flights from Manila serve Siargao. As the island gains in popularity for its tropical beaches and surfing sites, resorts have taken root, as well. In General Luna, start with the Siargao Island Villa (www.siargaoislandvilla.com), which can arrange access to water sports in the area.

**BELOW:** *nipa* hut, Siargao Island.

# ZAMBOANGA AND THE SULU ISLANDS

The Philippines' southwestern tip is a rich cultural mosaic: a variety of indigenous peoples share its wealth of fertile agricultural land and the bounty of its seas.

Manila

**M**indanao's westernmost provinces of Zamboanga del Norte and Sur, Basilan, Sulu, and Tawi-Tawi share a long history of unyielding resistance to foreign control. This far-flung region was once part of the Sultanate of Sulu, the oldest seat of government, at a time when "Manila was a swamp and Cebu was a beach," at least according to historian Oswalda Cadel. Spain captured Sulu in the 1870s, transferring the seat of power to Zamboanga. American forces established the Department of Mindanao and Sulu in 1914, making Zamboanga a province. In 1952, it was split into Norte and Sur. Like most of the country, the local economy is based on fishing, including aquaculture, and farming, with coconuts, coffee, citrus fruits, and rubber on the harvest list.

The Moro Islamic Liberation Front (see page 329) and violent splinter groups still occupy patches of southwest Mindanao and its outlying islands. But the region's major city, Zamboanga, is generally considered safe, allowing tourists to see indigenous people in the village of Rio Hondo and farther away in the Yakan Weaving Village. Other attractions are the beaches at Great Santa Cruz Island, which radiate a pink hue, while a tiny brick-walled city

awaits travelers to Jolo, and those who reach the stilt-built town of Sitangkai can munch tropical fruits at the southwestern extreme of the Philippines.

Flights from Manila and Cebu reach the cities of Dipolog, Pagadian, and Zamboanga. Various ferry services call at Zamboanga City and Dipolog. Highlights of the region are accessible via the national highway through Ozamis, connecting Dipolog to any point in Mindanao. Jeepneys and pedicabs operate around Zamboanga,

**Main attractions**
GREAT SANTA CRUZ ISLAND'S PINK BEACH
YAKAN WEAVING VILLAGE, ZAMBOANGA
WALLED CITY OF JOLO
BADJAO SEA GYPSY VILLAGE, TAWI-TAWI

**LEFT:** Plaza Pershing. **RIGHT:** colorful *vinta* boat, Santa Cruz Island.

**TIP**

Though Zamboanga City has a list of places of typical interest to tourists, its past security problems with Muslim insurgents have made it an unpopular stopover. Before visiting, check the latest situation with the local tourism department.

**BELOW:** Jose Rizal statue, Zamboanga City Hall.

while *kumpit* (long, deep, enclosed motorboats) connect outlying islands to mainland Mindanao.

## Zamboanga del Norte

Provincial capital **Dipolog City** ㉖ is considered the gateway to Western Mindanao. Christmas and New Year are the best times to visit, when Dipolog comes alive with fireworks. There is also the *Sinulog* festival in January, and special Holy Week celebrations in April. The city offers a range of hotels and discos, and at its heart stands **Holy Rosary Cathedral**, a century-old church designed by the Philippine national hero Jose Rizal. Though renovated, the basic design has been preserved. About 15 blocks across is **Punta Corro**, a cross to symbolize the religious character of the inhabitants.

Dipolog anchors the 6,600 sq km (2,550 sq mile) province of **Zamboanga del Norte** (pop. 750,000). Mt Dapiak (2,560 meters/8,399ft), south of Katipunan town, is the province's highest peak. The main inhabitants of its northern part are Christian

migrants from the Visayas, while in the south are the Muslim groups of Tausug, Samal, Yakan, and Kalibugan. Cebuano is the main dialect.

Visitors to Dipolog can climb 1,001 Concrete Steps to **Linabo Peak**, the city's highest point at 460 meters (1,500ft), offering a panoramic view of the twin cities of Dipolog and Dapitan. Visitors to *barangay* **Dicayas** often find their way to **Pamansalan Forest Park**, a 10-hectare (24-acre) restoration site and bird sanctuary, and the **Japanese Memorial Park**. Farther on are the Sicayab Beach and Miputak beaches. Miputak is known for scuba-diving safari packages and skim boarding (like surfing, but smaller boards), and Miputak Beach offers scuba diving, skim boarding, and beach camping. Local officials are also branding Dipolog as the sport fishing center of western Mindanao.

If driving east from Dipolog, stop in Ozamiz (there is also an airport here) to try the Hoyohoy Sky Line Zip some 20 minutes away from downtown. Stop by Dewberry Coffee on City Hall Drive for a meal and drinks.

## Dapitan City

Only 14km (9 miles) northeast of Dipolog is historical **Dapitan City** ㉗, site of the **Rizal Shrine** (daily 8am–5pm; charge) inside a 16-hectare (40-acre) estate where the leading nationalist hero spent his exile from 1892 to 1896 as a rural doctor, farmer, and painter, among other occupations. Visitors can see his former residence, clinic, school, and a water system, all built using indigenous materials. The adjacent Rizaliana, a modern, concrete building constructed in 1972, houses Rizal-related books, periodicals, and other historical exhibits.

Beyond the Rizal Shrine is **Dakak Beach Resort** (tel: 02-664-7266; www.ilink.ph/dakak-resort), a 750-meter (245ft) private beach blanketed with powdery white sand. Natural spring

water and tumbling waterfalls feed the resort's two pools. **Dapitan Bay** stretches along the northern coast of the city and is another popular swimming and diving site. **Ilihan Hill** and **Fort de Dapitan**, a Spanish military fortress built in 1762, overlook the bay. The island *barangay* of **Aliguay** and **Silinog**, located 10km and 14km (6 and 9 miles) respectively from Tagolo Point, have white-sand beaches and rich aquatic resources.

## Zamboanga del Sur

The coastline of **Zamboanga del Sur** is scattered with bays and a flat, coastal plain that gives way to interior mountains. The provincial capital **Pagadian City** ㉘ is the only Christian-dominated place in the province. The mostly Muslim ethnic groups Tausug, Yakan, Badjao, Samal, and Subanon populate the rest of the province. The Subanon set up a fishing and trading village near the coast and called it Pagadian, a corruption of the Maguindanao word *padian*, meaning marketplace.

A 10-minute pumpboat ride across the city wharf is Dao-Dao Island, or **Pajares Island**, ideal for swimming and sunbathing. Southeast of the seaport look for **White Beach**, with clear, deep water. **Pulacan Falls** is a picnicking and camping site in the town of **Labangan**, 12km (8 miles) from Pagadian City.

Along the Pagadian–Zamboanga City national highway is Mt Palpalan (210 meters/690ft). The mountain offers views of the urban center and the clear waters of **Pagadian Bay**. The 18-meter (60ft) Lison Valley Falls, in *barangay* Lison Valley, 40km (25 miles) from Pagadian, has a catchment pool area of 1,500 sq meters (1,800 sq yards).

**Zamboanga City** ㉙, capital of Mindanao throughout the Spanish regime, sits at the southern tip of the island's westernmost arm. Chavacano, a dialect of pidgin Spanish and Cebuano, is the lingua franca. The

inhabitants are Christians, Tausug, Yakan, Badjao, Samal, and Subanon.

Behind the wharf lies **Plaza Pershing**, named after Governor John Pershing, the first American governor in the region. The quasi-Baroque city hall, completed in 1907, stands at the southeast corner of the plaza and houses the post office. From here, along Valderros Street, head for the Lantaka Hotel to get briefed by the local Department of Tourism (DOT) office located within. Local tourism officials will go out of their way to stress Zamboanga's relative safety despite risks to travelers in offshore islands such as Basilan. A 15-minute walk away is **Fort Pilar**, built in 1635 by a Jesuit priest to ward off attacks from Moros and foreign invaders.

A short distance to the east, **Rio Hondo,** a 23-hectare (57-acre) coastal colony, shows passers-by how the Tausug, Samal, and Badjao live in houses on stilts. These 1,200 common households along a river as well as the sea coast serve as a snapshot of the region's indigenous people.

**TIP**

Try the Samal's unique manner of serving coffee, which involves the use of two identical glasses, one placed inside another.

**BELOW:** Fort Pilar, Zamboanga.

*Zamboanga City is known for its colorful vinta boats, made by the Baja and Moros peoples.*

**BELOW:** Muslim girls at Taluksangay Mosque.

## Around Zamboanga

Make arrangements at Lantaka landing (behind Lantaka Hotel) to rent a pumpboat for the 25-minute voyage to **Great Santa Cruz Island** . The site is known for its pinkish-sand beach colored by pulverized organ-pipe coral. A lagoon and fishing village also stand out on the island. The surrounding seas host an extensive variety of coral formations, which in turn support a medley of tropical fish.

Some 20km (12 miles) east of the city it is also possible to visit **Taluksangay**, a quieter village on stilts. Its mosque, with silvery dome and turrets, is particularly photogenic. Westward from Zamboanga, a road immediately enters the 2km (1.2-mile) -long **Cawa Cawa Boulevard**. This pocket-sized version of Manila's Roxas Boulevard, lined by old acacia trees, is the favorite gathering place of the locals. At the far end of the boulevard save your sobriety for any of several beer parlors. **Yellow Beach**, where American forces landed in March 1945 to liberate Zamboanga, lies not far beyond.

The 19th-century Spanish-built **San Ramon Prison and Penal Farm,** to the east, sells souvenirs, mainly woodcarvings.

A 7km (4-mile) drive north of Zamboanga City is **Pasonanca Park**, 150 meters (500ft) above sea level. Most travelers find it more interesting for the view than its scout camp and swimming pools. Also on a hill, in a 1.5-hectare (2.5-acre) lot at the Regional Government Center in Cabatangan, 5km (3 miles) from Zamboanga City, is **Astanah Kasannangan** (Palace of Peace), a mosque-like government office. About 7km (4 miles) along the west coast, the **Yakan Weaving Village** brings visitors together with members of a tribe originally from the nearby but war-racked island of Basilan. The Yakan weave fabrics in rainbow patterns, a supplement to their agriculture-based tribal economy.

A one- to two-hour voyage south from Zamboanga City, across the 25km (16-mile) Strait of Basilan, brings travelers to **Basilan Island** . The island has been the site of fierce fighting between the Philippine government and the terrorist group Abu Sayyaf. Visit with caution, or skip it.

Before reaching **Isabela**, the Basilan capital and port, boats pass through a 1km (0.6-mile) -wide mangrove channel banked by palm trees and adorned with *nipa* huts on stilts. In the Strait, look for **Malamaui Island,** a white-sand beach with one resort considered expensive for such a far-flung location. Basilan Hotel, an alternative place to stay, is conveniently located downtown in Isabela but, for security reasons, not recommended.

Basilan itself remains a haven for Muslim rebels. If it sheds that reputation some day, visitors will find

a strong local character defined by the ethnic Yakan, Tausug, Samal, and Zamboangueños.

A rough road southward from Isabela through rubber, palm-oil and coconut plantations, and past stands of coffee and pepper, leads, after 32km (20 miles), to **Maluso** fishing village, which the national tourism department advises visitors to avoid. A similar road to the northeast passes citrus groves and rubber plants. After 30km (20 miles), it reaches Basilan's relatively peaceful town of **Lamitan**, where **Datu Kalu's Park and Shrine** is located. The Yakan, the town's inhabitants, hold the **Lami-Lamihan Festival** every June to celebrate their cultural heritage. Travelers may catch a sunset over the rubber plantation in Menzi, with swaying rubber trees reflected in a nearby lagoon.

## The Sulu Archipelago

Comprising over 400 scattered islands, stretching from the tip of Zamboanga southwestward towards Borneo, the Sulu Archipelago is the Philippines' farthest frontier. As in Basilan and Tawi-Tawi, Muslims dominate. The local soil and climate allow it to grow a greater variety of agricultural products than elsewhere in the country, and the area abounds in timber resources. Major industries are fishing, boat building, coffee processing, and fruit preservation. Sulu remains one of the poorest provinces in the country in large part because of Muslim-vs-government strife. Despite some of the most idyllic beaches in the region, tourism has not been developed and the area remains largely off-limits due to the insurgency.

**Jolo** ㉜ (pronounced "Ho-Lo"), capital of **Sulu Province**, is accessible from Zamboanga City by a nine-hour ferry ride or three-hour fast boat. It has never been a particularly safe place to visit, with reports of kidnapping dating back even to millennia-old Chinese trade records. In 1974,

Jolo was burned to the ground when fighting broke out between rebelling Muslims and government troops.

The brick **Walled City of Jolo** deterred enemies for many centuries despite its relatively miniature scale. At its entrance are four gates – once used as watchtowers – and several mounds used as burial grounds for Spanish and American soldiers who died at the hands of Muslim warriors. The Provincial Capitol, built by Governor Murphy Sangkula, features a Moorish-inspired architectural design. The **American Cavalry Monument** (Mon–Fri 8–11am, 2–5pm; free), which commemorates the US soldiers who fought here in World War II, sits just outside Jolo. Off the mainland is the Pearl Farm at **Marungas Island**, a 30-minute pumpboat ride away.

## Tawi-Tawi

The Sulu Sea to the north and Celebes Sea to the south surround the 300-plus islands of Tawi-Tawi, the Philippines' southernmost province. **Bongao** ㉝, the provincial capital, is accessible by

*Zamboanga City is home to one of the Philippines' oldest golf courses. The Zamboanga Golf and Country Club was built by US General John "Blackjack" Pershing, in the early 1900s.*

**BELOW:** Yakan Weaving Village, Zamboanga.

*A Zamboanga market vendor displays a ripe marang fruit, unique to this region of Mindanao.*

**BELOW:** stilted fishing village on the outskirts of Zamboanga.

fast ferries and slower boats that regularly ply the Zamboanga–Bongao–Sandakan route. Several Cebu Pacific and Air Philippines flights per week connect Bongao to Zamboanga. In terms of attractions, a **monkey sanctuary** sits at Bongao Peak.

The Samal ethnic group dominates the local population. Locals usually wear colorful wrap-around sarongs, called *malong*.

**Badjao Village**, a series of simple houses tucked into a labyrinth of docks doubling as pathways, offers visitors direct access to handicrafts. The docks also provide a personal glimpse of the fabled Philippine sea gypsies at home.

Elsewhere in Tawi-Tawi, a mosque called Tubig Indangan, on the island of **Simunul**, was built by Arabian missionary Sheik Makdum in 1380. The Gusong Reef in **Cagayan de Tawi-Tawi** shelters gulls, locally called *tallah-tallah*, that settle by the thousands once a year to nest. If private boats are willing, go to small, uninhabited Palanjal Kam Balobok Rock for an undisturbed day at sea.

Tawi-Tawi's **Turtle Islands** offer a rare opportunity to observe the reptiles up close. It is being considered for future ecotourism development. But people's destructive practices already threaten the Turtle Islands. According to WWF, local extinction is imminent if the situation is not remedied quickly. Turtle Island itself is jointly administered with Malaysia, and Unesco recognizes this protected area as the Turtle Islands Wildlife Sanctuary.

Further out into the Celebes Sea, the island of **Sibutu** stakes its reputation on wild boars. Locals rumor that wild boars there swim over from Malaysia. The animals have been hunted by sports shooters from Manila. Not far from the sea border with Malaysia, visitors will find **Sitangkai**, a town built on stilts over crystal-clear waters and a coral reef. Try the native *kalawa* and *baulo* cakes while sitting over the water, watching the sun set at the western end of the Philippines.

## The Badjao Sea Gypsies

The Badjao, the smallest ethnic minority in the Sulu Archipelago, are struggling to hold on to a centuries-old legacy of living off their boats, as they fish the Sulu Sea.

These nomadic fishing people traditionally live along the coasts of Jolo, Siasi, Tapul Island, Sitangkai, Subutu, and Tawi-Tawi islands. Their boat is known as a *lipa*. Long and thin, the wooden vessel has a small stove at the stern for cooking the catch. But the so-called sea gypsies now face declining fish stocks. Many have moved to the relative comforts of stilt *nipa* or bamboo houses along the coast, but they have been generally unable to integrate successfully into society and are often forced to beg for money.

# A Regional Conflict

**Basilan Island, the Sulu islands, and other parts of the country's extreme southwest remain unsafe for travel due to a long struggle between the government and Muslim rebels seeking autonomy.**

The conflict in Mindanao has never been a simple one. The minority Muslim populations live in some of the most resource-rich areas in all of the Philippines, but they are among the last to receive the economic benefits. The country's highest poverty rates occur for that reason in Muslim Mindanao.

Being ruled by a Christian government in Manila doesn't help matters. Groups such as the Moro Islamic Liberation Front (MILF), founded in 1977, still take up arms against the government. Though the MILF has been involved in ongoing negotiations with the government and claims no link to terrorists or kidnap gangs in Mindanao, armed factions, splinter groups, and imitators make the area a dangerous and difficult destination. As of 2012, the MILF was trying to find kidnapped Australian expat Warren Rodwell as captors demanded ransom that his supporters had refused to pay since the December 2011 abduction.

## Terrorists' network

The most menacing of these smaller groups is the Abu Sayyaf, a band of terrorists operating around Basilan and the Sulu islands with suspected links to the infamous Al Qaeda terrorist network. Their tactics, such as kidnapping, ransoming, raping, and beheading foreign and Filipino civilians alike, have raised questions about the legitimacy of their political mission, which compares to that of the MILF.

Foreign governments have paid millions of dollars in ransom to the Abu Sayyaf, which the group quickly invested in faster speedboats, higher-powered weapons, and satellite phones to assist in their kidnapping operations. In anger, the Philippine government called off its talks with the group and sent thousands of troops to Basilan to rescue the two Americans and one Filipino held hostage since May 2001.

**RIGHT:** military police patrol the waters around Zamboanga.

On June 7, 2002, in a firefight between the Philippine military and the kidnappers, American hostage Martin Burnham and Filipino nurse Deborah Yap were killed. Burnham's wife Gracia was wounded but escaped alive. Since then, tensions in the area have remained high.

The conflict in Mindanao has reportedly cost at least 120,000 lives. Many of the children of those killed by government soldiers grow up harboring the same deep feelings of injustice that drove their fathers to arms.

## No-go area

The US, Australian, and Japanese governments, among others, have recommended against travel in Western and Central Mindanao and the entire Sulu archipelago from Zamboanga to Tawi-Tawi. *Fielding's World's Most Dangerous Places* guidebook describes Basilan as the lair of Abu Sayyaf. Recent cooperative exercises with American military forces have had some effect on scattering the Abus, but your Basilan beach vacation may still be a few years off.

President Benigno Aquino III's government has held a series of talks overseas with the MILF toward an end to the Muslim autonomy dispute. They candidly shared views on neutral ground in Malaysia – even as clashes with government forces continue.

**※ INSIGHT GUIDE**     **TRAVEL TIPS**

# PHILIPPINES

# TRANSPORTATION

# GETTING THERE AND GETTING AROUND

### By Air

Manila is a major international transport hub and more than 500 international flights arrive each week. **Ninoy Aquino International Airport** (NAIA), 7km (4 miles) from the city center, has three international terminals and two domestic terminals. **Terminal 1** serves most international flights except Philippine Airlines (PAL), Cebu Pacific, and a growing number of others that have splintered off toward other terminals. The **Centennial Terminal (Terminal 2)** is the base of all PAL and Air Philippines domestic and international flights.

The new **Terminal 3**, a hub for the growing domestic and international network of discount airline Cebu Pacific, features the spaciousness,

cleanliness, and expanses of shopping that put it in a league with airports in Bangkok and Hong Kong. As Cebu Pacific runs many of its flights at night and around sunrise, some airport restaurants and shops stay open 24 hours.

All other domestic flights originate from the **Domestic Terminal**, which is 3km (2 miles) from NAIA (about a 10–15-minute taxi ride away).

Passengers heading to the Visayas sometimes bypass Manila altogether and use the **Mactan Cebu International Airport** (MCIA) as a hub. MCIA has increased its international connections in recent years. Other cities with international airports are **Clark, Davao**, and **Puerto Princesa**.

Flights from Manila go to just about every major city in Asia, including Tokyo, Seoul, Beijing, Shanghai, Hong Kong, Taipei, Bangkok, Singapore, Jakarta, Kuala Lumpur, Hanoi, and Ho Chi Minh City. There are routes as

well to the Middle East, plus major European and North American cities.

### To/from the airports

**Arrival:** After clearing customs and claiming baggage, book a rented car inside the airport or take a taxi at the curb. Metered taxis queue up in Cebu, Davao, and Manila, with airport staffers forming lines of passengers and making notes on where they plan to go by cab to cut down on cheating by drivers. Though most drivers are reliable, airport taxis are notorious for asking passengers to pay a higher-than-normal fixed rate. Taxis take about 30 minutes and charge P200–250 to reach most parts of Manila and about the same rate from the airport in Cebu to the ferry pier or Fort San Pedro, also rides of about 30 minutes. Fares in Davao run cheaper, and rides within the urban center seldom exceed 20 minutes.

Most Manila hotels offer free or inexpensive shuttles. Look for people at the curb holding up small signs with the names of hotels. Free shuttles also take passengers from one terminal to another in Manila. **Departure:** It is easiest to reach the airport by private car or taxi, though jeepneys run from parts of Manila to the airport terminals. Give yourself plenty of time, especially during rush hour, typhoons, and holidays.

Most airline counters open 3 hours prior to departure. Manila airport's international departure tax is P550 and P200 for domestic flights.

### Airline contacts

**Cebu Pacific** (with flights from overseas to Boracay via Kalibo) www.cebupacificair.com
**Air Philippines** www.airphils.com

**BELOW:** Manila Airport.

ACCOMMODATIONS

EATING OUT

ACTIVITIES

A – Z

LANGUAGE

**Philippine Airlines**
www.philippineair.com
**Air France**
www.airfrance.com
**Amercian Airlines**
www.aa.com
**British Airways**
www.british-airways.com
**Cathay Pacific**
www.cathaypacific.com
**China Airlines**
www.china-airlines.com
**Emirates Airlines**
www.emirates.com
**EVA Airways**
www.evaair.com
**Japan Airlines**
www.jal.co.jp
**Korean Air**
www.koreanair.com
**Lufthansa**
www.lufthansa.com
**Northwest Airlines**
www.nwa.com
**Qantas Airways**
www.qantas.com
**Singapore Airlines**
www.singaporeair.com
**Thai International Airways**
www.thaiair.com

**ABOVE:** a domestic flight to Mindanao.

### By Sea

Though most travelers arrive by air, freighters, and cruise ships stop in Manila Bay. Cruise liners such as Cunard, Holland America, and Royal Caribbean make stops in the Philippine capital. Cruises may spend a day or more at sea between Manila and the next Asian city.

There are two sea routes from Mindanao to Southeast Asia frequented by backpackers, but the government discourages these excursions because of Moro rebels and piracy in the area.

**BELOW:** Cebu City buses.

The Philippines' Sampaguita Shipping Corporation operates a passenger ferry from Pagadian to Zamboanga (both in Mindanao), a quicker and safer alternative to overland travel. The ferry continues to Sandakan, Sabah, a few times weekly. Passengers are mostly Muslim Filipinos from Mindanao. Another company, Aleson Lines, runs a Sandakan–Zamboanga ferry service. Zamboanga also attracts the odd international cruise ship to its newer port facilities.

### GETTING AROUND

#### By Air

Transportation around the archipelago normally originates in the country's hub, Manila. Cebu City is coming into its own as a regional hub for flights going around the Visayas and into Mindanao. Flying is quick and cheap, with domestic airlines spanning much of the archipelago.

Flights leave hourly or even more frequently from Manila to Caticlan and Kalibo, the gateways to Boracay, as well as to Cebu's Mactan Island. Flights from Cebu, often on Cebu Pacific, go to other cities in the Visayas and to Mindanao destinations such as Cotabato, Davao, and Zamboanga. Other commonly served airports include Baguio, Coron, Dumaguete, Laoag, Legazpi, Puerto Princesa, and Virac. Air Phil Express runs flights between Coron and Puerto Princesa, connecting north and central Palawan. Most flights take little more than an hour, and airports tend to be close to city centers rather than in distant suburbs. Taxis (whether cars, tricycles, or motorcycles) wait outside arrival halls, and jeepneys serve some airports, such as in Laoag and Manila.

Domestic flight schedules are in constant flux; contact airlines directly for the latest update. Most airports charge a domestic flight departure tax of P40–200, which is paid before boarding rather than included in ticket prices.

**Cebu Pacific**
Tel: 02-702-0888; www.cebupacificair.com
**Air Philippines**
Tel: 02-855-9000; www.airphils.com
**Air Phil Express**
Tel: 02-855-9000; www.airphilexpress.com
**Philippine Airlines**
Tel: 02-855-8888; www.philippineair.com
**South East Asian Airlines (SEAIR)**
Tel: 02-884-1521; www.flyseair.com
**Zest Airways (Asian Spirit)**
Tel: 02-855-3333; www.zestair.com.ph

### Water Transport

Ferries, though once considered unsafe, now offer comfortable cabins and seats for all budgets with little

## Filipino Drivers Play the Numbers Game

Driving in Manila comes with its set of changing rules and responsibilities. As a result, visitors usually hire taxis or long-term drivers rather than getting behind the wheel. One rule – a measure to ease congestion in the capital – restricts vehicles to driving on certain days, though rentals are exempt. According to this Unified Vehicular Volume Reduction Program, the last digit on the car's license plate number determines the days it can or cannot hit the road. The number system is in effect from 7am to 7pm, and is strictly enforced, though it may be possible to take the car out from 10am to 3pm. Ask someone who drives locally what new scheme is in place at the time of your visit.

risk of mishaps at sea. They are the leading source of transit along Luzon's island-speckled south coast and throughout the Visayas. Tickets on major routes (e.g. Manila–Cebu, Cebu–Tagbilaran) can be booked through travel agencies. Check websites for special discounts, package tours, and e-ticket bookings.

If buying tickets straight from a ferry operator on the day of a journey, get to the pier early as printing and passenger registration procedures can be slow, lines long, and piers themselves so ancient that some lack even ceiling fans to keep the sweaty air circulating. Ferries, though frequent on popular routes, also fill fast.

Boats leave throughout the day from Manila, Batangas, Cebu, and Bohol, among others. The Cebu–Manila route takes 24 hours. Cebu–Bohol takes two hours, plus another to Dumaguete. Manila–Puerto Princesa takes more than 24 hours. **Cebu Ferries** serves Cebu, Cagayan, Iligan, Nasipit, Ormoc, Ozamiz, Surigao; tel: 032-233-7000; www.cebuferries.com/destinations.asp.
**Negros Navigation**'s ports of call include Bacolod, Cagayan de Oro, Coron, Dipolog, Dumaguete,

Dumaguit (Kalibo), Estancia, General Santos, Iligan, Iloilo, Manila, Ozamiz, Puerto Princesa, Roxas, and Tagbilaran (Bohol); Pier 2, North Harbor, Manila; tel: 02-245-5588; www.negrosnavigation.ph.
**Ocean Fast Ferries** covers Manila, Cebu, Davao, Bacolod, Dumaguete, Iloilo, Siquijor, Tagbilaran, Zamboanga; tel: 032-255-7560; oceanjet.net.
**Sulpicio Lines** sails to Baybay (Leyte), Cebu, Cotabato, Davao, Dumaguete, Iligan, Iloilo, Maasin, Masbate, Ormoc, Ozamis, Surigao, Tacloban, Zamboanga, General Santos City; 415 San Fernando, Binondo, tel: 02-241-9701; Pier 12, Manila, tel: 02-245-0616; www.sulpiciolines.com.
**SuperCat** (part of the WG&A Group) serves ports in Larena, Cebu, Tagbilaran, Dapitan, Calipan, Batangas; for a total of 50 trips per day; tel: 032-233-7000; www.supercat.com.ph.
**WG&A SuperFerry** sails to Bacolod, Cagayan de Oro, Cebu, Coron, Cotabato, Davao, Diplog, Dumaguete, Dumaguit, General Santos City, Iligan, Ozamis, Puerto Princesa, Surigao, Tagbilaran, Zamboanga; 12/F, Times Plaza, U.N. Avenue, Manila; tel: 02-528 7000; www.superferry.com.ph.

## By Bus

Highways and smaller roads make bus travel possible in the areas surrounding Manila and provincial capitals. Dozens of bus companies operate services to the main tourist centers and fares are low. Bus companies work out of their own stations rather than from a centralized depot in a given city, so before setting out ask a hotel clerk, taxi driver, or airport information counter which one is best. Buses rarely cheat on fares, and everyone gets a seat. Some operators blast the air-con, so take a light jacket. Long-distance buses make rest stops along the route for snacks and toilets.

Here are the major bus lines on Luzon, with stations in metro Manila. Most run to northern parts of the main island or out to the Bicol peninsula.
**Autobus**
Tel: 02-735-8098
**Baliwag Transit**
Tel: 02-912-3343
**Batangas Laguna Tayabas Bus Co (BLTB)**
Tel: 02-913-1525
**Dangwa Trans Co.**
Tel: 02-731-2879
**Farinas Transit**
Tel: 02-743-8582
**Maria de Leon Transit**
Tel: 02-731-4907
**Dominion Bus Lines**
Tel: 02-741-4146
**Victory Liner**
Tel: 02-833-5019-20; www.victoryliner.com

## Taxi Rates

Negotiate a price with the driver to hire a taxi for the day. A trip from Manila to Anilao, for instance, should cost under P3,000. For in-town rides, insist that the driver start the meter straightaway, or find another taxi, to avoid being cheated. Flagfall in Manila is P40, more at the airport, with an additional P2.50 for every 25 meters thereafter. Rates are cheaper in other cities. But in all but the biggest cities, motorcycles or tricycles equipped with jerry-rigged extra seats provide the only taxi service. They are never metered. Find out from a hotel clerk or tourist office how much the going rate is and fix on a reasonable price with the driver to avoid a foreigner overcharge.

**BELOW:** Metro Rail Transit Line, Manila.

## Rural transportation

Most of the far-flung white beaches and remote islands noted in this book require extensive transportation planning. The visitor first may need to hop on a bus or jeepney from a second-tier city for a ride of several hours, telling the driver exactly where to stop to find a motorcycle taxi, which may be obscured by trees at a small dirt-road intersection. The motorcycle will proceed to a pumpboat launch point, which could be something as simple as a muddy beach. Motorcycle fares are variable and highly negotiable. Check with locals about going rates. Private vans can do the city-to-pumpboat ride more comfortably in less time but for five or ten times the price, possibly P2,000 per group of passengers. Ask tourism offices for names of van operators. Visitors also might have to ask around for pumpboats, and should not be surprised when the only one around is a surly guy who speaks little English but wants P1,000 for a 10-minute ride.

## By Train

Train travel is only for the very brave with lots of time to spare. Manila's sole line runs from Tutuban Station in Tondo south to Legazpi City. The train is slow and costs the same as a bus. It is not recommended.

## Manila Public Transport

### Buses

Air-conditioned buses ply major thoroughfares such as EDSA, Ayala Avenue, Sen. Gil Puyat Avenue, Taft Avenue, and the South and North expressways. Air-conditioned bus terminals are located in Escolta, in Binondo, Manila, Ayala Center, Makati, and in Cubao, Quezon City.

Motorcycles with sidecars, called tricycles, may be available for short trips on the smaller streets. In many destinations, such as Boracay or Crown Town, these are the only form of transportation.

### Commuter rail

Manila's elevated rail system consists of two Light Rail Transit lines: LRT1 (yellow line) and LRT2 (purple line), and the Metro Rail Transit line, MRT3 (blue line). The oldest and most crowded of the light rail systems is the LRT1, which runs along Taft and Rizal avenues between Baclaran (near the

airport) and Monumento, providing access to many of Manila's historical attractions. The newest of Manila's light rail systems, the LRT2, has 11 stops running east–west along Aurora Avenue from Recto to M.A. Roxas in Marakina, meeting the LRT1 by Doroteo Jose Station, and the MRT3 at Cubao (Aurora) Station. LRT trains serve 579,000 passengers per day and cover a total of 31 stations. The MRT3 runs from Taft Avenue along EDSA to North Avenue in Quezon City.

### Taxis

White and yellow taxis work Manila at prices that range from less than P100 for a short hop around Ermita, for example, to P300 or more for a cross-town journey from one suburb to another. Despite a reputation for cheating passengers, drivers who agree to run the meter seldom cheat by taking detours, though some refuse to give change. Cabs cluster at airports, hotels, shopping malls, and tourist landmarks. They can also stop randomly at curbsides to pick up passengers who flag them down.

## Car Rental

Vehicle rental services arrange cars in the arrival halls of major Philippine airports, in some major hotels and at their own local headquarters. Prices range from P1,600 to P2,300 per day, plus a value added tax (VAT) of 12 percent, for a small car without a driver, and from P2,700 per day for a car with a driver. Fuel usually costs extra, and some companies require a deposit.
**Avis**
www.avis.com.ph
**Budget**
www.budget.com.ph
**Dollar Rent-A-Car**
www.dollar.com
**Safari Rent-A-Car**
www.safarirentacarinc.com
**Hertz Rent-A-Car**
www.hertzphilippines.com
**National Car Rental**
www.nationalcarph.ukf.net

## Private Car

For visitors willing to face challenges in finding parking and negotiating unwritten rules of traffic that may differ dramatically from the ones at home, airports and hotels rent cars to anyone with a vaild foreign or international driver's license.

Police stop drivers most often for unbuckled seatbelts and for going out in Manila on days they are banned as part of an effort to relieve congestion

## Jeepneys

In Metro Manila, like much of the country, non-air-conditioned bus and jeepney rates start at P7. For air-conditioned city buses, rates start at P9. Ask the conductor or fellow passengers how much the trip should cost. Payment can be made at any time during a ride, and drivers almost always give correct change without being reminded, regardless of how many people are squeezed on board.

The jeepney is the Philippines' most colorful mode of transport, originally constructed from American jeeps left behind after World War II. Routes are fixed, with the major stops written in block letters along vehicles' side panels.

(see page 334). A few police officers, known as *buwayas* ("crocodiles"), pull drivers over on spurious charges and demand a bribe. It is better to firmly yet respectfully bargain down and pay the bribe than it is to threaten to report the incident, which could cause the whole situation to get worse.

Getting out of Manila by car can pose another problem due to perpetually heavy traffic. In particular, avoid leaving Manila via the North and South expressways on Fridays, when many people escape the city. Conversely, avoid returning to Manila on Sunday evenings. It is often easier to fly out or take a ferry.

**BELOW:** jeepney transportation.

## ACCOMMODATIONS

# HOTELS, HOSTELS AND RESORTS

### Hotels

Lodging ranges vastly in the Philippines like anywhere else. Generally, the more you pay the more comfortable your stay. But an experienced hotel shopper can find rooms for just P1,500 (US$35) per night with almost everything.

In cities, smallish hotels (often labeled with the Spanish word "pension") charge just a few hundred pesos for a clean bed, fan (no air conditioning), desk, and shared bathroom. Pensions may be located away from city centers, though seldom too far. At just above P1,000 (US$25), lodgers can stay in standard hotels with air conditioning, television sets, and private baths. Breakfast may be included. Laundry costs P15 to P25 per item. Although almost everyone provides a tiny bar of soap, at this price level do not expect the free toothbrushes, combs, and shampoo packets found elsewhere in Asia. Wi-fi, if it works at all (see "Internet" under A–Z), usually performs better in common areas near the lobby than in the further-flung guestrooms.

Some hotel rooms in bigger buildings lack outdoor-facing windows, a consideration for the claustrophobe.

Prices of P1,500 to P2,000 (US$35–50) should fetch a breakfast, a swimming pool, and other amenities, such as a skilled restaurant chef and full bar. Rooms will come alive with sturdier beds, more lighting options, a host of cable TV channels (including English-language movies), and in-room internet service.

In major cities, particularly Manila, locally run, star-rated high-rises vie with multinationals, such as Hyatt, Marriott, and Shangri-la, for the top of the market: business travelers willing to spend well over P4,000 (US$100) per night for amenities comparable to what they get around the world. Those hotels also do conferences, set up weddings and even house mini-malls or casinos. Online bookings may shave money off the prices of locally owned high-end hotels.

In resort areas, book online early to avoid being turned away due to holidays. Lunar New Year, for example, packs resorts with Chinese tourists.

Guestroom break-ins are rare, by all accounts, but front desks may be willing to store valuables such as laptops and extra wads of cash. Safe deposit boxes come with some rooms. Front desks may also ask that keys be dropped off when guests go out. Most hotel staffers are used to fielding how-to questions from tourists, so don't hesitate to ask about the most oddball concern.

In larger cities and at tourist hotspots, apartelles have come of age as another option for long-stay vacationers. Rooms have the amenities of small apartments.

Philippine hotels do not favor the light sleeper. Old, thin walls conduct noise from hallways and neighboring rooms to every guest's bed. A hotel's own disco music may pulsate through the floors until after 11pm. Traffic, barking dogs, and hurried guests kick off their cacophony as early as 5.30am.

Rates quoted below are "rack rates." Hotels offer a multitude of different rates, from internet rates to walk-in and local resident rates. Promotions are also frequently offered, so always request the cheapest rates.

**BELOW:** a welcome drink.

# MANILA

**Aloha Hotel**
2150 Roxas Boulevard, Malate
Tel: 02-526-8088
www.alohahotel-manila.com
Conveniently placed bayside rooms along Roxas Boulevard, can get a little noisy. A choice of Chinese, Japanese, and Korean restaurants. **$$**

**Ascott Makati**
6F Glorietta 4, Ayala Center, Makati City
Tel: 02-729-8888
www.the-ascott.com
Massive rooms equipped with washing machines and dryers, furnished kitchens, and entertainment centers. Other amenities include a spa, salon, pool, and tennis courts. Guests are provided with butler service. **$$$$**

**Atrium Manila Hotel**
Taft Ave corner Gil Puyat, Pasay City
Tel: 02-552-0351
www.atriumhotel-manila.com
Newish boutique hotel. Music lounge, café, business center. Right next to an LRT station. **$$$**

**Bayview Park Hotel**
1118 Roxas Boulevard corner UN Avenue, Malate
Tel: 02-526-1555
www.bayviewparkhotel-manila.com
Good-value business hotel dating from 1960s, located opposite the US Embassy. Higher rooms have great bay views. Gym, small rooftop pool, café, bars. **$$$**

**Discovery Suites Ortigas**
25 ADB Avenue, Ortigas Center, Pasig City
Tel: 02-683-8222
www.discoverysuites.com
Optimal location for Ortigas-based business visitors with the CBD spread out right below. Some of the best malls in the city. Deluxe amenities and service. Breakfast buffet on the 22nd floor overlooking the city; lounge, conference rooms. **$$$$**

**Dusit Hotel**
Nikko, Ayala Center, Makati City
Tel: 02-867-3333
www.dusit.com
A stately hotel in the heart of Makati. Large rooms, full business service, peaceful

landscaped gardens in the midst of the city. Located near Glorietta mall complex. **$$$$**

**EDSA Shangri-La Hotel**
1 Garden Way, Ortigas Center, Pasig City
Tel: 02-633-8888
www.shangri-la.com
True Shangri-La style; close to Megamall. Tennis, fitness center, pool. Italian and Chinese dining, popular for business lunches. **$$$$**

**The Heritage Hotel Manila**
Roxas Boulevard corner EDSA Pasay City
Tel: 02-854-8888
www.millenniumhotels.com/ph/heritagemanila
Conveniently located; mainly Japanese clientele. Gym, pool, casino, Cantonese restaurant, sushi bar. **$$$$**

**Hotel Intramuros de Manila**
Plaza San Luis, General Luna Street, Intramuros
Tel: 02-524-6730
Small, cozy rooms in courtyard style. **$$$**

**Hotel Rembrandt**
26 Tomas Morato Extension, Quezon City
Tel: 02-373-3333 x 105
www.hotelrembrandt.com.ph
Caters to Japanese businessmen. Gym, spa, piano bar, café, penthouse suites, restaurant. **$$$**

**Hyatt Hotel and Casino Manila**
Pedro Gil corner M.H. Del Pilar, Malate
Tel: 02-245-1234
manila.casino.hyatt.com
The most Zen of Manila's luxury hotels. Impressive array of lounges, restaurants and amenities. On-site casino. **$$$$**

**Hyatt Hotel and Casino Manila**
2702 Roxas Boulevard, Pasay City
Tel: 02-833-1234
www.hyatt.com
Excellent value for money. Surprisingly stylish tourist hotel offering the most spacious rooms in the area. Fitness center, pool, casino. Japanese and Italian restaurants. **$$$$**

**Makati Prime Tower**
Kalayaan Avenue corner Mercade Street, Makati
Tel: 02-750-3010
www.makatiprimetowersuite.com
Pleasant business hotel near red-light P. Burgos Street district. Fully furnished condotel with a salon, spa, indoor pool, wine shop, and internet café. **$$$**

**Malate Pensionne**
1771 Adriatico Street, Malate
Tel: 02-523-8304
www.malatepensionne.com
Antique furniture, restaurant. A classic backpackers' haunt with a fresh facelift. Good location for fun. **$$**

**Mandarin Oriental Manila**
Makati Avenue corner Paseo de Roxas, Makati City
Tel: 02-750-8888
www.mandarinoriental.com/manila
Five-times winner of the Philippines' Best Business Hotel. High-class but warm service. Wi-fi, gym, beautiful pool and a luxurious spa. Restaurants and a Martini Bar. **$$$$**

**Manila Airport Hotel**
99 PAL Drive, Airlane Village, NAIA Terminal 1 Complex, Paranaque City
Tel. 02-854-7549/50
www.manila-airport-hotel.com
Comfortable rooms across from the international terminal. **$$$**

**Manila Diamond Hotel**
Roxas Boulevard corner Dr J. Quintos Street, Manila
Tel: 02-526-2211
www.diamondhotel.com
A bay view hotel, with soothing earth tones and dark woods decor. Japanese and continental dining. Lobby lounge with fountains, lush garden. Amenities include a fitness center, pool, and tennis. **$$$$**

**The Manila Hotel**
One Rizal Park, Roxas Boulevard, Manila
Tel: 02-527 0011
www.manila-hotel.com.ph
This legendary hotel will appeal to World War II history buffs. One of the oldest buildings in the capital, it once hosted General Douglas MacArthur. The

amenities and restaurants are top-notch and charming. **$$$$**

**Manila Pavilion Hotel**
United Nations Avenue corner Orosa Street, Ermita
Tel: 02-526-1212
www.waterfronthotels.com.ph
Rooms overlook Rizal Park or Club Intramuros. Attentive service; many repeat customers. Gym, pool, casino, spa, Chinese restaurant. **$$$**

**New Horizon Hotel Mandaluyong**
778 Boni Avenue, Mandaluyong
Tel: 02-532-3021
www.newhorizonhotel-manila.com
Mediterranean-inspired hotel on EDSA. Offers complementary Wi-fi, a gym, and a European-cuisine restaurant. **$$$**

**New World Renaissance Hotel**
Esperanza Street corner Makati Avenue, Makati City
Tel: 02-811-6888
renaissance-hotels.marriott.com
Good-value four-star hotel with five-star facilities. Large rooms in neutral tones. Fitness center. Continental, Chinese cuisines. **$$$$**

**Paco Park Oasis Hotel**
1032–34 Belen Street, Paco, Manila
Tel: 02-521-2371–4
www.oasispark.com
Dedicated tourist hotel, motel-style rooms open to central patio and pool. No elevator. Popular for its convenient location **$$**

**The Pan Pacific Manila**
Adriatico corner General Malvar Street, Malate
Tel: 02-536 0788
www.panpacific.com
Close to the World Trade Center, this offers sleek, contemporary-style rooms with butler service for all guests. All rooms come with bay views; the top-floor

Pacific Lounge provides the best city vistas. Fitness center, swimming pool, restaurants. **$$$$**
**Pension Natividad**
1690 M.H. del Pilar Street, Malate
Tel: 02-521-0524
pensionnatividad.multiply.com
Clean and well-kept, and tucked away from Malate's bustle. Antique furniture, restaurant. Simple, but charming. **$$**
**Ralph Anthony Suites**
Maria Orosa corner Engracia Reyes Street, Manila
Tel: 02-521-1107
www.ralphanthonysuites.com

Small friendly hotel a short walk from the Robinson's Place shopping mall in Ermita. **$$**
**Remington Hotel**
Tel: 02-908-8000
www.rwmanila.com/hotels-at-resorts-world-manila/remington
Part of Resorts World Manila complex across from the airport's Terminal 3. A luxury hotel connected to a casino, restaurants, and shopping. **$$$$**
**The Richmonde Hotel**
21 San Miguel Avenue, Ortigas
Tel: 02-638-7777
www.richmondehotel.com
Boutique hotel, close to

Megamall. Fitness center, pool. **$$$**
**Salem Domestic Guesthouse**
Salem Complex, Domestic Road, Pasay City
Tel: 02-851-6260
www.domesticguesthouse.com
Located across from the domestic airport. **$$**
**Sofitel Philippine Plaza**
CCP Complex,
Roxas Boulevard,
Pasay City
Tel: 02-551-5555
www.sofitel-asia.com
Cozy rooms overlooking Manila Bay and Intramuros. Amenities

include an outdoor pool in a tropical setting, excellent gym, tennis, and a driving range. Several restaurants in a garden setting. **$$$$**
**White Knight Hotel**
Plaza San Luis Complex, Gen. Luna Street at Urdaneta Street, Intramuros
Tel: 02-526-6539
www.whiteknighthotelintramuros.com
Boutique courtyard hotel inside the Intramuros city walls, opposite San Agustin Church. Spanish architecture and classic woods furnishings, Wi-fi, café. **$$**

# MANILA'S ENVIRONS

## Cavite

**Corregidor Hotel**
Corregidor Island
Tel: 02-831-8140
e-mail: suncruises@magsaysay.com.ph
Incomparable surroundings. There are cozy rooms, dark wood decor, a swimming pool, and a restaurant. A package includes ferry to Corregidor Island. **$$$**
**Days Hotel Tagaytay**
Aguinaldo Highway,
Silang Crossing, Tagaytay City
Tel: 046-413-2400
e-mail: daystag@arcon.com.ph
www.dayshotel.ph
Part of an American hotel chain with surprisingly luxurious rooms for a moderate price. Outdoor pool. **$$$**
**Island Cove Resort & Leisure Park**
Binakayan, Kawit

Manila tel: 02-810-3740, 810-3728
www.islandcovephil.com
Weekend getaway offering swimming pools, boating, fishing, mini-golf, basketball, volleyball, tennis. **$$$–$$$$**
**Taal Vista Hotel**
Km 60 Aguinaldo Highway, Tagaytay City
Tel: 046-413-1000
Manila tel: 02-886-4325
www.taalvistahotel.com
Rooms overlooking Lake Taal. Casino, dance performance, nightly entertainment, Filipino restaurant, pool. Volcano treks. **$$$**

## Batangas

**Coral Beach Club**
Matabungkay Beach,
Lian Town
Cell tel: 0917-901-4635

www.coralbeach.ph
Simple beach resort offering air-conditioned rooms with cable TV. PADI scuba-diving lessons. **$$**
**Sanctuary Spa at Maya-Maya**
Nasugbu, Batangas
Cell tel: 0918-909-7170/909-7167
www.mayamaya.com
Charming Filipino-style cottages. A comprehensive range of massages, scrubs, and treatments in the spa. Alfresco restaurant and bar, Maya Maya Yacht Club and Marina, pool, recreation areas, Wi-fi, PADI scuba lessons. **$$**

## Dive Resorts in Anilao, Batangas

**Bonito Island**
c/o Ms Bessie Vasquez
Tel: 02-812-2292
Beautiful private island resort in Mabini and Batangas. Diving and snorkeling, to view amazing corals. **$$–$$$**
**Vistamar Beach Resort and Hotel**
Anilao, Mabini
Tel: 02-821-8332
www.vistamaronline.com
Clean, simple rooms. A wide range of activities includes diving, windsurfing, and volleyball. **$$**

## Laguna

**Hidden Valley Springs**
Alamiños, Laguna

Tel: 02-840-4112–4
One of the more intriquing resorts, secluded at the foot of Mt Makiling, a dormant volcano that still heats hot springs in the area. These are complemented by cold springs, and giant fruit trees and primitive forest. **$$$$**
**Pagsanjan Rapids Hotel**
Gen. Taiño Street, Pagsanjan
Tel: 049-808-4258
Simple, clean, carpeted rooms overlooking Bumbugan River. Massage, pool. **$$**
**La Vista Pansol Resort Complex**
Brgy Pansol, Calamba
Tel: 049-545-1850, 834-1121
www.lavistapansolresort.com
Simple buildings; water slide, natural warm springs, tennis, mini-golf, view of Laguna de Bay, pool. Crowded on weekends. **$**

## Quezon

**Cote D'Azur Beach Resort**
Barangay Abiawin, Infanta
Tel: 042-535-3047
Manila tel: 02-948-7701
www.cotedazurbeachresort.com
Rugged setting 4km (2.5 miles) from the town center, air-conditioned rooms and bungalows, and a luxurious free-form swimming pool. **$$**
**Villa Escudero Plantations and Resort**
San Pablo City
Manila Tel: 02-523-0392

**BELOW:** there are numerous dive resorts near Manila.

www.villaescudero.com
Amenities include slide pools, bamboo rafts, carabao carts, and a museum. There are waterfalls nearby and native cottages, some on the lakefront. **$$$–$$$$**

### Rizal
**Seven Suites Hotel – Observatory**
convenient location. **$$–$$$**

Hollywood Street, Antipolo
Tel: 02-682-0330
www.cravingsgroup.com/seven
Near Valley Golf along Sumulong Highway. Seven romantic rooms overlooking Manila city lights. Pool, roof-deck lounge, Italian and Asian cuisines, bar. **$$$**

# CENTRAL PLAINS

### Pampanga
**Holiday Inn Clark**
Mimosa Leisure Estate, Clark Field
Manila tel: 02-845-1888
www.ichotelsgroup.com
Plush accommodations on the sprawling grounds of Mimosa. Golf course. Driving range, casino nearby. Beautiful pool, selection of restaurants. **$$$$**

**Juanita's Guest House**
F-1 Teodoro at Rina Street, Balibago, Angeles City
Tel: 045-892-3209
Close to the bar strip but on quiet street. Offers in-room Wi-fi and a breakfast bar. **$**

**Natalia Apartelle**
Fields Avenue between Club Camelot and Insomnia Bar, Balibago, Angeles City
Tel: 045-892-0661
www.nataliahotel.webs.com
Rooms for short and long stays in the thick of bar district. In-room Wi-fi. **$$**

**Oasis Hotel**
Clarkville Compound, Balibago, Angeles City
Tel: 045-625-8301–4
www.oasishotel.com.ph
Bright rooms with wicker furnishings. Pool, restaurant,

**The Swagman Narra Hotel**
S.L. Orosa Street, Diamond Subdivision Balibago, Angeles City
Tel: 045-322-5133
www.swagmanresort.com
Hotel tricycle for bar-hopping and daily van shuttles to Manila. Pool, spa, business facilities, and restaurants. **$$**

### Tarlac
**La Maja Rica Hotel**
MacArthur Highway corner Ligtasan Street, Tarlac City
Tel: 045-611-2053-7
www.lamajaricahotel.com
The hotel comprises 40 guestrooms, 20 drive-in units, pool, several dining facilities, and amenities for business travelers. **$$**

### Bataan
**Montemar Beach Club**
Bagac, Bataan
Tel: 02-892-6497, 811-5496
www.montemar.com.ph
Mediterranean-inspired rooms where the mountains meet sand and sea. Kayaking, pool, and restaurants. **$$$**

### Zambales
**By The Sea Resort**
Olongapo
99 National Highway, Barretto, Subic Bay, Olongapo City
Tel: 047-222-2888, 224-2494
www.bythesea.com.ph
Conference rooms, restaurants, and water sports. Expansive seaside lawns, plus private beach and picnic huts, bar with live music. **$$**

**Crown Peak Gardens**
Upper Cubi, Subic Bay, Olongapo City
Tel: 047-252-3144
enshotel.beachsubic.com
Sprawling hotel complex in a former marine barracks. Amenities include a swimming pool and restaurants. **$$$**

**Legenda Hotel**
Waterfront Rd, Subic Bay, Olongapo City
Tel: 047-252-1888
Manila tel: 02-732-9888
www.subiclegend.com
Business-style hotel with a casino. Spacious rooms featuring handmade Filipino furniture. Pool, health club, restaurants, disco, karaoke. **$$$$**

**Mango's Bayview Apartelles**
116 Beach Boulevard, Barretto, Olongapo City
Tel: 047-223-4139
www.mangossubic.com
Apartments overlooking Subic Bay with big remote-controlled televisions and air conditioning. Available daily, weekly, or monthly. **$$**

**White Rock Beach Resort Hotel**
Matain, Subic Bay
Tel: 047-222-2378, 232-2857
Manila tel: 02-421-2781
www.whiterock.com.ph
Leisure for a whole family, offering a wide range of activities from golf to bowling to water sports, all along Subic Bay. **$$$$**

**Zoobic Lodge**
Tiara (Crown Peak), Subic Bay, Freeport Zone
Tel: 047-252-2272
www.zoobic.com.ph
A stay at the Zoobic Lodge can be combined with a visit to the Zoobi Safari, and a chance to see tigers. The lodge motif is safari-inspired. **$$**

# ILOCOS

### Hundred Islands, Pangasinan
**Maxine by the Sea**
Lucap, Alaminos
Tel: 075-551-2537
Simple, clean, air-conditioned, and fan-cooled rooms, no hot water. Seafood restaurant. **$**

**Puerto Del Sol Beach Resort**
Barangay Ilog Malino, Bolinao
Manila tel: 02-637-8963
www.puertodelsol.com.ph
A boutique resort, massage gazebos, pool. Offers Hundred Island tour with options for island-hopping and snorkeling. **$$$$**

**SCL Garden Paradise Resort**
Barangay Ilog Malino, Bolinao
Manila tel: 02-536-1744
Cell tel: 0921-411-7983
Ask for the table in the treehouse for an interesting dining experience. **$$**

**100 Islands Pensionne House**
Lucap, Alaminos
Tel: 075-551-2505
Simple backpacker-style lodgings in front of where the boats to Hundred Islands depart in the morning. **$–$$**

### La Union
**Bali Hai Beach Resort**
Paringao, Bauang
Tel: 072-242-5679
www.balihai.com.ph
Private air-conditioned cabins in a tropical garden setting. Pool, 24-hour bar, German and Indonesian cuisines. **$$**

**Cabaña Beach Resort**
Paringao, Bauang
Tel: 072-242-5585
www.cabana.com.ph
Private nipa huts along beachfront. Pool, bar. Filipino, Chinese, Japanese, American cuisines. **$**

**San Juan Surf Resort**
238 Brgy Urbiztondo, San Juan
Tel: 072-720 0340
www.sanjuansurfresort.com.ph

### PRICE CATEGORIES
Price categories are for a standard double room.
**$** = less than US$20
**$$** = 20–50
**$$$** = 50–100
**$$$$** = over US$100

TRANSPORTATION | ACCOMMODATIONS | EATING OUT | ACTIVITIES | A – Z | LANGUAGE

Native cottages complete with mosquito nets. Restaurant, surfing, board rentals, hiking, internet. **$$**

### Ilocos Sur

**Ciudad Fernandina Hotel**
26 Mabini Street, corner Plaridel Street, Vigan
Tel: 077-722-3765/67
ciudadfernandinavigan.com.ph
Ornately redesigned Spanish-style hotel and restaurant in old Vigan, air conditioning, cable TV. **$$$**

**Cordillera Inn**
M. Crisologo Street corner Gen. Luna, Vigan
Tel: 077-722-2727/39
Clean, simple rooms in a large traditional house with rooftop, first-floor restaurant. All rooms are air-conditioned and come with cable TV. **$$**

**The Golden Pine**
Corner Carino and Legarda streets, Baguio City
Tel: 074-444-9965
www.goldenpinehotel.com
Centrally located full-service hotel, with a restaurant and business center. **$$**

**Gordion Hotel**
15 Salcedo Street, Vigan
Tel. 077-722-2526
www.vigangordionhotel.com

Lavish, preserved Spanish-style building. **$$**

**Palm Grove Hot Springs Mountain Resort**
Pelizloy Centrum, Lower Session Road, Baguio
Tel. 0918-800-7462
palmgroveresort@yahoo.com
Hillside resort complex with heated pools, coffee shop, and a recreation center. **$$**

**Vigan Plaza Hotel**
Plaza Jose Burgos, Vigan
Tel. 0917-799-9874
www.viganplazahotel.com
Wood furnishings, central location. **$$–$$$**

### Ilocos Norte

**Fort Ilocandia Resort & Casino**
Barrio Caylayab, Laoag City
Tel: 077-772-1166–70
www.fortilocandia.com.ph
Close to Laoag Airport. Spanish-style architecture coupled with elegant rooms. Golf course, massive pool, beach, tennis. **$$$$**

**Hannah's Beach Resort & Convention Center**
Barangay Balaoi, Malingay, Pagudpud
Cell tel: 0928-520-6255
www.hannahsbeachresort.com
Full-on resort near remote

Blue Lagoon. **$$–$$$**

**Saud Beach Resort**
Saud, Pagudpud
Tel: 077-764-1005
Manila tel: 02-921-2856
www.saudbeachresort.com
Relaxing resort offering ocean-swimming beach, karaoke, restaurant. **$$$**

**Palazzo de Laoag Hotel**
27 Paterno Street, Laoag City
Tel: 077-773-1842
www.thepalaciodelaoag.com
Comfortable hotel in the heart of town. Swimming pool. **$$**

**Plaza del Norte**
Barangay 41, Bacalad, Laoag
Tel. 077-670-8818
www.plazadelnorte.com.ph
Pool, restaurant, situated on a hillside near Laoag airport. **$$**

**Hotel Tiffany**
Gen. Segundo Ave corner M.H. del Pilar, Laoag
Tel: 077-770-3550
Fax: 077-771-4360
Located near the sinking bell tower. Whimsically decorated in pastels. **$**

**Playa Tropical Resort Hotel**
Barangay Victoria, Currimao
Tel: 077-670-1211

www.playatropical.com.ph
Guests stay in detached wooden huts by the sea; pool. **$$$**

### Batanes

**Batanes Resort**
Cell tel: 0918-273-6964
A nice 2km (1-mile) walk from Basco town proper. Eight maroon-roofed cottages; beautiful views of the hills, sea and sunrises over Mt Iraya. 

**Batanes Seaside Lodge and Restaurant**
Cell tel: 0981-993-613
www.batanesseasidelodge.com
At the end of Basco, right off the national road, this resort has 13 charming rooms tucked into a pocket cove poised to catch the sun, waves, and wind. Restaurant and vehicle rental. **$$**

**Pensionne Ivatan**
Basco, Batanes islands
Cell tel: 0921-442-8841
203.177.6.3/pensionivatan.net
Deck views from hill facing the South China Sea and the town of Basco. The closest lodging to Laoag airport; offering a variety of rooms. **$–$$**

# NORTHEAST LUZON

### Cagayan

**Hotel Andrea**
Don Jose Canciller Street
Cauayan City,
Isabela
Tel: 078-652-3972
An Art Deco-designed hotel in a central location. **$**

**Callao Cave Resort**
Peñablanca
Tel: 078-844-1801
Fax: 078-844-7658
A stone's throw from the cave, with basic facilities. The resort can arrange for caving guides. **$**

**Hotel Carmelita**
(Address, Tel)
hotelcarmelita@yahoo.com
Simple, comfortable rooms. **$**

**Ivory Hotel and Convention Center**
Buntun Highway,
Tuguegarao
Tel: 078-844-1275
Fax: 078-846-2179

www.ivoryhotelandsuites.com
Modest rooms, hot shower, pool, restaurant, and phone. Lobby garden sets the homely tone. **$**

**Hotel Lorita**
16 Rizal Street,
Tuguegarao City
Tel: 078-844-1390
Fax: 078-846-2179
Simple rooms with cable TV and hot water. Beside Tuguegarao Church. **$$**

**Hotel Roma**
Luna corner Bonifacio Street, Tuguegarao City
Tel: 078-844-2222
Fax: 078-844-7678
Spacious rooms and one of the best coffee shops in town. **$$**

### Isabela

**Carig Plaza Hotel**
Mabini, Santiago City
Tel: 078-682-7143
Santiago's biggest hotel, set

in a lush garden. Air conditioning, cable TV, hot showers, phone, restaurant, mini golf. **$**

**King George Hotel**
Bonifacio Avenue, Victory Norte, Santiago
Tel: 078-682-8434, 682-8743
Monolithic building. Air conditioning, hot showers, cable TV. Ballroom, restaurant. **$**

### Quirino

**Aglipay Caves and Campsite**
Villa Ventura, Aglipay
Tel: 078-692-5088
Cottages, budget dormitories. Pool, children's park, picnic sheds. Accessible from Aglipay's 37 caves. **$**

### Nueva Vizcaya

**Governor's Garden Hotel**
Manzano Street, Solano
Tel: 078-326-5166, 326-5200
Gardens, big pool, good

local reviews. **$**

**Saber Inn & Restaurant**
National Highway, Bayombong
Tel: 078-321-2222
Air-cinditioned rooms, pool, and restaurant. **$–$$**

**Villa Margarita Mountain Resort**
Busilac, Bayombong
Tel: 078-326-5083
Comfortable, with cool mountain air. Trekking nearby. Sunrise and sunset views from rooms. **$**

### Aurora

**Bahia De Baler**
Sabang, Baler
Cell tel: 0920-904 0177
Great rooms by the beach. **$**

**Bays Inn**
Sabang, Baler
Tel: 0918-926-6697
baysinnbaler.multiply
A mainstay for surfers – eat your breakfast while checking out the day's waves. **$**

# CENTRAL CORDILLERA

## Benguet

**Benguet Pine Tourist Inn**
82 Chanum corner Otek Street,
Baguio City
Tel: 074-442-7325
Quiet, backpacker lodging
near Burnham Park.
Restaurant. **$**

**Concorde Hotel**
Europa Center, Legarda Road,
Baguio
Tel: 074-443-2048
e-mail: concorde@mozcom.com
Among Baguio's best hotels.
Wood and brick interior,
lodge-like ambiance, good
views. Chinese, Japanese
restaurants, piano bar, kara-
oke. **$$$**

**Forest Inn**
Legarda Rd,

Baguio City
Tel: 074-442-2552
Fax: 074-443-8437
Pleasant, cozy rooms with
white wicker furniture; hot
showers. **$$**

**Safari Lodge**
Leonard Wood Road,
Baguio City
Tel: 074-442-2419
safarilodgebaguio.blogspot.com
Home of a former trophy
hunter, stuffed and
mounted wildlife fill the
room. Restaurant.
**$$$**

**Tam-awan Ifugao Village**
Tacay Road, Baguio City
Tel: 074-446-2949
www.tamawanvillage.com
Artists' village where

tourists stay in traditional
Ifugao homes. **$$**

## Mountain Province

**Mt Data Lodge**
Km 100, Halsema Highway,
Bauko
Manila tel: 02-524-2495
Simple, quiet lodge, cultural
performances. **$$**

**St Joseph's Guesthouse**
Sagada
Cell tel: 0918-559-5934
Simple Episcopalian-run
rooms. Restaurant, shared
bath. **$**

## Ifugao

**Banaue Hotel and Youth
Hostel**
Banaue, Ifugao

Tel: 074-386-4087
www.philtourism.gov.ph
Restaurant, pool, cultural
performances, far from
town center near Tam-an
Village. **$$$**

**Banaue View Inn**
Banaue, Ifugao
Tel: 074-386-4078
A favorite, offering open-air
views over terraces, plus a
museum of Ifugao artifacts
collected by American
anthropologist Otley Beyer.
Food, parking. **$$**

**Halfway Lodge and
Restaurant**
Banaue, Ifugao
Tel: 074-386-4082
Simple, clean, with great
terrace views; restaurant. **$**

# BICOL

## Camarines Norte

**Apuao Grande Island
Resort**
1085 Vicente Basil St.,
Mercedes, Daet
Tel: 054-721-1545
Resort on a private island
with bar and library. **$$**

**Canimog Hotel**
San Vicente Road,
Lag-on, Daet
Tel: 054-721-5318
Fax: 054-721-2602
Beautiful garden lends
ambiance. **$$**

**Wiltan Hotel**
Vinzon's Avenue, Daet
Tel: 054-721-2525
Standard amenities, pleas-
ant garden. **$$**

## Camarines Sur

**Aristocrat Hotel**
E. Angeles Street, Dinaga,
Naga City
Tel: 054-473-8832
Fax: 054-811-6605
Large, ornate building, with
views of Mt Isarog and Mt
Mayon. **$**

**Avenue Plaza Hotel**
Magsaysay Avenue, Naga
Tel. 054-473-9999
www.theavenueplazahotel.com
High-end hotel with a range
of rooms up to presidential
suite. **$$**

**Camarines Sur
Government Lodgings**
Inquire at the Camsur
Watersports Complex (tel: 054-
475-0854; www.
camsurwatersports_complex.com)
about the local lodging:
The Villa del Ray Villas come
with a spa, private garden,
swimming pool, and
upscale dining (**$$$$**). The
**Mansion Suites** is a
15-bedroom hotel with a
24-hour restaurant, Wi-fi,
and cable TV (**$$$**). The **Villa
del Rey Cabanas** is more
rudimentary, but with mod-
cons. It is within walking
distance of the Camsur
Watersports Complex,
Skatepark, and Bike Trail
(**$$**).

**Hotel Mirabella**
Caceres Street, Dinaga, Naga
Tel: 054-473-9537
Fax: 054-811-1379
Quiet, old, well kept. Nice
garden, pool, and an excel-
lent view of Mt Isarog. **$$**

**New Crown Hotel**
P. Burgos Street, San Francisco,
Naga

Tel: 054-811-7288
Fronts Quince Martires
Monument and San
Francisco Church. Air condi-
tioning, cable TV, hot show-
ers. **$$**

## Albay

**Albay Hotel**
88 Penaranda Street,
Legazpi City
Tel: 052-480-8660
Fax: 052-214-3642
Hotel offers airport transfer,
a pool, and parking. Superb
views of Mt Mayon. **$$$**

**Mayon International Hotel**
419 Quezon Avenue,
Legazpi
Tel: 052-245-5028, 480-1655
On the slope of Mt Mayon,
with exhilarating views of
the Pacific Ocean. Full trek-
king packages. **$$**

**Oriental Legazpi**
Taysan Hill, Santo Niño Village,
Legazpi
Tel: 052-435-3333
www.theorientalhotels.com
Hillside hotel with Mayon
Volcano views. **$$$$**

**Porta Azure**
Barangay Padang, Legazpi City
Manila tel: 02-807-8414
Well-decorated villas set on
the black sands of Legazpi
Bay, in the shadow of Mt
Mayon. Local food, mas-
sages. **$$$**

**Hotel la Trinidad**
Rizal Street,
Legazpi
Tel: 052-480-7469, 212-2951-
53
Fax: 052-214-3148
Simple rooms, air condition-
ing, restaurant. A 90-minute
drive to view the Donsol
whale sharks. **$$**

## Catanduanes

**Bosdak Beach Resort**
Magnesia del Sur, Virac
Tel: 052-633-1703
Wide range of rooms, air
conditioning or fan. Sports
facilities, disco, restaurant.
**$$**

**Kemji Resort and
Restaurant**
San Isidro Village, near Virac
airport
Tel. 0939-451-1494
Basic rooms, above-average
food. **$**

**Kosta Alcantara Beach
Resort and Restaurant**
Marilima, Virac
Tel: 052-811-1459
Clear water, good for swim-
ming. **$$**

**Puting Baybay Resort**
Puraran, Baras
Cell tel: 0919-512-9938
puraran-surf-putingbaybay.webnode.
com
Basic but comfortable, with
meals. **$**

**Fernandos Hotel**
Pareja Street,
Bitan-o
Tel: 056-211-1573
www.fernandoshotel.com
Calm, elegant ambiance;
diving and whale-watching

packages, tours of
Sorsogon, Bulusan Volcano.
**$**
**Rizal Beach Resort**
Rizal Gubat
Tel: 056-211-1056
Former school turned into a
resort, with spectacular

views of Rizal Beach. **$$**
**San Mateo Hot and Cold
Springs Resort**
San Benon,
Irosin
Native design in rural set-
ting. View of San Mateo
Springs. **$$**

**Villa Kasanggayahan
Pension**
Rizal Street, Sorsogon
Tel: 056-211-1275
e-mail: koriksl@hotmail.com
Well-preserved, colonial
house. Rustic, pleasant,
and green. **$**

# LUZON'S ISLANDS

**Blue Water Lodge**
White Beach, Puerto Galera
Manila tel: 02-714-6632
Cell tel: 0926-839-4222
www.bluewaterlodge.com.ph
Large air-conditioned rooms
with TV and hot shower.
Located about 60m (200ft)
from the beach. **$$**
**Coco Beach Resort**
Coco Beach, Puerto Galera
Tel: 0912-305 0476,
www.cocobeach.com
Nipa bungalows on
secluded beach. Amenities
include tennis, swimming,
diving; restaurants. **$$–$$$**
**La Gensol Plaza Hotel**
95 Natinal Road,

Mamburao
Tel: 043-711-1072
Antique beds, nice bath-
rooms, air conditioning,
cable TV, 24-hour restau-
rant. Friendly staff. **$$**
**Grace Island Resort**
Ambulong, San Jose, Occidental
Mindoro
Tel: 043-491-2533
graceisland_ambulong@yahoo.com
www.graceislandresort.com
Rooms over the water on
isolated Ambulong island,
floating conference halls,
canteen, banana boats.
**$$$**
**Hollywood Palm Beach
Resort**
White Beach, Puerto Galera

Cell tel: 0916-849-0495
A 50-room hotel, with air
conditioning, Wi-fi, cable TV,
private baths. Amenities
include a pool, bar, restau-
rant, and conference hall.
**$$–$$$**
**La Laguna Beach Club &
Dive Center**
Big La Laguna Beach, Puerto
Galera
Cell tel: 097-794-0323
www.llbc.com.ph
Native-style lodgings with
swimming pool; dive center
attached. **$$**
**Pandan Island Resort**
Sablayan, Mamburao
Cell tel: 0919-305-7821
www.pandan.com

Private bungalows made of
native materials.
Restaurant, dive center. **$$**
**Sikatuna Beach Resort
Hotel**
Barangay San Roque, San Jose
Tel: 043-491-4108
www.sikatunabeachhotel.com
Beachside rooms, restau-
rant, bar, conference space.
Located near boat launch,
five minutes from San Jose
airport. **$–$$**
**White House Beach
Resort**
Barangay San Roque, San Jose
Tel: 043-490-1656
Secluded rooms in large,
rambling beachside house.
**$$**

# EASTERN VISAYAS

**Asia Stars Hotel**
P. Zamora Street, Tacloban City
Tel: 053-325-5322
Near city center, nice interi-
ors, friendly staff. **$$**
**Dio Island Beach Resort**
San Jose, Tacloban
Tel: 053-323-2389
Seaside tranquility, near air-
port. Water sports. **$**
**Leyte Park Resort Hotel**
Magsaysay Boulevard,
Tacloban

Tel: 053-325-6000
www.leyteparkhotel.com.ph
Originally built for Imelda
Marcos's friends in her
hometown, just 15 minutes
from the airport. Overlooking
Samar's Mt Danglay, the
hotel is set in tropical gardens, with a guitar-shaped
pool. Restaurants, bars,
disco. **$$$**
**MacArthur Park Beach
Resort**
Government Ctr, Candahug,

Palo
Tel: 053-323-4095/96
Near MacArthur Memorial
Landing along Red Beach.
Native decor and well-
appointed rooms.
Sailboats, restaurant, pool.
**$$$**

**Leyte Park**
Marabut, Samar
Tacloban tel: 053-325-6000
Elegant cabins along pris-

tine shore, near rock forma-
tions. **$**
**The Surf Camp**
ABCD Beach, Calicoan Island,
Guiuan, Eastern Samar
Cell tel: 0917-530-1828
www.calicoansurfcamp.com
Cottages inspired by Thai,
Balinese, Indonesian, and
Filipino architecture. Infinity
pool, exquisite landscap-
ing, and instant access to
prime Pacific surfing waves.
**$$$$**

# CENTRAL VISAYAS

**Alona Palm Beach Resort
and Restaurant**
Alona Beach, Tawala, Panglao
Tel: 038-502-9141
www.alonapalmbeach.com
Attention to landscaping,
luxurious rooms, unique
swimming pool. **$$$$**
**Alona Tropical Beach
Resort**

Alona Beach, Tawala, Panglao
Tel: 038-502-9024
alonatropicalbeachresort.com
Filipino-style nipa
bungalows, sprawling gar-
den. **$$**
**Citadel Alona**
Lot 4480-A, Purok 7, Tawala,
Panglao
Tel: 038-502-9424
www.citadelalona.com

Clean, quiet, off beach,
shared bathrooms, shared
kitchen. **$**
**Panglao Bluewater Beach
Resort**
Tel: 038-416-0695
www.bluewater.com.ph/panglao
Seclusion along the beach,
near dive sites. **$$$$**
**Panglao Nature Resort**
Panglao Island

Tel: 038-411-5982
www.panglaoisland.com
Beachfront tribute to nature,
beautiful rooms, jacuzzi,
pool. **$$$$**
**La Roca Hotel**
Graham Avenue, Tagbilaran
Tel: 038-411-3179
www.bohollarocahotel.com
Central location, near
Bohol–Cebu ferry pier. **$**

**Sun Apartelle Luxury Apartment**
Alona Beach, Tawala, Panglao
Tel: 038-502-9063
www.sunapartelle.com
Sun Divers dive shop located on site; www.sun-divers.net
Business centre, kitchenette, DVD player, Wi-fi, and one of the most stunning pools in the Visayas. Long-term stays possible. **$$$**

## Cebu City

**Hotel Asia**
11 Don Jose Avila St.
Tel: 032-255-8534
www.hotelasiacebu.com
Central location, Japanese-style accommodations.
**$$–$$$**

**The Beverly Boutique Business Hotel**
F. Manalo Street corner of Queens Road
Tel: 032-254-8570
www.beverlyboutiquehotel.com
Comfortable, central location, near bar district. In-house steak restaurant.
**$$**

**City Park Inn**
Archbishop Reyes Avenue
Tel: 032-232-7311–13
Small tourist inn. **$**

**Marriott Cebu City**
Cardinal Rosales Avenue, Cebu Business Park
Tel: 032-232-6100
www.marriott.com
Centrally located inside Cebu Business Park. Good

**ABOVE:** Shangri-La's Mactan Island Resort.

restaurants and bars. Geared towards business travelers. **$$$$**

**Montebello Villa Hotel**
Banilad
Tel: 032-232-3589
www.montebellovillahotel.com
Spanish-inspired hacienda, with 145 guest rooms and suites. Two pools, tropical garden area. **$$**

**Verbena Pension House**
584 Don Gil Garcia St.
Tel: 032-253-4440
www.verbenapensionhouse.com
Cozy, central location. **$**

## Cebu Island

**Cabana Beach Club Resort**
Panangsama Beach, Moalboal
Cell tel: 0927-950-9968

Classy, ocean-view rooms, with private pier and decks.
**$$$**

**Malapascua Exotic Island Dive and Beach Resort**
Malapascua Island
Tel: 032-437 0983
Cell tel: 0917-327-6689
www.malapascua.net
Resort organizes three- and four-day diving expeditions.
**$$**

**Ravenala Beach Bungalows**
White Beach
Tel: 032-232-5452, 474-0075
www.ravenala.net
Quaint bungalows a few steps from White Beach. Diving equipment. **$$**

## Mactan Island

**Bluewater Maribago**

Buyong Maribago
Tel: 032-492-0100
www.bluewater.com.ph
Rooms, bungalows; near airport. **$$$$**

**Plantation Bay**
Marigondon, Mactan
Tel: 032-340-5900
Manila tel: 02-844-5024/25
sales@plantationbay.com
www.plantationbay.com
Luxurious rooms with private garden, gazebo, whirlpool. Swimming lagoons, water sports. Beach-side dining. **$$$$**

**Shangri-La's Mactan Island Resort**
Punta Engaño Road, Lapu-Lapu City, Mactan
Tel: 032-231-0288
www.shangri-la.com
Resort near airport. Rooms overlook pool, beach, and sea. International, Filipino, and Chinese cuisines. **$$$$**

**Waterfront Mactan Island Hotel & Casino**
Airport Road, Lapu-Lapu City, Mactan
Tel: 032-340-4888
www.waterfronthotels.com.ph
Several restaurants including Korean, casino, cigar and whiskey bar, nightclub.
**$$$$**

**BELOW:** Cebu City.

# WESTERN VISAYAS

## Negros Oriental

**Bethel Guest House**
Rizal Boulevard, Dumaguete City
Tel: 035-225-2000
bethelguesthouse.com
Elegant lobby, spartan rooms. Fast-food restaurant overlooks sea. $-$$

**Bahia de Bais Hotel**
Dewey Island Hilltop, Capiñahan, Bais City
Tel: 035-402-8850–1
Garden with a panoramic view of Bais Bay. Mini-bar and small restaurant. Trips to sandbar, mangrove park, and Tañon Strait for whale- and dolphin-spotting. $

**Liberty's Lodge/Apo Island**
Off Zamboangita/Dauin
Tel: 035-321-1036
Cell tel: 0920-238-5704
www.apoisland.com
Simple rooms and package deals for divers, snorkelers, or explorers. $$

**La Planta Hotel**
Mabini Street, Bais City
Tel: 035-541-5755
Manila tel: 02-899-8756
www.laplanta.com.ph
Bright, airy rooms. Golf, dolphins, and inviting waters nearby. $$$

**La Residencia Al Mar**
Rizal Boulevard, Dumaguete City
Tel: 035-225-7100–1, 422-8449
www.laresidenciaalmar.com
Some rooms have balconies facing the sea. Free breakfast. $$

**South Sea Resort**
Bantayan, Dumaguete City
Tel: 035-225-2409
Seaside garden setting, swimming pool, restaurant. Shuttle to city center just 10 minutes away. $$

**Sta Monica by the Sea**
Banilad, Dumaguete City
Tel: 035-225 0704
Seaside cottages, good restaurant by the beach. Shuttles to city center 20 minutes away. $$

**Wellbeach Resort**
Mojon, Maluay km 22
Zamboanguita
Tel: 035-400-3159; cell tel: 0917-300-4674
www.wellbeach.com

Swiss chalet-style beach-side resort and launch site for diving trips. $$

**The Worldview Pension Plaza**
Dumaguete
Tel. 035-225-4110, 0917-700-7079
Air-conditioned rooms, coffee shop, Wi-fi. $

**Wuthering Heights Hotel**
San Jose
Dumaguete tel: 035-225 0487
Beachfront hotel 16km (10 miles) north of Dumaguete. Terrace restaurant and deck overlook Tañon Strait and surrounding countryside. Air conditioning, bathtub, cable TV. $$

## Negros Occidental

**Bacolod King's Hotel**
San Sebastian corner Gatuslao Street, Bacolod
Tel: 034-433-0572
Popular tourist inn. $-$$

**L'Fisher Hotel**
14–15 Lacson Street, Bacolod
Tel: 034-433-3731
lfisherhotelbacolod.com
Small lobby and atrium, fine restaurant and café around a cozy pool. $$$

**Sugarland Hotel**
Araneta Street, Sinagcang, Bacolod
Tel: 034-435-2691
Near airport. A favorite among locals and golfers. $$

**Tamera Plaza Inn**
79 Lacson Street, Bacolod
Tel: 034-709-0886
www.tameraplazainn.com
Wi-fi, restaurant, bar, coffee shop, function room. $

## Iloilo/Kalibo

**Amigo Terrace Hotel**
Iznart corner Delgada Street, Iloilo
Tel: 033-335-0908
During Dinagyang festival, hotel balconies are in demand for views of the events. Restaurant, swimming pool, disco. $$-$$$

**Harbor Town Hotel**
J.M. Besa corner Aldeguer Street, Iloilo
Tel: 033-337-2384
Luxury hotel 10 minutes from the harbor. Traditional Ilonggo hospitality. $$-$$$

**Marzon Hotel Kalibo**
Santa Monica, Andagao, Kalibo
Tel: 036-268-2188
www.marzonhotelkalibo.com
Motel-style, spacious rooms, pool, spa, Wi-fi. $

**Ong Bun Pension House**
Ong Bun Building, near Quezon-Ledesma intersection, Iloilo
Tel: 033-335-1271
www.ongbun.com/pensionhouse-iloilo
Ultra-cheap rooms. $

**Sarabia Manor Hotel**
General Luna Street, Iloilo
Tel: 033-335-1021
www.sarabiamanorhotel.com
Large pool, restaurant, carpeted rooms. $$

## Guimaras

**Costa Aguada Island Resort**
Inampulugan Island, Sibunag
Tel: 02-890-5333 ext. 615/6
www.costaaguadaislandresort.com
Pleasant resort with beaches, turtle park, mini-zoo, hilltop jungle park, pool, horseback riding. Located off Guimaras Island; access by pumpboat. $$

**Nagarao Island Resort**
Jordan, Guimaras
Cell tel: 0912-520-0343
www.nagaraoresort.com
Located on a 10-hectare (25-acre) island with sandy beach, snorkeling. Pool, tennis court, restaurant with lounge, bar, library, business center. 2 hours from Iloilo by boat and jeep. $$$

## Antique

**Barrio House Resort**
Madrangca, San Jose
Tel: 036-540-7024
Dining hall, picnic facilities. $$

## Boracay

Rates are those of peak season November–May. Off-season rates often drop 50 percent. More than 100 budget inns are available, most offering rooms with fans, away from the beach.

**Angol Point**
Boat Station 3, White Beach
Cell tel: 0947-324-1969

angolpointbeach.com
Quiet, fan-cooled thatched huts along beach. $$

**Boracay Regency Beach Resort & Spa**
Station 2, Boracay
Tel: 036-288-6111
www.boracayregency.com
Free breakfasts, help with transportation. $$$

**Cocomangas Beach Resort**
White Beach
Tel: 036-288-3409
Renowned for Moondog's Shooters Bar. $$$

**Friday's Boracay Resort**
Tel: 036-288-6200
www.fridaysboracay.com
Guests stay in cottage-style rooms or luxurious suites. The beachfront restaurant, serving Asian and Filipino cuisines, has a barbecue buffet on Friday. $$$$

**Manadla Spa & Villas**
Malay, Aklan
Tel: 036-288-5858
mandalaspa.com
Award-winning spa and detox resort, with villas tucked into landscaped greenery. $$$$

**The Panoly Resort**
Punta Bunga
Tel: 036-288-3134
www.thepanoly.com
Clustered cottages. Restaurants, pools, bar, disco. $$$$

**Sandcastles Beach Resort**
Tel: 036-288-3207
Manila tel: 02-823-2725
www.boracaysandcastles.com
Arranges kayaking and sailing. Refurbished rooms, apartments, Thai restaurant. $$$$

**Villa Camilla**
Boat Station 3, White Beach
Tel: 036-288-3354
www.villacamilla.com/boracay
A range of rooms just off beach, small swim-up bar at pool. $$

# PALAWAN

## Puerto Princesa

**The Legend Palawan**
Malvar Street
Manila tel: 02-638-9256
www.legendpalawan.com.ph
A business hotel that organizes island cruises and tours of the Underground River. **$$$**

**Puerto Pension**
No. 35 Malvar Street, Puerto Princesa
Tel: 048-433-2969
www.puertopension.com
Centrally located bed-and-breakfast; protection from power outages. **$**

**Sabang Balay-Balay Travel Lodge**
Sabang, Cabayugan, Puerto Princesa
Tel. 0920-628-9946
Scenically located hotel near the Underground River. **$–$$**

**Villa Leonora Beach Resort**
Km 60 on highway toward Roxas
Tel: 0999-413-3247
Air-conditioned rooms and huts with fans. Restaurant, bar, and a beach ideal for snorkelers. **$$**

## Northern Palawan

**Amanpulo**
Pamalican Island
Manila tel: 02-759-4040
www.amanpulo.com
Secluded island getaway. White-sand beach, water sports, cycling, tennis, picnics, massage. **$$$$**

**Busuanga Seadive Resort**
Coron
Cell tel: 0918-400-0448
www.seadiveresort.com
Range of seaside rooms, restaurant, bar, amenities for divers. **$**

**El Nido Resorts**
Miniloc and Lagen Islands, Bacuit Bay
Manila tel: 02-894-5644
www.elnidoresorts.com
High-end accommodations near the sea cliffs of El Nido. **$$$$**

**Modessa Island Resort**
Roxas
Tel: 048-434-1584
www.modessaisland.com
Huts on the beach, water sports, hammocks, electricity from dusk to dawn. **$$**

**Oriental Lodging House**
Mao Bldg. (in front of Tourism Center Bldg.), Coron
Tel. 0919-828-2934
coronorientallodge.webs.com
Hotel located in central Coron. Tours arranged. Massages, internet café, restaurant, Wi-fi. **$**

# SOUTHERN AND CENTRAL MINDANAO

## Davao City

**Casa Leticia**
J. Camus Street, Davao
Tel: 082-224 0501
www.casaleticia.com
A Spanish-style hotel in the city center; studio rooms. **$$**

**Hotel Galleria**
Gov. Duterte Street, Davao
Tel: 082-221-2480
Situated in the financial/entertainment district. Spanish-Mediterranean-inspired structure, with waterfall-fed swimming pool. **$$**

**My Hotel**
San Pedro Street at Legaspi Street
Tel: 082-222-2021
www.myhoteldavao.com
Centrally located hotel with air conditioning, restaurants, Wi-fi. **$**

**Royal Mandaya Hotel**
J. Palma Gil Street, Davao
Tel: 082-225-8888
theroyalmandayahotel.com

**BELOW:** many upmarket hotels offer spa treatments and massages.

Centrally located hotel, contemporary design; transfers arranged for the 30-minute drive from the airport. Amenities include a business center and pool. **$$–$$$**

**Villa Margarita Hotel**
J.P. Laurel Avenue, Bajada, Davao
Tel: 082-221-5674/75
www.villamargaritahotel.com
A cozy, peaceful hotel, with restaurant-bar and pool. Located halfway between town and airport. **$$**

**Waterfront Insular Hotel**
J.P. Laurel Avenue, Lanang, Davao
Tel: 082-233-2881–87
www.waterfronthotels.com.ph
A Davao institution, offering beachside location, restaurants, jogging path, poolside gym, private pier, weaving center. Close to airport, Lanang Golf Course, casino, and Davao Museum. **$$$**

**White Mansion**
14 Alaminos Street, Rolling Hills Bacaca Road, Davao
Tel: 082-222-1048
www.whitemansion.com
Self-contained, home-like rooms with kitchens. Internet; parking **$$$**

## Samal Island

**Bluewaters Beach Resort**
Tel/Fax: 082-225-4009
Centrally located. White sandy beachfront with shaded tables and huts. Mediterranean-style guest-rooms with terrace and view. **$$**

**Paradise Island Park and Beach Resort**
Samal, 1181-Km 9, Sasa, Davao
Tel: 082-233 0251/52
www.paradiseislanddavao.com
Rooms with fan or air conditioning. Seafood restaurant near beach. Bar, sports facilities, mini-zoo, and park. **$$**

**Pearl Farm Beach Resort**
Damosa Complex, Lanang, Davao
Tel: 082-221-9970
Manila tel: 02-750-1896–8
www.pearlfarmresort.com
The 11-hectare (27-acre) former pearl farm has modern facilities in native-inspired rooms and cottages. Arranges transfers from Davao. **$$$$**

## South Cotabato/Gen. Santos City

**Hotel Delores**
Santiago Boulevard, General Santos City
Tel: 083-552-4139
doloreshotels.rdgroup.com.ph
Close to public market and financial center. Air-conditioned rooms, cable TV, business services; restaurant. **$**

**Above:** waiter at the Waterfront Insular Hotel, Davao City.

**Durian Garden ATBP**
Awas, Sulit, Polomolok, South
Cotabato, 24km (15 miles)
northwest of General Santos City
Cell tel: 0921-686-1729
duriangarden.blogdrive.com
Rooms in the shadow of Mt
Matutum on a durian
orchard, with pomelo and
other fruit trees, birds and
animals. **$**

**Family Country Hotel and
Convention Center**
Mateo Road, Lagao, General
Santos City
Tel: 083-552-8895–7
e-mail: fchcc@bayandsl.com
Spread out over two com-
plexes. Simple, affordable
rooms and cheery staff. **$–$$**

**Sydney Hotel**
Pioneer and Roxas avenues,
General Santos City
Tel: 083-552-5478–81
Excellent service and good
accommodations with views

of the city and Mt Matutum
or Sarangani Bay. Piano bar
and ballroom. Vancouver
Plaza Restaurant serves
seafood. **$$**

## North Cotabato

**Highlander Hotel**
Osmena Drive, Kidapawan
Tel: 064-288-1445
Conveniently located, pri-
vate, with tribal design; res-
taurant. **$$**

## Maguindanao

**Hotel Cerilona**
Sinsuat Avenue,
Cotabato
Tel: 064-421-7523–24
Elegant hotel, Islam-
inspired lobby. **$$**

**Estosan Garden Hotel**
Gov. Gutierrez Street, Cotabato
City
Tel: 064-421-6777
www.estosanhotel.com
Sprawling venue with flower
garden. Modern conveni-
ences with nostalgic
touches, away from city
center. **$$**

**Evie's Gardenville**
Second Streeet at Don E. Sero
Street, Cotabato
Tel: 064-421-2271
Set in tropical garden.
Sunrise view from terrace.
**$**

**Pacific Heights Hotel**
66 Don Juliano Avenue,
Cotabato
Tel: 064-421-7517
Air-conditioned rooms with
cable TV and free shuttles to
airport and downtown.
Steam bath, spa, seminar
facilities, food and beverages services, business
center. **$$**

# NORTHERN MINDANAO AND CARAGA

## Misamis Oriental

**Cha-Li Beach Resort**
Cugman, CDO
Tel: 08822-732-929, 732-840
www.chalibeach.com
Near Macajalar Bay,
surrounded by cottages,
convention halls. Rooms
have air conditioning, cable
TV. **$**

**D'Budgetel**
Corrales Extension, CDO
Tel: 088-856-4200
info@budgetel.ph
budgetelcdo.brinkster.net
Family-friendly budget hotel,
shared bathrooms, air con-
ditioning. **$**

**Dynasty Court Hotel**
Tianno Hayes Street, CDO
Tel: 08822-724-516
Downtown location;
Chinese-inspired interior.
Live band. Internet access.
**$$**

**Malasag Resort**
Alwana Business Park, Cugman,
CDO

Tel: 088-855-2198
e-mail: marco@alwana.com
Full amenities, including a
ballroom, restaurant, business center, pool, and
jacuzzi. Big lawn and fine
views. **$$$**

**Parkview Hotel**
Tirso Neri Street, CDO
Tel: 08822-726-565
Simple, new, centrally
located lodgings. **$**

**River View Inn**
Vamenta Boulevard, CDO
Tel: 088-858-4245/46
Located along Cagayan
River, 20-minute drive from
airport and seaport.
International cuisine and
open-air café; internet. **$**

**Southwinds Hotel**
Captain Vicente Roa Ext., CDO
Tel: 08822-727-623
This white-washed hotel has
hardwood floors, garden,
and a small lawn. Parking.
Live jazz band. Near shop-
ping malls. **$**

## Camiguin

**Camiguin Beach and
Country Club**
Yumbing,
Mambajao
Tel: 088-387-9028
www.camiguinbeachandcountryclub.
com
Fronting White Island. Pool,
tree-lined beach, telephone,
parking, restaurant, pump-
boat, bar. **$$**

**Casa Grande Hotel and
Café**
Poblacion Mambajao
Tel: 088-387-2075
Renovated old Spanish
house opposite the municipal building. Reservations
recommended, especially
during Lanzones Festival
(October) and Lenten sea-
son. **$$**

**Caves Dive Resort**
Agoho, Mambajao
Tel: 088-387-9040
www.cavesdiveresortcamiguin.com
Opposite White

Island; scenic view from
native-design rooms. Air
conditioning or fan, nipa
and bamboo cottages.
Walking distance to Ardent
Spring. **$**

## Misamis Occidental

**Minerva Tourist Inn**
Washington Street, Ozamis City
Tel: 088-521-0065
Clean, busy inn. Simple,
tasteful designs and furni-
ture **$**

**Plaza Beatriz Hotel**
Port Road, Ozamis
Tel: 088-521-1394–5
Picture windows give views
of bustling city and nearby
port area. **$$**

**Royal Garden Hotel**
Burgos Corner Zamora Street,
Ozamis City
Tel: 088-521-2888–9
www.royalgardenozamis.com
Large hotel with well-
appointed rooms in city
center. **$**

## Lanao del Norte

**Bukidnon**

**Haus Malibu**
Bonifacio Drive corner Camisio Street, Malaybalay
Tel: 088-221-5741
hausmalibu.blogspot.com
Garden setting, clean, comfortable. Fan, cable TV, fridge, phone, hot showers. **$**

**Caprice Pensionne House**
Badelles corner Lluch Street, Iligan
Tel: 063-221-2018
Clean hotel. Close to fast food and public transport. **$**

**Corporate Inn**
5 Sparrow Street, Isabel Village, Pala-o, Iligan
Tel: 063-221-4456–8
Secluded inn at the foothills of Mt Agad-Agad. Lobby bar and dinette looks onto mountain. **$$**

**Maria Cristina Hotel**
Gen. Aguinaldo Street, Iligan
Tel: 063-221-5308, 221-3352
Iligan's oldest hotel, fronts city plaza. Near mall and transport. Café, live band. **$$**

**Pine Hills Hotel**
Fortich Street, Malaybalay
Tel: 088-221-3211
Ornamental plants; café-cum-bistro in the lobby – perfect for lounging. **$**

## Agusan del Norte

**Almont Hotel**
San Jose Street, Butuan City
Tel: 085-342-5263/64
View of Rizal Park; café in a garden setting with artificial waterfall. **$$**

**Hotel Karaga**
Montilla Boulevard, Butuan
Tel: 085-341-5405, 342-8387
www.hotelkaraga.com
A popular hotel offering air conditioning, cable TV, phone, restaurants, bar, and internet access. **$–$$**

**Red Palm Suites and Restaurant**
Villa Kanangga Road, Butuan City
Tel: 085-341-2000
Central location, behind provincial capitol building; restaurant, convention center. **$**

## Agusan del Sur

**Diwata Training Center and Resort**
Purok 3, San Isidro, San Francisco
Tel: 085-343-8185
Handicraft training center converted into a sprawling resort of native design. Fishpond, karaoke bar. **$**

## Surigao del Sur

**Royal Christian Hotel**
Tandag
Tel: 086-211-3140, 211-5002
Spacious and cozy, with a garden at the back. Beds made of rare Philippine hardwood. **$**

## Surigao del Norte

**Cabuntog Lodge & Cottages**
Takbo, General Luna, Siargao
Cell tel: 0919-363-2507
Basic accommodation on a lagoon, between Gen. Luna and Cloud 9. **$**

**Grande Suites**
Ramon Kaimo St.,San Juan, Surigao City
Tel: 086-826-6396
www.thegrandesuites.com
Cozy rooms, restaurant. **$$**

**Ocean 101**
Cloud 9, Gen. Luna, Siargao
Cell tel: 0910-848-8093
www.ocean101cloud9.com
Clean simple rooms, cable TV, food; geared toward surfers. **$$**

**Pansukian Tropical Resort**
Gen. Luna, Siargao Island
Cell tel: 0918-903-9055
www.pansukian.com
Manila: 02-813-8718, 817-0169
Native furnishing (bamboo, rattan basketry, wood decoration), restaurant, kayaking, open-air massage hut, beachfront hammocks. **$$$$**

**Philippine Gateway Hotel**
Km. 2 Checkpoint, Surigao
Tel: 086-232-4257
www.gatewayhotel.com.ph
Large hotel with air conditioning, cable TV, parking, a flower garden in front, and rural views. **$**

**Sagana**
Cloud 9, Gen. Luna, Siargao
Cell tel: 0919-809-5769
www.cloud9surf.com
Well-decorated rooms, with world-famous surf breaks 200 meters' (650ft) walk away. Restaurant. **$$–$$$**

# ZAMBOANGA

## Zamboanga del Norte

**Camila Hotel**
General Luna Street, Dipolog City
Tel: 065-212-3009
Tribal design. Big lawn with children's playground, babysitting services. **$$**

**Dakak Park and Beach Resort**
Dakak, Brgy Taguilon, Dapitan
Echaves Street corner Quezon Avenue, Dipolog
Cell tel: 0918-595-0713/16
e-mail: philt@world.net
White beach facing Sulu Sea, waterfalls, spring-fed pool, modern facilities and amenities, plus aqua sports center. **$$$**

**Ramos Hotel**
Rizal Avenue corner Magsaysay Street, Dipolog
Tel: 065-212-3504
Garden terrace with excellent view of Sulu Sea. Seafood restaurant. **$**

**Top Plaza Hotel**
Quezon Avenue, corner Echavez Street, Dipolog
Tel: 065-212-5888
Near Dipolog's shopping and business center; 10 minutes from Dipolog Airport and 30 minutes from Pulawan Port in Dapitan City. **$$**

## Zamboanga del Sur

**Anson's Hotel**
Sumagdang, Isabela City, Basilan
062-200-3302
Central location. **$**

**Argamel Hotel**
Governor Camins Avenue, Zamboanga City
Tel: 062-991-2023
Nice view of the city at night. Rooftop restaurant, cable TV, shuttle service. **$**

**D'Iaville Orchard Park**
Sunrise Village, Pagadian City
Tel: 062-215-2123
Convention facility with 300-person capacity, piano bar, swimming pool; floating and non-floating cottages. **$**

**Garden Orchid Hotel**
Governor Camins Avenue, Zamboanga
Tel: 062-991-0032
www.gardenorchidhotel.com
Situated near the airport. Business center, pool, bar. **$$**

**Grand Astoria Hotel**
Major Jaldon Street, Zamboanga
Tel: 062-991-2510–15
grand.astoria.ph
Ideally located; 5–10-minute drive from the airport. Amenities include mini-bar, cable TV, restaurant, car rental, café, boutique, shuttle service, business center. **$$**

**Hotel Guillermo**
Rizal Avenue, Pagadian
Tel: 062-214-1471
Spanish-inspired look, touts ballroom dancing facility. Located at center of city, but has retained a secluded ambiance. **$$**

**Hotel Juana**
Datu Halum Street, Bongao
Tel: 068-268-1018
Central location, restaurant. **$**

**Lantaka Hotel by the Sea**
Mayor Valderrosa Street, Zamboanga
Tel: 062-991-2033
Central location. Seafood restaurant with view of wharf, bar, pool. Docked nearby are small boats to ferry tourists to Great Santa Cruz Island. **$$**

**Mardale Hotel and Convention Center**
Cabrera Street, San Francisco District, Pagadian City
Tel: 062-215-4366
www.mardalehotel.com
Range of room sizes, central location. **$$**

## PRICE CATEGORIES

Price categories are for a standard double room.

**$** = less than US$20
**$$** = 20–50
**$$$** = 50–100
**$$$$** = over US$100

TRANSPORTATION

ACCOMMODATIONS

EATING OUT

ACTIVITIES

A – Z

LANGUAGE

# EATING OUT

# RECOMMENDED RESTAURANTS, CAFES & BARS

**ABOVE:** fast food, Manila-style.

Lavish ambiance best characterizes higher-end restaurants. Specific hallmarks are tropical landscaping, live bands, or dozens of bamboo-woven outdoor tables. These restaurants often specialize in a particular type of cuisine. Better restaurants in popular resort areas are attached to the posh hotels.

Foreigners are always welcome to eat with the masses at the low and middle end. Market stall diners or roadside restaurants with wobbly pockmarked tables serve a range of local food, usually with an emphasis on grilled meats. A meal big enough to last all day may cost less than P250 (US$6). The food is often served buffet style from trays or vats.

One tip: Pick back-ups before ordering, as restaurants often run out of core ingredients, or even beer, and are slow to replace them.

For those on shoestring budgets, fruits and vegetables can be bought very cheaply at markets to supplement packaged soups and noodles.

## What to Eat

American, French, Italian, and Thai eateries can be found in the bigger cities. German cuisine has sprung up in resort areas to serve northern European long-stay travelers. The Yellow Cab chain makes international-caliber pizza nationwide. Large, gaudy Chinese restaurants are common in Manila. The nationwide ChowKing chain churns out more pedestrian Chinese dishes. (See page 86.)

Fast food is prominent. Local chains such as Jollibee and Chooks use flashy facades to sell fried or roasted chicken, vying with Western fast-food conglomerates. The nationwide Mang Insasal chain has added traditional Filipino rice dishes and *sinigang* soups to the mix. At the Mall of Asia in Manila, where a pair of food courts are so long one can't see from end to end, smaller chains make regional specialties such as Bacolod's chicken recipes or the Ilocos favorite veggie dish *pinakbet*. One sells *bibingka*, a rice-based dessert cake. Fast-food chains keep long, late hours (often open 24 hours in Jollibee's case), while business at other restaurants waxes and wanes with conventional meal times until 9 or 10pm.

## Restaurant Listings

Restaurants are listed by area in the same order as they appear in the Places section of the book. Hotel restaurants in Manila are among the best. In smaller cities, dining options may be limited, though resorts often hire professional chefs and it pays to follow your nose in lively downtown areas where eateries abound. For the latest information on Philippine restaurants, visit www. munchpunch.com.

Manila restaurants are categorized by the type of food served; restaurants elsewhere are listed alphabetically.

# MANILA

## Filipino

**Andok's Lechon Manok**
Tel: 02-372-4033
www.andokscorp.com/
Numerous Andok's outlets are located throughout Manila and beyond – look for the yellow sign with a heart. They serve excellent roasted chicken (*manok*) and *lechon* (roast pig). Carry out; cash only. **$**

**The Aristocrat**
432 San Andres Street corner Roxas Boulevard, Malate
Tel: 02-524-7671–80
www.aristocrat.com.ph
Delicious barbecued chicken and *kare-kare* (oxtail); 24-hour takeout counter. **$**

**Casa Xocolat**
B. Gonzales Street, off Katipunan, by Ateneo University, Quezon City
Tel: 02-929 -4186
www.xocolat.com.ph
A wonderful little place celebrating the Pinoy love for cacao and chocolate in their different forms, from churros to rich hot drinks, to fondues that will put a smile on your face. Focaccia sandwiches and other creative entrées are on the menu too. There's also Wi-fi internet access and a pleasant patio. **$**

**Gerry's Grill**
12 branches around Manila and Luzon, including:
20 Jupiter Street corner Antares Bel-Air, Makati
Tel: 02-332-1111
www.gerrysgrill.com/
Ultra-cheap Filipino food. Request a seat outside – it can be noisy inside. The chargrilled (*inihaw*) squid and tuna belly, tuna or traditional *tanigue kinilaw* (marinated raw fish) and *kilawin puso ng saging* (marinated heart of banana) are recommended. For dessert, try *leche* flan custard or the refreshing *pandan-buko* dessert. Reservations recommended. **$**

**Ihaw-Ihaw, Kalde-Kaldero**
(Singing Cooks and Waiters)
Roxas Boulevard corner Gil Puyat Avenue (Buendia), Pasay City
Tel: 02-832-0658, 831-5015
J.P. Rizal corner Makati Avenue, Makati
Tel: 02-899-7528
Quezon Boulevard, Quezon City
Tel: 02-372-3204
The food is Pinoy and the waiters even more so, entertaining you with song while you wait. **$**

**Kamayan**
47 Arnaiz Avenue (Pasay Road), Makati
Tel: 02-892-8897
Use your fingers to lift rice and meats off the banana leaf. Recommended are the *lechon de leche* (roasted piglet), crispy *pata* (fried ham hocks) and *kare-kare*. The other branches are located at West Avenue (Quezon City), Greenhills, Pasay Road (Makati), Megamall, Glorietta, and Robinson's. **$**

**Lami Barbecue**
South Road corner Parade Street, Luneta Park, Intramuros
Tel: 02-400-7440
Charcoal-roasted Cebuano food is served here. A second, smaller branch (no phone) has recently opened along the Baywalk stretch of Roxas Boulevard, perfect for watching Manila's famous sunsets. Two great locations near the waterfront. **$**

## Chinese

**Chuan Kee**
G/F, 650 Ongpin corner Nueva Street, Binondo
Tel: 02-242-9759
This Chinatown institution has served home-made soups and special brews for more than 70 years. Cash only. **$**

**Gloria Maris**
10 branches in the Metro area, including Greenhills Shopping Center, Ortigas Avenue, San Juan,
Tel: 02-722-5508
G/F, Rockwell Powerplant
Tel: 02-897-8310
Try the fried crab, baked lobster or Peking duck. *Dim sum* all day. **$$**

**The Legend (Hong Kong) Seafood Restaurant**
Boom na Boom Compound, CCP Complex, Roxas Boulevard, Pasay City
Tel: 02-833-1188, 833-3388
Choose your fish or other seafood from the aquarium, Hong Kong style. Salt-and-pepper squid and fish lip soup are among the most popular here. **$**

**North Park**
1200 Makati Ave
Tel: 02-897-9039
www.northpark.com.ph
Check the website to find the nearest branch of this ever-expanding chain. Well-priced Chinese food in clean, ambient surroundings makes this a favorite until the 3am closing time. **$$**

**Pot and Noodle House**
Level 4 Building A, SM Megamall EDSA, Mandaluyong
Tel: 02-634-1260/61
Jupiter Place, 136 Jupiter Street, Makati
Tel: 02-899-8999
SM Manila
Tel: 02-522-8840/9159
Hand-pulled noodles in soup, dumplings, and claypot meals. Good for business lunches. **$**

**Quick Snack**
637–639 Carvajal Street, Binondo
Tel: 02-851-0226
A favorite, quick lunchtime spot with Chinatown locals. *Lumpia* (spring rolls) that are fresh, not fried, and *kunchay-ah* (pastries filled with meat and vegetables). **$**

**BELOW:** Korean restaurants abound in Manila.

## PRICE CATEGORIES

Prices are for a meal per person:
**$** = under US$5
**$$** = US$5–10
**$$$** = US$10–25
**$$$$** = over US$25

**Seafood Market Restaurant**
1190 Jorge Bocobo,
Ermita
Tel: 02-524-5761, 521-6969
Choose your own live seafood and vegetables, and then tell the chef precisely how you like it. **$$**

**Seafood Wharf Restaurant**
Army-Navy Club Compound, South Drive, Luneta Park
Tel: 02-536-3522
Choose your own fresh ingredients and let the chef get to work. Relax on the open-air deck overlooking Manila Bay, or take a quick dip in the pool before dinner. Great sunset view. **$**

**Tin Hau**
Mandarin Oriental Hotel, Makati
Tel: 02-750-8888
Delicate Chinese food at hotel prices. Try the steamed or baked crab and garoupa (*lapu-lapu*), Peking duck, and Sichuanese specialties. *Dim sum* from 11.30am–2.30pm. **$$**

## Japanese and Korean

**Furusato Japanese Restaurant**
Level 1, Glorietta, Ayala Center Makati
Tel: 02-892-5115
1712 Roxas Boulevard, Pasay City
Tel: 02-525-1005
Authentic Japanese cuisine. **$$**

**Inagiku**
Makati Shangri-La Hotel, Ayala corner Makati Avenue
Tel: 02-81-8888
Order sushi by the set or sit by the grill. **$$$**

**Kaya Korean Restaurant**
6 branches, including:
62 Jupiter Street, Bel-Air, Makati
Tel: 02-895-0404
Korean barbecue. Try the *bulgogi* (roasted beef), *kalbi gui* (short ribs), and *japchae* (clear sweet potato noodles). **$$**

**Korea Garden**
128 Jupiter Street, Makati
Tel: 02-895-5443, 896-4361
Popular Korean restaurant. **$–$$**

**Shinjuku Ramen House**

7853 Makati Avenue corner Hercules Street, Makati
Tel: 02-890-6107
www.shinjukuramenhouse.com/homewp/about-us/branch
Great bowls of ramen; *gyoza* (dumplings) is a specialty. A favorite among Japanese residents. **$**

**Wasabi Bistro and Sake Bar**
7912 Makati Avenue, Makati
Tel: 02-840-4223, 892-3707
Stylish atmosphere, updating traditional Japanese delicacies with a modern twist. Try signature dishes such as #1 Special and Dynamite Sushi Rolls. **$$$**

## Southeast Asian

**Benjarong Royal Thai Restaurant**
Mezzanine Level, Dusit Hotel Nikko, Makati
Tel: 02-867-3333, 867-3888, 238-8888
Some of the best Thai food in Makati. Open daily for lunch and dinner. **$$$**

**Phobac Vietnamese Specialties**
Level 1, Robinson's Galleria, Ortigas Center, Pasig City
Tel: 02-632-9460
Level 2, Glorietta
Tel: 02-894-4308
Level 1, Robinson's Place, Ermita
Tel: 02-586-3176
G/F, Fort Bonifacio, Global City
Tel: 02-815-6529
A popular noodle shop chain with hearty meals at good prices. **$**

**Soms Thai Noodle House**
5921 Alger Street, Makati; Maysilo Street, Mandaluyong City
Tel: 02-757-8079
Cheap Thai food. Must-tries are the Thai milk tea, catfish salad, and the curries. Open daily 9am–11pm. **$**

**Spices**
The Peninsula Manila, Ayala corner Makati Avenue, Makati
Tel: 02-887-2888
www.peninsula.com/Manila/en/Dining/Spices/default.aspx
Asian selections, including Thai and Indian, in lush, luxurious setting. **$$**

## Indian and Middle Eastern

**Hossein's Persian Kebab**
7857 Ikv Building, Makati Avenue (near Jupiter), Makati
Tel: 02-890-5928, 890-8503
Classy Middle Eastern dining. Kebabs, hummous, and vegetarian entrées. **$$**

**Ziggurat Restaurant**
Ground Level, Sunette Tower, Durban Street, Makati
Tel: 02-897 5179
www.zigguratcuisine.com
Varied menu with samplings from the Mediterranean, India, Africa, and the Middle East. This oasis in the bustling P. Burgos Street area has an outdoor patio with comfortable seating. **$$**

## Italian

**California Pizza Kitchen**
Alabang Town Center, 2nd Level, Alabang Commercial Corporation, Alabang-Zapote Road, Muntinlupa
Tel: 02-850-5771
www.cpk.com.ph/
Shangri-la Plaza Mall, 2nd Level, EDSA corner Shaw Boulevard, Mandaluyong City
Tel: 02-687-7841–2
243 Tomas Morato corner Fuentabella Street, Quezon City
Tel: 02-372-7371–2
Glorietta, 1st Level, Glorietta 3, Ayala Center, Makati
Tel: 02-893-9898
Greenhills Promenade, Ground Level, San Juan
Tel: 02-725-7377
Pizzas are regarded as gourmet; salads are among the best in town. **$$**

**Il Ponticello**
2/F, Antel 2000, 121 Valero Street, Makati
Tel: 02-887-7168, 887-4998
Trendy Italian eatery. Try Chef Romeo Garchitorena's *risotto del Boscaiolo* and *ai funghi Porcini con Gorgonzola*. The restaurant turns into a modern late-night bar. **$$**

**L'Opera**
26th Street corner 5th Avenue, Fort Bonifacio, Taguig
Tel: 02-889-3963, 889-2784
www.loperagroup.com
Home-made pizzas and pastas; good ravioli. Open daily for lunch and dinner. **$$**

**Mi Piace**
The Peninsula Manila, Makati
Tel: 02-810-3456
Exquisite Italian dining with the focus on seafood. Try the grilled seabass. **$$$**

**Paparazzi**
2/F, Shangri-La EDSA Hotel, Ortigas Center
Tel: 02-633-8888
www.shangri-la.com/manila/edsashangrila/dining/restaurants/paparazzi/
A popular business lunch destination featuring northern Italian specialties. Try the pasta and rib-eye steak. **$$–$$$**

**Portico 1771**
Serendra Piazza, Ground Level, Fort Bonifacio, Taguig
Tel: 02-856-0581–5
Creative Italian food in a fabulous music bar setting. **$$**

## Continental

**Barbara's Restaurant**
Plaza San Luis, Gen. Luna Street, Intramuros
Tel: 02-527-3893
www.barbarasrestaurantandcatering.com
Spanish and Filipino cuisine. Try the seafood bonbon, wrapped in filo pastry and baked in lemon butter. **$$**

**Casa Armas**
J. Nakpil Street corner Bocobo Malate
Tel: 02-523-5763
*Bocarones* (marinated sardines with garlic), Spanish sausage, garlic shrimp and olives; paella, garlic chicken (order in advance) and unbelievable crab. Reservations recommended. **$$**

**Casa Armas Tapas Bar y Restaurante**
132 Jupiter Street, Bel-Air Makati City
Tel: 02-897-3605, 897-3542
With more space than the original Malate restaurant, Makati's Casa Armas offers the same food as the original. Reservations recommended. **$$**

**Chateau 1771**
El Pueblo Real, ADB Avenue corner Vargas, Ortigas Center, Pasig City
Tel: 02-729-9761
www.chateaugroup.com/

TRANSPORTATION · ACCOMMODATIONS · EATING OUT · ACTIVITIES · A–Z · LANGUAGE

Featuring "no borders" cuisine, from seafood jambalaya and steak to beef fondue and soufflés. **$$$**

**El Cirkulo**
900 Arnaiz Avenue (Pasay Road) corner Paseo de Roxas, Makati
Tel: 02-810-8735
www.elcirkulo.com
Innovative Spanish cuisine with excellent tapas. **$$**

**Florabel**
G/F, The Podium, 18 ADB Avenue, Ortigas Center, Manadaluyong
Tel: 02-638-7527, 667-3220
Continental cuisine in a low-key, cozy environment. Signature dishes are the Wagyu rib eye, the crispy prawn salad, and the foie gras burger. **$$$**

**Gaudi**
Greenbelt 3, 4th Level, Makati
Tel: 02-757-2710, 757 2711
Serendra Piazza, G/F, Fort Bonifacio, Taguig
Tel: 02-854-0474, 856-0473
Spanish cuisine from some of the best Castilian chefs this side of Madrid. **$$$$**

**Ilustrado**
744 Calla Real del Palacio Intramuros (formerly Gen. Luna)
Tel: 02-527-3674
www.ilustradorestaurant.com.ph
Evokes the lifestyle of well-traveled Filipinos of the Spanish era; the *ilustrados* knew how to dine, and this

establishment features period cuisine, specializing in oysters, scallops, baked eggplant, and fine wines. **$$**

**Le Soufflé**
The Fort Bonifacio Entertainment Center, Makati
Tel: 02-890-7630, 887-5106
Seared tuna, steaks, and, of course, soufflés. Reservations recommended. **$$$$**

**Mag:net Gallery**
ABS-CBN Compound, Quezon City
Tel: 02-410-0995
Paseo de Roxas Avenue corner Sedeno Street, Makati
Tel: 02-817-7895
335 Katipunan Avenue, Quezon City
Tel: 02-929-3191
www.magnetgalleries.com
Mag:net offers a taste of the Philippines arts scene. The flagship Katipunan branch is a mix of bookstore, nightspot, gallery, and restaurant with reasonable prices. **$**

**M Café**
Ayala Museum, Greenbelt 4 Ground Level, Makati Avenue corner Legaspi Street, Makati
Tel: 02-757-3000, 757-6000
Spacious indoor seating and outdoor patios. Asian and international cuisines at a bustling weekend nightspot. **$$**

**Melo's Steak and Seafood**
58 Bohol Avenue, Quezon City
Tel: 02-924-9168
22 Jupiter Street, Makati
Tel: 02-899-9403, 899-2456
Steaks made from certified Angus beef. Reservations recommended. **$$$**

**Mexicali**
Current branches located at Greenhills (tel: 02-725-3921); Glorietta (tel: 02-894-0987); Robinsons Manila (tel: 02-400-6869); SG Megamall (tel: 02-635-6079) and other areas
www.mexicali-phil.com
Baja California cuisine in unpretentious surroundings but in hearty portions. **$**

**Old Swiss Inn**
Olympia Towers, Makati Avenue
Tel: 02-818-8251, 818-0098
Garden Plaza Hotel, Belen Street Paco
Tel: 02-522-4835
Madrigal, 2/F, BMW Building, Alabang
Tel: 02-809-2326, 809-2342
www.oldswissinn.com/location.php
Enjoy traditional Swiss pork knuckles, lamb chops, rosti potatoes, and sauerkraut. **$$**

**Patio Guernica**
1856 Jorge Bocobo Street Remedios Circle, Malate
Tel: 02-521-4415, 524-2267
www.patio-guernica.com
An old Spanish church

turned into a stylish Spanish restaurant. Cozy and romantic. **$$**

**Red Restaurant**
Makati Shangri-La Hotel, Ayala corner Makati Avenue
Tel: 02-813-8888
French and international cuisine by a Provencal chef. Try the halibut or lamb. **$$$$**

**Sala**
610 J Nakpil Street, Malate
Tel: 02-524 6770
The menu is constantly changing, and it was last listed as a Thai restaurant. Desserts include rhubarb crème brûlée and home-made ice cream. Reservations are recommended. **$$$**

**Schwarzwälder German Restaurant**
Atrium Center, Makati Avenue, Makati
Tel: 02-893-5179
Authentic German food. **$$**

**Top of the Citi/Le Soufflé**
34/F citibank Tower, 8741 Paseo de Roxas, Makati
Tel: 02-750-5810/11
Some of the best food in town served at the highest elevation. Open to non-members for dinner, Monday to Friday. A great place for evening drinks, with a commanding view over Makati. **$$$$**

# MANILA'S ENVIRONS

## Tagaytay
**Josephine's Restaurant**
Km 58, Gen. E. Aguinaldo Highway, Tagaytay
Tel: 046-871-5627
www.josephinerestaurant.com
Filipino dining with a view over Lake Taal and volcano. Try the *lechon de leche* (traditional roast piglet) and *pinakbet*, a vegetable stew with fish sauce. **$–$$**

**Sonya's Garden**
Aguinaldo Highway, west of Tagaytay
Tel: 0917-532-9097
www.sonyasgarden.com
Sonya welcomes visitors to her house, where pre-set, home-cooked lunches and dinners are served with fresh fruit

juice, in a garden. Call in advance. **$$**

## Calamba, Laguna
Various restaurants serve local *binalot* – the original Pinoy fast food in banana leaf wrappers. Usually includes fried rice, pork or chicken, and an egg. Lift the first layer of banana leaf to uncover the salt with which to dip the egg.

**Dura-Fe Restaurant**
General Jaina Street, Pagsanjan
Excellent Filipino food. **$**

**Exotic Restaurant**
National Highway, Longos, Kalayaan (near Paete)
Tel: 049-557-1036
Serves deer, wild boar,

python, turkey, eel, and monitor lizard. Visitors have captured a resident anaconda on film. **$**

**Samaral Seafood Restaurant**
National Highway, Calamba (near Pansol)
Decent seafood in a pleasant outdoor setting. **$**

## Rizal
**Balaw-Balaw Restaurant**
Doña Justa Village, Angono
Tel: 02-651-0110
Restaurant-cum-art gallery of artist-chef-owner Perdigon Vocalon. Try the game dishes – wild boar, python, monitor lizard, and frogs' legs. **$$**

**Padi's Point**
Sumulong Highway, Antipolo
Tel: 02-240-5088/89
www.padispoint.com/branches
A cluster of a bar and several restaurants popular among locals and foreigners on this mountain ridge. Among the choices, Dad's, Nipa Hut Restaurant, The Balcony, Cycling Station, Motoyori Japanese, and Leonardo's. **$**

**PRICE CATEGORIES**
Prices are for a meal per person:
**$** = under US$5
**$$** = US$5–10
**$$$** = US$10–25
**$$$$** = over US$25

## CENTRAL PLAINS

### Pampanga

**Aling Cely's Carinderia**
Nepo Complex, Angeles City
Tel: 045-888-0014
Let *Aling* (Auntie) Cely feed
you the best of
Kapampangan (local
Pampanga) cuisine. **$$**

**Aling Lucy Panciteria**
158 Pineda Street, C.M. Recto,
Angeles City
Tel: 045-874-5686
A Pampanga institution
serving Angeles for almost
50 years. Try the regional
dish *sisig* – pig's ears. **$**

**Cottage Kitchen Café**
582 Don Juico Avenue (Perimeter
Road), Clarkview Subdivision,
Balibago, Angeles City
Tel: 045-322-3366
cottagecafe.tripod.com
Cajun and American soul
food from a former US Air
Force major who is right
when he says his barbecue
is so good "it'll make you go
home and slap your
momma." **$**

**Ituro Mo Iluto Ko**
Olongapo–Gapan Expressway,
San Fernando
Tel: 045-961-5417/18
The name translates as "I
point it, you cook it," in ref-
erence to the restaurant's
original set-up. This is the
original branch of the
Cabelen chain in Manila.
Filipino food. **$**

**Blue Boar Inn**
Tel: 045-892-6256
www.margarita-station.com/hotels/
lacasa.html
Owned by an American
expat, this quiet, dim, multi-
chamber restaurant serves
Western food, pours beers,
and mixes drinks. Pool;
darts. **$–$$**

### Zambales

**Golden Dragon**
Aguinaldo Street corner Canal
Road, Subic Bay
Tel: 047-252-2222
Authentic Chinese food pre-
pared by Hong Kong chefs.
Large setting good for ban-
quets. **$$**

**Magic Lagoon**
Building 716,
Bicentennial Park,
Rizal Highway,
Subic Bay
Tel: 047-252-1475
Fish caught in the
restaurant's lake are
cooked Filipino style for
atmospheric outdoor
dining. Open 24 hours.
**$$**

## ILOCOS REGION

### Hundred Islands, Pangasinan

**Maxine by the Sea**
Lucap, Alaminos
Tel: 075-551-2537
Simple cuisine, including
fresh seafood. Overlooks
the Hundred Islands. Similar
to other hotel restaurants in
the area. **$**

### La Union

**Fat's Bar and Grill**
Se-Bay Resort, Urbiztondo,
San Juan
Tel: 072-888-4075
Typical Filipino food with a
view of sea and surfers. **$**

**S.O.U.L. Café**
Camp 1, Main Highway,
Rosario, by the Shell Station
Tel: 072-712-0852
Highway stop, right before
(or after) the demanding zigzags of Kennon Road that
goes to Baguio. Pastries and
coffee, including a variety
that has been partly fer-
mented in the stomach/
intestines of a civet. **$**

### Ilocos Sur

**Café Leona**
Near plaza, Crisologo Street,
Vigan
Tel: 077-722-2212
Chicken barbecue, squid
salad, Thai food buffets. **$**

**Ciudad Fernandina Hotel**
26 Mabini Street,
Vigan
Tel: 077-722-3765
Beer and Western foods,
including soups, pastas,
and burgers, in quiet colonial garden environment.
**$$**

### Ilocos Norte

**Chinese Full Moon**
Ft Ilocandia Resort,
Barrio Caylayab,
Laoag City
Tel: 077-772-1166–70
Hotel restaurant serving
Taiwanese cuisine. **$$–$$$**

**La Preciosa**
Rizal Street,
Laoag
Tel: 077-773-1162
Ilocano dining, not far from
Texicano Hotel. **$**

**Stone House Cafe**
Airport Road, Laoag City
Coffees, chocolate des-
serts, pastas, salads in
cozy, rustic European-style
setting. **$$**

## NORTHEAST LUZON

### Cagayan

**Bali Leisure Club/The Port**
Pallua Road,
Tuguegarao City
Tel: 078-844-7808,
846-3283
Japanese and local cui-
sines, *pulutan* (finger food
that accompanies drinks). **$**

**Family Fastfood and Bakeshop**
College Avenue at Taft Street,
Tuguegarao City
Tel: 078-844-2110
Buttered chicken, fish fillet,
adobo, pork roll, and other
dishes in university area. **$**

**Kusina Cagayuna**
Pengue Ruyu,
Tuguegarao City
Tel: 078-844 2880
Down-home Ilocano food,
such as *pinakbet* (meat and
vegetable stew), *inabrao*
(vegetable stew), and *bag-
net* (deep-fried pork). **$**

**Pampangueña Restaurant**
Bonifacio Street,
Tuguegarao
Tel: 078-844-1829
Modest, with specialties like
*kare-kare* and *sinigang*.
Open 7am–8pm. **$**

### Isabela

**King George Hotel**
Bonifacio Avenue, Victory Norte
Santiago
Tel: 078-682-8743
Tenderloin and Spanish
omelet. Request King
George Sunriser special.
**$**

**Vanda Café**
Paguirigan Street,
Ilagan
Tel: 078-624-2050
Serves deer and steak;
weekly exotic specialties.
**$**

### Nueva Vizcaya

**Bread N' Bites Bakery & Restaurant**
National Highway,
Solano
Tel: 078-326-6085
A competitive likeness to
Jollibee. Very popular. **$**

**FTM Fastfood & Restaurant**
Bayombong,
Nueva Vizcaya
Tel: 078-321-2572
Serves Filipino, Japanese,
and Chinese food.
Ballroom, big-screen TV,
karaoke. **$**

### PRICE CATEGORIES

Prices are for a meal per
person:
**$** = under US$5
**$$** = US$5–10
**$$$** = US$10–25
**$$$$** = over US$25

# CENTRAL CORDILLERA

## Benguet

**Bliss Café**
Munsayac Inn, Leonard Wood
Road (across Teachers Camp),
Baguio
Tel: 0917-846-4729
blissnbaguio.multiply.com, also
Facebook
Art and music space offer-
ing lacto-vegetarian and
vegan food, taking advan-
tage of Baguio's fresh pro-
duce. **$**

**Café by the Ruins**
Shuntug Road, in front of
Baguio City Hall
Tel: 074-442-4010
This garden café also takes
advantage of Baguio's
fresh produce. With its own

bakery and an Igorot-style
*ato*, it is the perfect place
for drinking mountain tea.
**$$**

**Le Fondue Bar and
Restaurant**
112 Session Road,
Baguio
Shares space with food
stalls until dinner, when it
has the second-floor deck
all to itself until 9pm, or
later if there is live music.
Fondue dishes lead the
menu. **$**

**OMG (Oh My Gulay)**
4th Floor, La Azotea Building,
Baguio
Vegetarian restaurant
("*gulay*" means veggies)

with artistic delivery. Organic
salads, pasta, desserts, and
a non-alcoholic drinks list.
Theme park-like layout. **$**

**PNKY Café**
13 Leonard Wood Road, Baguio
Tel: 074-446-7094
pnkyhome.com/pnkycafe
Part of a bed-and-breakfast
accommodation, the café
serves all-day Filipino and
American breakfasts as well
as a large selection of
dishes from steaks and
burgers to pizzas and pas-
tas. **$**

## Mountain Province

**Log Cabin Bar & Café**
Uphill from the jeep parking

plaza, Sagada
Tel: 0920-520-0463; also on
Facebook
French chef; order from a
special menu before 4pm
for dinner later that night.
**$**

**Yoghurt House**
Downhill from the Town Hall,
Sagada
Home-made yogurt, hearty
Western-style breakfasts.
**$**

## Ifugao

For restaurants in Banaue,
see Accommodation list-
ings, page 341.
Independent restaurants
are rare in these parts.

# BICOL

## Camarines Norte

**Louie's Restaurant**
Daet, Camarines Norte
Tel: 054-571-2801
Local cuisine served in
native setting. Fast service,
clean. **$**

## Camarines Sur

**Molino Grill**
G/F SM City Naga, Ninoy and
Cory Avenues, Naga
Tel: 054-472-8011
A simple places for Filipino
dishes and beer. **$**

**Naga Restaurant**
Gen. Luna Street, Naga City

Tel: 054-473-8736
Filipino and Chinese dishes.
**$$**

**Patio Magdelena**
Burgos Street, Sta Cruz,
Naga
Tel: 054-473-9828
Filipino cuisine by the pool-
side in Hotel Mirabella.
Open 4pm–midnight. **$**

**Plaza Grill**
Hernandez Street,
Naga City
Tel: 054-473-6534
Local food in an elegant set-
ting. Nightly entertainment.
**$**

## Albay

**Café Ola**
88 Penaranda Street, Legazpi
Tel: 052-214-3640
A 24-hour seafood restau-
rant. **$**

**Chili Peppers**
Rizal Street at Doña Aurora, Old
Albay District
Tel: 052-481-7142
Filipino food. **$**

**Lobby Lounge**
Casablanca Hotel
Peñaranda Street, Legazpi
Tel: 052-480-8334–5
Grilled prawns and tender-
loin steaks. **$**

## Sorsogon

**Kalunduan Seafood
Restaurant**
Pareja Street, Bitan-o Sorsogon
town
Tel: 056-211-1573
Fresh seafood, native cuisine, Western fare and
wholesome entertainment
by the sea. **$**

**Rizal Beach Restaurant**
Rizal Gubat, Sorsogon
Tel: 056-211-1056, 0917-418-
8233
Fresh seafood and native
dishes; overlooks Rizal
Beach. **$**

# LUZON'S ISLANDS

## Mindoro

**La Gensol Restaurant**
95 National Road,
Mamburao
Tel: 043-711-1072
Seafood galore in a marine
setting. Open 24 hours. **$**

**Traveler Restaurant**
120 National Road
Payompon,
Mamburao
Tel: 043-711-1136
Serves chop suey, pork
*tapa, calderatang usa*

(deer), and other local specialties. **$**

**Doña Lina, The Carabao,
The Dolphin, The Palmera
Café, The Barracuda**
Coco Beach,
Puerto Galera

Tel: 097-377-2115
These restaurants offer
Filipino, French, and Indian
cuisines, plus seafood, with
tropical drinks and wines.
The resort is French-owned.
**$**

# EASTERN VISAYAS

## Leyte

**Giuseppe's Restaurant**
Avenida Veteranos,
Tacloban
Tel: 053-321-8758
Italian and Filipino cuisine. **$**

**Greenhouse Kitchen**
Fatima Village,
Tacloban
Tel: 053-321-2463
Filipino dishes served in a
garden setting. **$**

**San Pedro Bay Seafoods
Restaurant**
Magsaysay Boulevard,
Tacloban
Tel: 053-325-6000
A wide variety of seafood. **$$**

**ABOVE:** the Ayala shopping mall in Cebu City has numerous eateries.

## Cebu

**Mr A's Bar & Restaurant.**
Sitio Maasmum, Busay, Lahug, Cebu
Tel. 032-232-5200
Filipino food in indoor-outdoor settings overlooking Cebu. **$$**.

**Café Laguna**
Ayala Center, Cebu Business Park
Tel: 032-233-8600
Regional and home-style Filipino cooking. Specialties include *puto bumbong* (colored rice flour steamed in bamboo tubes), *pancit palabok* (traditional noodle dish), vegetable rolls, and *sinigang* stew. **$**

**Formo Restaurant & Lounge**
Banilad Town Center, Banilad
Tel: 032-416-1990
Mexican, Vietnamese cuisine. Acoustic and Latin music at night. **$$**

**Giuseppe Pizzeria and Sicilian Roast**
Mancao Compound, Maria Luisa Road, Banilad, Cebu City
Tel: 032-343-9901
Pizza and pasta on the menu here, made with love. **$$**

**Golden Cowrie**
Salinas Drive, Lahug
Tel: 032-233-4243
www.goldencowrienativerestaurant.com

Inexpensive seafood. Native setting with pebble floors and bamboo decor. Specialties include baked mussels, lobster, sizzling squid, and grilled blue marlin. **$**

**Goodah.Gud Grill & Seafood**
#935-B Salinas Drive, Lahug
Tel: 032-234-2716
Fresh seafood, barbecue. Where the night owls go when they start getting hungry. Open 24 hours. **$**

**Gustavian**
Maria Luisa Road, Banilad
Tel: 032-344-7653
Swedish ambiance and mixed European fare. Breakfasts and a set menu. **$$**

**Ichiriki Chaya**
A.S. Fortuna Street, Banilad
Tel: 032-345-1300
Japanese restaurant, sake, and sushi bar, Korean-style barbecue, and even massage facilities. **$$**

**Kaishu**
168 Buot Punta Engano, Lapu Lapu City, Mactan
Tel: 032-495-2888
Japanese restaurant with sashimi and sushi. **$$**

**La Marea**
The Walk, Asiatown IT Park, Lahug
Desserts in cental location; try the warm brownie cup. **$$**

# CENTRAL VISAYAS

**La Tegola Cucina Italiana**
Banilad tel: 032-345-6080
Mactan tel: 032-340-9070
Upper Busay tel: 032-419-2220
Several branches around Cebu serving Italian cuisine, including one up on the hilltop park Tops, which has a view of Cebu. **$$**

**Red Moon**
GQS Building, between Petron and UFC, Banilad
Tel: 032-232-4367
Pinoy-Chinese restaurant. Specialties include honey spring chicken, *kiampong* (fried rice), and oyster omelets. **$**

**SPICE Fusions**
Banilad Town Center
Tel: 032-344-2923
www.baniladtowncentre.com/stores/food/spice-fusion
Never empty, this restaurant offers dishes from around Asia: Thai curry, Malay sate, Singaporean desserts, Filipino offerings. The *roti* (bread) may start a meal. **$$**

**STK**
Near Mactan Island Shangri-La
This assortment of foodstalls overlooking a mangrove swamp serves fresh seafood from the adjacent wet market. S for *sinugba*

(grilled food), T for *tinola* (stewed), or K for *kinilaw* (fresh food in vinegar). **$**

**Tinderbox**
Banilad Road, next to Crossroads Mall
Tel: 032-234-1681
Well-stocked wine and cigar rooms, continental menu, and a connected store with imported meats, vegetables, and other goods. **$$$**

## Bohol

**Garden Café**
J.S. Toralba St, Tagbilaran City
Tel: 038-411-3761
Western food, desserts, and a place to rest next to St Joseph's Cathedral between ferries and land transit to other parts of Bohol. **$$**

## Boracay

**Mango-Ray Boracay Resort**
Tel: 036-288-6129
www.mango-rayboracay.com
Swiss-style restaurant-bar by the beach. **$$**

**Surfside Boracay Resort**
White Beach, Angol Boracay
Tel: 036-288-3324
www.surfsideboracay.com
Continental and Japanese food, gourmet coffee by the sea. **$$**

**BELOW:** family dining, Mactan Island.

# PALAWAN

## Puerto Princesa

**Bilao at Palayok**
Rizal Avenue,
Puerto Princesa

Tel: 048-433-6910
Seafoods and native cuisine, country-style atmosphere with cottages, **$$**

**KaLui Restaurant**
369 Rizal Avenue, Puerto Princesa
Tel: 048-433-2580

www.kaluirestaurant.com
Seafood in a *nipa*-hut atmosphere. Remove shoes and lounge on floor cushions. **$$**

# SOUTHERN AND CENTRAL MINDANAO

**ABOVE:** barbecues are popular at many beach resorts.

## Davao

**Ah Fat Seafood Plaza**
Victoria Plaza Compound, Bajada
Tel: 082-224-0002
Chinese food. So popular it opened a second branch next door. **$$**

**Claude's Café de Ville**
Habana Compound,
29 Rizal Street
Tel: 082-222-4287
French cuisine, steaks, clams, and Jambalaya gumbo. **$**

**Colasa's Barbecue**
Rotunda Magallanes
Tel: 082-305-1924
Barbecue food; kamayan-style dining. Stays open late. **$**

**Luz Kinilaw Place**
Salmonan Quezon Boulevard
Tel: 082-226-4612
Grilled tuna and *kinilaw* (marinated fish dish). **$**

**Mandarin Tea Garden**
With locations in Uptown Plaza, Guerro Street, Amgar Plaza, SM Mall, and Gaisano Mall, offering affordable dim sum. **$**

**Tsuru Japanese Restaurant**
J. Camus
Tel: 082-221-0901
tsuru.com.ph
Japanese cuisine with an accent on seafood including sashimi; native coffee. **$$**

## South Cotabato

**The Garden Grill**
Anchor Hotel, Cagampang Ext. Street, General Santos
Tel: 083-552-4660
Grilled and steamed *pompano*, smoked *bangus sinigang*, grilled *bangus* belly. **$**

**Nanay Bebeng**
Gaisano Mall, J. Catolico Street, General Santos
Cell tel: 0926-326-1571
Various *viand* (rice toppings) from Cagayan/Ilocos region. **$**

**Rooftop Grill**
6/F, Sydney Hotel, Pendatun Street, General Santos
Tel: 083-552-5479/80
Sergeant fish: grilled, *kinilaw*, *sashimi*. Views overlooking bay. **$**

## North Cotabato

**Rock Star Café**
Osmeña Street, Kidapawan
Tel: 064-288-1445/46
Food and live music on some nights. **$**

**Maguindanao**
Casa Blanca
Sinsuat Avenue, Cotabato City
Tel: 064-421-2126
Local Filipino cooking in colonial wooden house. **$**

# NORTHERN MINDANAO AND CARAGA

## Misamis Oriental

**Café Alexandria**
Captain Vicente Roa Ext., Cagayan de Oro City
Tel: 08822-727-623
Red-carpet treatment, seafood, coffee. **$**

**Consuelo Steakhouse**
192 Corrales Avenue, Cagayan de Oro City
Tel: 08822-725-736
Buffets and giant desserts. **$**

**Kagay-anon Restaurant**
Rosario Arcade, Limketkai Center Lapasan, CDO
Tel: 08822-729-003
Recipient of "Kalinisan (Cleanliness) Award of Excellence." Fresh crab, Filipino delicacies: *pinakbet*
served inside squash, *kinilaw* in clam shell, *sinagang* rice in bamboo tube. **$**

**Pecan Tree Café**
Rosario Arcade, Limketkai Center Lapasan, CDO
Tel: 08822-729-292
Continental cuisine: ostrich steak, grilled pink
Tasmanian salmon. Pecan pie and gourmet coffee. **$**

**Sasutukil Seafood Grill**
Cugman, CDO
Tel: 08822-732-929
Trademark grilled seafood in a beach setting. **$**

## Camiguin

**Casa Grande Hotel and Café**
Poblacion Mambajao
Tel: 088-387-2075
Only place here for international cuisine; caters to foreigners. **$**

**RJ Pension and Restaurant**
Mabajao
Tel: 088-387-0089
Fast food, seafood. **$**

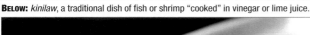

**BELOW:** *kinilaw*, a traditional dish of fish or shrimp "cooked" in vinegar or lime juice.

### PRICE CATEGORIES

Prices are for a meal per person:

**$** = under US$5
**$$** = US$5–10
**$$$** = US$10–25
**$$$$** = over US$25

**ABOVE:** Traditional Zamboangan dishes.

### Misamis Occidental

**Lapyahan Seafoods**
Bliss, Sta Cruz, Ozamis
Seafood by the beach. **$**

**La Veranda Restaurant**
Burgos corner Zamora Street,
Ozamis.
Tel: 088-521-2888/89
Seafood eatery. **$**

### Lanao del Norte

**Dear Manok**
Quezon Avenue Ext. corner La
Salle Street, Iligan City
Tel: 088-221-9221
Grilled chicken on banana
leaves. Also *kinilaw* and
*buko* juice. **$**

**Pagoda Fastfood
Restaurant**
Quezon Avenue, Iligan

Tel: 088-221-3163
Try Iligan's hottest *sepo
guisado*, a fiery mixture of
squid, fish, shrimp, vegetables, and chili. **$**

### Lanao del Sur

**Marawi Resort Hotel
Restaurant**
MSU, Marawi
Tel: 063-520-981
Maranao and non-Maranao
dishes served in traditional
Islamic ware. **$**

### Bukidnon

**Town Café and Bar**
Fortich Street, Malaybalay
Tel: 088-221-3211
Seafood in Chinese-Filipino
style. **$**

### Agusan del Norte

**Aling Cora's Lutong
Bahay**
R. Calo Street
Tel: 085-342-5281
Native delicacies. Your mom
would cook this food if she
were Cebuana. **$**

**Weegol's Garden**
Doongan, City Hall Drive,
Butuan
Tel: 085-342-5558
Garden restaurant with *nipa*
huts; serves chicken barbe-
cue on banana leaves. Also
wild boar and deer. **$**

### Surigao del Sur

**Almont Inland Resort and
Hotel**
Rizal Park, Corner San Jose

Street, Butuan City
Tel: 85-342-5263
Food by sea, pool. **$$**

### Surigao del Norte

**Berna & Carol Drive Inn**
Borromeo Street,
Surigao
Tel: 086-231-7300
Barbecued food on banana
leaves. Crowded 6–7pm.
Native setting. **$**

**Mario's Garden Grille and
Restaurant**
Next to Town Hall,
Surigao City
Tel: 086-826-2003
Garden restaurant with
live music at nights.
Barbecue and grilled sea-
food. **$**

## ZAMBOANGA

### Zamboanga del Norte

**Golden Pot Restaurant**
Arellano Street,
Dipolog
Tel: 065-212-3451
Filipino cuisine and sea-
food; home-made ice
cream. Ballroom dancing in
the evenings. **$**

### Zamboanga del Sur

**Alavar Seafood House**
Don Alfaro Street,
Tetuan

Tel: 062-991-2483
Popular seafood
restaurant, romantic
setting, sunset views.
**$**

**Café Bianca**
34 Barcelona Street,
Zamboanga City
Tel: 062-991-2514
Coffee and Filipino
cooking; balcony views.
**$**

**BELOW:** freshly cooked fish at Alavar Seafood House.

# ACTIVITIES

# FESTIVALS, THE ARTS, NIGHTLIFE, SHOPPING, AND SPECTATOR SPORTS

## CULTURE

### General

As you might expect, Manila has the country's richest mix of music, theatre, and cinema, but a smaller scene can be found in Cebu. Rock, jazz, and other popular music performances often follow tourists to hotspots such as Boracay.

A number of free magazines and websites list current happenings in the rest of the Philippines. *City Guide* (www.city-guide.ph) is a comprehensive publication, a resource for information with maps, schedules of events and business listings. The website www.bandstand.ph covers event schedules for rock and world music. The site Philippine Entertainment Portal (www.pep.ph) covers a range of musical events.

Check the **National Commission for Culture and the Arts** (NCCA) website, www.ncca.gov.ph, for events such as the Philippines Arts Festival, held every February at venues nationwide.

When in Cebu, pick up a free copy of *Bite* magazine (tel: 032-344-7047; bitemagazine.multiply.com), a pocket-sized monthly guide to music gigs, art exhibitions, live performances, and other events. It is available in top hotels, cafés, bars, and restaurants.

### Dance

**Ballet Philippines** is the country's foremost company, followed by the **Philippine Ballet Theater**. The **Bayanihan National Dance Company** and **Ramon Obusan Folkloric Group** excel in cultural and folk dancing.

These companies perform regularly at the **Cultural Center of the Philippines** (CCP). More information is available on the ccp website www.culturalcenter.gov.ph.

### Theater and Concerts

The following venues also host theatrical and musical performances:
**GSIS Theater**
GSIS Building, CCP Complex, Manila
Tel: 02-891-6161 x 4021
**Manila Metropolitan Theater**
Liwasang Bonifacio, Manila
Tel: 02-527 0892
manilamet.webs.com
**Meralco Theater**
Ortigas Avenue, Pasig City
Tel: 02-632-8848, 631-2222
Plays and musicals year-round.
**Tanghalang Pilipino**
CCP Complex, Roxas Boulevard, Manila
Tel: 02-842 0137, 832-3704
www.tanghalangpilipino.org.ph
**William J. Shaw Theater**
5/F, Shangri-La Plaza, EDSA corner

### Buying Tickets

For information about concerts and plays, call **Ticketworld** (tel: 02-891-1000; www.ticketworld.com.ph). Tickets can be purchased over the phone with credit cards, then picked up at outlets in Manila such as National Bookstores, or at Glorietta cinemas.

Ticketworld handles events held by the Cultural Center of the Philippines and the Philippine Basketball Association (PBA) games in Manila.

Shaw Boulevard, Mandaluyong
Tel: 02-633-4821-5
Performances by Repertory Philippines (www.repertory.ph).

### Music

**The Philippine Philharmonic Orchestra**, **Philippine Madrigal Singers**, and **UST Symphony Orchestra** perform regularly

**BELOW:** Buklog performance at the Cultural Center of the Philippines.

at the **Cultural Center of the Philippines** (tel: 02-832-1125; www.culturalcenter.gov.ph). Various open-air concerts are held in Rizal Park and in Paco Park.

## Movies

Movie-going is one of the best entertainment bargains in town: tickets cost P90–150. American films are the most popular. For more on movies, see page 80.

Tagalog cinema is a big deal for locals, though many of the films are of doubtful merit. The glamor inspires many young Filipinos to dream of becoming film stars.

With the opening of Mall of Asia in 2006 came the country's first IMAX movie theater (www.smcinema.com). Its eight-story screen and bone-shaking sound make for a great family trip out. Tel: 02-556-4629.

For information about movies at the various Robinsons Malls around Manila and the country (Galleria, Ermita, etc), check out www.robinsonsmovieworld.com.

ShoeMart (SM) Malls around the country, such as Megamall, Mall of Asia, and Clark, offer SM Dial-a-Movie service. Tel: 02-833-9999.

Information about Ayala Malls movie tickets (Glorietta, Greenbelt, Alabang Town Center, Ayala Center Cebu, etc) can be found at www.sureseats.com.

## Cultural Centers

**Alliance Française de Manille** (209 Nicanor Garcia Street, Bel-Air II, Makati; tel: 02-895-7585, 895-7441; www.alliance.ph) hosts cultural events, most notably French Spring and Fête de la Musique, both held in June. It's also a lunch spot.

Get in touch with the Philippines' Spanish heritage at the **Cervantes Institute** (manila.cervantes.es), a Spanish government program that has helped protect the last vestiges of the 300-year Spanish colonial rule. Check schedules for music, film, lectures, and book launches.

For those wanting a more active cultural experience, enquire at the **Clara Ramona Centro de Danza Flamenca** (5917 Alger Street, parallel to Rockwell Drive; tel: 02-890-8030 or cell tel: 0915-434-5789, www.clararamona.com) for instruction in flamenco, sevillana, and Andaluzi dancing. Classes are offered for kids, teens, and adults.

**ABOVE:** Blue Room jazz bar.

## NIGHTLIFE

Bars in the Philippines look much like those in Western countries. Almost all carry the local beers San Miguel Pilsen and San Mig Light. Barkeepers can stir up a mean rum and coke, using the local Tanduay brand. Whiskey and other hard liquors abound; wine is harder to find. Sodas and canned fruit juices usually top non-alcoholic drink lists.

## General

Manila by night is a swinging town with a flurry of ballroom dances, cinemas, bars, and casinos. Quezon City and Malate are particularly well known, but the opening of Greenbelt and the Fort have made Makati shine brightest under the Manila moonlight. Smokers take note: Makati has a no-smoking ordinance that prohibits smoking in non-designated areas of restaurants and bars.

Don't assume that beach clothes will also work on a night out in Manila; Filipinos do not always embrace casual dress for the evening.

## Manila

### Bar and Clubs

(See manilaclubbing.com for more listings and detailed descriptions.)
**Absinth**
3rd Level, Greenbelt 3, Makati
Tel: 02-757-4967
Hip hop, live and house music-fueled hip hangout.
**Blue Room**
615 Nakpil Street, Malate
Tel: 02-524-6870
**Mall of Asia, G/F**
Tel: 02-556-0288
A club for 30-somethings, piped-in jazz music.

**Café Havana**
1903 Adriatico corner Remedios, Malate
Tel: 02-521-8097, 524-5526
1st Level, Greenbelt, Makati
Tel: 02-757-4370
Cuban music and dancing. Grab a mojito and swing, or head upstairs to Hemingway's for cigars.
**Capone's**
G/F Fraser Place, Valero Street, Salcedo Village, Makati
Tel: 02-818-1818
Crowds, and an ever-changing line-up of music.
**Fez**
Piazza Serendra, Fort Bonifacio, Taguig
Tel: 02-901-1840
Plays house music, with variations during the week; Moroccan food.
**Government**
7840 Makati Avenue
House music, powerful sound system. Gay-oriented.
**Handlebar**
31 Polaris Street, off Jupiter Street, Makati

**BELOW:** there is no shortage of bars in Manila.

Tel: 02-898-1976; 898-2189
www.handlebar.com.ph
Rock 'n Blues expat hangout. Billiards;
sporting events aired on a big screen.
**Nuvo**
G/F Greenbelt 2
Tel: 02-757-3698
Swank setting for people-watching.
**Penguin Café and Gallery**
604 Remedios Circle, Malate
Tel: 02-521-2088
Alternative artists' bar; changing
exhibits.
**Piedra Bistro Bar**
3rd Floor, Fort Boni Strip, The Fort,
Taguig
Tel: 02-856-0318-20
At around 11pm, this restaurant turns
into a nightspot that spins house,
R&B, and retro music.
**Vida de Malate Restaurante**
612 Julio Nakpil Avenue, Malate
Tel: 02-523-4561
Contemporary minimalist ambiance;
bands and DJs.
**7th High**
The Fort (Bonifacio Global City),
Manila.
Cell tel: 0917-585-2164
Large club, restaurant, lounge.

*Live Music*

**Arcadia**
542 Remedios Street, Malate
Tel: 02-400-9776
Live rock music.
**70's Bistro**
46 Anonas Street, Project 2, Quezon
City
Tel: 02-434-3597
www.70sbistro.com
Live bands after 10pm.
**Hobbit House**
1801 Mabini Street, Malate
Tel: 02-521-7604
www.hobbithousemanila.com
Folk-music bar staffed by midgets.
**Ratsky Manila**
1663 Bocobo Street, Malate
Tel: 02-523-8608
Like its cousin in Cebu, this is where
rockers hang out.
**Strumm's**
110 Jupiter Street, Bel-Air, Makati
Tel: 02-895-4636, 890-1054
Live retro music after 9pm.

*Cabaret*

**Jools Cabaret**
5043 P. Burgos Street, Makati
Tel: 02-897-9061
www.jools.ph
Burlesque shows almost every night.
Naughty, but not over the top.
**The Library**
1779 Adriatico Street, Malate
Tel: 02-522-2484
www.thelibrary.com.ph

Stand-up comedy, usually in Tagalog.
You may be part of the act.

*Cafés*

**Bo's Coffee**
www.boscoffee.com
Nineteen branches in Manila (part of
a nationwide network) offer a local
alternative to international coffee
chains. Freshly roasted coffee.
**Café Breton**
European foods.
Café Bretons operate in Greenbelt,
Alabang, Podium, and Mall of Asia.
Tasty late-night eats. Call 02-771-
2114 for location details.

## Angeles City

Fields Avenue, just outside the former
Clark Air Force base, remains a major
nightlife district for foreigners and
Filipinos. Some of the most popular
go-go bars in the area are **Brown
Sugar** and **King of Diamonds**, while
huge Bangkok-style bars, such as
**Blue Nile** and **Ponytails**, have joined
the party. There are plenty of other
types of bars in Angeles as well,
including **Margarita Station** (www.
margaritastation.com), where you
will find no dancing girls but good
Thai and Mexican food. Filipino pool
personality Bata Reyes sometimes
graces the tables. At the **Blue Boar
Inn**, a familial ambience dominates
as customers eat, drink, play darts,
and crash in an attached guesthouse.

## Baguio

Baguio has a reputation for
accomplished singer-musicians, and
many a surprise can be found while
strolling up Session Road, or in other
artist nests around the city.
**Alberto's Music Lounge**
Otek Street, opposite Mt. Crest Hotel,
Baguio
Tel: 074-443-3467
Live bands from Baguio and Manila,
open daily.
**Nevada Square**
2 Loakan Road, Baguio City
Tel: 074-443-5904
Karaoke, acoustic bars, dance club,
cafés.
**Rumours**
Session Road, Baguio
Tel: 074-442-8153
Hangout for artists, writers; one of a
few bars on this strip offering acoustic
and rock music.

## Subic

Remnants of the nightlife that once
boomed during US Navy days remain

in this coastal city. It is more low-key
than Angeles. One will find friendly
seaside bars in Barrio Barretto such
as **Islander Bar**, run by a military
veteran who used to serve on US
submarines. Expats working at the
Subic Freeport gather in the evenings
at the **Rock Lobster**. The **Midnight
Rambler** is popular with European
travelers and features classic rock-
and-roll CD collections.

## Puerto Galera

**Coco Aroma Restobar**
cocoaromawhitebeach.com
Music, drinks on White Beach.
**Utopia Resort & Spa**
Barangay Palangan
Tel: 043-287-3681
www.utopiaresort.ph
Restaurant, bar just off the beach.

## Cebu City

**Paseo** (F. Cabahug Street, in Mabolo)
is the city's first year-round night
market and entertainment center,
with over 30 F&B outlets, 100 market
stalls, and a big open-air stage with
covered seating capacity of up to
2,000 people.

*Bars and Clubs*

**After Hours Tapas Lounge**
Crossroads Arcade,
Banilad
Tel: 032-233-4089
A hair salon by day literally folds up
into the walls and transforms into a
chill-out venue for food, booze, and
live soul music.
**Badgers Sports and Dining Pub**
RCBC Building, Gov. M. Cuenco
Avenue
Tel: 032-345-2199
Comfortable *Cheers*-like ambiance.
Meat pies, billiards, and draft beer.
**The Loft**
Skyrise Building, Asia Town I.T. Park
Tel: 032-345-2199
DJs play house, chill-out, and R&B
music.
**Handuraw**
460 Gorordo Avenue
Tel: 032-232-6401
Old Coaco Building, Cuenco Avenue,
Mabolo
Tel: 032-233-8678
www.handurawpizza.com
Ska, rock, acoustic, and other genres
of music; bills itself as a "pizza and
events" café.
**Jazz'n bluz**
F. Cabahug Street
Tel: 032-232-2698
www.jazznbluzcebu.com
As the name suggests, this

establishment offers live jazz and blues.

**Sunflower City**
Salinas Drive, Lahug, Cebu City
Tel: 032-231-8413
Cavernous beer hall, live music, and dancing.

**Café Teatro**
Crossroads Mall, Archbishop Reyes, Banilad
Pocket bar, house music, and piano bar, with pianist ready to play requests.

### Boracay

**Luna Negra**
White Beach, Station 2
Salsa bar in comfortable surroundings.

**Wreck Bar**
White Beach (Mangayad) Calypso Diving Resort
Tel: 036-288-3206
Fashioned to look like a wrecked ship; drinks, cigars.

### Davao City

**Blue Posts Bar & Billiards**
J.P. Laurel Avenue
Tel: 082-224-6349
Billiards and exotic *pica-pica*.

**Matina Town Square**
McArthur Highway, Matina
Tel: 082-300-1780
Live bands, both local and from Manila, sports bars, jazz, cultural shows, and stand-up comedy.

**Pag-asa Piano Bar**
G/F, The Apo View, J. Camus Street
Tel: 082-221-6430
Live band entertainment.

**Summit Bar**
9/F, Royal Mandaya Hotel, Palma Gil corner Reyes Street
Tel: 082-225-8888
A high-end sound/lighting system for

DJs and local bands.

**The Venue**
Jacinto Extension Street
Tel: 082-224-4150
Collection of disco and live band venues.

### FESTIVALS

Festival dates change from year to year. Check with local officials or visit the Philippine Department of Tourism website (www.dotpcvc.gov.ph/VPY-calendar/vpy-octdec.html) for up-to-date information. For full descriptions of the bigger events, see Fiesta Fantastica, page 69.

### January

**January 1** New Year's Day.
**First Sunday** Three Kings' Pageant, Santa Cruz and Gasan, Marinduque.
**January 9** Feast of the Black Nazarene. Quiapo, Manila.
**Third weekend** Ati-Atihan (Landing of the 10 Bornean Noblemen), Kalibo, Aklan: colorful processions; Fiesta de Santo Niño (Sinulog, the Feast of the Christ Child), Cebu City.
**January 25** Feast of St Paul, Vigan, and Vigan City Fiesta.
**Fourth weekend** Dinagyang, Iloilo (similar to Ati-Atihan).
**Variable** Appey (planting festival), Bontoc, Mountain Province.
**Variable** Santo Niño Festival: processions of images of the Child Jesus. Chinese New Year (any time between third week of Jan and mid-Feb).

### February

**February 11** Feast of Our Lady of Lourdes, Quezon City.

**Second week** Bamboo Organ Festival, Las Piñas. International Hot Air Balloon Fiesta, Clark Field.
**February 22–25** People Power at EDSA Manila: celebrates overthrow of Ferdinand Marcos.
**February 23** Sibug-Sibug Festival, Zamboanga: tribal street dances, harvest rituals.
**Last weekend** Panagbenga Flower Festival, Baguio.
**Variable** Hari Raya Hadji: Muslims mark pilgrimage to Mecca; Kaamulan Festival in Bukidnon, north Mindanao.

### March & April

**First weekend** Paraw Regatta Iloilo: race of native sailboats.
**March 10–16** Araw ng Dabaw, Davao City: town fiesta.
**April 9** Araw ng Kagitingan (Day of Valor), nationwide: commemorates the Death March.
**Lenten Week** Moriones Festival Boac, Marinduque.
**Variable** Good Friday and Easter. Seven Last Words Festival, Pampanga.

*April*
**Variable**: Butanding Festival, Donsol and Sorsogon: street parade celebration of the whale shark and its blessings to the local people.

### May

**Entire month** Santacruzan: procession of St Helena of Constantinople; Flores de Mayo: floral parades; Bohol Fiesta: pilgrimage to the Shrine of Our Lady of Peace and Good Voyage, Antipolo, Rizal.
**May 1** Labor Day, nationwide.
**May 2** Salubong (Holy Cross Festival), Bauan, Batangas.
**May 14–15** Carabao Festival, Pulilan, Bulacan, and Angono, Rizal.
**May 15** Pahiyas Festival, Sariaya and Lucban, Quezon.
**May 15–17** Kailonawan (fertility rites), Obando, Bulacan.

### June

**Entire month** Rizal Arist Festival (art shows geared toward foreign travellers), Angono, Rizal.
**June 12** Independence Day.
**June 24** Feast of St John the Baptist, San Juan, Manila.
**June 24** Parada ng Lechon (parade of roast pigs), Balayan, Batangas.
**June 27** Our Lady of Perpetual Help, Baclaran, Manila.

**BELOW:** Cebu City nightlife.

**ABOVE:** Matina Town Square, Davao City.

**June 29** Apung Iru Fluvial Parade (honors St Peter), Apalit, Pampanga.
**June 28–30** Pintados Festival, Tacloban, Leyte.
**Last Friday** Feast of the Sacred Heart, Lucban, Quezon.
**Variable** Maolod En Nabi (birthday of Prophet Mohammed); Fête de la Musique, Manila.

### July

**First Sunday** Pagoda sa Wawa (Fluvial Procession), Bocaue, Bulacan.
**July 29** Fluvial Festival for St Martha, Pateros, Manila.
**Fourth Sunday** Santa Ana Kahimonan Abayan (Abayan Festival for St Anne), Butuan, Agusan del Norte.
**Variable** Apuy and Pisit (harvest rituals), Ifugao and Mountain provinces.

### August

**August 19** Gigantes Festival, Lucban, Quezon.
**August 18–31** Kadayawan sa Dabaw (Fruit and Flowers Festival), Davao, Davao del Sur.
**August 27–28** Cagayan de Oro Fiesta, Cagayan de Oro.
**Variable** Lesles and Fagfagto (planting rites); Sumbali (Aeta Festival), Bayombong, Nueva Vizcaya.

### September

**Third weekend** Peñafrancia Festival (fluvial procession), Naga City, Camarines Sur; T'boli Festival, Lake Sebu, South Cotabato.
**September 29** Señor San Miguel, Iligan, Lanao del Norte.
**Variable** Sunduan. Procession of marriageable lads and ladies, Parañaque, Manila.

### October

**October 1–12** Zamboanga Hermosa Festival: native sailboat regatta.
**October 2** Kinilaw Festival, Surigao City: show on how to make the raw fish dish.
**October 7–8** Halaran Festival, Roxas City, Capiz.
**Second Sunday** La Naval de Manila, Quezon City.
**Fourth weekend** Masskara (Festival of Smiling Masks), Bacolod City; Lanzones Festival, Mambajao, Camiguin.
**Last Sunday** Feast of Christ the King, nationwide.

### November

**November–December** Intramuros Festival, Manila.
**November 1** All Saints' Day, nationwide.
**November 23** Gigantes Festival, Angono, Rizal.
**November 23** Benguet Foundation Day: native festival, including ritual sacrifices.
**November 30** Binabayani, Zambales.
**November 30** Bonifacio Day, nationwide.

### December

**December 2** Kalamay Festival, San Enrique, Iloilo: celebrates the sugar industry, including ecotourism benefits.
**December 8** Feast of the Immaculate Conception, nationwide; fluvial parade, Malabon, Manila.
**December 8** Coco Festival, San Teodoro, Mindoro Oriental: honors the Immaculate Conception and gives thanks to the coconut, the area's agricultural staple.
**December 8–9** Feast of Our Lady of Caysaysay. Fluvial parade, Taal, Batangas.

**December 16** Misa de Gallo. Start of nine pre-Christmas dawn Masses in Catholic regions.
**December 16–24** Simbang Gabi. Midnight Masses.
**Week before Christmas** Giant Lantern Festival, San Fernando, Pampanga.
**December 25** Christmas Day.

## SHOPPING

### What to Buy

The Philippines is an old Asian shopping emporium, dating back to the days when its coastal towns sold pearls, beeswax, and tortoise shells to trading vessels from China and Arabia. Tourists today generally pursue handicrafts and woodcarvings, with prices lower in the provinces but available for a fair trade in major cities as well.

#### Basketry

Popular Philippine baskets sell just about everywhere. Made from natural rattan, *nipa*, bamboo, abaca, and palm, the baskets come in a range of sizes and purposes. They are both functional and decorative. When every basket on a shelf looks slightly different, a shopper can be sure they are handmade.

#### Mats and Handbags

Handbags and mats are often made of *pandan* or abaca, although the UK's Prince Charles ordered his in *buri*, an indigenous grass. Check the stock at the Ilalim ng Tulay (Under the Bridge) market in Quiapo, Manila.

#### Handicrafts

Tourist shops in Manila's airport, the Makati commercial center, and Ermita sell piles of abaca hats, placemats, coasters, bamboo trays, shells, and ceramic pots. Travelers may run across handmade picture frames made from coconut husks and bamboo, and *capiz*-shell Christmas ornaments.

#### Embroidery

Travelers can seldom help stopping to inspect the untucked, no-tie-required *barong Tagalog*. Ask the hotel concierge to suggest a tailor. Choose either the translucent pineapple fiber, *piña*, with the finest hand embroidery, or the cheaper *ramie* or cotton with machine embroidery. Women can get embroidered *terno* dresses, with matching scarves, bags, and handkerchiefs.

### Jewelry

Philippine jewelry is made usually of pearl, shell, and silver. But visitors are advised not to purchase items made from coral or tortoise shell, as the harvest of both contributes to the degradation of Philippine seas. Moreover, trade in some items is illegal.

The best silver jewelry is found in Baguio, while wood and vine jewelry occur in the specialty shops of Ermita and Makati along with tribal beadwork such as necklaces, earrings, and ornamental hairpieces of the T'boli, Mangyan, and Ifugao people.

### Pearls

Quality pearls from Mindanao are for sale at V-Mall in Greenhills, San Juan, Manila. Most of the strands are freshwater pearls in irregular shapes, exotically beautiful and selling for prices that are just as other-worldly. Cultured pearls are available as well. Also look for South Sea black pearls sold at bargain prices compared to the international market. Serious pearl shoppers can drop by Jewelmer's showroom in Megamall B. Jewelmer (www.jewelmer.com) is the world's second-largest producer of salt-water pearls.

### Furniture

Wicker and rattan furniture normally weighs little enough to ship without spending large amounts of money. Angeles City is the shopper's best bet and offers made-to-order items, while Cebu has emerged as the country's main source of export-quality furniture. In Manila, drop by a FIRMA Home Accessories shop (www.firma.com.ph) for the latest in decor.

**BELOW:** trinkets for sale, Borocay Island.

**ABOVE:** SM City Baguio.

### Antiques

Shoppers can find Chinese vessels used to store wine, water, and vinegar as well as Spanish religious items (including *santos*, the Christ child). Old Chinese and Indonesian furniture occurs with similar frequency. Antiques are sold in Manila, from roadside stalls in Laguna, and in historic towns such as Vigan.

### Brassware

The first craftspeople of the Philippines are from Mindanao. To this day, they still make gongs, jewel boxes, betel nut boxes, brass beds, and cannon replicas. Ermita's tourist belt area hawks a fair amount of brassware, though the true collector will head to Mindanao.

### Woodcarving

Travelers can purchase hardwood carvings by the mountain-dwelling Ifugao of Luzon Island or wooden sculptures of the rice granary god (*bulol*) and animal totems from Palawan. Snoop around the Ermita tourist belt for shops that sell woodcarvings. Hardwoods become more precious by the day, and the Philippines has its fair share of fine narra and molave. If up north in Luzon, visit the woodcarving village in Baguio or browse the streets of Banaue.

## Where to Buy

### Handicrafts

**Balikbayan Handicrafts**
1010 Antonio Arnaiz, Makati
Tel: 02-893-0775–7
HK Sun Plaza, Diosdado Macapagal Avenue, Pasay
Tel: 02-831-0044
www.balikbayanhandicrafts.com
**Kayumanggi Arts and Crafts**
Ninoy Aquino Avenue,
Parañaque
Tel: 02-820-6916, 852-9813

**Narda's Handwoven Arts & Crafts**
5781 Felipe Street, Makati
Tel: 02-896-7372
Also in NAIA, Baguio, La Trinidad, Cebu, Alabang.
**Silahis Center**
744 General Luna Street, Intramuros
Tel: 02-527-2111,-527-2114
Fax: 02-527-2112
Also at: Iri Plaza N. Garcia Street, Makati
Tel: 02-898-2125
Alabang Town Center
Tel: 02-842-1505
**Tesoro's International**
1325 Mabini Street, Ermita
Tel: 02-524-3936
Also at: The Landmark, tel: 02-812-1945; Arnaiz Avenue, tel: 02-844-4253; Manila Hotel, tel: 02-527-5341.

### Antiques

**Jo-Liza Antique Shop**
664 Jose Abad Santos, Little Baguio, San Juan
Tel: 02-725-8303, 725-8151
Megamall tel: 02-635-3013
Alabang tel: 02-807-2256
**Glorietta Goldcrest Village Square**
Ayala Center, Makati. Several antiques vendors.
**The Legaspi Collection**
2/F, Textron Building, 168 Luna Mencias Street, San Juan
Tel: 02-724-3477
918 L. Mencias Street, Addition Hills Mandaluyong
Tel: 02-717-0900
**La O' Center**
Makati corner Antonio Arnaiz Avenue Makati
**Via Antica Export & Trading**
1411 Mabini Street, Ermita
Tel: 02-524-7726
Parañaque tel: 02-852-8776

## Shopping Malls

Shopping malls abound in Manila, most open from around 8am to mid-evening. Expect to find a range of clothiers, bookstores, fast food, snacks, travel accessories, and home electronics at variable prices.

Near the airport, visit the **Duty Free Philippines Fiesta Mall** and **Duty Free Philippines** (check-out lines can be exasperating). Just north, in the Malate-Ermita tourist belt, are **Robinson's Place** (www.robinsonsmalls.com) and **Harrison Plaza**, on Mabini Street. North of the Pasig, check out the flea market-esque **Tutuban Center** (www.tutuban.com.ph), in the heart of **Divisoria market**.

Quezon City's shopping options include **Araneta Center** – including **Ali Mall** and **SM Shoemart** (www.smdeptstore.com) – in Cubao to **Time Zone-Eastwood Mall**. South, in San Juan, the **Greenhills Shopping Center** stands along Ortigas Avenue, with pearls available at **V-Mall**, and many restaurants nearby. In Mandaluyong City, shoppers can stroll the **SM Megamall** on EDSA. Other area malls include the upscale **Shangri-La Plaza Mall** (www.shangrila-plaza.com), **Rustan's** (www.rustans.com.ph) and **Crossings Department Store**.

In Makati, **Ayala Center** (ayalamalls.com.ph) includes department stores such as **Landmark** and **Rustan's**. **Makati Cinema Square** rounds out the list of regular malls, while the upscale boutiques of **6750 Ayala Avenue** carry internationally known brands at internationally recognized prices. The **Greenbelt Shopping Complex** has redefined the Manila shopping experience with additional cutting-edge shops.

The **SM Mall of Asia** (tel: 02-556-0680; www.smmallofasia.com), located in Pasay at the end of EDSA, is the largest shopping mall in the country and the sixth largest in the world.

Southward, in the residential community of Ayala Alabang in Muntinlupa City, shoppers frequent the **Alabang Town Center**, **Festival Mall** (Corporate Avenue corner Civic Drive, Alabang), and **SM Southmall** (smsupermalls.com).

## SPORT AND OUTDOOR ACTIVITIES

### Basketball

Thanks to American influence, basketball is a well-loved national sport played by younger men in local leagues throughout the Philippines. Metro Manila has three semi-professional leagues, with the **Philippine Basketball Association**, or PBA (www.pba-online.net), sometimes traveling across the country in an outreach program. For game tickets, tel: 02-638-1815 or call Ticketworld (tel: 02-891-1000; www.ticketworld.com.ph). For more on basketball, see page 91.

### Boxing

Boxing is big in the Philippines and takes place year-round. The public can watch professional bouts in Metro Manila at the Elorde Sports Complex in Paranaque and SM Mall of Asia Arena in Pasay City. The Baguio City Convention Center and Surigao del Norte's Washington Gymnasium also host competitions. For details on upcoming matches, visit philboxing.com/boxers/schedules.php.

### Cockfighting

Two roosters enter the ring; usually just one emerges. Watching their battle is a favorite national pastime, as the audience makes bets, pigs out, and spends a long night watching the bloody duels between birds – not for the faint of heart. For a schedule of fights at two major "cockpits" in Manila, see www.sabong.net.ph, or check directly with the **Araneta Coliseum** in Cubao (tel: 02-911-3101; www.aranetacoliseum.com). In smaller towns, fights usually take place on Sunday afternoon. For more on cockfighting, see page 93.

### Golf

For many visitors, golf is the flagship attraction, as the country has some of the finest courses in the world, including championship ones. The authoritative website www.golfph.com lists 77 courses. Attractions include teeing off amid lush tropical vegetation resorts covered in pools waiting to snag balls hit in the wrong direction.

Manila's most accessible course is **Club Intramuros**, which winds around the stone walls of the old Spanish fort. Its 18 holes are open to the public daily, last tee-off is at 7pm (Bonifacio Drive corner Aduana Street, Intramuros, tel: 02-527-9594, 527-6613).

Golf also plays a part in tourism in Angeles City (Clark) and Subic Bay, Luzon, and in Boracay. From its low-key start of a few thousand golfers in the 1920s, golf has grown with the advent of international golf tournaments and well-appointed country clubs. Many golf courses purport to be for "members only," but visiting tourists can often make a case for themselves. Caddies, carts, clubs, and "umbrella girls" are usually available for hire on site.

### Horse Racing

Horse races generally take place at San Lazaro Leisure Park (tel: 02-914-4838, www.manilajockey.com) and Santa Ana Race Track (tel: 02-890-4015) in greater Manila. Betting on horses is a big-time operation. Major races include the Gran Copa, National Grand Derby, the Founder's Cup, and the Presidential Cup. For more on horse racing, see page 94.

## Outdoor Activities

(For further information, see The Sporting Life, page 91.)

### Caving

For stalactites, rock galleries, mountains of marble, and in some cases underground rivers, visitors can delve into the numerous dark caves of the Philippines. Local guides are usually hired on the spot.

### Diving

The Philippines has more than 28,000 sq km (10,808 sq miles) of coral reefs, making it a perfect site for diving and underwater exploration. Despite destructive practices in some areas, many once sedate towns have exploded with diving schools and coastal resorts for overnight stays. Alona Beach in Bohol, Moalboal in Cebu, and Apo Island in Negros Oriental are among the hip diving centers. The coral offshore shelters sea snakes, sharks, turtles, lion fish, and a multitude of other species. Diving promotes ecological awareness of underwater life and because of that in many places it has helped bring damaged reefs back from the brink of extinction. (For a broader description, see A Diver's Haven, page 97.)

Many divers rent their equipment on site. Although this is generally safe, check out your provider. For a list of certified scuba-diving organizations, contact the Philippine Commission on Sports Scuba Diving at the Department of Tourism in Manila, tel: 02-524-1703.

Dive operators in or near Manila include **Aquaventure Reef Club** (tel: 02-584-1328; aquareefclub.com) and **Scuba World** (Makati tel: 02-895-3551; www.scubaworld.com.ph). Those looking to probe the depths off Puerto Galera, check out **South**

Sea Divers (tel: 043-287-3052; www. southseadivers.com), **Capt'n Greggs Dive Shop** (tel: 043-287-3071; www. captngreggs.com), and **Blue Ribbon Dive Resort** (tel: 043-287-3561; www.blueribbondivers.com).

At Alona Beach in Bohol, contact the **Bohol Divers Club** (tel: 038-502-9050; www.boholdiversclubl.com), **Sun Divers** (tel: 038-502-9171; www.sun-divers.net), and **Polaris Beach Dive Resort** (cell tel: 0918-903-7187; www.polaris-dive.com).

In Boracay, look for **Scotty's Action Sport Network** (Cebu tel: 032-231-0288; www.divescotty. com), **New Wave Divers** (tel: 036-288-5265; www.boracaydiver.com) and **Watercolors Boracay Diving Adventures** (tel: 036-288-6745; www.watercolors.ph)

### Hiking

Trails lurk in most of the country's uplands. Some belong to national parks; others are chiselled out by locals. Most are safe, legal, and obviously scenic. Guide services are unnecessary for day hikes, though transportation from coastal cities to staging areas may take some careful planning.

Those in good physical shape may tackle one of the country's volcanoes for a view into the crater and clear down to the coast. Proper gear is needed and guides are recommended. For a list of recommended hikes, see page 95.

### Wildlife spotting

Numerous coastal areas of the Philippines lend themselves to watching and recording migratory birds. Inland, visitors may find a range of wildlife, though it takes patience to spot the more exotic beasts. Philippine Trails (www.philippinetrails. com) leads birdwatching tours.

### Wind Sports

Water and weather conditions are perfect for windsurfing and kiteboarding. Travelers in Boracay, for example, will find ample rental equipment available. The island hosts the Boracay Funboard Cup every January or February. It is open to windsurfers of all ages and abilities. Check out www.kiteboardingboracay.com

### Tour Operators

For official tour operators and guides registered with the Department of Tourism (DOT), call 02-524-1703 or check with the Philippine Tour Operators Association (PHILTOA), tel:

02-812-4553.
**250K Kiteboarding Adventures**
Tel: 949-498-9460; www.kiteboarding-philippines.com
Equips visitors for kiteboarding.
**Annset Holidays**
Tel: 02-354-4101; www. annsetholidays.com.ph
Offers adventure, culture, and sightseeing tours.
**Banca Safaris**
Tel: 0920-387-5837; www. bancasafaris.com
Operates boat tours to some of the farthest corners of the country such as Batanes, Palawan, and Mindanao.
**Bataan Tours**
Tel: 0917-697-7671, 047-237-1877
Runs tours throughout Bataan and to Corregidor island.
**Blue Horizons Travel & Tours**
Tel: 02-988-5000; www.bluehorizons. travel
Arranges flights, hotels, diving, golfing, sightseeing, and conventions.
**Calamian Islands Travel & Tours**
Tel: 939-569-659; www.coron-travel. com
Organizes packages in Coron.
**Chico River Quest, Inc.**
Tel: 920-205-2680; www. chicoriverquest.com
Specializes in rafting trips in Kalinga and elsewhere.
**Filipino Travel Center**
Tel: 02-528-5407; www.filipinotravel. com.ph
Arranges day trips and longer, exploratory tours.
**Freeport Service Corporation**
Tel: 047-252-2313–15
Operates tours to Subic Bay – the former military base – incorporating jungle treks and the survival skills of native Aeta people.
**KR Travel & Tours**
Tel: 032-239-7571; www. cebutourguide.com
Specializes in trips in Cebu and Bohol.
**Scorpio Travel and Tours Philippines**
Tel: 02-6874812; www.scorpiotravel. com
Takes visitors on sightseeing and "divine healing" trips.
**Uncharted Philippines**
Tel: 02-621-5399; www. unchartedphilippines.com
Organizes adventure tours.

**ABOVE:** Manila Golf Course.

### Guides

The following guide services can arrange treks and cave tours as well as links to emerging outdoor sports such as white-water rafting and mountain biking.
**Imaginative Traveler**
UK tel: +44-1728-885561; www. imaginative-traveller.com
Organizes treks.
**Philippine Adventure Tours**
Tel: 02-887-0047; www.philippine adventures.com
Organizes hikes, treks.
**Planet Action Adventure**
Tel: 032-474-0068; www.action-philippines.com
An outdoor sports company based in Moalboal; arranges waterfall drops, horseback riding, caving, and kayaking. It may also lead visitors to indigenous villages and to treks around Cebu.
**Tribal Adventures**
Tel: 036-288-3207, tribaladventures. com
Organizes treks, hikes, white-water rafting, mountain bike rides.

### Cultural Center of the Philippines (CCP)

The sprawling **Cultural Center of the Philippines** complex on Roxas Boulevard, Manila, houses theaters, museums, a library, restaurants, galleries, and exhibition rooms.

Most of the city's plays, ballets, and concerts take place here. It was built on the instigation of former first lady Imelda Marcos. Tel: 02-832-1125; www.culturalcenter.gov.ph

# A – Z

## A HANDY SUMMARY OF PRACTICAL INFORMATION, ARRANGED ALPHABETICALLY

### A

#### Addresses

Buildings are identified in the Philippines by number followed by a street name, much as they are in the United States. Large institutions may skip the number, as they're easy to find by street name alone. Under the street name, a "barangay" name may also appear. Barangay means village in rural areas and district, or borough, in cities.

#### Admission charges

Fees to enter galleries, museums, and parks vary from free to several hundred pesos per person, with an average around P100. Some institutions just ask for donations to keep the place running. Day of the week seldom affects admission price. Tour packages may include these fees, but special cards that buy discounted admission to multiple places are rare.

### B

#### Budgeting for your trip

Here are average prices for common expenses (P40–42 = US$1):
Coffee, juice, or beer: P21–80 per can or bottle
Glass of house wine: P100–200
Restaurant meal, per person: P200 budget, P500 moderate, P800 expensive
One night in a hotel: P800 cheap,

P1,500 moderate, above P3,500 deluxe
Taxi fare from Manila's airport complex to downtown: P275
In-town tricycle-taxi and jeepney fares: P7–15

#### Business Hours/ Opening Times

Shops are open Monday–Saturday, 9am to 7 or 8pm. Outside Manila, the Philippine attitude of *bahala na* (whatever happens) prevails; paid-admission parks and museums are lackadaisical about schedules but tend to open after 8am, break for a 90-minute lunch and close before 5pm. If an attraction is closed, ask around; it might very easily be opened if you ask the right person. Shops may stay open into the evening in busy areas, as long as customers are coming in.

Government and business hours are Monday–Friday, 8am–5pm and workers break for lunch noon–1pm. Businesses are usually open on Saturday. Banks are open Monday–Friday, 9am–3pm.

### C

#### Children

Filipinos love children and will be more than happy to accommodate yours. Talking about your family is a good icebreaker in conversation.

Larger resorts and major shopping malls are among the more child-friendly places in the Philippines. Resorts expect full-family vacations, while malls may have activities for

kids. Basketball courts in public parks also attract older children to practice the sport. Manila has a dedicated children's museum, and the capital's Mind Museum (tel: 02-909-6463) features interactive science exhibits. Some institutions let younger children in for free or reduced entrance fees.

Megamall Powerplant and Mall of Asia have bowling alleys, ice-skating rinks, and video arcades geared toward children. A family with young ones can make a day trip to the top of Taal Volcano.

#### Climate

A tropical country, much of the Philippines has a hot and dry climate from March to May. Generally, the southwest monsoon – and the typhoons it brings – predominates from June to October. The dry, cooler season during the northeast monsoon period lasts from November to February. Year-round temperatures range from 78°F (25°C) to 90°F (32°C); mean annual humidity is at 83 percent.

Rainfall varies with the region:
**Type 1** has two seasons, dry November–May and wet June–October. Type 1 areas are found mainly in the western half of Luzon (including Manila), Palawan, Coron, Cuyo, and the lower part of Antique, Iloilo, and Negros.
**Type 2** lacks a distinct dry season but has a pronounced maximum rain period December–February. Areas include eastern Bicol, eastern Mindanao, northern and eastern Samar, and southern Leyte.
**Type 3** areas, which do not have a pronounced maximum rain period

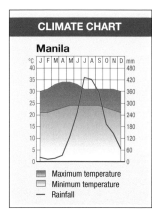

### CLIMATE CHART

**Manila**

Legend:
- Maximum temperature
- Minimum temperature
- Rainfall

but a short dry season of one to three (November–January) months, include central Luzon, Visayas, and western Mindanao.

**Type 4** sees even rainfall throughout the year and is found in the eastern coast of Luzon, Leyte and Bohol, and in central Mindanao.

The Philippines has about 15 typhoons each year. High season is June–October, with the peak in July–September, coinciding with the height of the southwest monsoon.

### What to Wear

Dress in loose, lightweight clothing to beat the heat. Few locals wear shorts or sleeveless shirts in the city, but tourists can bend the rules somewhat. To blend in better, dress like the locals – in jeans and T-shirts. If visiting a church, make an effort to dress conservatively.

Umbrellas are useful against sun and rain. If heading to the mountains, pack a fleece jacket, as chilly conditions surprise many travelers.

### Customs

Each arriving passenger is allowed 400 cigarettes (20 packs) or two tins of tobacco, and two 1-liter bottles of alcohol.

Filipinos living overseas bring home huge amounts of goods – many of them dutiable – to their families back in the Philippines. As a result, you will see passengers walking stacks of boxes through the "Nothing to Declare" Customs line at the Manila airport. In general, customs regulations are not strictly enforced but officials will sometimes use the rule of law on a selective basis, particularly when it comes to bringing electronics into the country.

### D

### Disabled Travelers

Despite its every effort, the Philippines remains a Third World country struggling to feed its own people. Sidewalks are often crumbling and streets usually pockmarked with potholes. Far be it for them to offer wheelchair ramps.

However, owing to Filipino hospitality and a genuine willingness to help, disabled travelers with a noble amount of patience (and keen sense of adventure) can navigate the city with little difficulty.

For a broader look at vacation choices for disabled people, check out www.handidivers.com.

### E

### Embassies and Consulates

**Australia:** 23/F, Tower 2, RCBC Plaza, 6819 Ayala Avenue, Salcedo Village, Makati City; tel: 02-757-8100; www.australia.gov.ph
**Canada:** 6/F, Tower 2, RCBC Plaza, 6819 Ayala Avenue, Salcedo Village, Makati City; tel: 02-857-9000; philippines.gc.ca
**European Union Commission:** 30/F, RCBC Plaza, Tower 2, Makati City; tel: 02-859-5100; eeas.europa.eu/delegations/philippines
**France:** 16/F, Pacific Star Building, Sen. Gil Puyat (Buendia) corner Makati Avenue, Makati City; tel: 02-857-6900; www.ambafrance-ph.org
**Germany:** 6819 Ayala Ave., Makati City; tel: 02-702-3000; www.manila.diplo.de
**Italy:** 6/F, Zeta Building, 191 Salcedo Street, Legazpi Village, Makati City; tel: 02-892-4531; www.ambmanila.esteri.it
**New Zealand:** 23/F, BP1 Buendia Center, Sen. Gil Puyat Avenue (Buendia Avenue Extension), Makati City; tel: 02-891-5355; www.nzembassy.com/philippines
**Singapore:** 35/F, Tower One, Enterprise Center, Ayala Avenue,

### Electricity

The standard voltage in the Philippines is 220 volts AC, 60 cycles. Many areas also have 110 volts capability. Major hotels will provide adapters. Plugs are of the North American configuration, without the grounding slot.

Makati City; tel: 02-751-2345; www.mfa.gov.sg/manila
**United Kingdom:** 120 Upper McKinley Road, Taguig City; tel: 02-858-2200; ukinthephilippines.fco.gov.uk
**United States:** 1201 Roxas Boulevard, Ermita; tel: 02-528-6300; manila.usembassy.gov

### Philippine embassies abroad

**Australia:** Level 1 Philippine Center, 27–33 Wentworth Ave., Sydney; tel: 02-9262-7377; www.philippineconsulate.com.au
**New Zealand:** 50 Hobson Street, Thorndon; tel: 04-472-9848; www.philembassy.org.nz
**United Kingdom:** 6–8 Suffolk St., London; tel: 020 7451-1780; www.philembassy-uk.org
**United States:** 1600 Massachusetts Ave. NW, Washington, DC; tel: 202-467-9300; www.philippineembassy-usa.org

### Etiquette

Filipinos tend to take things slow and easy unless there's an actual emergency. They're also conscious of losing face, so avoid pushing in line or asking twice if a meal order takes longer than expected. To give other people face, locals tend to answer every question as best they can, even if they don't know how, which can generate erroneous street directions. If someone starts giving short or hesitant answers, drop the topic to avoid pressing for more details they probably don't have. In casual conversation, people enjoy telling strangers about their families: who's-who lists, where relatives are working, and even where they're struggling. It's OK to discuss the country itself, including its political and developmental problems. Foreigners who have spent considerable time in the Philippines suggest avoiding discussion of religion, except in support of Christianity, and mentions of homosexuality until after two people know each other. As in other Asian cultures, the topics of major illness and death are also best shelved until a friendship is cemented.

### G

### Gay and lesbian travelers

Although homosexuality is not the first topic a traveler should broach with a new acquaintance in the largely Catholic country, same-gender displays are widely tolerated and the topic hardly taboo among friends. Manila's gay-friendly nightspots cluster around Julio Nakpil and Maria Orosa streets. One is the BED Bar and Club (tel: 02-536-3045) in Malate. On Roxas Boulevard, look for White Bird Disco Theater and KTV (tel: 02-851-2088). For more information on the LGBT scene, visit www.pinkmanila.com or www.utopia-asia.com.

## H

## Health & Insurance

Yellow fever vaccination is necessary for those arriving from an infected area. Do note that outside some parts of Palawan and Mindanao, malaria is fairly rare in the Philippines. However, there is a risk of malaria year-round below 600 meters (2,000ft) in elevation, except in urban areas; the malignant *falciparum* strain is present, and is highly resistant to chloroquine. Anti-malarial drugs are suggested for travel in remote areas. Mosquito-borne dengue fever has seen a resurgence in recent years; wear insect repellent and cover exposed skin to prevent insect bites.

Hospitals admit uninsured foreigners. A drop-in tourist will be asked to fill out papers, pay a P50 to P500 consultation fee and wait an hour or more, depending on how busy the doctors are. Any prescriptions cost extra. Payment must usually be guaranteed before treatment. It's up to each foreign insurer how much coverage to offer in the Philippines.

Although pharmacies such as Mercury Drug are clustered near hospitals and in city centers, visitors may be unable to find the selection of medications available at home. Drugs, including common painkillers and anti-itch creams, can be expensive and often mean standing in line at a prescription counter even if no doctor's order is legally needed. Mercury Drug (www.mercurydrug.com) is open 24 hours at certain branches around the country. In Manila, a centralized 24-hour outlet is at 2625 Aurora Avenue, tel: 02-711-5575 or 02-741-6927.

Foreigners sometimes go to Manila for laser eye surgery, which is cheaper there than elsewhere. Choose clinics carefully.

Carry a first-aid kit with necessary prescription drugs, plus aspirin, anti-inflammatory tablets, Imodium (anti-diarrhea pills), and antibiotics.

It is best to avoid drinking tap water; stick to bottled water.

### Manila hospitals

**Asian Hospital**: Filinvest Corporate Center, Alabang; tel: 02-771-9000.
**Cardinal Santos Medical Center**: Wilson Street, Greenhills, San Juan; tel: 02-727-0001–46.
**Makati Medical Center**: 2 Amorsolo corner de la Rosa Street, Makati City; tel: 02-888-89991, 892-5544.
**Manila Doctor's Hospital**: 667 United Nations Avenue, Ermita; tel: 02-524-3011–77.
**Medical Center Manila**: 1122 General Luna Street, Ermita; tel: 02-523-8131/65.
**Philippine General Hospital**: Taft Avenue, Manila; tel: 02-521-8450.
**St Luke's Medical Center**: 279 Rodriguez Boulevard, Quezon City; tel: 02-723-0301, 723-0101.

### Davao hospital

**Davao Doctors Hospital**, General Malvar Street; tel: 082-222-0850, local tel: 106.

### Cebu hospitals

**Ching Hua Hospital**, Fuente Osmeña; tel: 032-253-9409

**Cebu Doctors Hospital**, President Osmeña Boulevard; tel: 032-255-5555.

### Emergencies, hotlines

**Police/Fire/Medical Emergency:** 117
**National police headquarters (24 hours):** 02-723-0401. Camp Crame, EDSA, Metro Manila
**Manila Police:** 02-523-3378
**Makati Police:** 02-899-9014
**Pasay City Police:** 02-831-1544
**Quezon City Police:** 02-921-5267
**Manila fire department:** 02-410-6254
**Manila coastguard:** 02-527-3877
**Tourist police assistance (24 hours):** 02-524-1660, 02-524-1728
**Tourist information:** 02-524-2384, 02-525-2000.

### Diving emergencies

Go with a buddy or guide and stay within the charted dive area. In a diving emergency, contact:
**Manila** Armed Forces of the Philippines (AFP) Medical Center, V. Luna Road, Quezon City, Metro Manila. Attention: Sgt. Ricardo Mengua, Senior Recompression Technician. Tel: 02-426-2701 x 6745, cell tel: 0919-572-2676.
Coastguard Action Center. Tel:

**BELOW:** English-language newspapers are widely available.

02-527-8481 x 6136.
**Batangas** Dr Mike Perez. Cell tel: 0917-536-2757.
**Cavite** Philippine Coast Guard Medical Center. Tel: 02-527-8481 x 6321–3.
**Cebu** VISCOM Station Hospital, Camp Lapu-Lapu, Lahug, Cebu City. Tel: 032-232-2464, 253-2325.

## I

### Internet

Don't promise family back home that you will e-mail them from the Philippines. Most mid-range hotels offer free Wi-fi, but due to telecom outages and poor signal penetration, travelers often can't go online when needed. Successful connections may be aggravatingly slow. In second-tier hotels, the lobby or restaurant internet often works better than in guestrooms. The business centers of larger hotels have Net-enabled computers. Airport waiting halls seldom offer free Wi-fi, though it sometimes pops up in Cebu and at Manila's Terminal 3 and even on some long-distance buses. Upscale cafés and resort bars usually let guests use free Wi-fi (always ask for the password), but subject to the same problems facing hotels.

## L

### Lost property

Report the loss of valuable items, such as cameras or high-end mobile phones, to authorized police stations. A detective will ask questions and make a report – if only with pen and paper – and ask for a contact number in case the lost item is found. Small police offices may not be able to take a report but will refer travelers to larger stations that can.

## M

### Maps

Most airport arrival halls and some ferry piers, especially in tourist-heavy areas, give away up-to-date local maps, which travelers can show to locals when asking for directions. Maps do not show every dirt track, but most cover essential roads as well as markers for public institutions. To get maps in one part of the country before traveling to another, try a branch of the National Book Store chain. The chain also sells country maps for less than P200.

### Media

*The Philippine Daily Inquirer, Manila Bulletin,* and other English-language newspapers are circulated widely, with in-depth national news about corruption, accidents, and celebrity moves. The papers carry foreign news from overseas wire services. News-stands sell *Newsweek, Time,* and internationally circulated consumer magazines with focuses such as automotive and high-tech. Radio stations from abroad include the BBC World Service and Voice of America. BBC broadcasts often appear on hotel TVs.

### Money Matters

The peso (P) is the monetary unit and there are 100 centavos to one peso. The US dollar, euro, pound sterling, Canadian dollar, Australian dollar, and Japanese yen are easily convertible – though the US dollar is most widely accepted.

The exchange rate usually hovers just above 40 pesos per US dollar, around 42 in mid-2012. Banks, including their outlets at major airports, offer the fairest rates. Hotels also change money, but not always on the most favorable terms.

Especially outside Metro Manila and Cebu, the Philippines is a cash economy. Even traveler's checks can present something of a challenge in Manila; bring your purchase receipt and passport to a bank and be prepared for a queue.

ATMs are open 24 hours and easily found in major cities, although international banks may not be accessible. Maximum daily withdrawal is about P20,000. During holidays, withdraw early, before ATMs run out of cash. Smaller towns, including popular beach resort areas, may have just one ATM, if any.

International credit cards are widely accepted throughout Manila, although service charges prevail. In more rural areas, only major establishments accept plastic. Many a traveler has cut short a trip in the provinces for lack of money.

#### Public toilets

All restaurants, bars, hotels, and shopping malls have toilets for customers. Large hotels, which offer some of the cleaner restrooms, won't stop a non-guest from using the facilities. Shopping malls are another clean, reliable, option. All transit centers offer restrooms, as well, though bus depots do little upkeep and ironically may charge small fees for use. Restrooms unconnected to another business are rare in the Philippines.

#### Taxes

When shopping, taxes are included in the listed price. Major restaurants and hotels add a 10 percent service charge; hotels tack on an additional 12 percent VAT. Ask whether one or both is already included in prices listed on the menu.

#### Tipping

Larger establishments will add a service charge. Smaller establishments leave tipping to discretion, but it is best to leave something. The local habit is to leave a token fee rather than a percentage of the total bill, usually less than P100. The relatively low cost of travel here makes it easier for foreign visitors to be generous.

## P

### Postal Services

Post offices are open Monday–Friday, 8am–5pm, Saturday 8am–noon. The Philippine Postal Corporation is at Lawton Plaza (Liwasang Bonifacio), Intramuros, Manila. Hotel desks provide the most convenient services for purchasing stamps and posting letters. At Ninoy Aquino International Airport, the post office is in the arrival area.

The Philippine mail system is slow and unreliable. It is fine for postcards but not much use for anything else. Private courier services like **DHL** (tel: 1800-1888-0345), **Fedex** (1800-10-855-8484), **UPS** (tel: 1800-10-742-5877), and **TNT** (tel: 02-551-5632) offer inexpensive and reliable mail service within the Philippines, as well as speedy overseas deliveries.

#### Post Offices in Manila

**Manila Post Office** Liwasang Bonifacio, Manila
**Makati Post Office** corner Gil Puyat Avenue (Buendia) and Ayala Avenue
**Pasay Post Office** F.B. Harrison, Pasay
**San Juan Central Post Office** Pinaglabanan, San Juan
For other branches, see www.philpost. gov.ph (list on lower left side of the home page).

### Public Holidays

**January 1** New Year's Day. Fireworks and celebratory gunfire ring in the new year.
**April/May** Maundy Thursday, Good Friday Flagellants in the streets, processions and *Cenaculos* (passion plays). In Pampanga and elsewhere, devout Catholics are voluntarily crucified.
**April/May** Easter Sunday Morning processions; family celebration.
**April 9** Araw ng Kagitingan (Day of Valor/Bataan and Corregidor Day). Celebrations at Fort Santiago in Intramuros commemorate the bravery of Filipino soldiers during World War II.
**May 1** Labor Day. A tribute to the Philippine worker.
**June 12** Independence Day – from Spain in 1898. Parades at Rizal Park in Manila.

**October/November** Eid al Fitr – a recently declared public holiday passed to respect the country's other dominant religion, Islam. Marks the ending of Ramadan.
**November 1** All Saints' Day. Most Filipinos travel home to visit ancestral tombs and spend the day with their family.
**November 30** Bonifacio Day celebrates the birth of nationalist leader Andres Bonifacio.
**December 25** Christmas Day.
**December 30** Rizal Day. Wreath-laying ceremony at National Hero's Monument in Rizal Park (Manila), in honor of the revered Jose Rizal.
**December 31** New Year's Eve.
Note: In the Muslim provinces of western Mindanao, four other Islamic holidays are also recognized.

Travel during the holiday season – especially Easter and Christmas – can be difficult and chaotic. Make reservations far in advance, or avoid travel during these periods. One interesting exception to this rule is Easter in Manila. This is the biggest travel time of the year in the Philippines and the capital city empties. Though many stores and museums are closed, the usually congested city is nearly vacant. Many smaller Manila hotels offer discounts because there are so few customers.

## R

### Religious Services

Historically, the Filipinos have embraced two of the world's great religions: Islam and Christianity. The former is mostly confined to the south while the latter has followers all over the country.

Most Christian church services are held on Sunday morning and evening, while Friday is the Muslim day of worship. Details of services are available at hotel desks and tourist information centers.

## S

### Security & Crime

The Philippines is generally safe for travelers, despite appearances such as drunks or beggars loitering around dark, abandoned buildings in big cities. In many cases, traveling in the provinces is safer than Manila, where petty theft, not violent crime, is the main concern. Keep valuables safe. Always lock car and taxi doors once inside. Wear a money belt under clothing; use safety deposit boxes.

There have been occurrences of kidnapping both in Manila and Mindanao. Taxi drivers can be scam artists, though not necessarily criminals in the legal sense; if a driver refuses to start his meter, find another cab. Pretend to know the city better than you do and be wary of anyone who seems overly friendly – lest they catch you off guard and slip a sedative into your drink in order to rob you, a common scam in Manila. Don't play cards or betting games with groups of strangers. Drunk people walking around at night are also targets for robbery and other crimes.

**BELOW:** security is an issue in Mindanao.

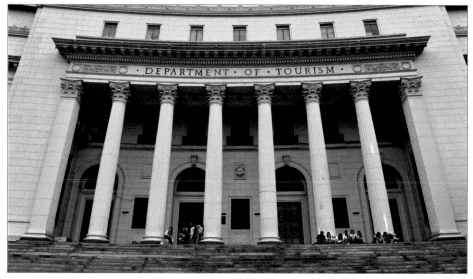

**ABOVE:** Department of Tourism, Manila.

Travelers should be aware of sporadic problems with Muslim separatists such as the MILF (Moro Islamic Liberation Front) and the Abu Sayyaf in Mindanao plus some of its surrounding islands. Ask locals for accurate updates on security issues; people not in Mindanao might over-dramatize.

Parts of Mindanao always remain sketchy for foreign travelers, including the remote islands of Sulu and Basilan, where foreigners have been kidnapped. Before traveling to the countryside, check with an embassy or a local tourism office.

## T

### Telecommunications

Most of the larger Philippine hotels have IDD, fax, and internet facilities available to guests at a small charge.

Public payphones require P2–3 or prepaid telephone cards. Some small shops also provide informal phone services.

### Cellular phones

The Philippines, which has always had notoriously bad telephone service, has embraced cellular phones wholeheartedly. Mobile phones are now as reliable as, or in fact more reliable than, many land lines. Coverage extends from remote regions of Mindanao in the south to the northern islands of Batanes.

The competition for cell-phone users is intense, with Smart and Globe commanding the lion's share of the market; Sun Cellular is a recent entry into the market. Cellular phone prefixes are 4 digits, and start with 09, the 0 to be dropped when dialing from overseas. Another seven digits follow each prefix.

Cellular phones in the Philippines use the GSM network. If your cell phone has a roaming facility, it will automatically hook up to one of the country's networks. Mobile phones from some countries are not compatible.

A simple and convenient telecommunications solution is to buy a cheap (US$40 new, US$20 used) cellular phone upon arrival and use it with prepaid calling cards, available just about everywhere, even in villages with just a store or two. The phone can be resold upon departure from the country at small cellular shops for about half of its original purchase price if it is still in good condition.

If compatibility is not an issue, you can also make calls on your cell phone with a prepaid local SIM card that includes a local phone number. The set-up costs around US$10 for the card and one round of stored value. Major airports sell the cards.

### Telephone Codes

International access code: 00
International operator: 108
Domestic operator: 109
Directory assistance: 114 or 187
Philippines country code: 63
City codes:
**Manila** 02
**Angeles** 045, 0455
**Bacolod** 034
**Baguio** 074
**Batangas** 043
**Boracay** 036
**Cagayan de Oro** 088, 08822
**Cebu** 032
**Clark** 045
**Davao** 082
**General Santos** 083
**Iloilo** 033
**Subic** 047

The prefix 0 must be dialed for all calls made within the Philippines. When calling the Philippines from overseas, dial the international access code, followed by 63 and the phone number (without the preceding 0).

### Tourist Offices

#### Europe

**United Kingdom:** Philippine Department of Tourism, 146 Cromwell Road, London SW7 4EF; tel: 4420-7835-1100; www.wowphilippines. co.uk; e-mail:_infotourism@ wowphilippines.co.uk

#### North America

**Canada:** Philippine Department of Tourism, 151 Bloor Street, West Suite 1120, Toronto, Outario, M5S1S4; tel: 416-924-3569; www.wowphilippines. ca; e-mail: info@wowphilippines.ca

**Chicago:** Philippine Consulate General, 30 N Michigan Avenue, Suite 913; tel: 1312-332-6458; www. chicagopcg.com; e-mail: pdotchi@ aol.com
**Los Angeles:** Philippine Consulate General, 3600 Wilshire Boulevard, Suite 500; tel: 1213-639-0980; www.philippineconsulatela.org; e-mail: pdotla@aol.com
**New York**: Philippine Center, 556 Fifth Avenue; tel: 1212-575-7915; www.experiencephilippines.org; e-mail: pdotny@aol.com
**San Francisco:** Philippine Consulate General, 447 Sutter Street, Suite 507; tel: 1415-956-4060; www. philippinessanfrancisco.org; e-mail: pdotsf@aol.com

### Asia-Pacific

**Australia:** Philippine Department of Tourism, Level 1, Philippine Centre, 27-33 Wentworth Avenue, Sydney; tel: 612-9283-0711; www.emanila. com/ptsydney; e-mail: cgjones@pdot. com.au
**Hong Kong:** Philippine Consulate General, 6/F, Room 602, United Centre, 95 Queensway, Hong Kong; tel: 852-2823-8500; www. philcongen-hk.com, e-mail: pdothk@ netvigator.com
**Singapore:** Philippine Tourism Office, #06–11 Orchard Towers, 400 Orchard Road; tel: 65-6738-7165; e-mail: www.philippine-embassy.org.sg, philtours_sin@pacific. net.sg

### Regional Tourist Offices
**Metro Manila**
Department of Tourism (DOT), DOT Building, Room 207, T.M. Kalaw Street, Ermita; tel: 02-524-2345.
DOT, Ninoy Aquino International Airport branch; tel: 02-832-2964.

**Southern Luzon**
DOT, DOT Building, Room 208, T.M. Kalaw Street, Ermita, Manila; tel: 02-524-1969.

**Central Luzon**
DOT, Paskuhan Village, San Fernando, Pampanga; tel: 045-961-2665.

**Ilocos**
DOT, Oasis Country Resort National Highway, Bgy, Sevilla San Fernando, La Union; tel: 072-888-2411.
DOT, Ilocano Heroes Memorial Hall, Laoag City; tel: 077-771-1473.

**Cotabato**
DOT, 2/F, Comse Building, Quezon Avenue, Cotabato City; tel:

## Time Zone

The Philippines is 8 hours ahead of Greenwich Mean Time (GMT). There is no daylight savings adjustment. Sunrise and sunset occur around 6am and 6pm.

064-421-1110; e-mail: dot12@ mozcom.com

**Northeastern Luzon**
DOT, 2/F, Tuguegarao Supermarket, Tuguegarao, Cagayan; tel: 078-844-1621.

**Cordillera Administrative Region**
DOT, DOT Complex, Gov. Pack Road, Baguio City; tel: 074-442-6708; e-mail: dotcar@mozcom.com

**Bicol**
DOT, Regional Center Site, Rawis, Legazpi; tel: 052-482-0712; e-mail: dotr5@globalink.net.ph

**Eastern Visayas**
DOT, G/F, Foundation Plaza Building, Leyte Park Resorts Compound, Magsaysay Boulevard; tel: 053-321-4333; e-mail: dotev@skyinet.net

**Central Visayas**
DOT, G/F, LDM Building, Lapu-Lapu Street, Cebu; tel: 032-254-2811.
Airport office; tel: 032-340-8229; e-mail: dotr7@cvis.net.ph

**Western Visayas**
DOT, Western Visayas Tourism Center, Capitol Ground, Bonifacio Drive, Iloilo; tel: 033-337-5411; e-mail: deptour6@ iloilo.net
Boracay Field Office, Balabag (by Boat Station 2); tel: 036-506-0094.

**Southern Mindanao**
DOT, Door No. 7, Magsaysay Park Complex, Sta. Ana District, Davao; tel: 082-221 6955; e-mail: dotr11@ philwebinc.com

**Northern Mindanao**
DOT, A. Velez Street, Cagayan de Oro; tel: 08822-726-394; e-mail: dot10@ cdo.weblinq.com

**Caraga**
DOT, D & V Plaza Building, Butuan; tel: 085-225-5712.

**Zamboanga**
DOT, Lantaka Hotel By the Sea, Valderosa Street, Zamboanga City; tel: 062-991-0218; e-mail: dotr9@jetlink. com.ph

## Visas & Passports

Everyone entering the Philippines from abroad must hold a valid passport. Visitors from nations with diplomatic ties are granted a 21-day visa upon arrival. All visitors must hold onward or return tickets.
Visitors who wish to extend their stay from 21 to 59 days should contact the Bureau of Immigration, Magallanes Drive, Intramuros, in Manila (Mon–Fri 8am–5pm). Some overseas missions issue 59-day visas before arrival. Check with immigration at your first point of arrival for the latest information on how to extend visas while in the Philippines.

## Women Travelers

Foreign women should experience little trouble traveling independently. Most Filipinos will be surprised at lone female travelers – theirs is a culture that travels in groups. However, your independence will only increase their admiration. Filipinos are generally friendly and helpful.
Local men enjoy whistling and giving out catcalls. No disrespect is meant. Any response on the woman's part may be seen as an invitation or, more likely, would embarrass the perpetrator.
Life is different here: even seven-year-old girls describe themselves as "sexy" before family and friends – a term synonymous with "beautiful" and just as harmless.
At times, a woman may be inclined to invent a boyfriend she is on her way to meet. Filipina women are wary of traveling alone and may invite themselves to sit next to you on the bus or in the lobby to ward off unwelcome male attention.
Tampons are not easily available outside Manila, so bring your own. The same goes for birth control pills.

## Weights/Measures

Though the metric system predominates, the imperial system is well understood. Temperatures are listed in Centigrade, with weight expressed in grams and kilograms. Distances are listed in meters and kilometers.

## LANGUAGE

# UNDERSTANDING THE LANGUAGE

### General

Pilipino and English are national languages. Much of Pilipino is derived from Tagalog, the language of Manila and nearby provinces. Other major languages are Ilocano, Visayan, Cebuano, and Maguindanao, although at least 110 languages prevail throughout the archipelago.

Listed below are some useful Tagalog expressions. Tagalog is pronounced phonetically, with no distinct accents on any particular syllables. "Siy" is pronounced "sh," "ts" becomes "ch," and "ng" takes on a nasal, guttural sound.

### Greetings

**Welcome** *Mabuhay*
**How are you?** *Kumusta ka?*
**Fine. And you?** *Mabuti. At ikaw?*
**Fine also** *Mabuti rin*
**Good morning** *Magandang umaga (po)*
**Good afternoon** *Magandang hapon (po)*
**Good evening** *Magandang gabi (po)*
**Goodbye** *Paalam*
**Thank you** *Salamat (po)*
**You're welcome** *Walang anuman*

### Shopping

**How much is this?** *Magkano ito?*
**expensive** *mahal*
**cheap** *mura*
**I want...** *Gusto ko ng...*
**Do you have...?** *Meron ba kayong...?*
**How much per meter?** *Magkanong metro?*
**How much of a discount?** *Magkanong tawad?*
**OK, wrap it up.** *Pakibalot nga.*
**Bill, please.** *Ang bill nga.*

### Useful Phrases

**What is your name?** *Anong pangalan mo?*
**My name is...** *Ang pangalan ko ay...*
**How old are you?** *Il ng taon ka na?*
**Just a moment, please.** *Sandali lang.*
**May I take a photo?** *Maari po. bakayong kunan ng retrato?*
**What time is it?** *Anong oras na po?*
**I don't know.** *Hindi ko alam.*
**Where did you come from?** *Saan po kayo galing?*
**Where are you from?** *Taga saan po sila?*
**Where do you live?** *Saan po kayo nakatira?*
**Have you eaten yet?** *Kumain na po ba sila?*
**Excuse me.** *Ipagpaumanhin ninyo ako.*
**Sorry.** *Paumanhin (po)*
**Please come in.** *Tuloy po kayo.*
**I will take care of you.** *Aalagaan kita.*
**I am leaving tomorrow.** *Aalis ako bukas.*
**The airplane leaves at four o'clock in the afternoon.** *Aalis ang eroplano ng alakuwatro ng hapon.*
**The flight leaves in 30 minutes.** *Aalis ang flight sa loob ng tatlumpung minuto.*
**The bus leaves at 5.15** *Aalis ang bus sa alas singko kinse.*
**Where's the toilet?** *Nasaan ang kasilyas (banyo, CR)?*
**Straight ahead.** *Deretso.*
**On the right.** *(Sa) kanan.*
**On the left.** *(Sa) kaliwa.*
**In front.** *(Sa) harap.*
**Turn around.** *Umikot.*
**At the back, behind.** *(Sa) likod/likuran.*
**There, on that side.** *Diyan lang po sa tabi*
**Fire!** *Sunog!*
**Call the police!** *Tumawag ka ng pulis!*
**Leave me alone.** *Iwanan mo ako mag-isa! Hayaan mo ko mapag-isa.*
**Good luck.** *Suwertehin ka sana.*

**Merry Christmas.** *Maligayang Pasko.*
**How do you say ... in Tagalog?** *Paano mo sabihin ang ... sa tagalog?*
**I don't understand.** *Hindi ko naiintindihan*
**Please speak more slowly.** *Pwede mo bang bagalan ang iyong pagsasalita?*
**yes/no** *oo/hindi*
**good/bad** *mabait/masama*
**many** *marami*
**who** *sino*
**what** *ano*
**when** *kailan*
**where** *saan*
**sweet** *matamis*
**sour** *maasim*
**cold/hot** *malamig/mainit*
**water** *tubig*
**old/young** *matanda/bata*
**new/old** *bago/luma*
**big/small** *malaki/maliit*
**clean/dirty** *malinis/masama*
**man/woman** *lalaki/babae*
**father/mother** *tatay/nanay*

### Numbers

**1** *isa*
**2** *dalawa*
**3** *tatlo*
**4** *apat*
**5** *lima*
**6** *anim*
**7** *pito*
**8** *walo*
**9** *siyam*
**10** *sampu*
**11** *labin-isa*
**12** *labin-dalawa*
**20** *dalawampu*
**30** *tatlumpu*
**40** *apatnapu*
**50** *limanapu*
**100** *isang daan*
**200** *dalawang daan*
**500** *limang daan*
**1000** *isang libo*

# FURTHER READING

TRANSPORTATION

## Travel

**Insight Pocket Guide: Manila and Environs** by Julie Gaw. Apa Publications, 2000. A companion guide to this volume, with focused tours of the Philippine capital.

## History & Politics

**Comfort Woman: A Filipina's Story of Prostitution and Slavery Under the Japanese Military** by Maria Rosa Henson. Rowman & Littlefield, 1999. The powerful autobiography of a teenage girl captured by the Japanese in April 1943 and forced to be a "comfort woman" for countless Japanese soldiers during World War II. A simply told account of triumph over adversity.

**In Our Image: America's Empire in the Philippines** by Stanley Karnow. Ballantine Books, 1990. A Pulitzer Prize-winning look at America's sometimes blundering steps in the dance of colonialism. An invaluable perspective on the past.

**Developing as a Democracy: Reform and Recovery in the Philippines, 1992–1998** by Fidel V. Ramos. St Martin's Press, 1999. A history of the Philippines under the Ramos administration.

**Bataan: Our Last Ditch: The Bataan Campaign, 1942** by John W. Whitman. Hippocrene Books, 1990. A comprehensive history of the Death March.

**Corazon Aquino and the Brushfire Revolution.** Louisiana State University Press, 1995. An unflinching account of the failures of the Aquino administration written by a reporter who covered it in its entirety.

**Noynoy: Triumph of a People's Campaign** by Wilfrido V. Villacorta. Anvil Publishing, 2011. Thin paperback on the election of President Benigno Aquino III.

**Testament from a Prison Cell** by Benigno Aquino III. Philippine Journal, 1989. The Philippine President elected in 2010 writes about his days of incarceration under Marcos.

**Rizal without the Overcoat** by Ambeth R. Ocampo. Anvil Publishing, 2008. A sober journalist's retrospective of the national hero.

**Waltzing with a Dictator: The Marcoses and the Making of American Policy** by Raymond Bonner. Vintage Books, 1988. Using extensive documentation obtained through the Freedom of Information Act in the United States, this account outlines the tragic folly of the Marcos years as well as any.

**You know you're Filipino if —: A Pinoy Primer** by Neni Sta. Romana-Cruz and Dindo Llana. Tahanan Books, 1997. If more than 50 people are on your Christmas shopping list or if you make a cross every time you pass a church, you're Filipino – just some of the examples.

**The King of Nothing to Do** by Luis Joaquin M. Katigbak. Milflores Publishing, 2007. Ironic, humorous essays that reflect trends in modern society.

## Literature & Fiction

**Manila Boy** by Patrick Everard. Book Guild Publishing, 2010. Story of a gay man in Manila whose adventure lands him in a criminal world.

**The Best Philippine Short Stories of the 20th Century**, edited by Isagani R. Cruz. Tahanan Books, 2000. An anthology of stories, a hallmark of Filipino literary tradition.

**More Tales (supernatural & otherwise) From the Barrio** by T.P. Boquiren. New Day Publishers, 1999. Stories about legal and other struggles in poor neighborhoods of the Philippines.

**Dusk: A Novel** by F. Sionil José. Modern Library, 1998. An epic novel set in the late 19th century, following the difficult lives of a tenant family after the expulsion of the Spaniards by American forces.

**Noli Me Tangere** (Shaps Library of Translation) by Jose P. Rizal. Edited by Raul L. Locsin; translated by Ma Soledad Lacson-Locsin. University of Hawaii Press, 1997. National hero Rizal's semi-autobiographical account of the harshness of life under Spanish rule. Required reading, along with his follow-up, *El Filibusterismo*.

**Ghost Soldiers** by Hampton Sides. Doubleday 2001. The bestselling book and soon-to-be Hollywood movie tells the story of the Bataan death march and a heroic mission to rescue its survivors. An important part of Philippine history told in riveting detail.

## Send Us Your Thoughts

We do our best to ensure the information in our books is as accurate and up-to-date as possible. The books are updated on a regular basis using local contacts, who painstakingly add, amend and correct as required. However, some details (such as telephone numbers and opening times) are liable to change, and we are ultimately reliant on our readers to put us in the picture.

We welcome your feedback, especially your experience of using the book "on the road". Maybe we recommended a hotel that you liked (or another that you didn't), or you came across a great bar or new attraction we missed.

We will acknowledge all contributions, and we'll offer an Insight Guide to the best letters received.

Please write to us at:
**Insight Guides**
**PO Box 7910**
**London SE1 1WE**
Or email us at:
**insight@apaguide.co.uk**

ACCOMMODATIONS · EATING OUT · ACTIVITIES · A – Z · LANGUAGE

# ART AND PHOTO CREDITS

# INDEX

*Main references are in bold type*

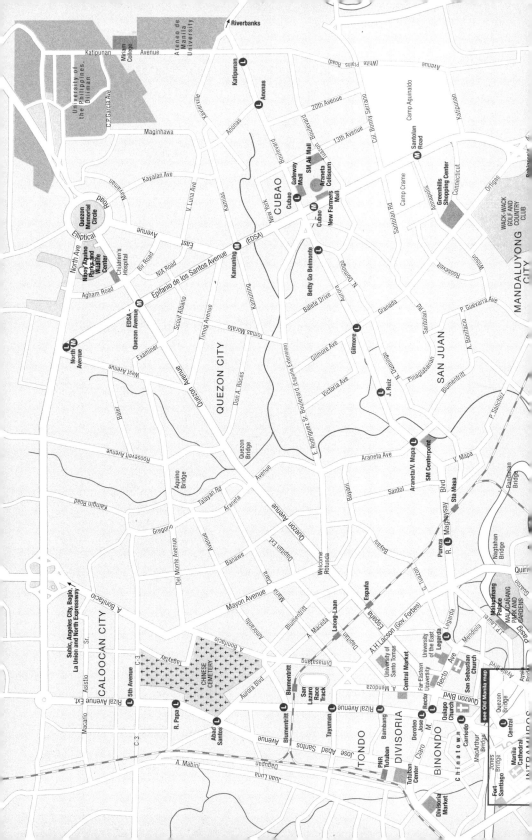